W9-AYE-606

The Visual Miscellaneum

THE BESTSELLING CLASSIC, Revised & Reimagined

The Visual Miscellaneum

A Colorful Guide to the World's Most Consequential Trivia

David McCandless

HARPER DESIGN
An Imprint of HarperCollinsPublishers

The Visual Miscellaneum: Revised and Reimagined

Published in 2012 by:
Harper Design
An Imprint of HarperCollins*Publishers*
10 East 53rd Street
New York, NY 10022
Tel (212) 207-7000
harperdesign@harpercollins.com
www.harpercollins.com

First published in 2009 by:
HarperCollins*Publishers*

Library of Congress Control Number: 2012943296
ISBN: 978-0-06-223652-4

Printed in Hong Kong, 2012

FSC
www.fsc.org

MIX
Paper from responsible sources
FSC™ C007454

FSC™ is a non-profit international organisation established to promote the responsible management of the world's forests. Products carrying the FSC label are independently certified to assure consumers that they come from forests that are managed to meet the social, economic and ecological needs of present and future generations, and other controlled sources.

Find out more about HarperCollins and the environment at
www.harpercollins.co.uk/green

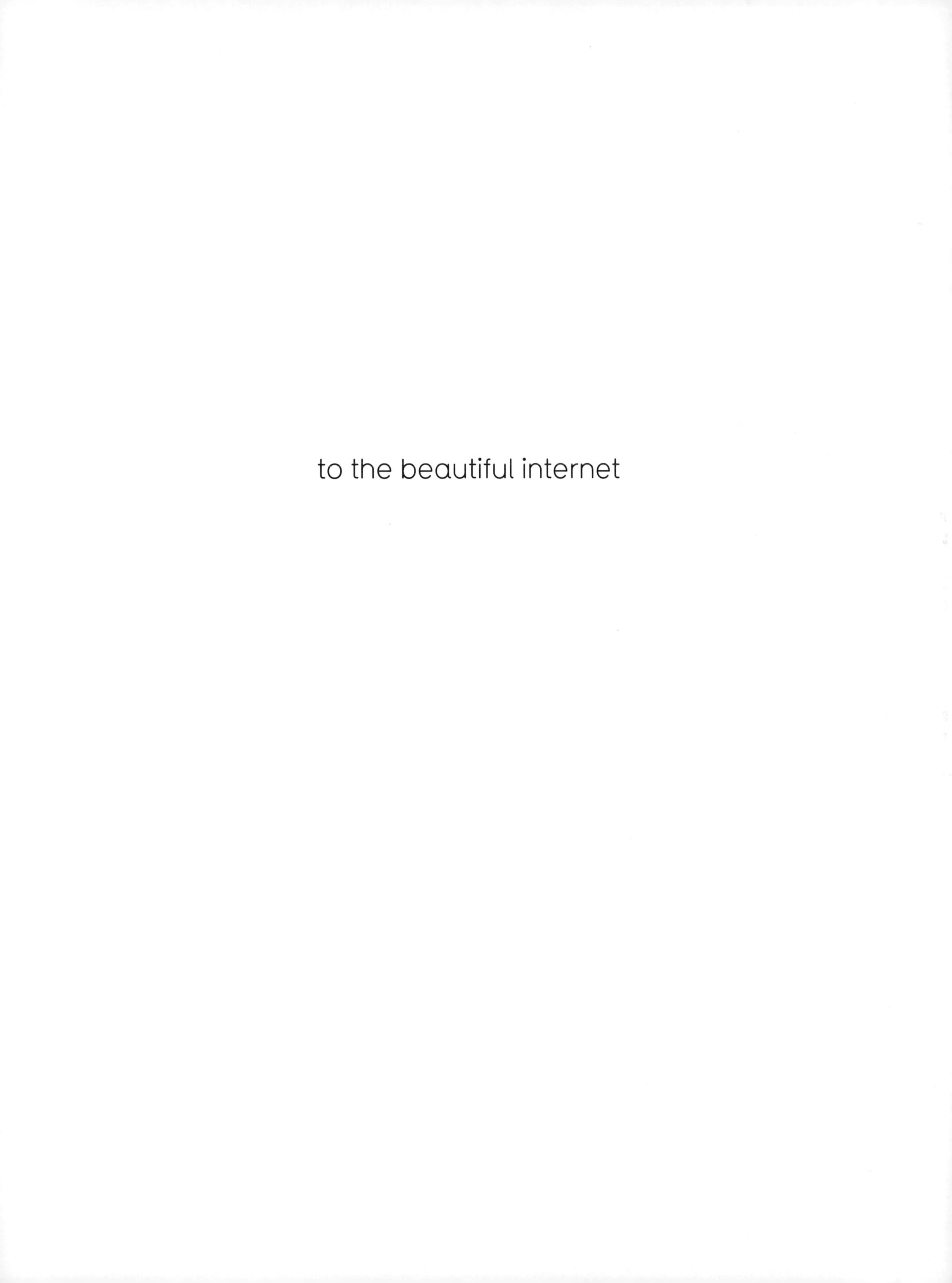

to the beautiful internet

Introduction

This book started out as an exploration. Swamped by information, I was searching for a better way to see it all and understand it. Why not visually?

In a way, we're all visual now. Every day, every hour, maybe even every minute, we're seeing and absorbing information via the web. We're steeped in it. Maybe even lost in it. So perhaps what we need are well-designed, colourful and — hopefully — useful charts to help us navigate. A modern-day map book.

But can a book with the minimum of text, crammed with diagrams, maps and charts, still be exciting and readable? Can it still be fun? Can you make jokes in graphs? Are you even allowed to?

So I started experimenting with visualizing information and ideas in both new and old ways. I went for subjects that sprang from my own curiosity and ignorance — the questions I wanted answering. I avoided straightforward facts and dry statistics. Instead, I focused on the relationship between facts, the context, the connections that make information meaningful.

So, that's what this book is. Miscellaneous facts and ideas, interconnected visually. A visual miscellaneum. A series of experiments in making information approachable and beautiful. See what you think.

David McCandless

POP

WEB

THOUGHT

NATURE

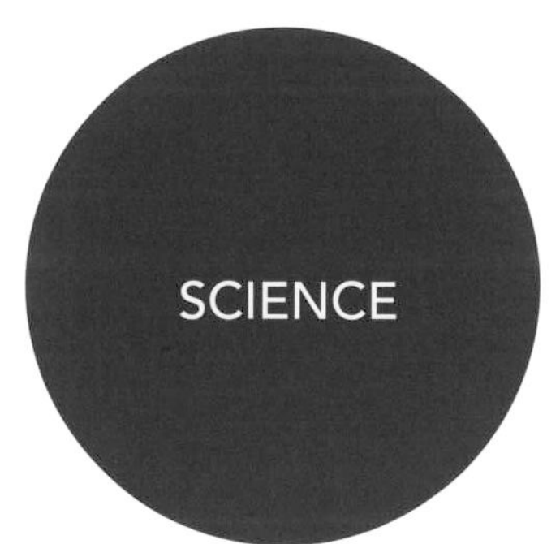
SCIENCE

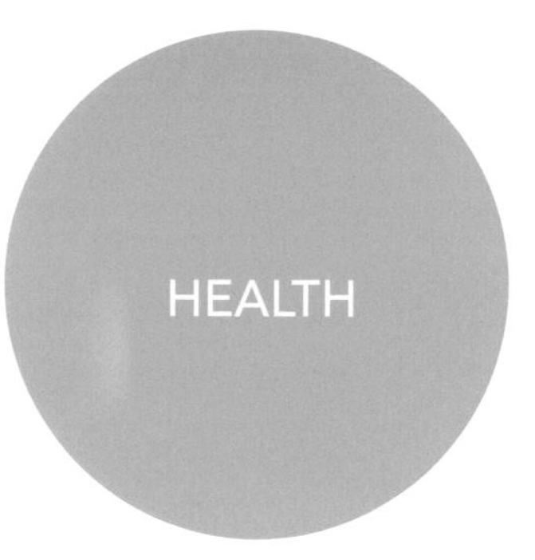
HEALTH

FOOD

POWER

LIFE

FILM

MEDIA

MUSIC

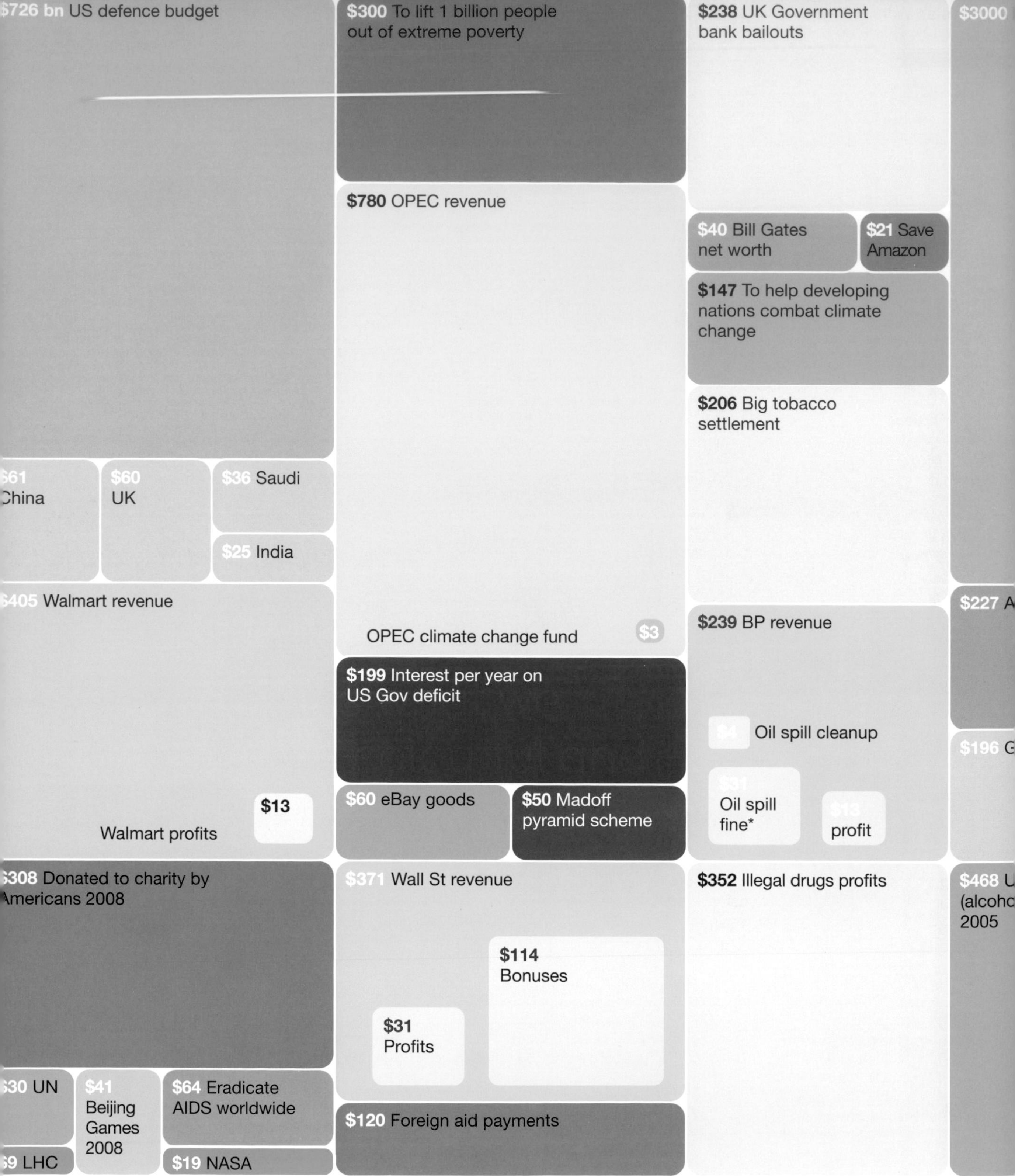
$726 bn US defence budget
$300 To lift 1 billion people out of extreme poverty
$238 UK Government bank bailouts
$3000
$780 OPEC revenue
$40 Bill Gates net worth
$21 Save Amazon
$147 To help developing nations combat climate change
$206 Big tobacco settlement
$61 China
$60 UK
$36 Saudi
$25 India
$405 Walmart revenue
OPEC climate change fund
$3
$227
$239 BP revenue
$199 Interest per year on US Gov deficit
$4
Oil spill cleanup
$196
$31
Oil spill fine*
$13
profit
$13
Walmart profits
$60 eBay goods
$50 Madoff pyramid scheme
$308 Donated to charity by Americans 2008
$371 Wall St revenue
$352 Illegal drugs profits
$468
2005
$114
Bonuses
$31
Profits
$30 UN
$41
Beijing Games 2008
$64 Eradicate AIDS worldwide
$120 Foreign aid payments
$9 LHC
$19 NASA

Billion-Dollar-O-Gram

Billions spent on this. Billions spent on that. It's all relative, right?

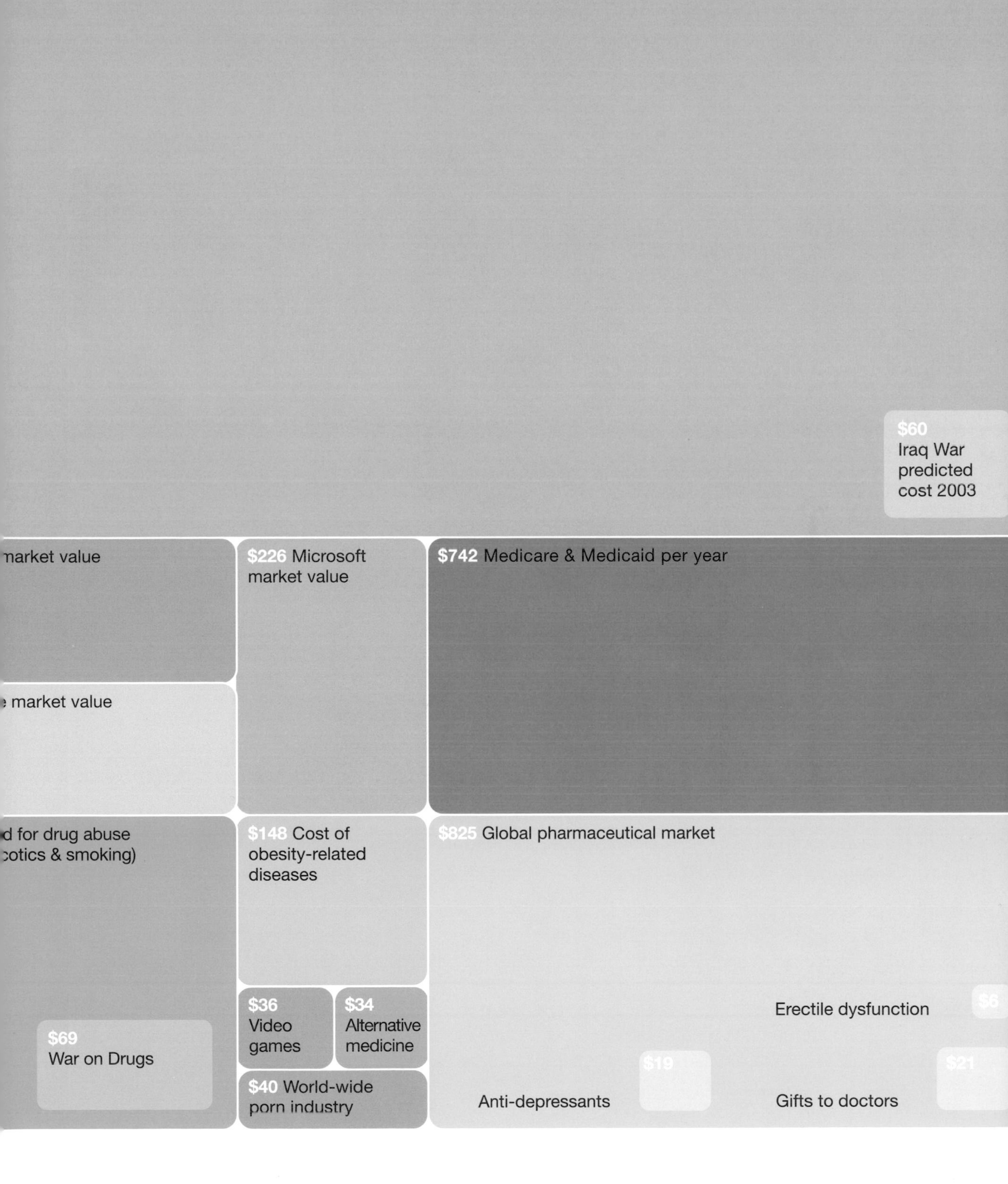
Afghanistan Wars total eventual cost*
$60
Iraq War
predicted
cost 2003
narket value
$226 Microsoft
market value
$742 Medicare & Medicaid per year
market value
d for drug abuse
cotics & smoking)
$148 Cost of
obesity-related
diseases
$825 Global pharmaceutical market
$36
Video
games
$34
Alternative
medicine
Erectile dysfunction
$6
$69
War on Drugs
$40 World-wide
porn industry
$19
Anti-depressants
$21
Gifts to doctors

* estimated

source: MSNBC, Guardian, Washington Post, Forbes, UNODC, BBC News. All figures 2009 unless otherwise stated.

$12,700bn Worldwide cost of the financial crisis

source: Wikipedia, Guardian, Business Week, Ritzholtz.com

Left

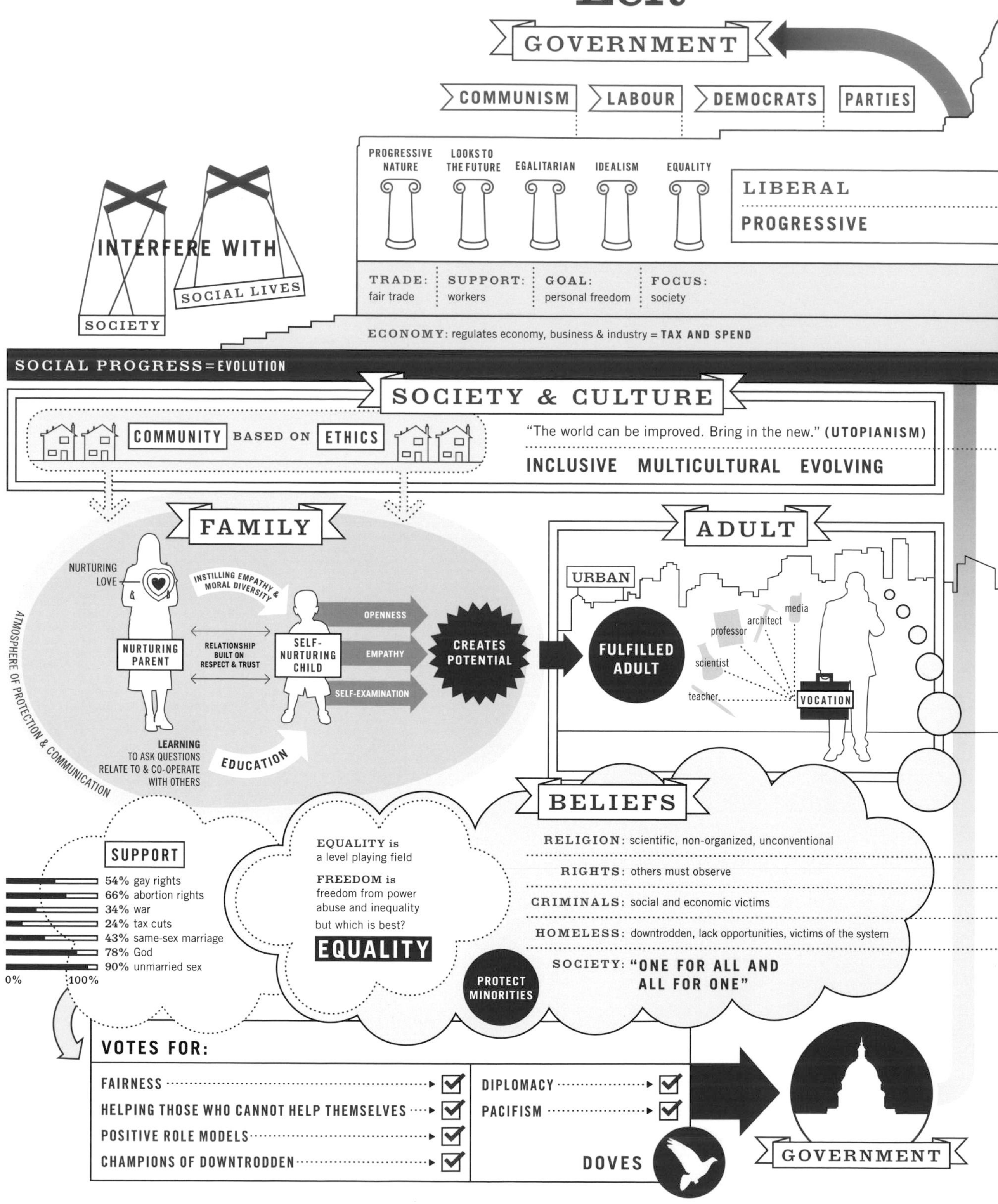

GOVERNMENT
COMMUNISM
LABOUR
DEMOCRATS
PARTIES
PROGRESSIVE NATURE
LOOKS TO THE FUTURE
EGALITARIAN
IDEALISM
EQUALITY
LIBERAL
PROGRESSIVE
INTERFERE WITH
SOCIETY
SOCIAL LIVES
TRADE: fair trade
SUPPORT: workers
GOAL: personal freedom
FOCUS: society
ECONOMY: regulates economy, business & industry = TAX AND SPEND
SOCIAL PROGRESS=EVOLUTION
SOCIETY & CULTURE
COMMUNITY BASED ON ETHICS
"The world can be improved. Bring in the new." (UTOPIANISM)
INCLUSIVE MULTICULTURAL EVOLVING
FAMILY
NURTURING LOVE
INSTILLING EMPATHY & MORAL DIVERSITY
NURTURING PARENT
RELATIONSHIP BUILT ON RESPECT & TRUST
SELF-NURTURING CHILD
OPENNESS
EMPATHY
SELF-EXAMINATION
CREATES POTENTIAL
LEARNING TO ASK QUESTIONS RELATE TO & CO-OPERATE WITH OTHERS
EDUCATION
ATMOSPHERE OF PROTECTION & COMMUNICATION
ADULT
URBAN
FULFILLED ADULT
media
architect
professor
scientist
teacher
VOCATION
BELIEFS
RELIGION: scientific, non-organized, unconventional
RIGHTS: others must observe
CRIMINALS: social and economic victims
HOMELESS: downtrodden, lack opportunities, victims of the system
SOCIETY: "ONE FOR ALL AND ALL FOR ONE"
SUPPORT
54% gay rights
66% abortion rights
34% war
24% tax cuts
43% same-sex marriage
78% God
90% unmarried sex
0%
100%
EQUALITY is a level playing field
FREEDOM is freedom from power abuse and inequality
but which is best?
EQUALITY
PROTECT MINORITIES
VOTES FOR:
FAIRNESS
HELPING THOSE WHO CANNOT HELP THEMSELVES
POSITIVE ROLE MODELS
CHAMPIONS OF DOWNTRODDEN
DIPLOMACY
PACIFISM
DOVES
GOVERNMENT

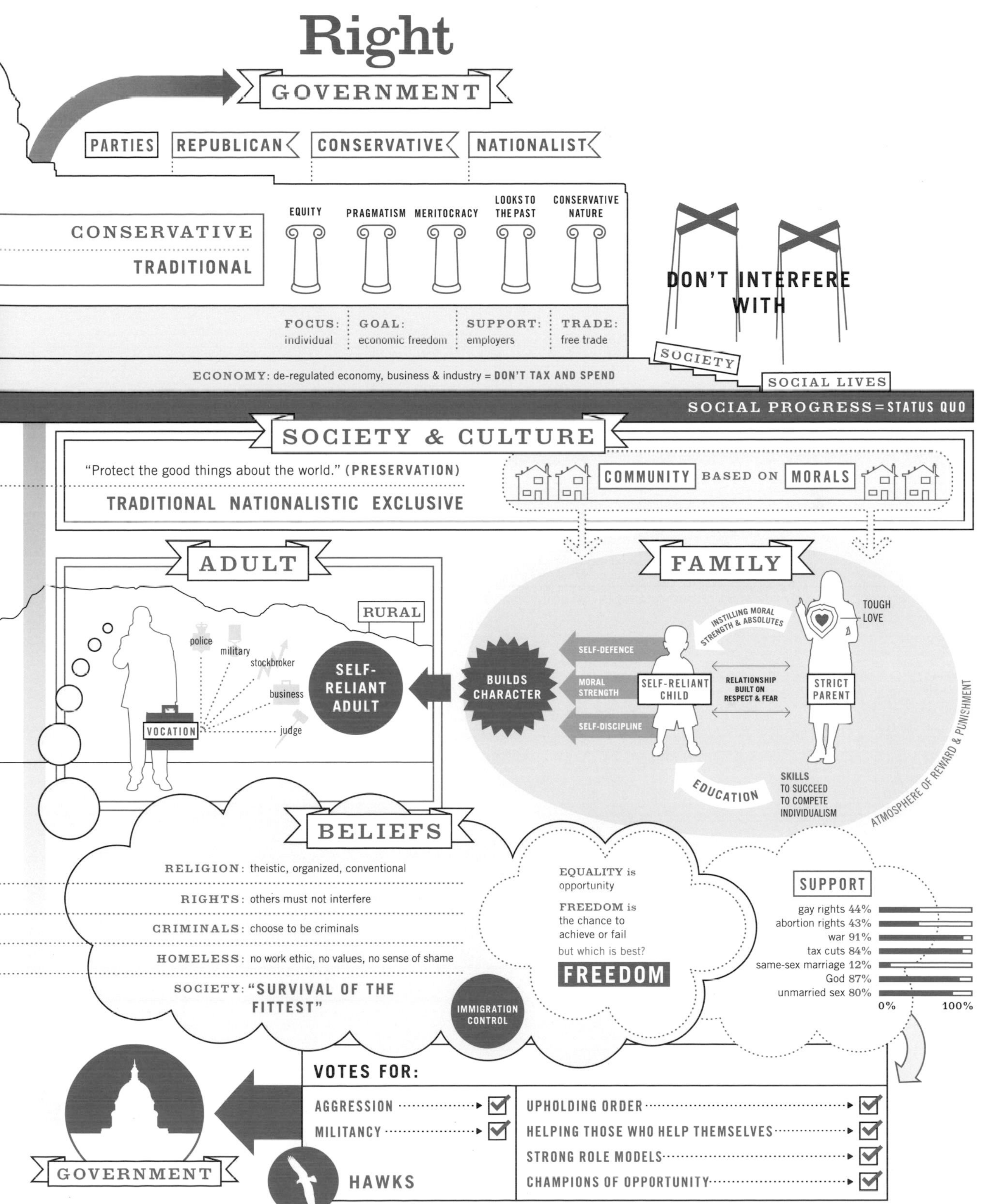

Right
GOVERNMENT
PARTIES
REPUBLICAN
CONSERVATIVE
NATIONALIST
CONSERVATIVE
TRADITIONAL
EQUITY
PRAGMATISM
MERITOCRACY
LOOKS TO THE PAST
CONSERVATIVE NATURE
FOCUS: individual
GOAL: economic freedom
SUPPORT: employers
TRADE: free trade
ECONOMY: de-regulated economy, business & industry = DON'T TAX AND SPEND
DON'T INTERFERE WITH
SOCIETY
SOCIAL LIVES
SOCIAL PROGRESS = STATUS QUO
SOCIETY & CULTURE
"Protect the good things about the world." (PRESERVATION)
TRADITIONAL NATIONALISTIC EXCLUSIVE
COMMUNITY BASED ON MORALS
ADULT
RURAL
police
military
stockbroker
business
judge
VOCATION
SELF-RELIANT ADULT
BUILDS CHARACTER
FAMILY
SELF-DEFENCE
MORAL STRENGTH
SELF-DISCIPLINE
INSTILLING MORAL STRENGTH & ABSOLUTES
SELF-RELIANT CHILD
RELATIONSHIP BUILT ON RESPECT & FEAR
STRICT PARENT
TOUGH LOVE
EDUCATION
SKILLS TO SUCCEED TO COMPETE INDIVIDUALISM
ATMOSPHERE OF REWARD & PUNISHMENT
BELIEFS
RELIGION: theistic, organized, conventional
RIGHTS: others must not interfere
CRIMINALS: choose to be criminals
HOMELESS: no work ethic, no values, no sense of shame
SOCIETY: "SURVIVAL OF THE FITTEST"
IMMIGRATION CONTROL
EQUALITY is opportunity
FREEDOM is the chance to achieve or fail
but which is best?
FREEDOM
SUPPORT
gay rights 44%
abortion rights 43%
war 91%
tax cuts 84%
same-sex marriage 12%
God 87%
unmarried sex 80%
0%
100%
VOTES FOR:
AGGRESSION
MILITANCY
UPHOLDING ORDER
HELPING THOSE WHO HELP THEMSELVES
STRONG ROLE MODELS
CHAMPIONS OF OPPORTUNITY
HAWKS
GOVERNMENT

source: Wikipedia, Britannica.com, New Scientist, Conservative-resources.com

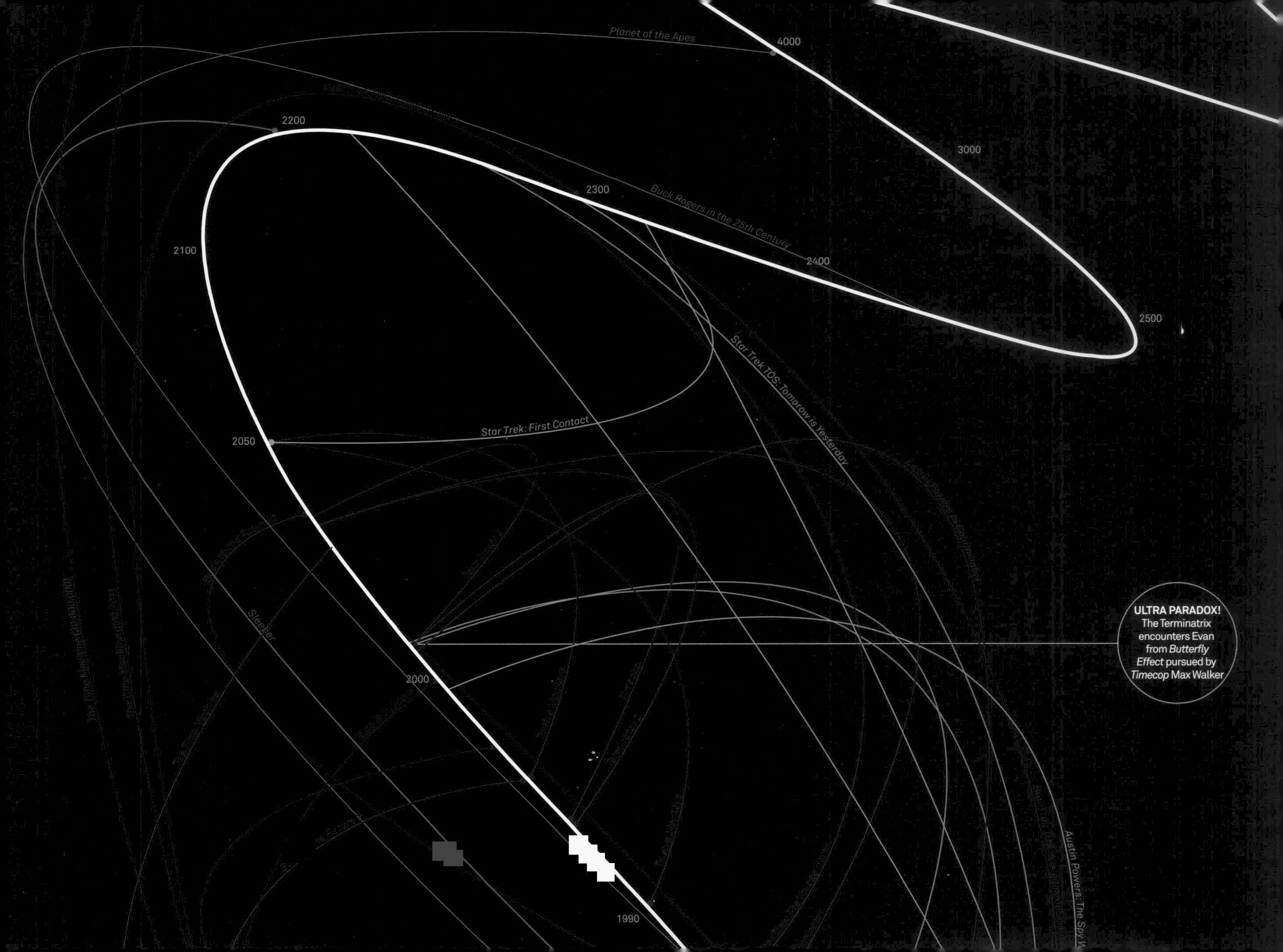

Planet of the Apes
4000
3000
2500
2400
Buck Rogers in the 25th Century
2300
2200
2100
2050
Star Trek: First Contact
Star Trek TOS: Tomorrow is Yesterday
ULTRA PARADOX!
The Terminatrix encounters Evan from *Butterfly Effect* pursued by *Timecop* Max Walker
2000
Sleeper
1990
Austin Powers: The Spy W

ULTRA PARADOX!
Marty McFly meets the Star Trek crew and both battle The Terminator
PARADOX!
The Time Bandits meet Evan from Butterfly Effect
PARADOX!
DCI Sam Tyler arrests (and beats) Miles Munroe from Sleeper
Method Of Time Travel
Alien Tech
Force of Nature
Time Machine
Deep Freeze
Life on Mars
Star Trek TNG: Time's Arrow 1&2
Star Trek TOS: City on the Edge of Forever
Red Dwarf
Back to the Future 1&2
Bill And Ted's Excellent Adventure
Time Bandits
800
1000
1200
1400
1600
1800
1850
1900
1950
1960
1970
1980
Time Lines
Time travel plots in TV and film

Snake Oil?

Scientific evidence for popular dietary supplements showing tangible health benefits when taken orally by an adult with a healthy diet.

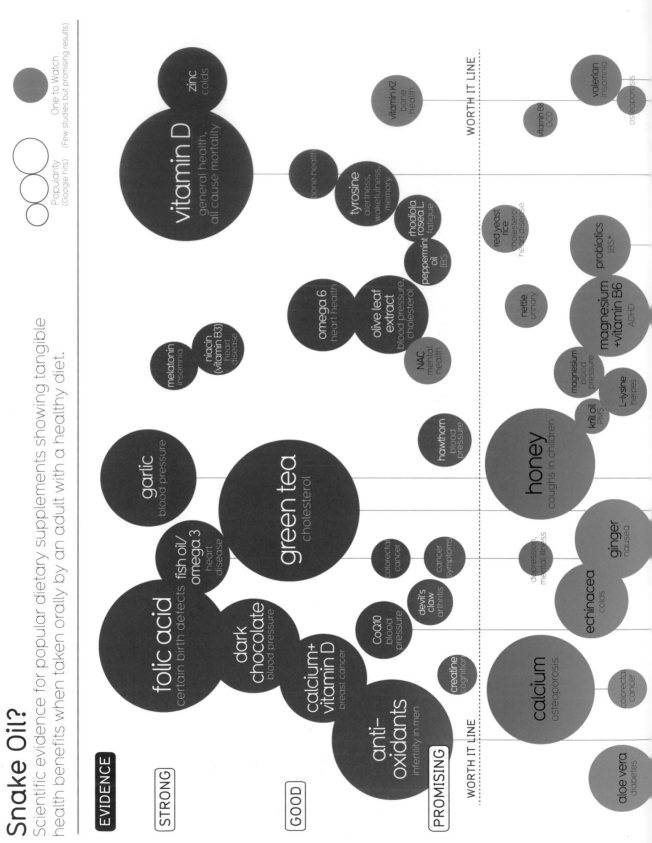

Popularity
(Google hits)

One to Watch
(Few studies but promising results)

EVIDENCE

STRONG

GOOD

PROMISING

WORTH IT LINE

folic acid
certain birth defects

fish oil/ omega 3
heart disease

garlic
blood pressure

melatonin
insomnia

niacin (vitamin B3)
heart disease

vitamin D
general health, all cause mortality

zinc
colds

dark chocolate
blood pressure

green tea
cholesterol

calcium+ vitamin D
breast cancer

omega 6
heart health

bone health

tyrosine
alertness, wakefulness, memory

anti-oxidants
infertility in men

CoQ10
blood pressure

colorectal cancer

olive leaf extract
blood pressure, cholesterol

vitamin K2
bone health

devil's claw
arthritis

cancer symptoms

NAC
mental health

peppermint oil
IBS

rhodiola rosea L.
fatigue

creatine
cognition

hawthorn
blood pressure

red yeast rice
cholesterol heart disease

nettle
urinary

calcium
osteoporosis

depression, mental illness

honey
coughs in children

vitamin B8
OCD

magnesium
blood pressure

echinacea
colds

krill oil
PMS

magnesium +vitamin B6
ADHD

probiotics
IBS*

valerian
insomnia

ginger
nausea

aloe vera
diabetes

colorectal cancer

L-lysine
herpes

osteoporosis

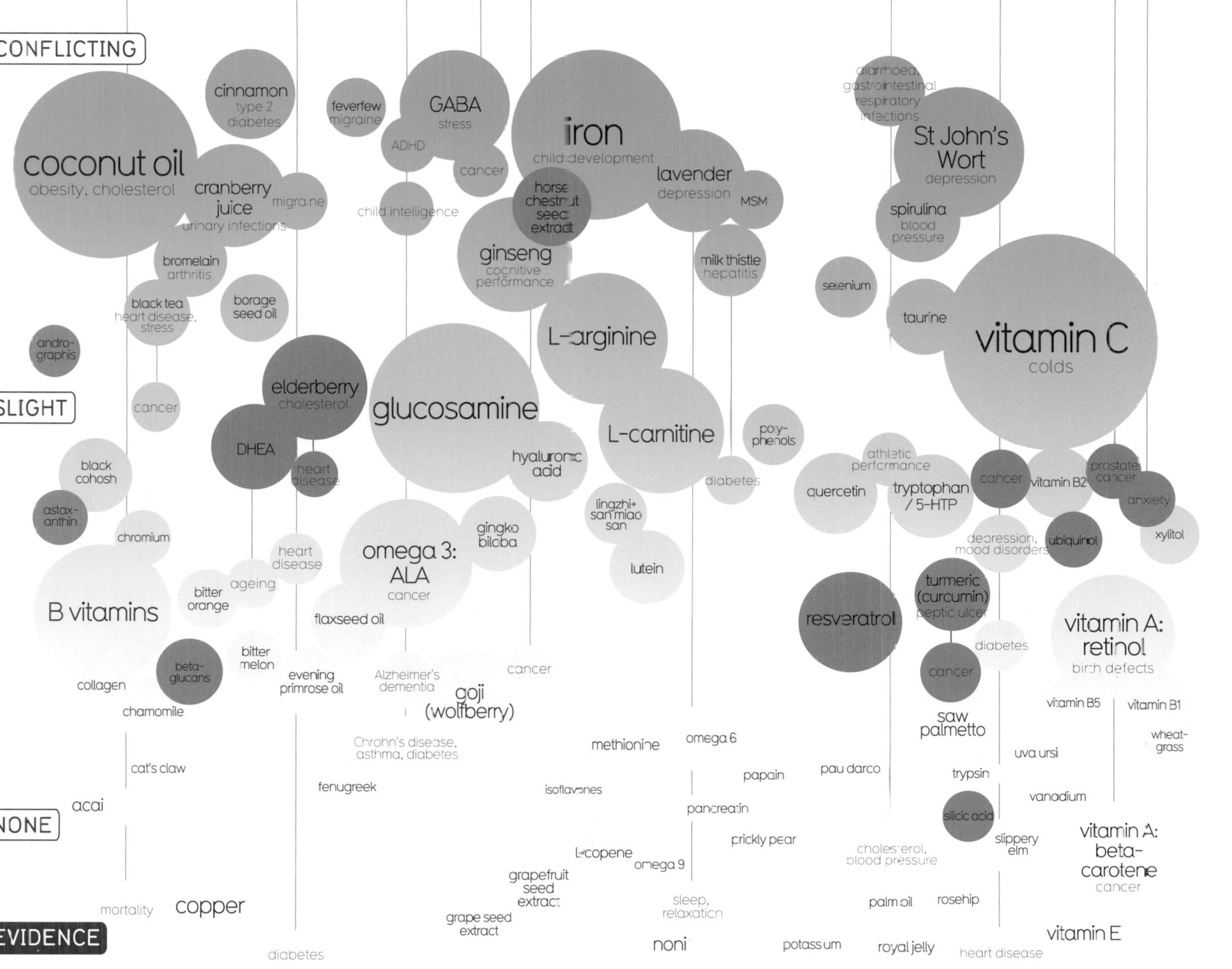
CONFLICTING
SLIGHT
NONE
EVIDENCE
coconut oil
obesity, cholesterol
cinnamon
type 2 diabetes
cranberry juice
urinary infections
migraine
bromelain
arthritis
black tea
heart disease, stress
borage seed oil
andro-graphis
cancer
feverfew
migraine
GABA
stress
ADHD
cancer
child intelligence
iron
child development
horse chestnut seed extract
ginseng
cognitive performance
lavender
depression
MSM
milk thistle
hepatitis
diarrhoea, gastrointestinal, respiratory infections
St John's Wort
depression
spirulina
blood pressure
selenium
taurine
vitamin C
colds
elderberry
cholesterol
DHEA
heart disease
glucosamine
L-arginine
L-carnitine
poly-phenols
diabetes
hyaluronic acid
black cohosh
astax-anthin
chromium
heart disease
ageing
bitter orange
B vitamins
omega 3: ALA
cancer
gingko biloba
lingzhi+ san miao san
lutein
flaxseed oil
quercetin
athletic performance
tryptophan / 5-HTP
cancer
vitamin B2
prostate cancer
anxiety
xylitol
depression, mood disorders
ubiquinol
turmeric (curcumin)
peptic ulcer
resveratrol
diabetes
cancer
vitamin A: retinol
birth defects
beta-glucans
bitter melon
evening primrose oil
Alzheimer's dementia
cancer
goji (wolfberry)
collagen
chamomile
Chrohn's disease, asthma, diabetes
methionine
omega 6
saw palmetto
vitamin B5
vitamin B1
wheat-grass
cat's claw
papain
pau darco
uva ursi
trypsin
fenugreek
isoflavones
pancreatin
vanadium
acai
silicic acid
prickly pear
slippery elm
vitamin A: beta-carotene
cancer
Lycopene
omega 9
cholesterol, blood pressure
grapefruit seed extract
sleep, relaxation
palm oil
rosehip
mortality
copper
grape seed extract
noni
potassium
royal jelly
heart disease
vitamin E
diabetes

source: English language placebo-controlled double-blind human trials on PubMed.org and Cochrane.org, The US Office of Dietary Supplements, Herbmed.org, European Medicines Agency

International Number Ones

Because every country is the best at something

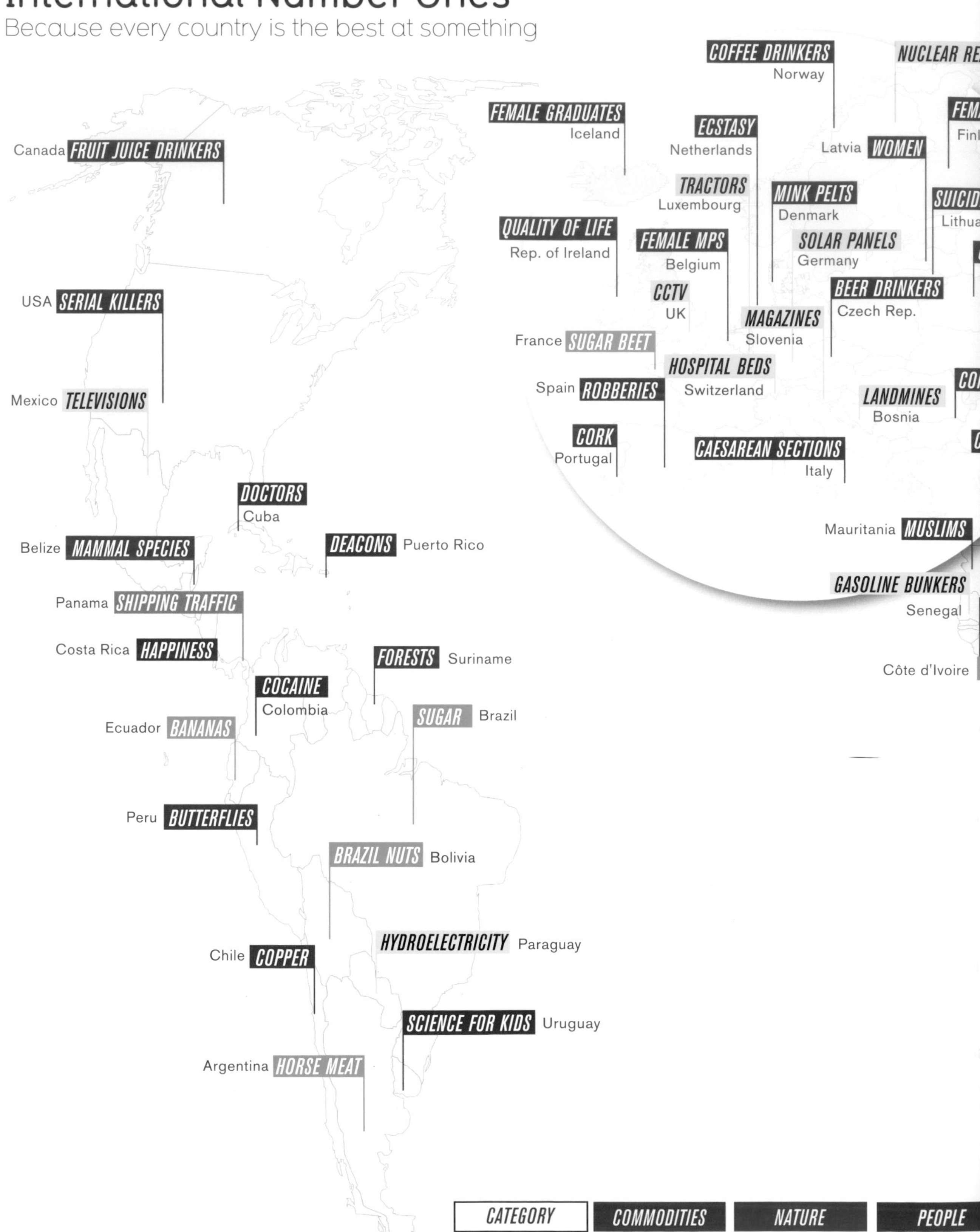

COFFEE DRINKERS
Norway
NUCLEAR RE
FEMALE GRADUATES
Iceland
ECSTASY
Netherlands
Latvia
WOMEN
FEM
Finl
Canada
FRUIT JUICE DRINKERS
TRACTORS
Luxembourg
MINK PELTS
Denmark
SUICID
Lithua
QUALITY OF LIFE
Rep. of Ireland
FEMALE MPS
Belgium
SOLAR PANELS
Germany
USA
SERIAL KILLERS
CCTV
UK
BEER DRINKERS
Czech Rep.
MAGAZINES
Slovenia
France
SUGAR BEET
HOSPITAL BEDS
Switzerland
Mexico
TELEVISIONS
Spain
ROBBERIES
LANDMINES
Bosnia
CORK
Portugal
CAESAREAN SECTIONS
Italy
DOCTORS
Cuba
Mauritania
MUSLIMS
Belize
MAMMAL SPECIES
DEACONS
Puerto Rico
GASOLINE BUNKERS
Senegal
Panama
SHIPPING TRAFFIC
Costa Rica
HAPPINESS
FORESTS
Suriname
Côte d'Ivoire
COCAINE
Colombia
Ecuador
BANANAS
SUGAR
Brazil
Peru
BUTTERFLIES
BRAZIL NUTS
Bolivia
HYDROELECTRICITY
Paraguay
Chile
COPPER
SCIENCE FOR KIDS
Uruguay
Argentina
HORSE MEAT
CATEGORY
COMMODITIES
NATURE
PEOPLE

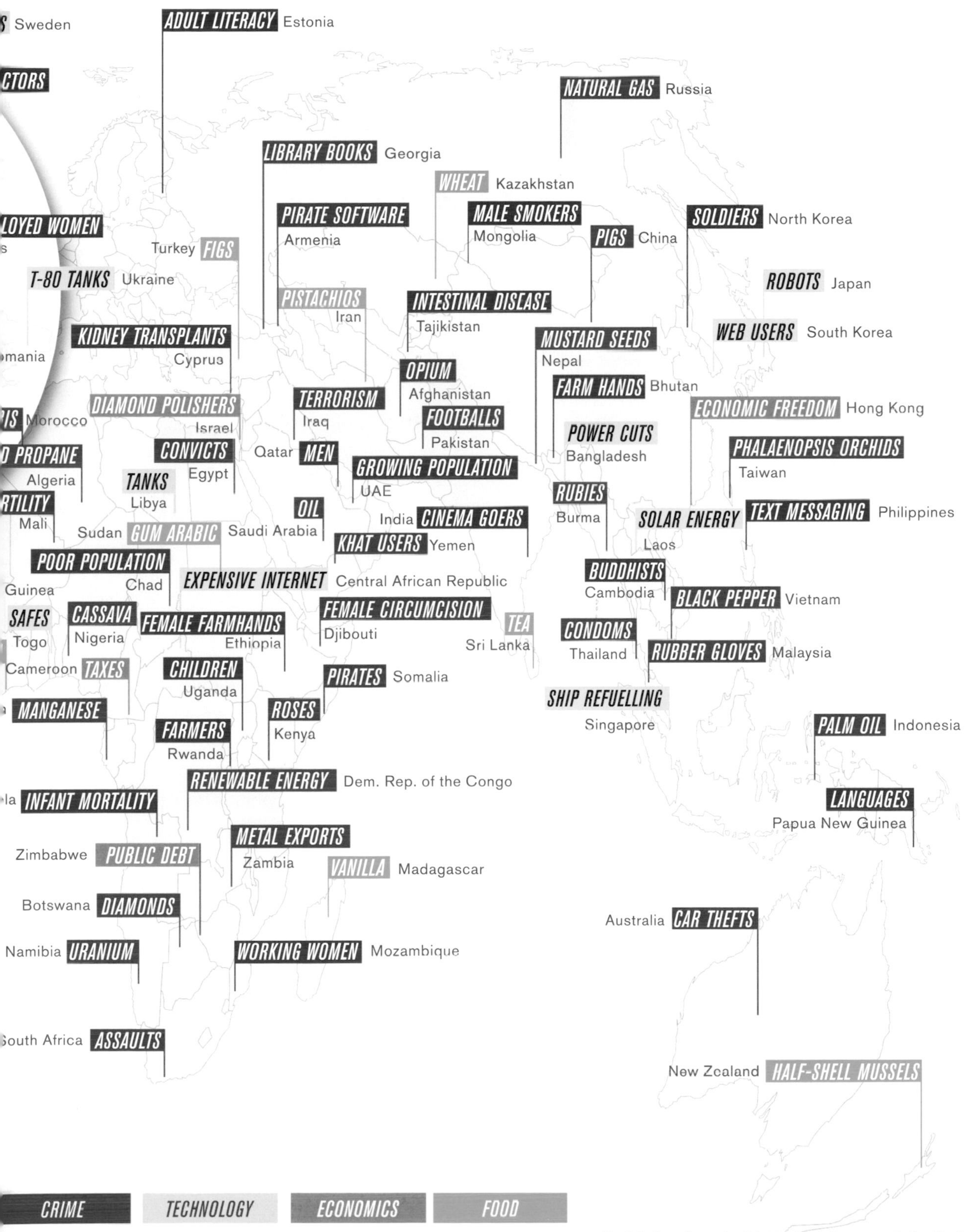
Sweden
ADULT LITERACY Estonia
NATURAL GAS Russia
LIBRARY BOOKS Georgia
WHEAT Kazakhstan
PIRATE SOFTWARE Armenia
MALE SMOKERS Mongolia
PIGS China
SOLDIERS North Korea
Turkey FIGS
T-80 TANKS Ukraine
ROBOTS Japan
PISTACHIOS Iran
INTESTINAL DISEASE Tajikistan
WEB USERS South Korea
KIDNEY TRANSPLANTS Cyprus
MUSTARD SEEDS Nepal
OPIUM Afghanistan
FARM HANDS Bhutan
DIAMOND POLISHERS Israel
TERRORISM Iraq
FOOTBALLS Pakistan
ECONOMIC FREEDOM Hong Kong
Morocco
POWER CUTS Bangladesh
PHALAENOPSIS ORCHIDS Taiwan
CONVICTS Egypt
Qatar MEN
GROWING POPULATION UAE
Algeria
TANKS Libya
RUBIES Burma
OIL Saudi Arabia
Mali
India CINEMA GOERS
SOLAR ENERGY Laos
TEXT MESSAGING Philippines
Sudan GUM ARABIC
KHAT USERS Yemen
POOR POPULATION Chad
EXPENSIVE INTERNET Central African Republic
BUDDHISTS Cambodia
Guinea
BLACK PEPPER Vietnam
FEMALE CIRCUMCISION Djibouti
SAFES Togo
CASSAVA Nigeria
FEMALE FARMHANDS Ethiopia
TEA Sri Lanka
CONDOMS Thailand
RUBBER GLOVES Malaysia
Cameroon TAXES
CHILDREN Uganda
PIRATES Somalia
SHIP REFUELLING Singapore
MANGANESE
ROSES Kenya
FARMERS Rwanda
PALM OIL Indonesia
RENEWABLE ENERGY Dem. Rep. of the Congo
INFANT MORTALITY
LANGUAGES Papua New Guinea
Zimbabwe PUBLIC DEBT
METAL EXPORTS Zambia
VANILLA Madagascar
Botswana DIAMONDS
Australia CAR THEFTS
Namibia URANIUM
WORKING WOMEN Mozambique
South Africa ASSAULTS
New Zealand HALF-SHELL MUSSELS
CRIME
TECHNOLOGY
ECONOMICS
FOOD

source: per capita data from NewScientist.com, Unstats.un.org, NationMaster.com

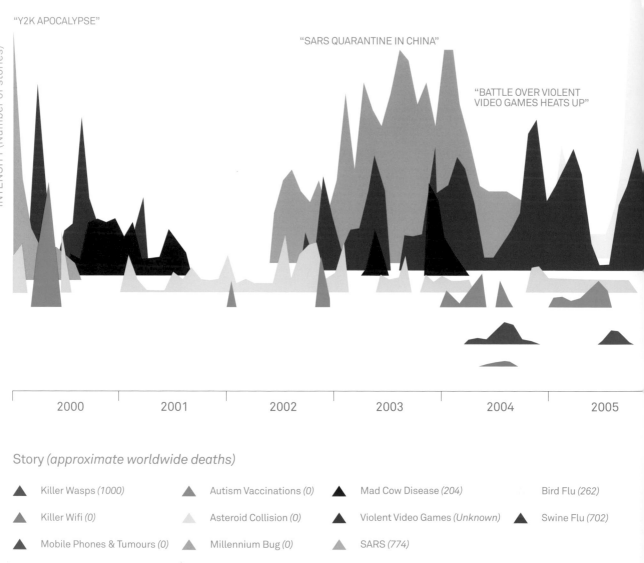

"Y2K APOCALYPSE"

"SARS QUARANTINE IN CHINA"

"BATTLE OVER VIOLENT VIDEO GAMES HEATS UP"

INTENSITY (Number of stories)

2000
2001
2002
2003
2004
2005

Story *(approximate worldwide deaths)*

- Killer Wasps *(1000)*
- Killer Wifi *(0)*
- Mobile Phones & Tumours *(0)*
- Autism Vaccinations *(0)*
- Asteroid Collision *(0)*
- Millennium Bug *(0)*
- Mad Cow Disease *(204)*
- Violent Video Games *(Unknown)*
- SARS *(774)*
- Bird Flu *(262)*
- Swine Flu *(702)*

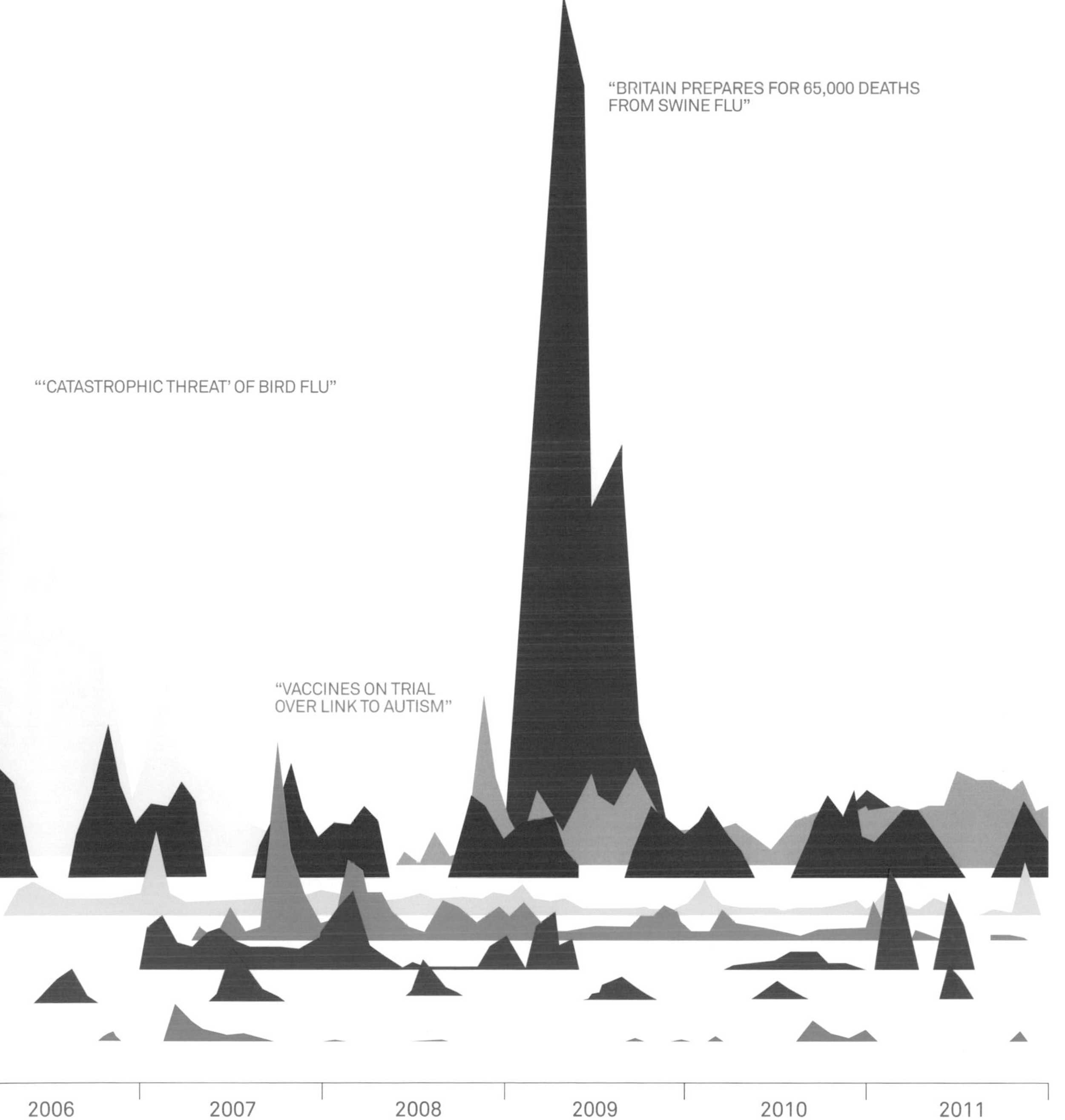
"BRITAIN PREPARES FOR 65,000 DEATHS FROM SWINE FLU"
"'CATASTROPHIC THREAT' OF BIRD FLU"
"VACCINES ON TRIAL OVER LINK TO AUTISM"
2006
2007
2008
2009
2010
2011

Mountains out of Molehills

A timeline of global media scare stories

source: Google News and Insights for Search (worldwide deaths at time of print)

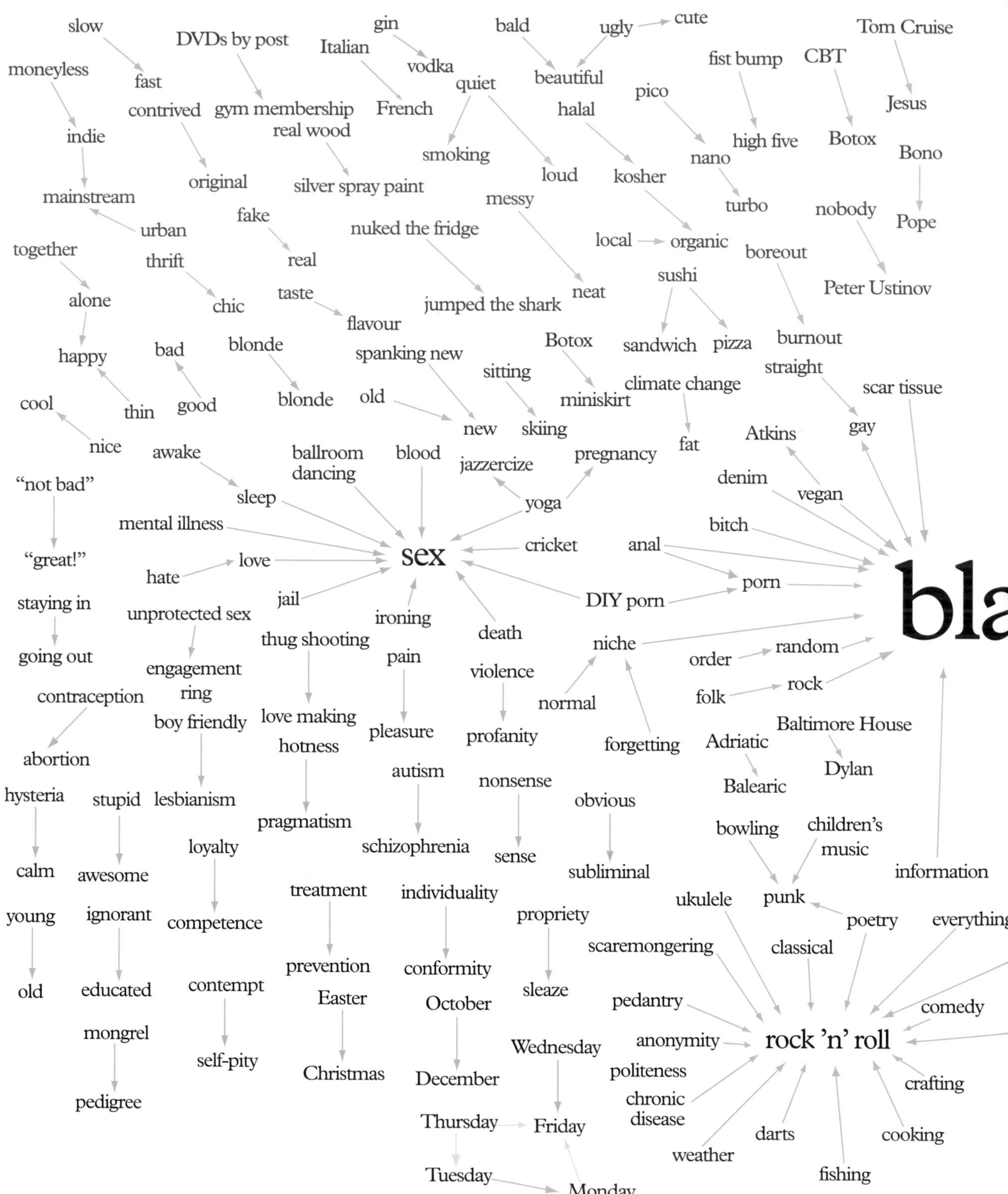
slow
fast
moneyless
indie
mainstream
urban
DVDs by post
gym membership
contrived
original
gin
vodka
Italian
French
real wood
silver spray paint
quiet
smoking
loud
bald
beautiful
ugly
cute
halal
kosher
pico
nano
turbo
fist bump
high five
CBT
Botox
Tom Cruise
Jesus
Bono
Pope
nobody
Peter Ustinov
together
alone
happy
thin
fake
real
thrift
chic
taste
flavour
nuked the fridge
jumped the shark
messy
neat
local
organic
sushi
sandwich
pizza
boreout
burnout
bad
good
blonde
blonde
spanking new
old
new
sitting
skiing
Botox
miniskirt
climate change
fat
straight
gay
scar tissue
cool
nice
awake
sleep
ballroom dancing
blood
jazzercize
yoga
pregnancy
Atkins
vegan
denim
bitch
"not bad"
"great!"
mental illness
sex
cricket
anal
porn
DIY porn
bla
hate
love
jail
ironing
death
niche
order
random
folk
rock
staying in
going out
unprotected sex
engagement ring
thug shooting
love making
pain
pleasure
violence
profanity
normal
forgetting
contraception
abortion
boy friendly
lesbianism
hotness
pragmatism
autism
schizophrenia
nonsense
sense
obvious
subliminal
Baltimore House
Dylan
Adriatic
Balearic
hysteria
calm
stupid
awesome
loyalty
competence
bowling
children's music
punk
information
young
old
ignorant
educated
treatment
prevention
individuality
conformity
propriety
sleaze
ukulele
poetry
everything
scaremongering
classical
contempt
self-pity
Easter
Christmas
October
December
pedantry
comedy
mongrel
pedigree
Wednesday
Friday
anonymity
rock 'n' roll
politeness
chronic disease
crafting
Thursday
Tuesday
Monday
weather
darts
fishing
cooking

X "is the new" Black

A map of clichés

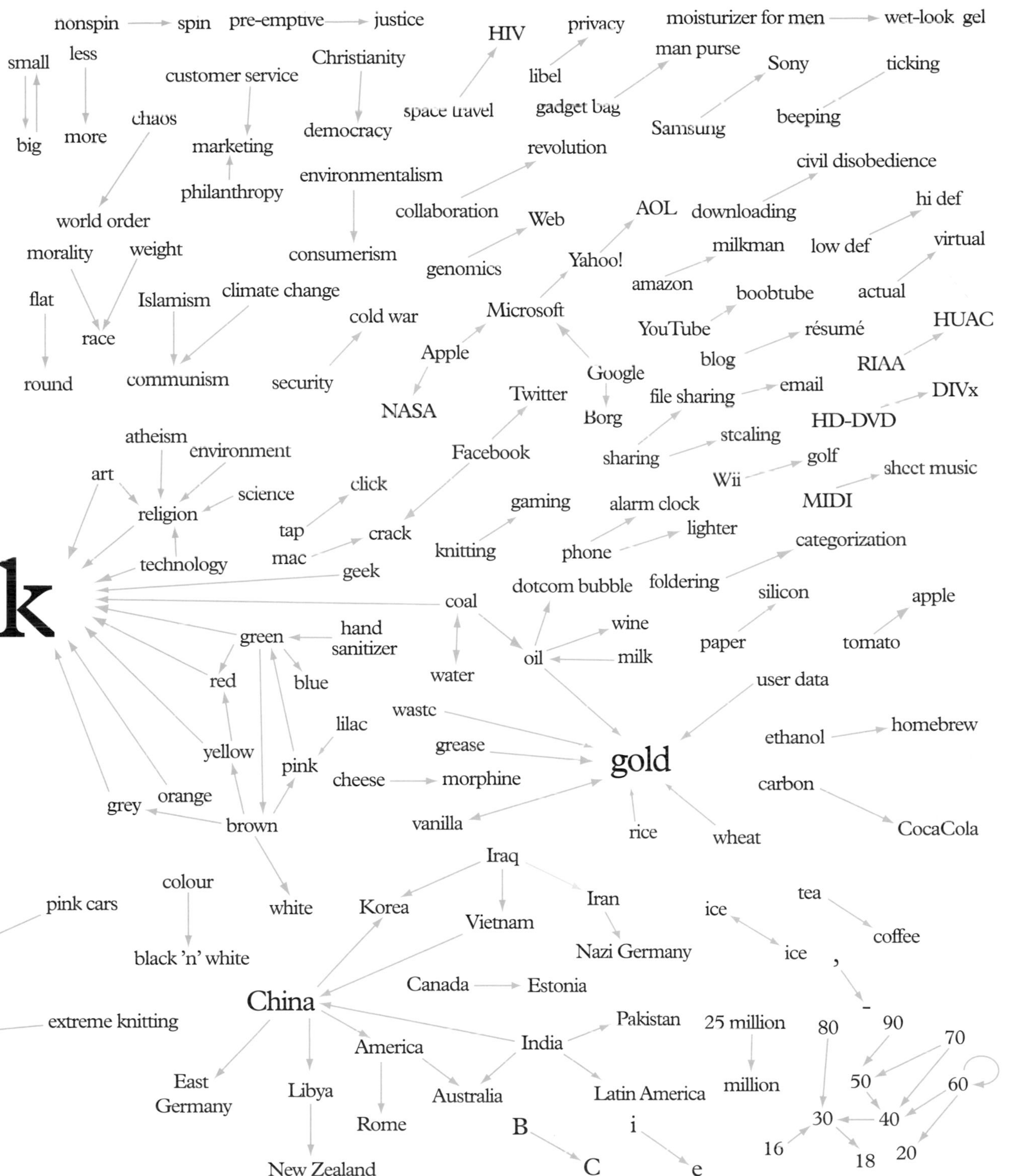
nonspin
spin
pre-emptive
justice
HIV
privacy
moisturizer for men
wet-look gel
small
less
Christianity
libel
man purse
Sony
ticking
customer service
space travel
gadget bag
beeping
big
more
chaos
democracy
Samsung
marketing
revolution
civil disobedience
environmentalism
philanthropy
collaboration
AOL
downloading
hi def
world order
Web
milkman
low def
virtual
morality
weight
consumerism
genomics
Yahoo!
amazon
actual
flat
Islamism
climate change
boobtube
cold war
Microsoft
HUAC
race
YouTube
résumé
Apple
blog
RIAA
round
communism
security
Google
email
NASA
Twitter
file sharing
DIVx
Borg
HD-DVD
atheism
stealing
environment
Facebook
sharing
golf
art
sheet music
click
Wii
science
religion
gaming
alarm clock
MIDI
tap
crack
lighter
knitting
categorization
mac
phone
technology
geek
ck
dotcom bubble
foldering
silicon
coal
apple
wine
hand sanitizer
green
paper
tomato
oil
milk
red
blue
water
user data
waste
lilac
ethanol
homebrew
grease
yellow
gold
pink
cheese
morphine
carbon
orange
grey
vanilla
brown
rice
wheat
CocaCola
Iraq
colour
Iran
tea
pink cars
white
Korea
ice
Vietnam
coffee
black 'n' white
Nazi Germany
ice
,
Canada
Estonia
-
China
extreme knitting
Pakistan
25 million
80
90
70
America
India
50
60
East Germany
Libya
Australia
Latin America
million
30
40
Rome
B
i
16
18
20
C
e
New Zealand

Searches for the phrase "is the new" on various media websites.

idea: Randall Szott // source: Google, Guardian.co.uk, NewScientist.com, Wired.com, Nytimes.com

Kilograms of Carbon

Emissions per year

2,100
average meat-based diet
750
your facebook page
1,500
to heat the average hom
1,200
vegetarian diet
100
vegan diet
360
breathing
50
electric kettle
210
cappucino
(one a day)
90
low energy bulb
80
toilet roll
0
drying washing
on line
720
21" iMac computer
200
laptop
500
incandescent bulb
180
electric shower
(once a day)
310
tumbledryer
(3 times a week)
140
emails
(20 a day)
1,250
80
cremation
40
burial
1 TON
amount absorbed by a
tree in its lifetime
150
wine
140
28" LCD TV
50
mobile phone calls
(2 mins per day)
mobile phone calls
(1 hour per day)

Tons of Carbon

Emissions per year

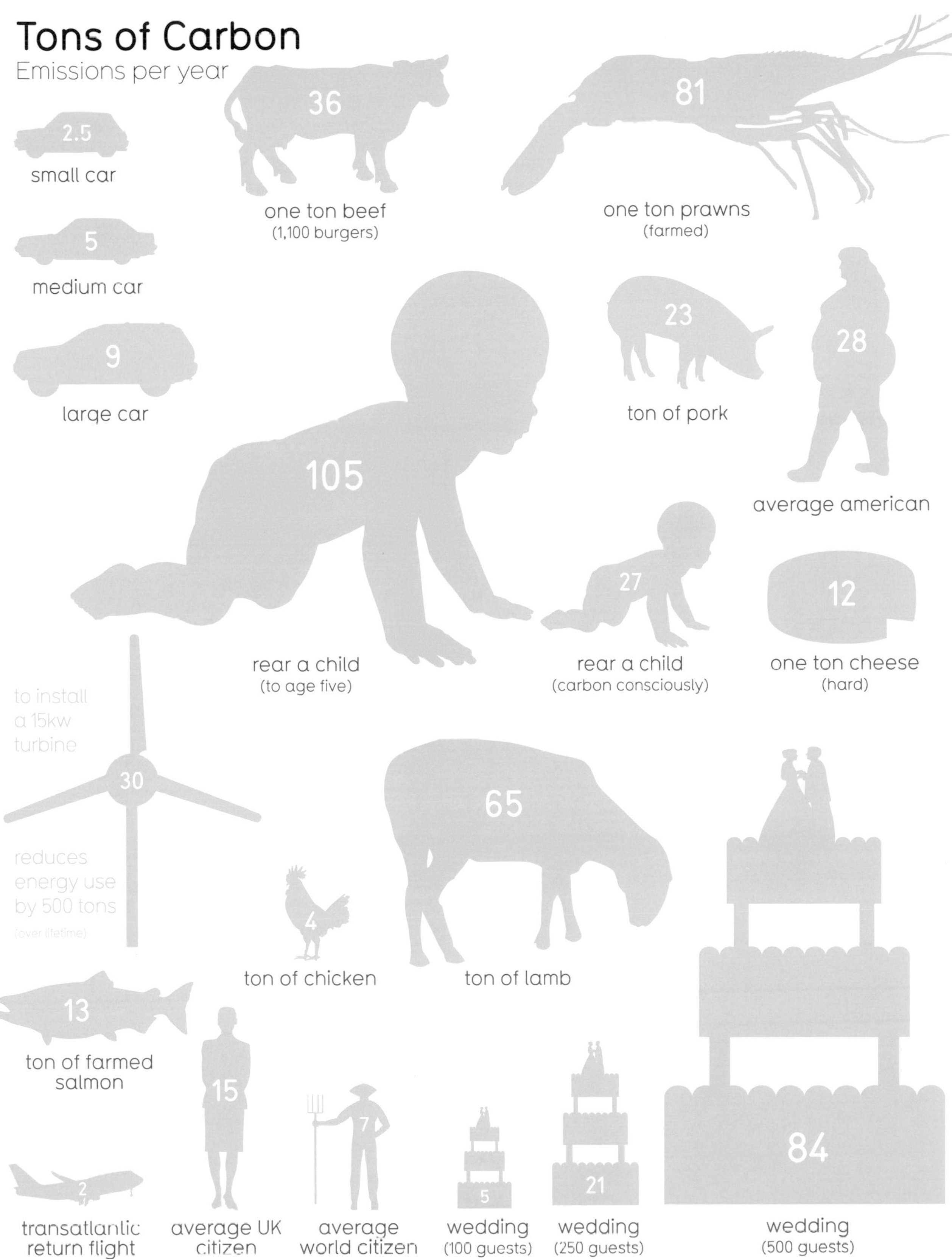
2.5
small car
5
medium car
9
large car
36
one ton beef
(1,100 burgers)
81
one ton prawns
(farmed)
105
rear a child
(to age five)
23
ton of pork
28
average american
27
rear a child
(carbon consciously)
12
one ton cheese
(hard)
to install
a 15kw
turbine
30
reduces
energy use
by 500 tons
(over lifetime)
4
ton of chicken
65
ton of lamb
13
ton of farmed
salmon
2
transatlantic
return flight
15
average UK
citizen
7
average
world citizen
5
wedding
(100 guests)
21
wedding
(250 guests)
84
wedding
(500 guests)

source: New York Times, Environmental Protection Agency, IPCC, Energy Information Administration, UNESCO

Books Everyone Should Read

A consensus cloud

All Quiet on t
Anne of Green Gables Emma Th
Of Mice and Men
The Jungle Lonesome Dove Life of Pi
Midnight's Children The Time Traveler's Wi
The Da Vinci Code Persuasion
The Fountainhead The Stranger Remembranc
Sense and Sensibility M
Underworld Love in the Time of Cholera Lord of t
The Remains of the Day The Handmaid's Tale
Invisible Man Scoop His Dark Materials One H
Watership Down The Leopard Winnie the Pooh The Sound and the Fury The Name of
A Thousand Splendid Suns
The Three Musketeers The Adventures of Huckle
The Lord of the Rings To Kill
The Life and Opinions of Tristram Shandy, Gentleman
The Scarlet Letter
Blood Meridian The Hitchhiker's Guid
The Color Purple The Chronicles of Narnia Lolita
A Prayer for Owen Meany Harry Potter Crash Vanity Fair
Siddhartha Tess of the D'Urbervilles Crime and
A Farewell to Arms Pride and Prejudice Les
Don Quixote The Hobbit Jane Eyre David
The Tin Drum Gone with the Wind Great Ex
Alice's Adventures in Wonderland Heart of Da
The Brothers Karamazov The Grape
Middlemarch
The Unbearable Lightness of

estern Front
ıre of Dorian Gray Atonement
ıdame Bovary A Clockwork Orange
Vuthering Heights Of Human Bondage
East of Eden Fahrenheit 451
f Things Past The Road The Little Prince
x Disgrace The Curious Incident of the Dog in the Night-Time
Flies On the Road The Kite Runner The Bell Jar
ndred Years of Solitude Dracula
ose One Flew Over the Cuckoo's Nest Little Women
rry Finn Beloved 1984 Stranger in a Strange Land
Moby-Dick
Mockingbird The Old Man and the Sea
The Master and Margarita Frankenstein
to the Galaxy War and Peace
ne The Glass Bead Game Twilight Do Androids Dream of Electric Sheep?
ve New World A Confederacy of Dunces Foundation
A Tale of Two Cities
unishment Catch-22 Possession
Cold Comfort Farm Memoirs of a Geisha
sérables Anna Karenina The Wind in the Willows
Atlas Shrugged
pperfield Slaughterhouse-Five Ender's Game
ions Ulysses
The Amazing Adventures of Kavalier and Clay
ess Animal Farm Rebecca
f Wrath For Whom the Bell Tolls
Oscar and Lucinda
The Good Earth

source: Desert Island Discs, Pulitzer Prize, AskMetafilter.com, World Day Book Poll, Booker Prize, BBC Big Reads, Oprah's Book Club List & the author's own top five

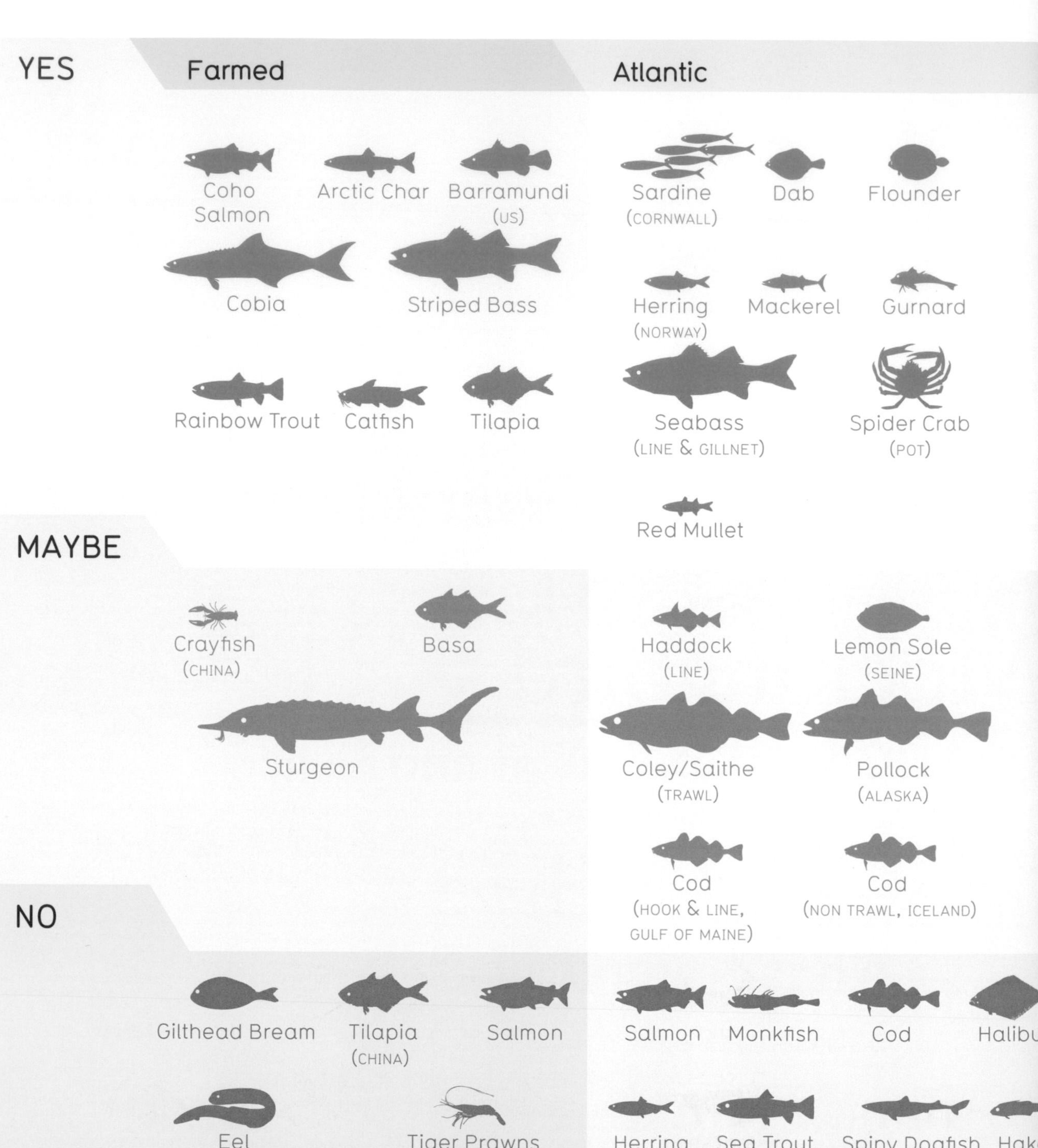

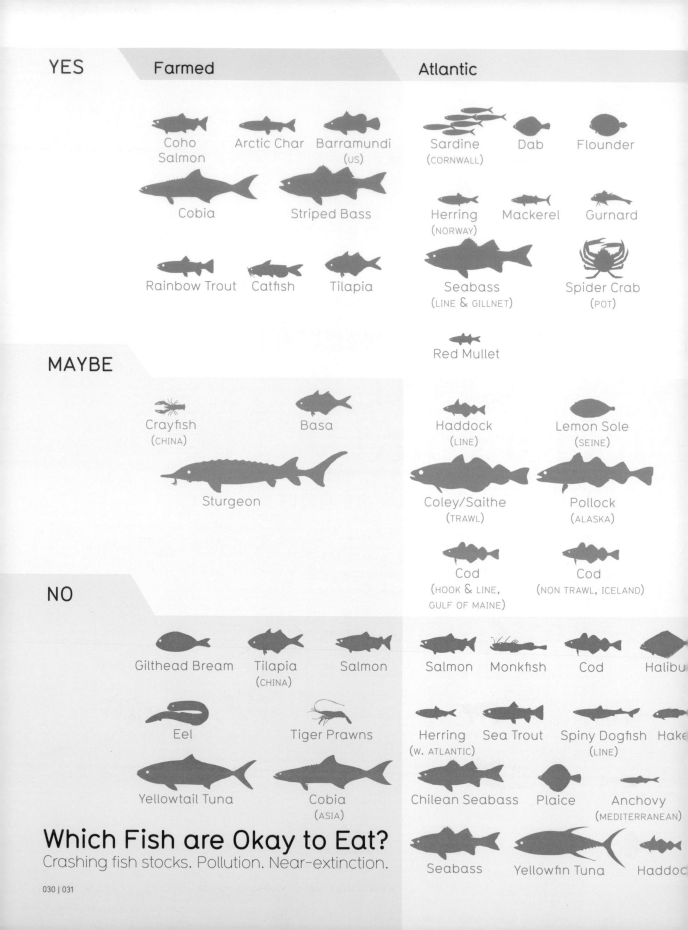

YES
Farmed
Atlantic
Coho Salmon
Arctic Char
Barramundi (US)
Cobia
Striped Bass
Rainbow Trout
Catfish
Tilapia
Sardine (CORNWALL)
Dab
Flounder
Herring (NORWAY)
Mackerel
Gurnard
Seabass (LINE & GILLNET)
Spider Crab (POT)
Red Mullet
MAYBE
Crayfish (CHINA)
Basa
Sturgeon
Haddock (LINE)
Lemon Sole (SEINE)
Coley/Saithe (TRAWL)
Pollock (ALASKA)
Cod (HOOK & LINE, GULF OF MAINE)
Cod (NON TRAWL, ICELAND)
NO
Gilthead Bream
Tilapia (CHINA)
Salmon
Eel
Tiger Prawns
Yellowtail Tuna
Cobia (ASIA)
Salmon
Monkfish
Cod
Halibu
Herring (W. ATLANTIC)
Sea Trout
Spiny Dogfish (LINE)
Hake
Chilean Seabass
Plaice
Anchovy (MEDITERRANEAN)
Seabass
Yellowfin Tuna
Haddoc

Which Fish are Okay to Eat?

Crashing fish stocks. Pollution. Near-extinction.

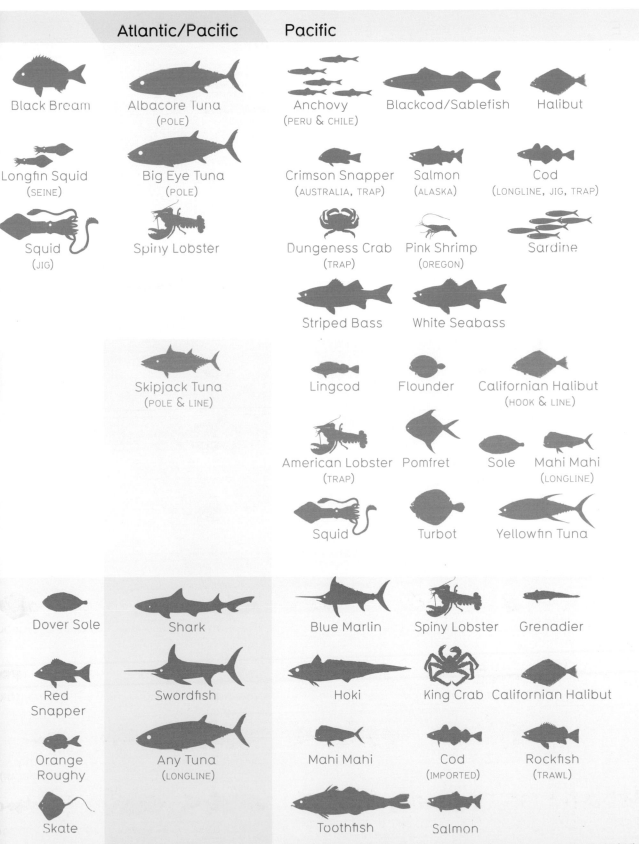

	Atlantic/Pacific	Pacific
Black Bream Longfin Squid (SEINE) Squid (JIG)	Albacore Tuna (POLE) Big Eye Tuna (POLE) Spiny Lobster	Anchovy (PERU & CHILE) Blackcod/Sablefish Halibut Crimson Snapper (AUSTRALIA, TRAP) Salmon (ALASKA) Cod (LONGLINE, JIG, TRAP) Dungeness Crab (TRAP) Pink Shrimp (OREGON) Sardine Striped Bass White Seabass
	Skipjack Tuna (POLE & LINE)	Lingcod Flounder Californian Halibut (HOOK & LINE) American Lobster (TRAP) Pomfret Sole Mahi Mahi (LONGLINE) Squid Turbot Yellowfin Tuna
Dover Sole Red Snapper Orange Roughy Skate	Shark Swordfish Any Tuna (LONGLINE)	Blue Marlin Spiny Lobster Grenadier Hoki King Crab Californian Halibut Mahi Mahi Cod (IMPORTED) Rockfish (TRAWL) Toothfish Salmon

source: Marine Conservation Society, Greenpeace, Seafood Watch // data:bit.ly/whichfish

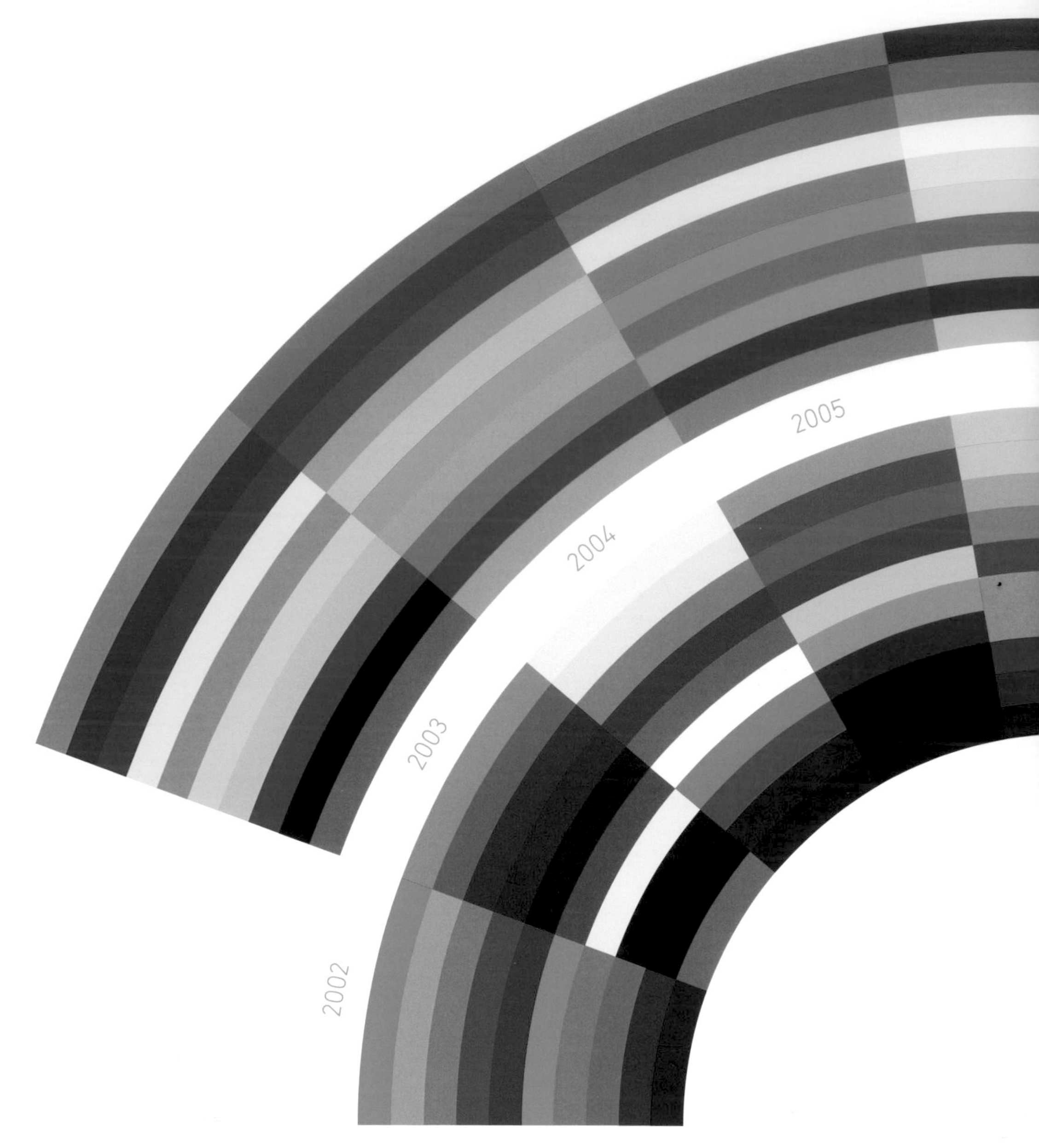
2005
2004
2003
2002
SUMMER | WINTER

The "In" Colours

Women's fashion colours

2007
2008
2009
2010
2011

source: pantone.com

The “Interesting” Colours

Selected women’s fashion colours

SUMMER

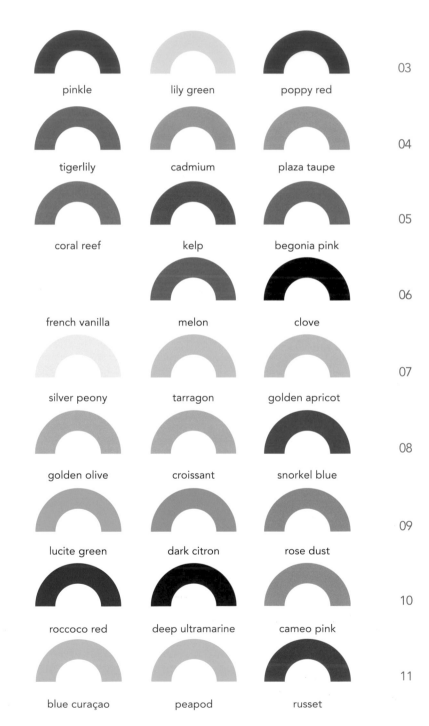

2002

pinkle	lily green	poppy red	03
tigerlily	cadmium	plaza taupe	04
coral reef	kelp	begonia pink	05
french vanilla	melon	clove	06
silver peony	tarragon	golden apricot	07
golden olive	croissant	snorkel blue	08
lucite green	dark citron	rose dust	09
roccoco red	deep ultramarine	cameo pink	10
blue curaçao	peapod	russet	11

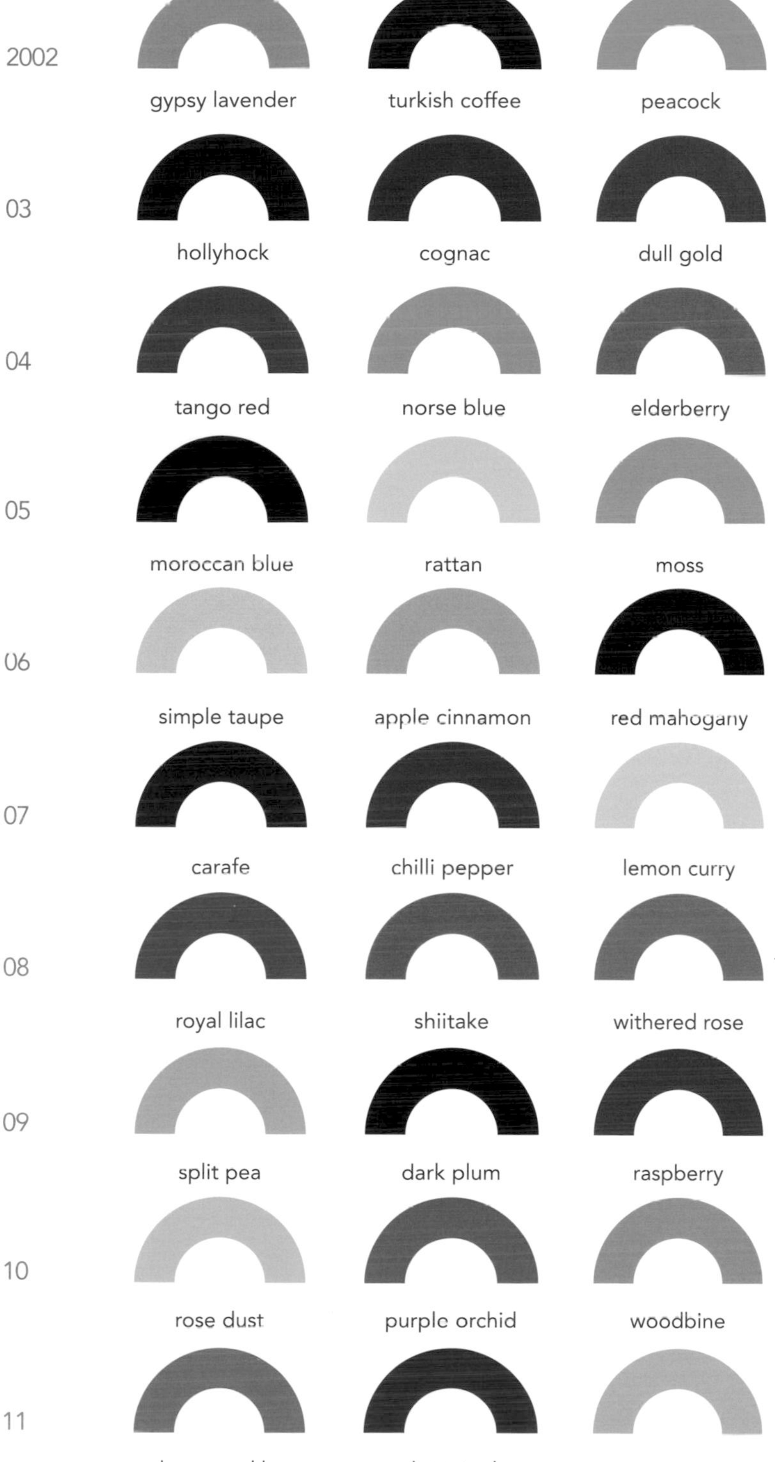
2002
gypsy lavender
turkish coffee
peacock
03
hollyhock
cognac
dull gold
04
tango red
norse blue
elderberry
05
moroccan blue
rattan
moss
06
simple taupe
apple cinnamon
red mahogany
07
carafe
chilli pepper
lemon curry
08
royal lilac
shiitake
withered rose
09
split pea
dark plum
raspberry
10
rose dust
purple orchid
woodbine
11
honeysuckle
deep teal
quarry

WINTER

source: pantone.com

Three's a Magic Number

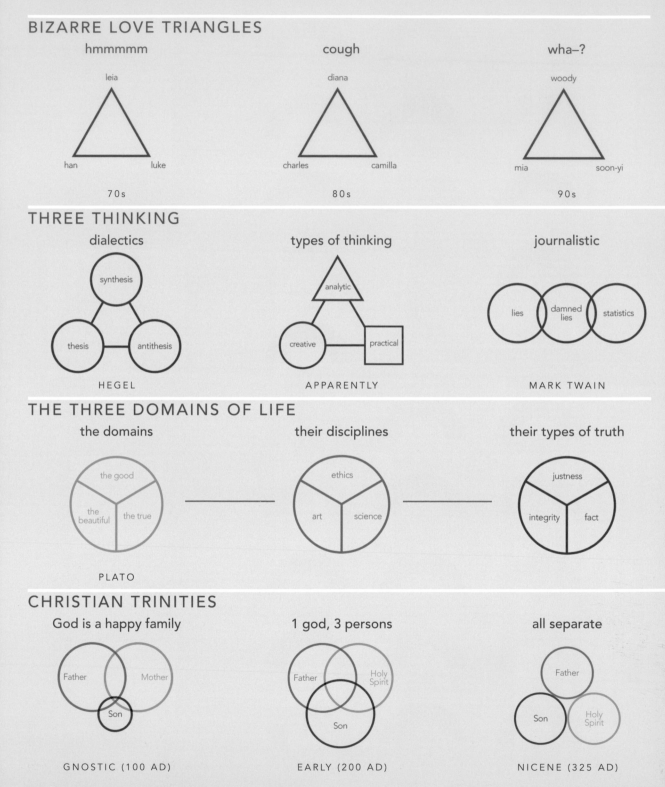

BIZARRE LOVE TRIANGLES

hmmmmm

leia
han
luke

70s

cough

diana

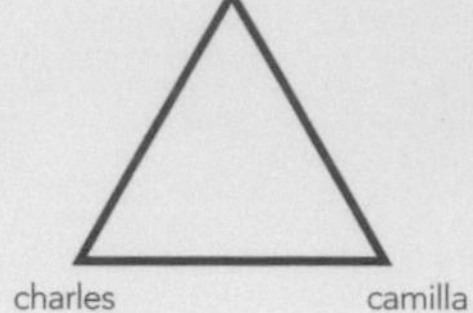
charles
camilla

80s

wha–?

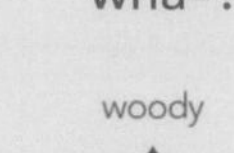
woody

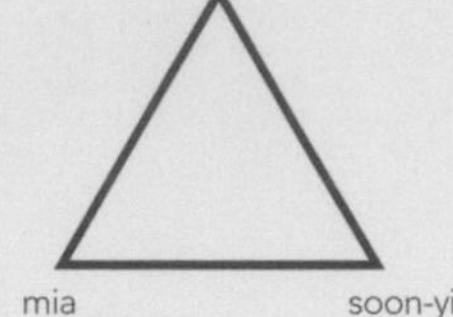
mia
soon-yi

90s

THREE THINKING

dialectics

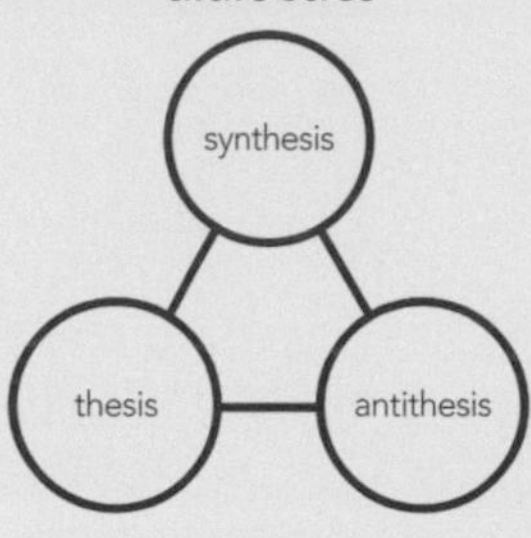
synthesis
thesis
antithesis

HEGEL

types of thinking

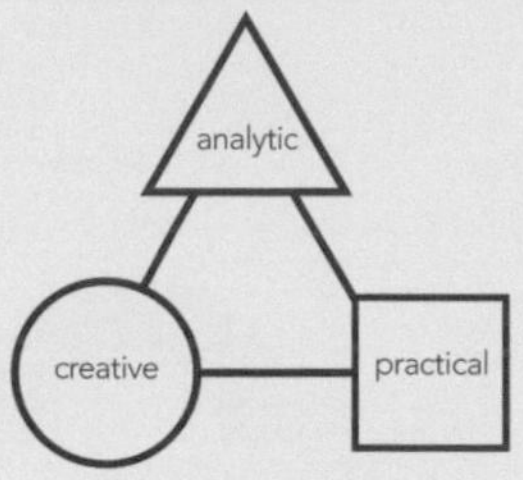
analytic
creative
practical

APPARENTLY

journalistic

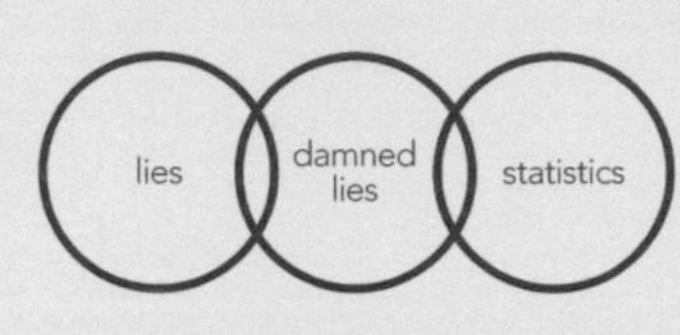
lies
damned lies
statistics

MARK TWAIN

THE THREE DOMAINS OF LIFE

the domains

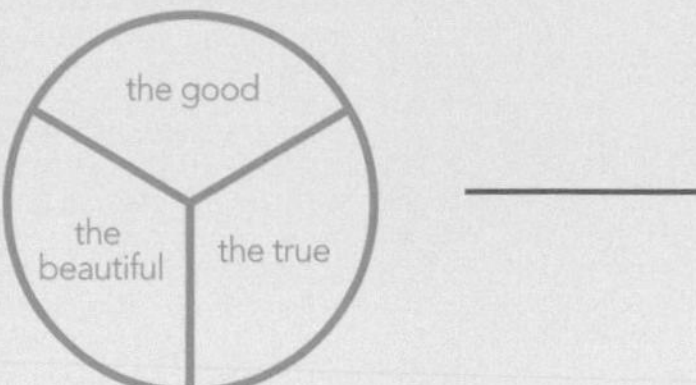
the good
the beautiful
the true

PLATO

their disciplines

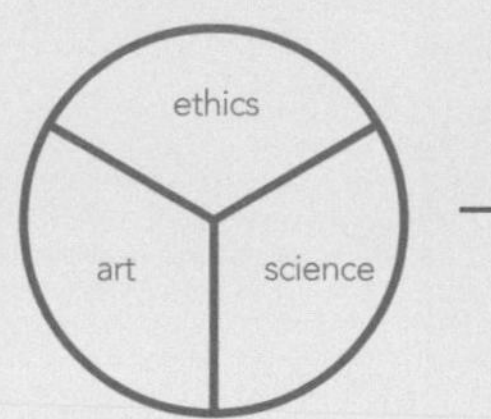
ethics
art
science

their types of truth

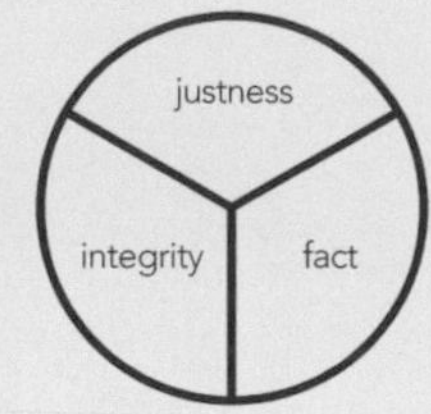
justness
integrity
fact

CHRISTIAN TRINITIES

God is a happy family

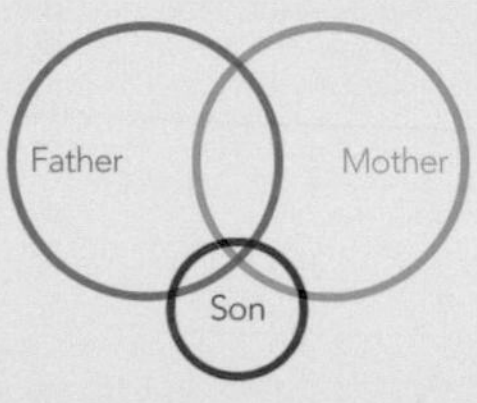
Father
Mother
Son

GNOSTIC (100 AD)

1 god, 3 persons

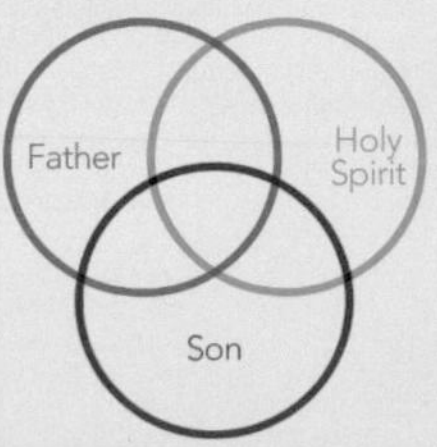
Father
Holy Spirit
Son

EARLY (200 AD)

all separate

Father
Son
Holy Spirit

NICENE (325 AD)

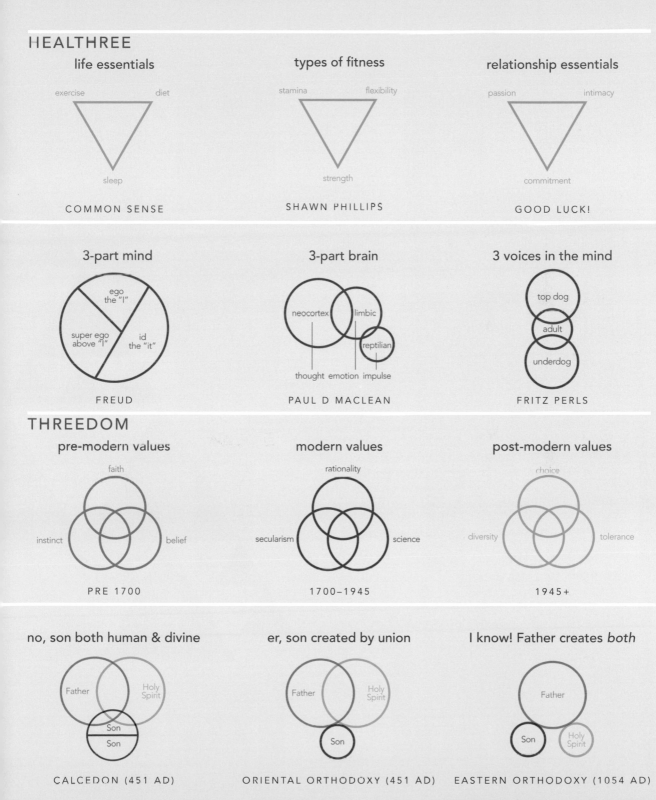

HEALTHREE

life essentials

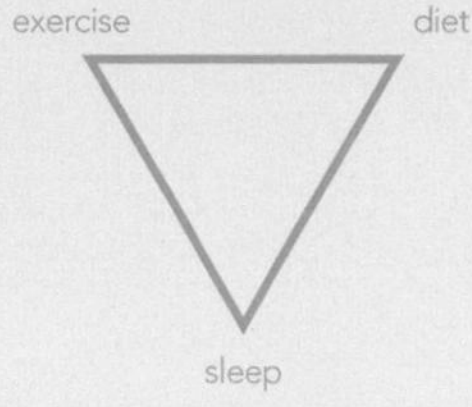
exercise
diet
sleep

COMMON SENSE

types of fitness

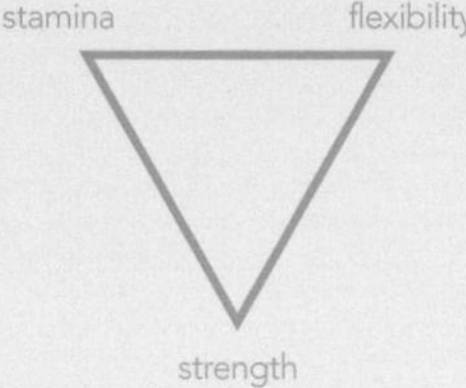
stamina
flexibility
strength

SHAWN PHILLIPS

relationship essentials

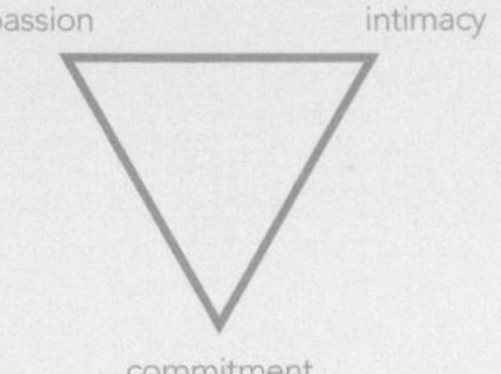
passion
intimacy
commitment

GOOD LUCK!

3-part mind

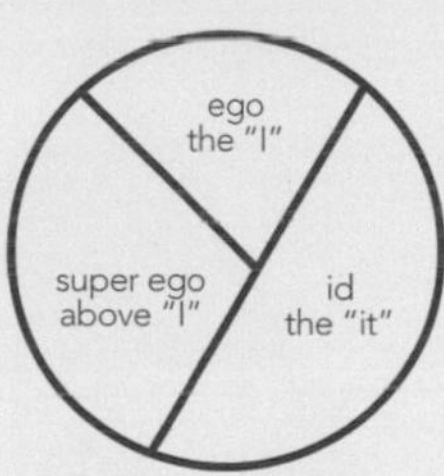
ego
the "I"
super ego
above "I"
id
the "it"

FREUD

3-part brain

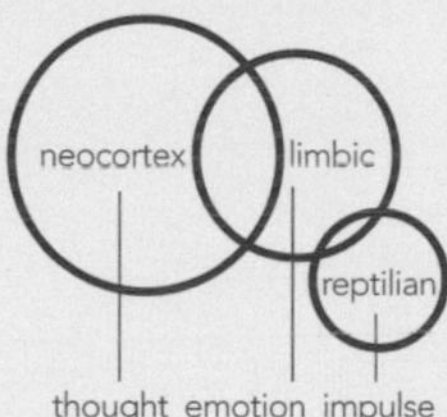
neocortex
limbic
reptilian
thought
emotion
impulse

PAUL D MACLEAN

3 voices in the mind

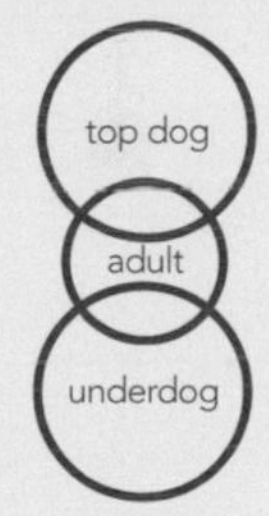
top dog
adult
underdog

FRITZ PERLS

THREEDOM

pre-modern values

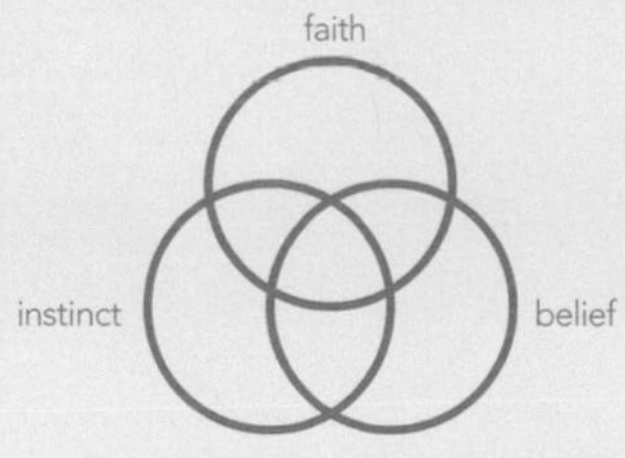
faith
instinct
belief

PRE 1700

modern values

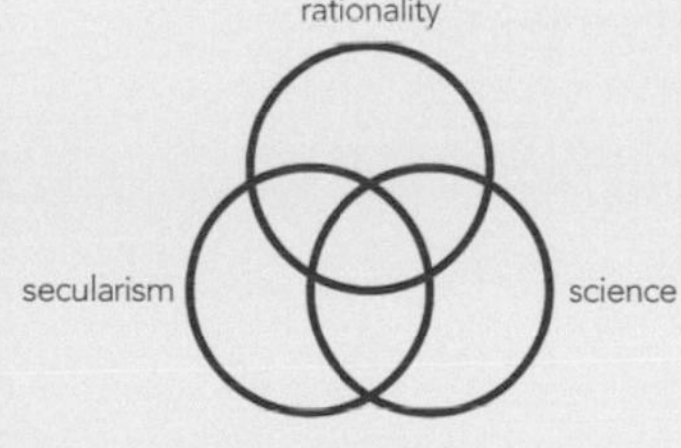
rationality
secularism
science

1700–1945

post-modern values

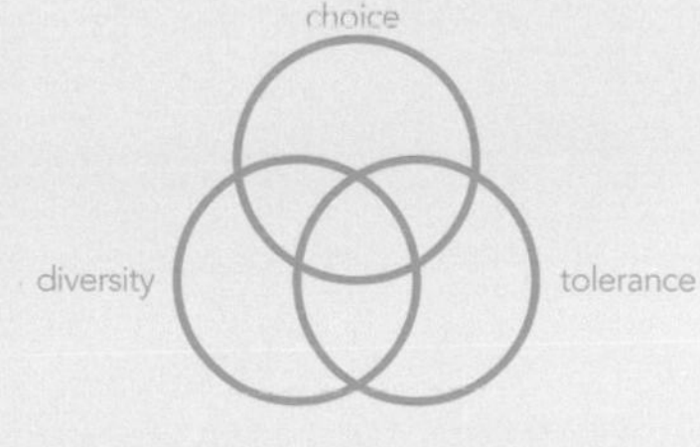
choice
diversity
tolerance

1945+

no, son both human & divine

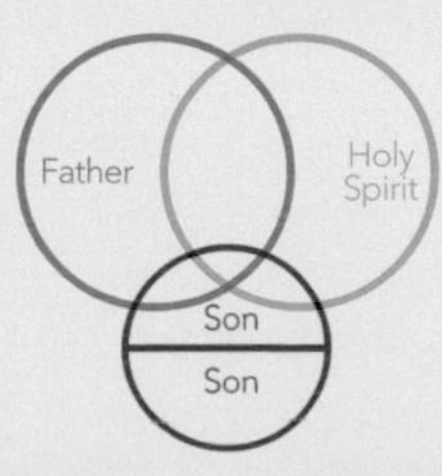
Father
Holy Spirit
Son
Son

CALCEDON (451 AD)

er, son created by union

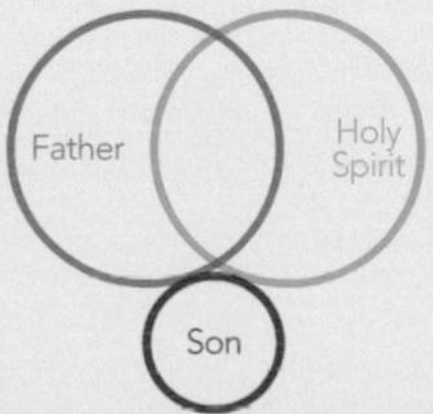
Father
Holy Spirit
Son

ORIENTAL ORTHODOXY (451 AD)

I know! Father creates *both*

Father
Son
Holy Spirit

EASTERN ORTHODOXY (1054 AD)

source: Wikipedia, The Gale Encyclopedia of Religion

Who Runs the World?

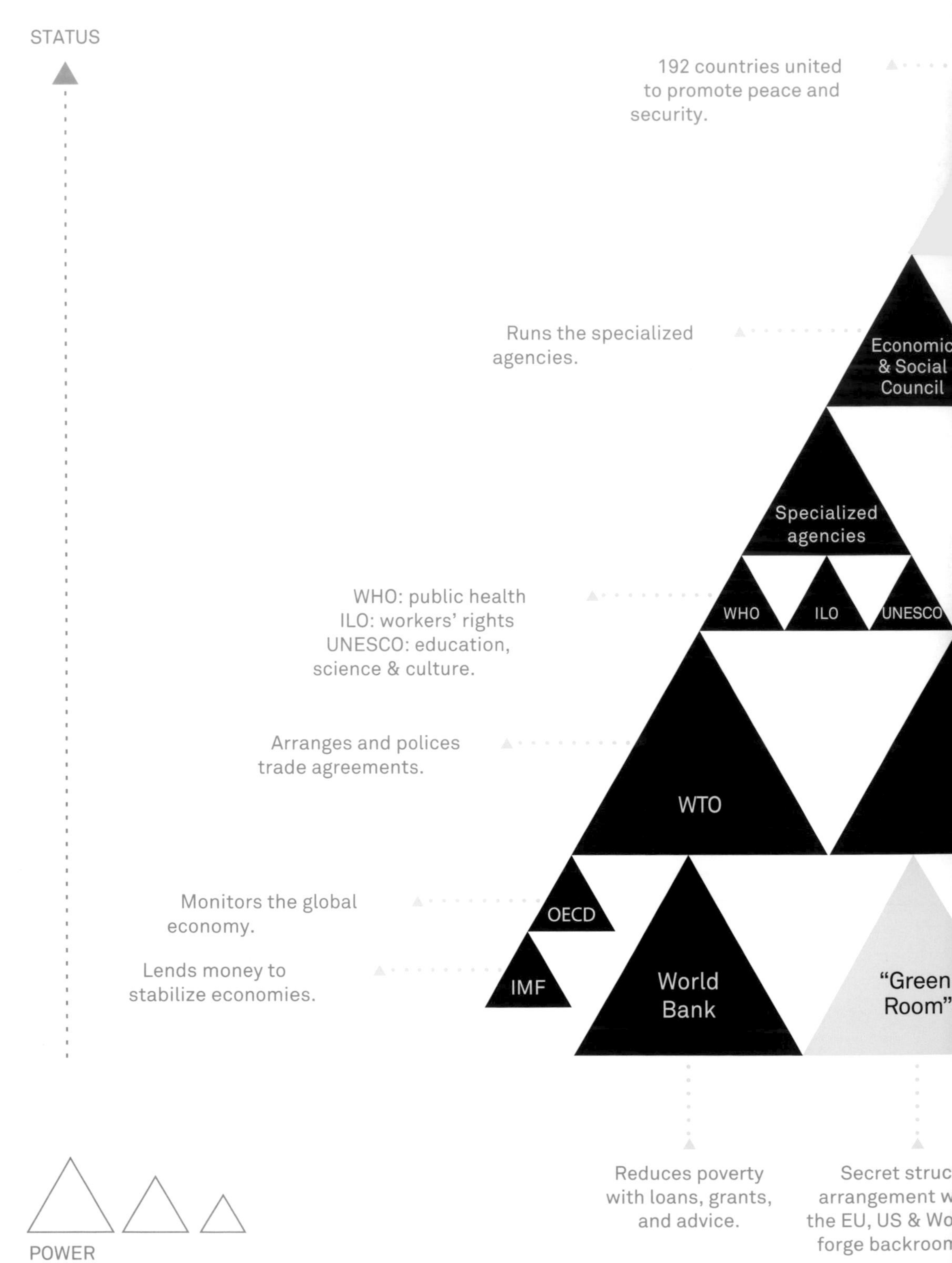
STATUS
192 countries united to promote peace and security.
Runs the specialized agencies.
Economic & Social Council
Specialized agencies
WHO: public health
ILO: workers' rights
UNESCO: education, science & culture.
WHO
ILO
UNESCO
Arranges and polices trade agreements.
WTO
Monitors the global economy.
OECD
Lends money to stabilize economies.
IMF
World Bank
"Green Room"
Reduces poverty with loans, grants, and advice.
Secret struct
arrangement w
the EU, US & Wo
forge backroom
POWER

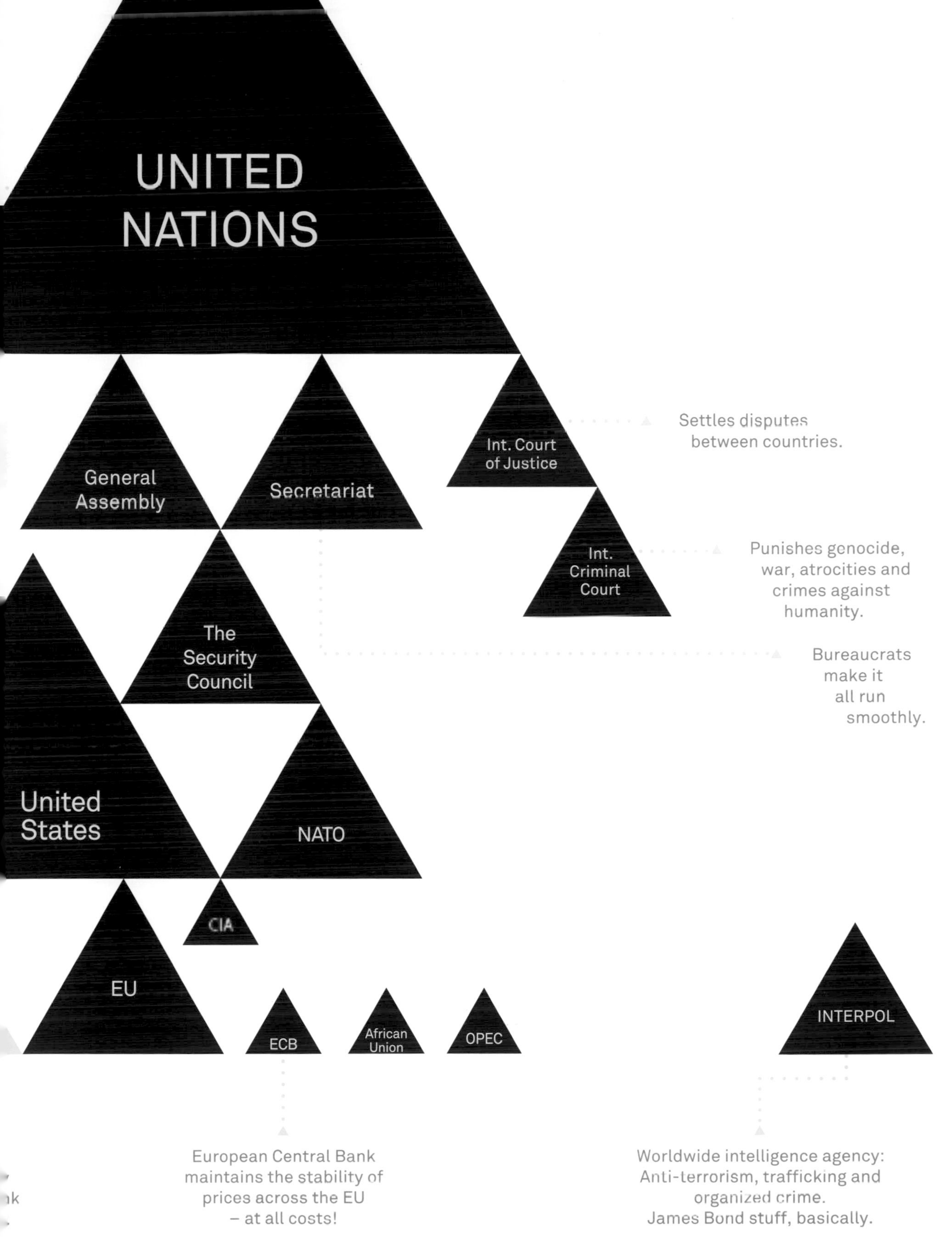
UNITED NATIONS
General Assembly
Secretariat
Int. Court of Justice
Settles disputes between countries.
Int. Criminal Court
Punishes genocide, war, atrocities and crimes against humanity.
The Security Council
Bureaucrats make it all run smoothly.
United States
NATO
CIA
EU
ECB
African Union
OPEC
INTERPOL
European Central Bank maintains the stability of prices across the EU – at all costs!
Worldwide intelligence agency: Anti-terrorism, trafficking and organized crime. James Bond stuff, basically.

source: Wikipedia, UN.org

Who *Really* Runs the World?

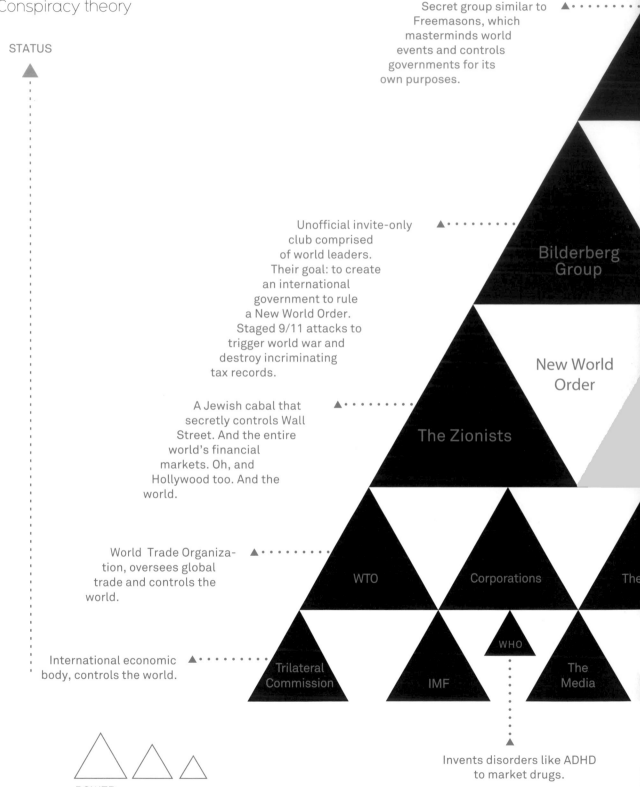

Conspiracy theory

STATUS
Secret group similar to Freemasons, which masterminds world events and controls governments for its own purposes.
Unofficial invite-only club comprised of world leaders. Their goal: to create an international government to rule a New World Order. Staged 9/11 attacks to trigger world war and destroy incriminating tax records.
Bilderberg Group
New World Order
A Jewish cabal that secretly controls Wall Street. And the entire world's financial markets. Oh, and Hollywood too. And the world.
The Zionists
World Trade Organization, oversees global trade and controls the world.
WTO
Corporations
The
WHO
International economic body, controls the world.
Trilateral Commission
IMF
The Media
Invents disorders like ADHD to market drugs.
POWER

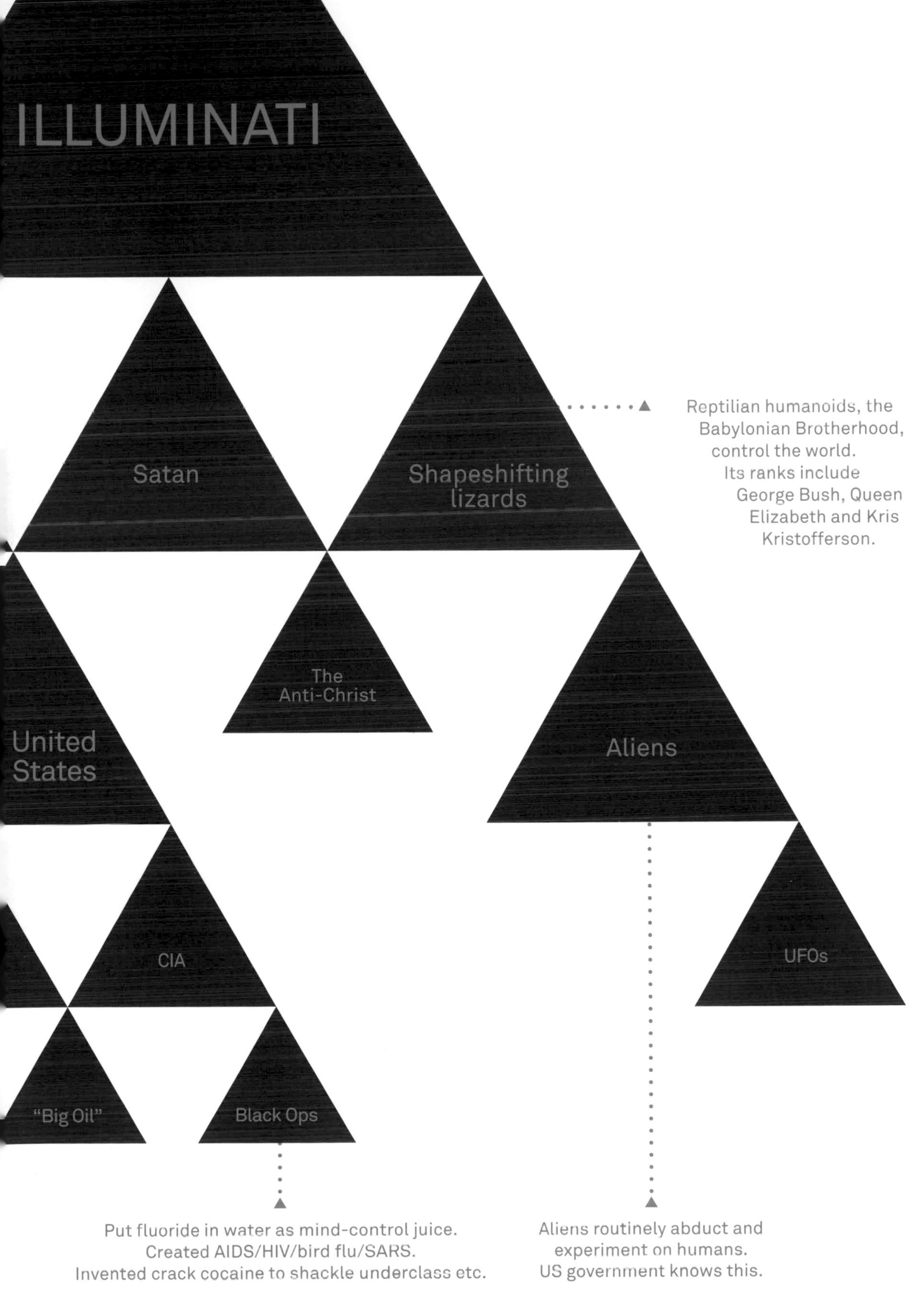

ILLUMINATI
Satan
Shapeshifting lizards
Reptilian humanoids, the Babylonian Brotherhood, control the world. Its ranks include George Bush, Queen Elizabeth and Kris Kristofferson.
The Anti-Christ
United States
Aliens
CIA
UFOs
"Big Oil"
Black Ops
Put fluoride in water as mind-control juice. Created AIDS/HIV/bird flu/SARS. Invented crack cocaine to shackle underclass etc.
Aliens routinely abduct and experiment on humans. US government knows this.

Stock Check

Estimated remaining world supplies of non-renewable resources

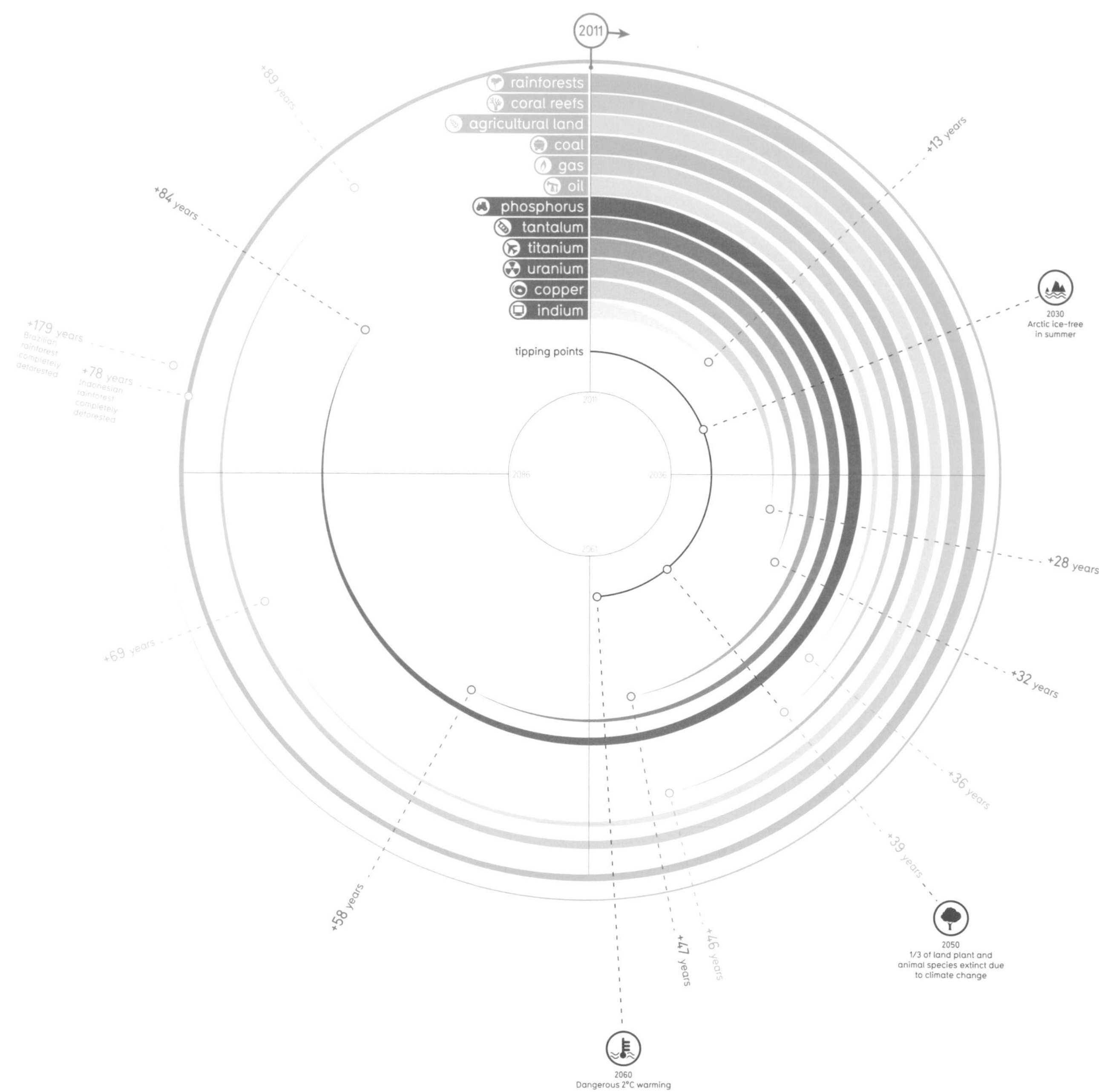

2011
rainforests
coral reefs
agricultural land
coal
gas
oil
phosphorus
tantalum
titanium
uranium
copper
indium
tipping points
+13 years
2030
Arctic ice-free in summer
+28 years
+32 years
+36 years
+39 years
2050
1/3 of land plant and animal species extinct due to climate change
+46 years
+47 years
2060
Dangerous 2°C warming
+58 years
+69 years
+78 years
Indonesian rainforest completely deforested
+179 years
Brazilian rainforest completely deforested
+84 years
+89 years

note: worst-case based on published estimates, assuming fixed % yearly consumption rate

source: UN TEEB, US Geological Survey, BP, Worm et al (2006), London Metal Exchange

$63,000 bn
Global Gross
Domestic Product
$50,800 bn
Value provided by the Earth
to the global economy
$93 bn
Needed to
preserve the
Earth's natural
capital

source: Costanza et al, World Bank (2010)

Amazon

COLOMBIA
AMAZON
PERU
BRAZIL
BOLIVIA

1979

COLOMBIA
AMAZON
PERU
BOLIVIA
BRAZIL

2009

source: Global Forest Watch

Creation Myths

How did it all start?

Ex Nihilo (Out of Nothing)

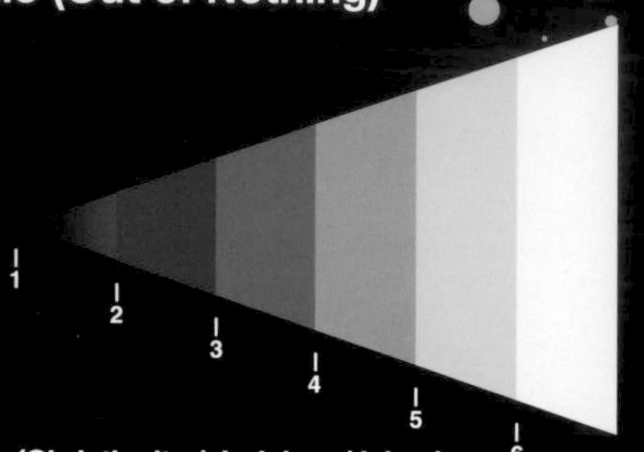
1
2
3
4
5
6

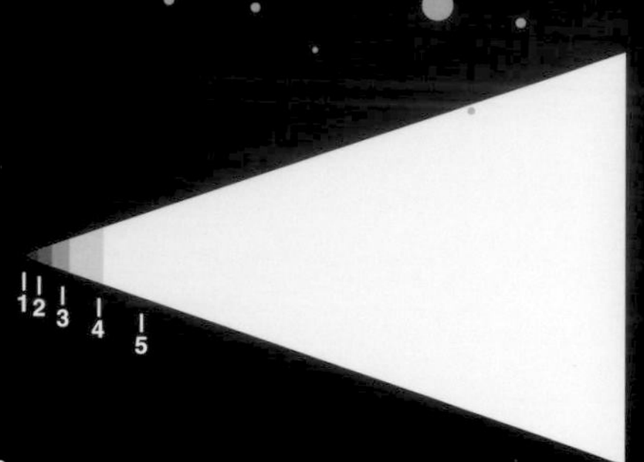
1
2
3
4
5

Abrahamic (Christianity / Judaism / Islam)

Day 1. God created light and darkness.
Day 2. He created water and sky.
Day 3. Separated dry ground from oceans, created all vegetation.
Day 4. Created sun, moon and stars.
Day 5. Created all water-dwelling creatures and birds.
Day 6. Created all creatures of the world.
Day 7. Had a nice rest.

The Big Bang

1. 15,000 million years ago all the matter in the Universe bursts out from single point. **2.** Inflates from the size of an atom to the size of a grapefruit in a microsecond. **3.** Three minutes in, the universe is a superhot fog, too hot for even light to shine. **4.** 300,000 years later, everything is cool enough to form the first atoms. Light shines! **5.** After a billion years, clouds of gas collapse. Gravity pulls them in to form the first galaxies and stars.

Primordial "Soup"

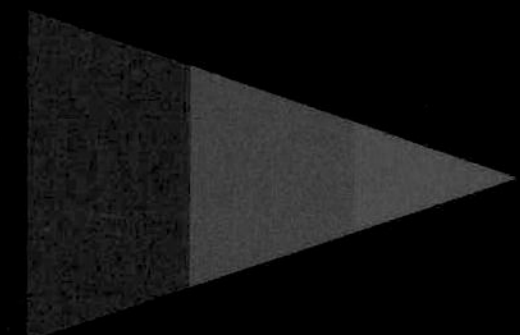

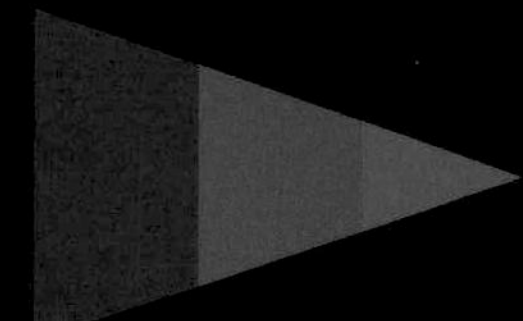

Hinduism

In a dark vast ocean, Lord Vishnu sleeps. A humming noise trembles. With a vast "OM!" Vishnu awakes. From his stomach blossoms a lotus flower containing Brahma, who splits the lotus flower into heaven, earth and sky.

Chinese (Taoist)

There was a mist of chaos. The mist separated and the light rose to heaven and the heavy sank and formed the earth. From heaven and earth came yin and yang, masculine and feminine. Together they keep the world in harmony.

Infinite Universe / Continuous Creation

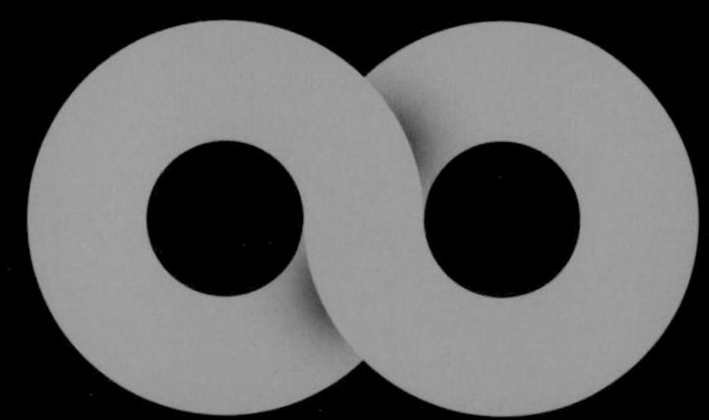

Steady State Theory

Matter is generated constantly as the universe expands. No beginning, no end.

Buddhism

The universe is not fixed in a state of "being", but of "becoming". At any moment some stars and galaxies are born while others die.

Infinite Universe / Cyclical

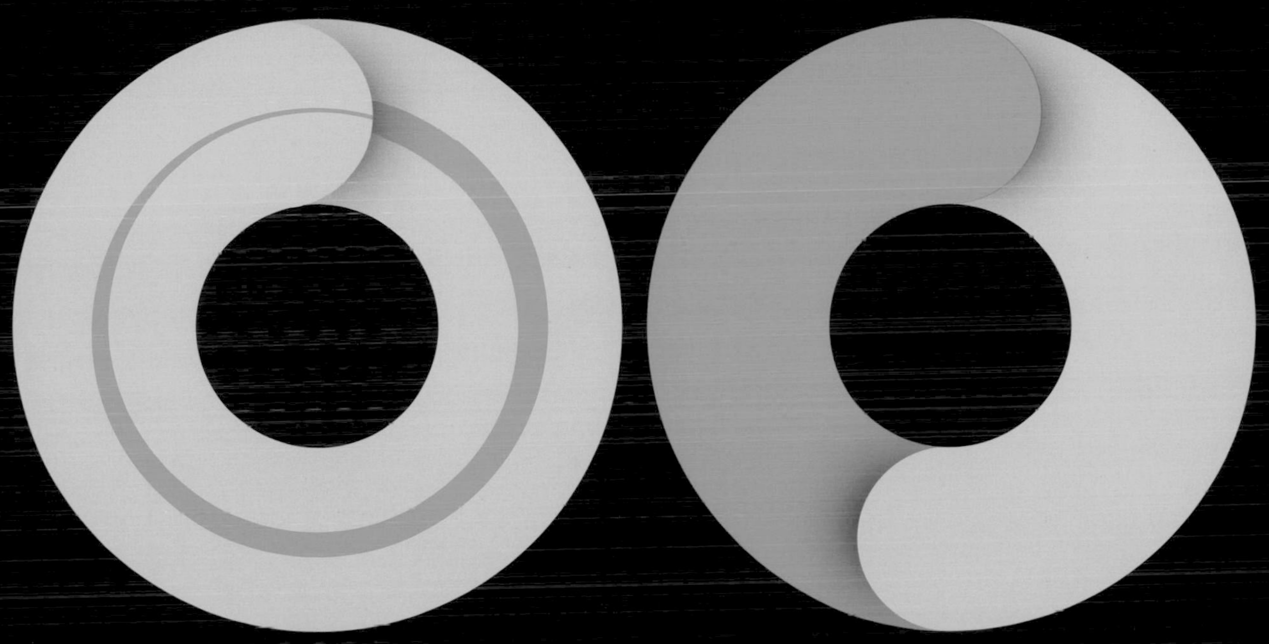

Big Bangs, Big Crunches
Endless cycles of big bangs and big crunches, with each cycle lasting about a trillion years. All matter and radiation is reset, but the cosmological constant is not. It gradually diminishes over many cycles to the small value observed in today's universe.

Involution / Evolution (Hinduism, Theosophy)
Infinite number of universes in an infinite cycle of births, deaths and rebirths. Each cycle lasts 8.4 billion years. The universe involves (in breath), gathers all the material, then 'evolves' (out breath) and expands. This cycle repeats infinitely.

Quasi Steady State (QSS) Theory
The cosmos has always existed. Explosions, of all different sizes, occur continuously, giving the impression of a big bang in our locality.

Bubble Universe
Our universe is a bubble spawned off a larger "foam" of other universes. Each bubble is different. Ours is finely tuned to support life.

source: Wikipedia, NewScientist.com

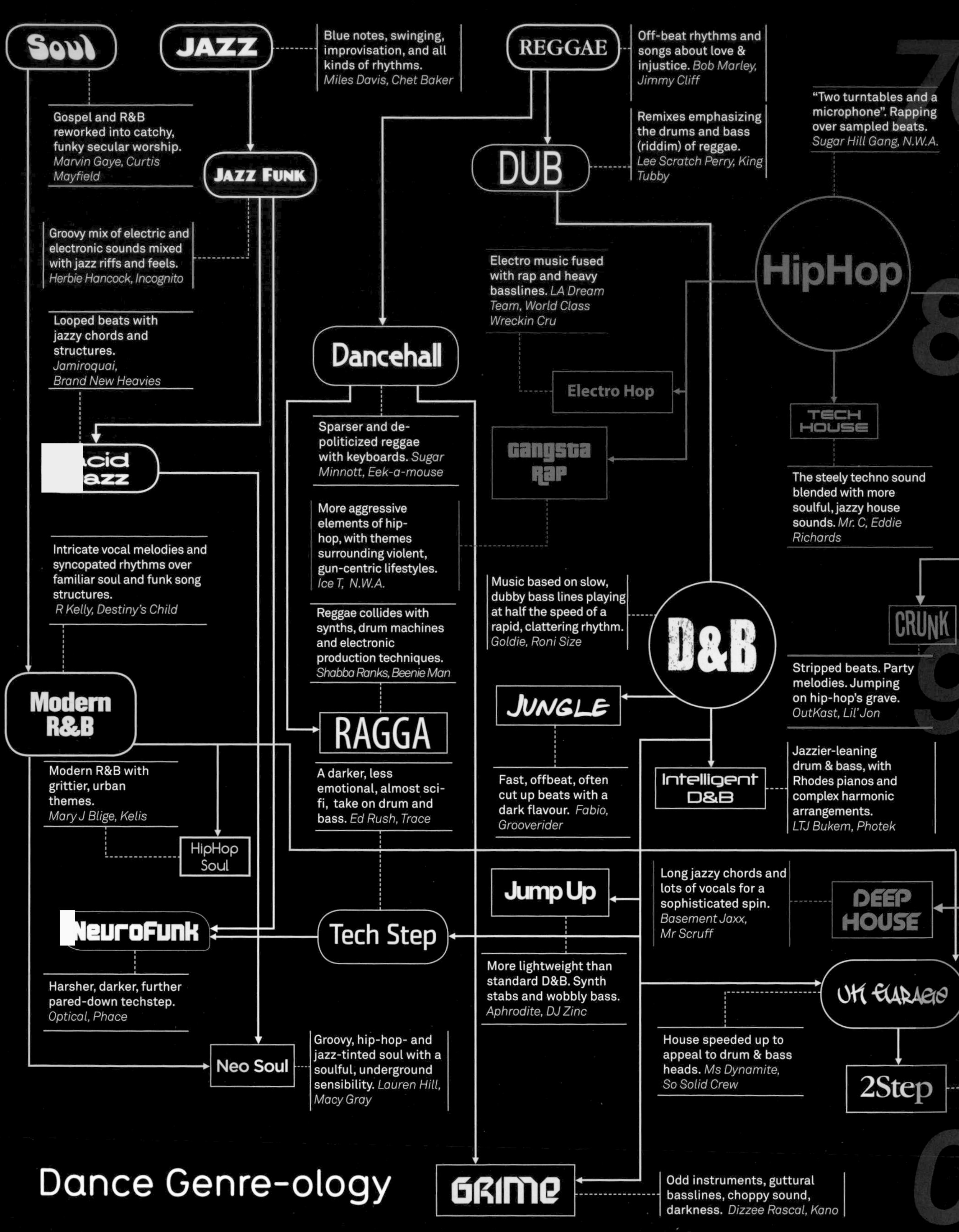
Soul
JAZZ
Blue notes, swinging, improvisation, and all kinds of rhythms. Miles Davis, Chet Baker
REGGAE
Off-beat rhythms and songs about love & injustice. Bob Marley, Jimmy Cliff
Gospel and R&B reworked into catchy, funky secular worship. Marvin Gaye, Curtis Mayfield
JAZZ FUNK
DUB
Remixes emphasizing the drums and bass (riddim) of reggae. Lee Scratch Perry, King Tubby
"Two turntables and a microphone". Rapping over sampled beats. Sugar Hill Gang, N.W.A.
Groovy mix of electric and electronic sounds mixed with jazz riffs and feels. Herbie Hancock, Incognito
HipHop
Electro music fused with rap and heavy basslines. LA Dream Team, World Class Wreckin Cru
Looped beats with jazzy chords and structures. Jamiroquai, Brand New Heavies
Dancehall
Electro Hop
TECH HOUSE
Sparser and de-politicized reggae with keyboards. Sugar Minnott, Eek-a-mouse
Gangsta Rap
The steely techno sound blended with more soulful, jazzy house sounds. Mr. C, Eddie Richards
More aggressive elements of hip-hop, with themes surrounding violent, gun-centric lifestyles. Ice T, N.W.A.
Intricate vocal melodies and syncopated rhythms over familiar soul and funk song structures. R Kelly, Destiny's Child
Music based on slow, dubby bass lines playing at half the speed of a rapid, clattering rhythm. Goldie, Roni Size
Reggae collides with synths, drum machines and electronic production techniques. Shabba Ranks, Beenie Man
D&B
CRUNK
Stripped beats. Party melodies. Jumping on hip-hop's grave. OutKast, Lil' Jon
Modern R&B
JUNGLE
RAGGA
Modern R&B with grittier, urban themes. Mary J Blige, Kelis
A darker, less emotional, almost sci-fi, take on drum and bass. Ed Rush, Trace
Fast, offbeat, often cut up beats with a dark flavour. Fabio, Grooverider
Intelligent D&B
Jazzier-leaning drum & bass, with Rhodes pianos and complex harmonic arrangements. LTJ Bukem, Photek
HipHop Soul
Jump Up
Long jazzy chords and lots of vocals for a sophisticated spin. Basement Jaxx, Mr Scruff
DEEP HOUSE
Tech Step
Harsher, darker, further pared-down techstep. Optical, Phace
More lightweight than standard D&B. Synth stabs and wobbly bass. Aphrodite, DJ Zinc
UK Garage
House speeded up to appeal to drum & bass heads. Ms Dynamite, So Solid Crew
Neo Soul
Groovy, hip-hop- and jazz-tinted soul with a soulful, underground sensibility. Lauren Hill, Macy Gray
2Step
GRIME
Odd instruments, guttural basslines, choppy sound, darkness. Dizzee Rascal, Kano
70
80
90
00

Dance Genre-ology

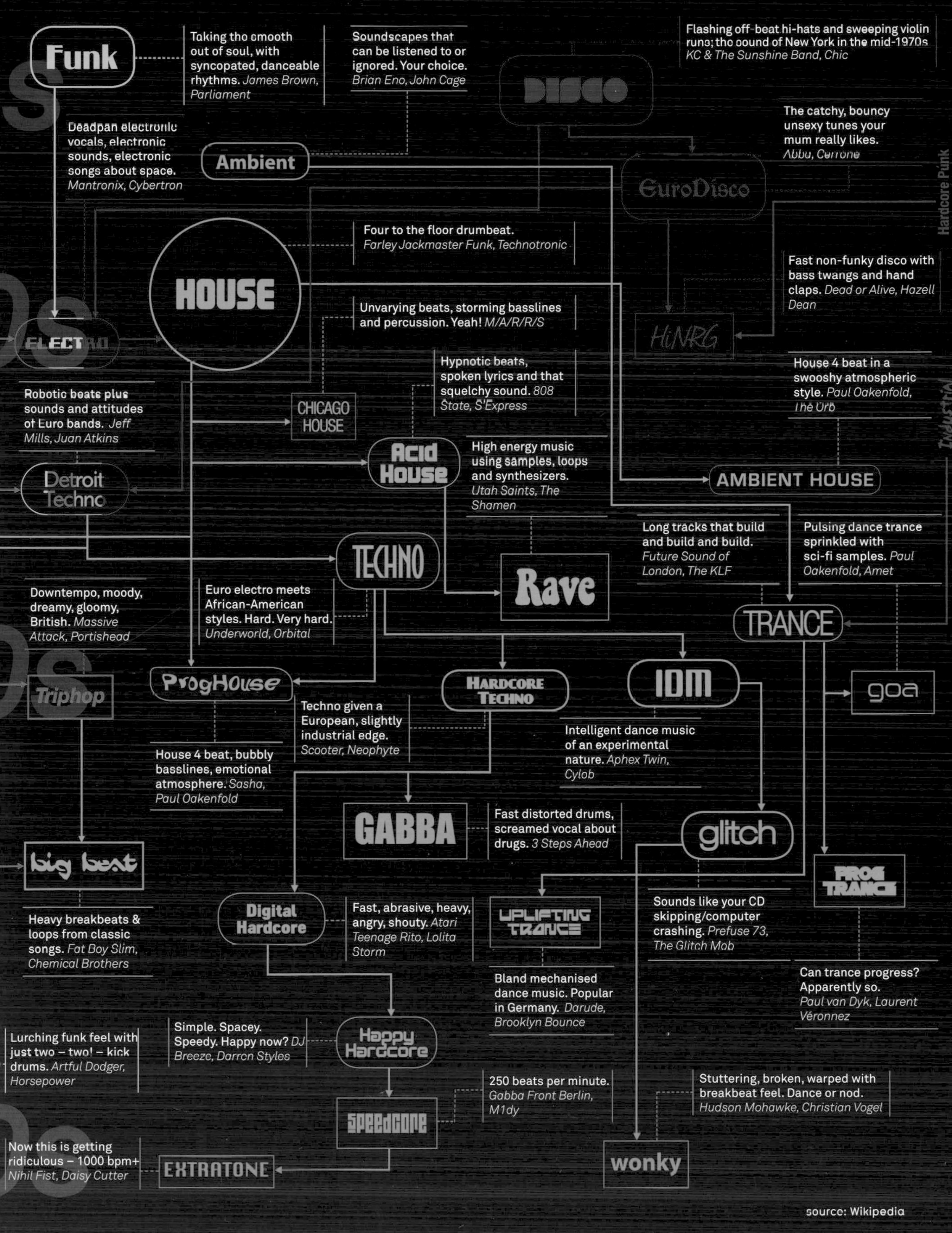

Funk
Taking the smooth out of soul, with syncopated, danceable rhythms. James Brown, Parliament
Soundscapes that can be listened to or ignored. Your choice. Brian Eno, John Cage
Flashing off-beat hi-hats and sweeping violin runs; the sound of New York in the mid-1970s. KC & The Sunshine Band, Chic
DISCO
Ambient
Deadpan electronic vocals, electronic sounds, electronic songs about space. Mantronix, Cybertron
The catchy, bouncy unsexy tunes your mum really likes. Abba, Cerrone
EuroDisco
Hardcore Punk
Four to the floor drumbeat. Farley Jackmaster Funk, Technotronic
HOUSE
Fast non-funky disco with bass twangs and hand claps. Dead or Alive, Hazell Dean
Unvarying beats, storming basslines and percussion. Yeah! M/A/R/R/S
ELECTRO
HiNRG
Hypnotic beats, spoken lyrics and that squelchy sound. 808 State, S'Express
House 4 beat in a swooshy atmospheric style. Paul Oakenfold, The Orb
Industrial
Robotic beats plus sounds and attitudes of Euro bands. Jeff Mills, Juan Atkins
CHICAGO HOUSE
Acid House
High energy music using samples, loops and synthesizers. Utah Saints, The Shamen
Detroit Techno
AMBIENT HOUSE
Long tracks that build and build and build. Future Sound of London, The KLF
Pulsing dance trance sprinkled with sci-fi samples. Paul Oakenfold, Amet
TECHNO
Rave
Downtempo, moody, dreamy, gloomy, British. Massive Attack, Portishead
Euro electro meets African-American styles. Hard. Very hard. Underworld, Orbital
TRANCE
Triphop
ProgHouse
Hardcore Techno
IDM
goa
Techno given a European, slightly industrial edge. Scooter, Neophyte
Intelligent dance music of an experimental nature. Aphex Twin, Cylob
House 4 beat, bubbly basslines, emotional atmosphere. Sasha, Paul Oakenfold
GABBA
Fast distorted drums, screamed vocal about drugs. 3 Steps Ahead
glitch
big beat
Prog Trance
Digital Hardcore
Fast, abrasive, heavy, angry, shouty. Atari Teenage Riot, Lolita Storm
Uplifting Trance
Sounds like your CD skipping/computer crashing. Prefuse 73, The Glitch Mob
Heavy breakbeats & loops from classic songs. Fat Boy Slim, Chemical Brothers
Bland mechanised dance music. Popular in Germany. Darude, Brooklyn Bounce
Can trance progress? Apparently so. Paul van Dyk, Laurent Véronnez
Lurching funk feel with just two – two! – kick drums. Artful Dodger, Horsepower
Simple. Spacey. Speedy. Happy now? DJ Breeze, Darren Styles
Happy Hardcore
250 beats per minute. Gabba Front Berlin, M1dy
Stuttering, broken, warped with breakbeat feel. Dance or nod. Hudson Mohawke, Christian Vogel
Speedcore
Now this is getting ridiculous – 1000 bpm+ Nihil Fist, Daisy Cutter
EXTRATONE
wonky
source: Wikipedia

The Book of You

A copy in every one of your 10,000,000,000 cells

The Book Your complete DNA (or "genome") – 3.2 billion words

Your Page
The only part that varies from person to person ("genotype")
0.06%

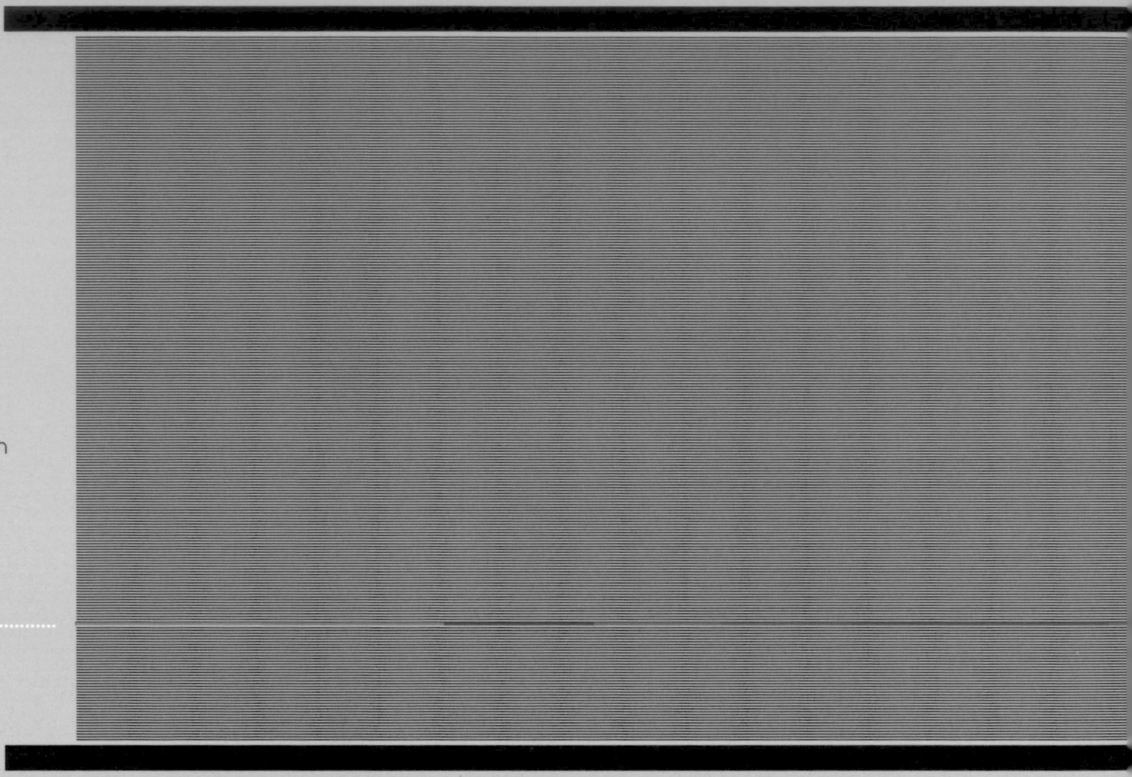

The Chapters
Organized sections inside the book ("chromosomes"). Made of genes
23 pairs

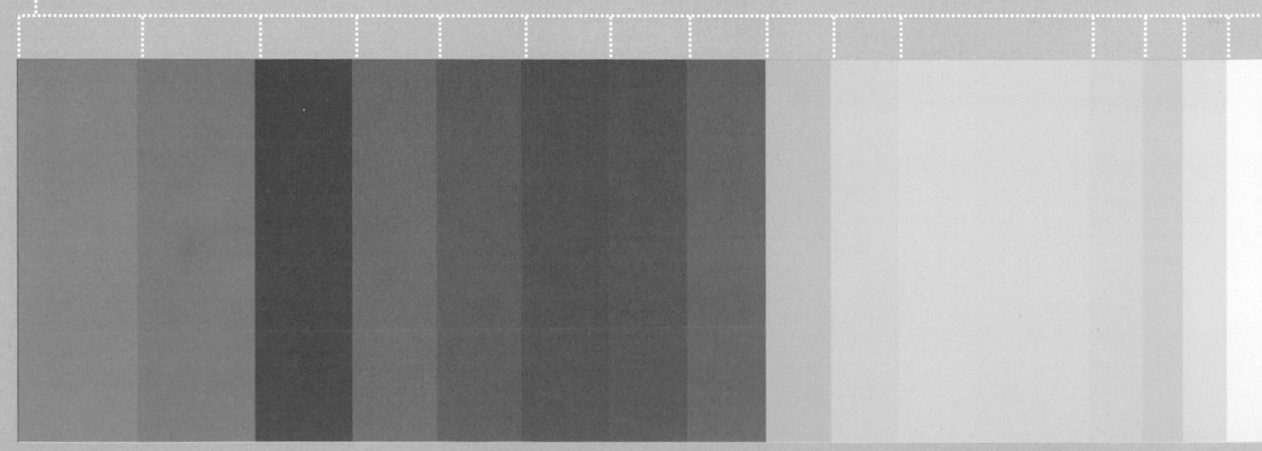

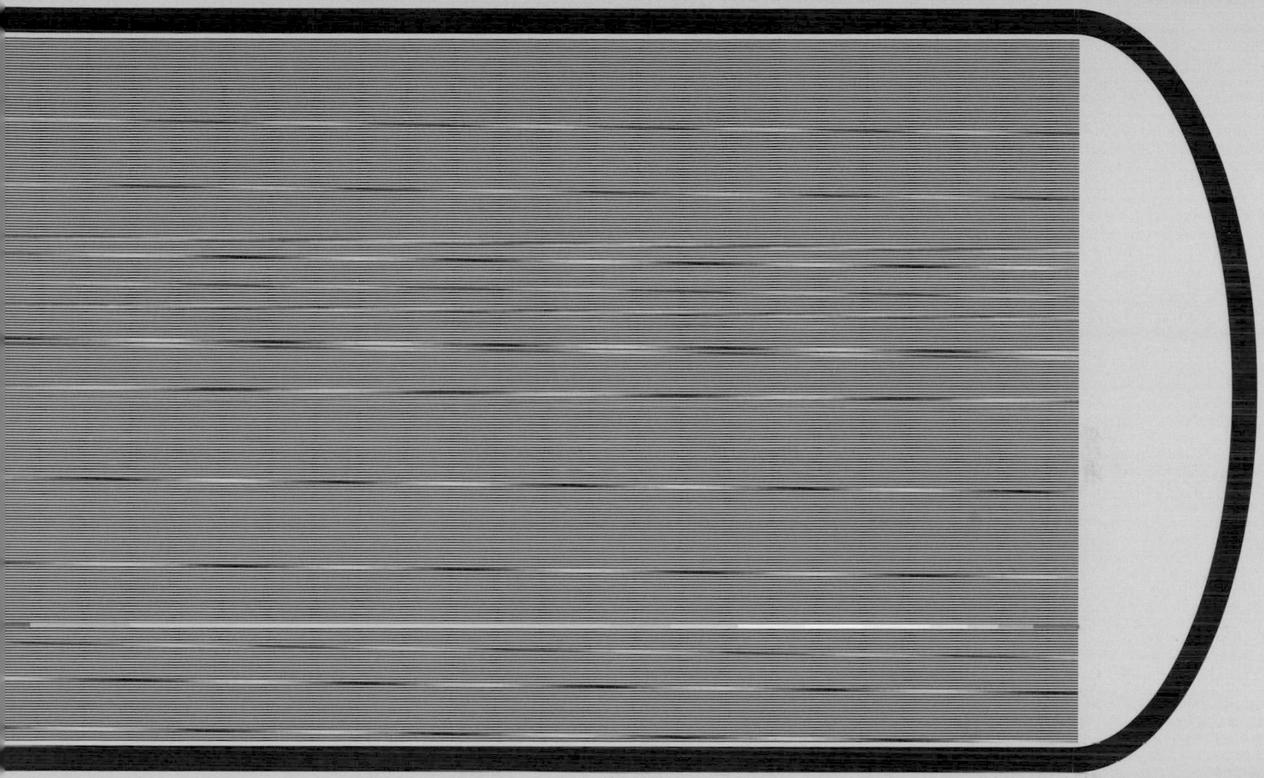

The Paragraphs

Genes are clumps of DNA made up of base pairs
20 – 25,000

The Words

Individual two letter "words" of DNA
2 million

The Letters

Letters made of just four individual molecules

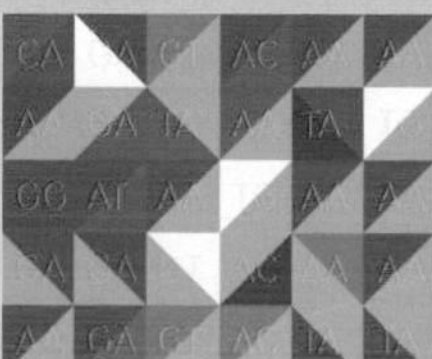

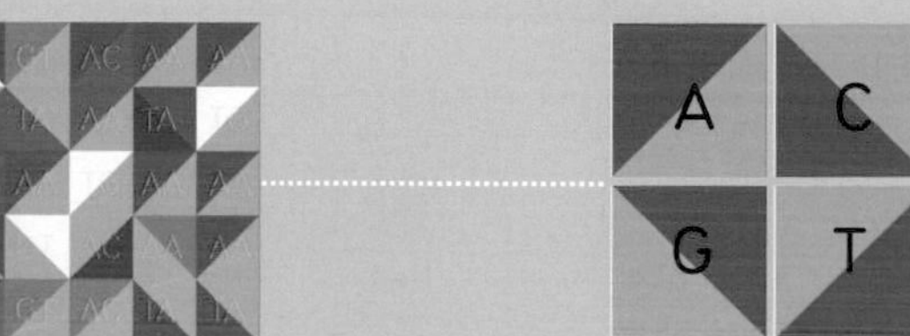
A
C
G
T

Responsible for all your physical characteristics, susceptibility to certain diseases, and even earwax
We have identified the effects of around 5000 out of 2,000,000 (0.25%)

source: Decodeme.com, Wikipedia

folate metabolism & several cancers

The Book of Me

My chromosomes sequenced (2 million letter combinations)

restless legs syndrome (5)

type 1 diabe

psoriasis (4)

Cr

obesity (10)

gallstones

prostate cancer (11)

rheumatoid arthr

coeliac disease (8)

venous thromboembolism

heart attack (4)

lactose intolerance

basal cell carcinoma (3)

parts of other sequences

Some conditions are influenced by several "letters" (DNA base pairs). Only the first letters of a sequence are labelled here with the number of base pairs in the sequence (brackets).

age-related macular degeneration (3)

breast cance

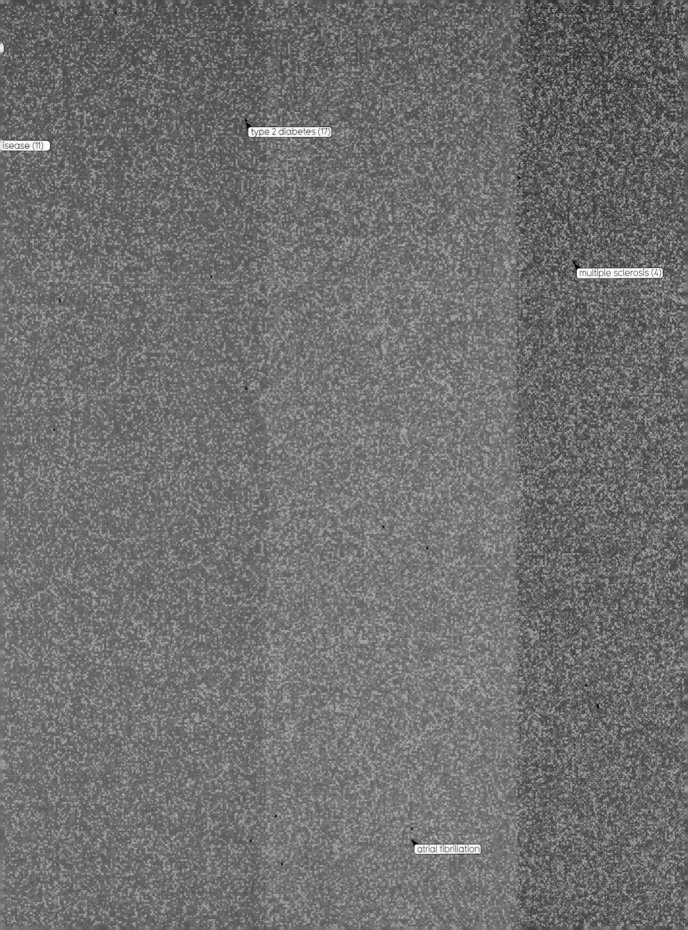

isease (11)

type 2 diabetes (17)

multiple sclerosis (4)

atrial fibrillation

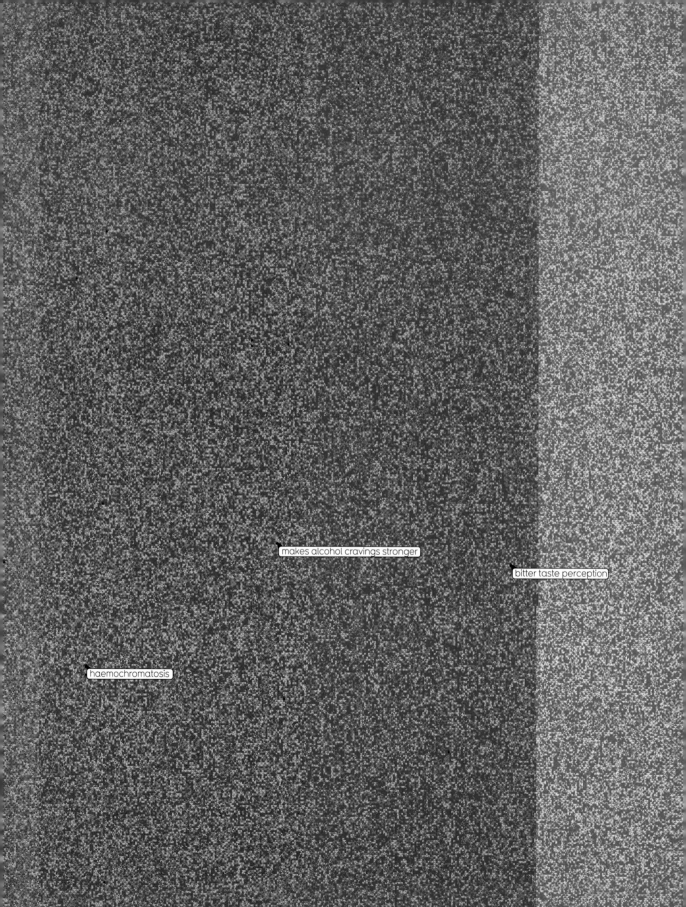

makes alcohol cravings stronger

bitter taste perception

haemochromatosis

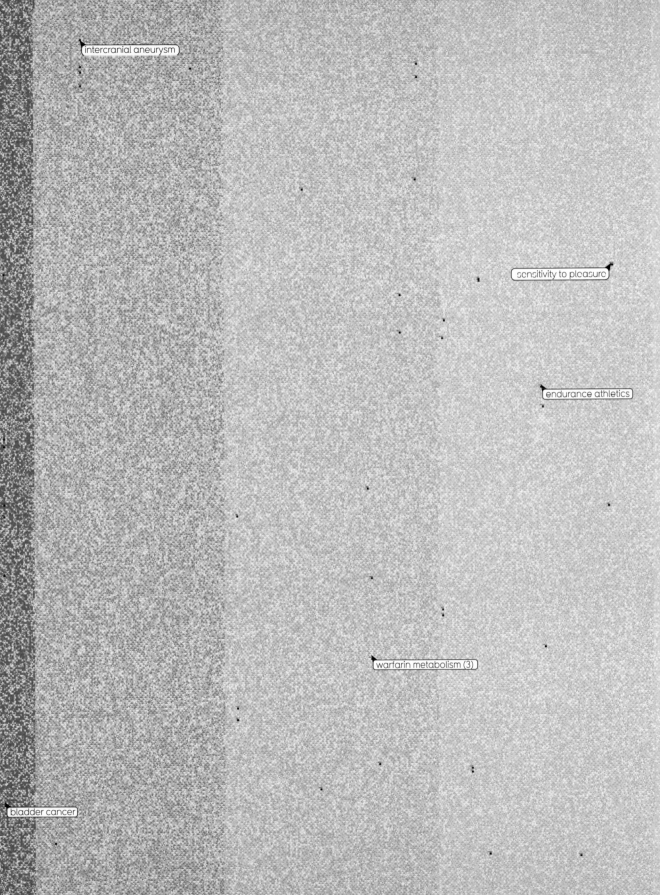

intercranial aneurysm

sensitivity to pleasure

endurance athletics

warfarin metabolism (3)

bladder cancer

colorectal cancer (6)

nicotine dependence

determines earw

alcoholic flush reaction

exfoliation glaucoma

green eye colour

blue eye colour

asthma

increased Alzheimer's risk (3)

baldness

source: Decodeme.com / programming : Mattias Gunnarås

varied cognitive effects

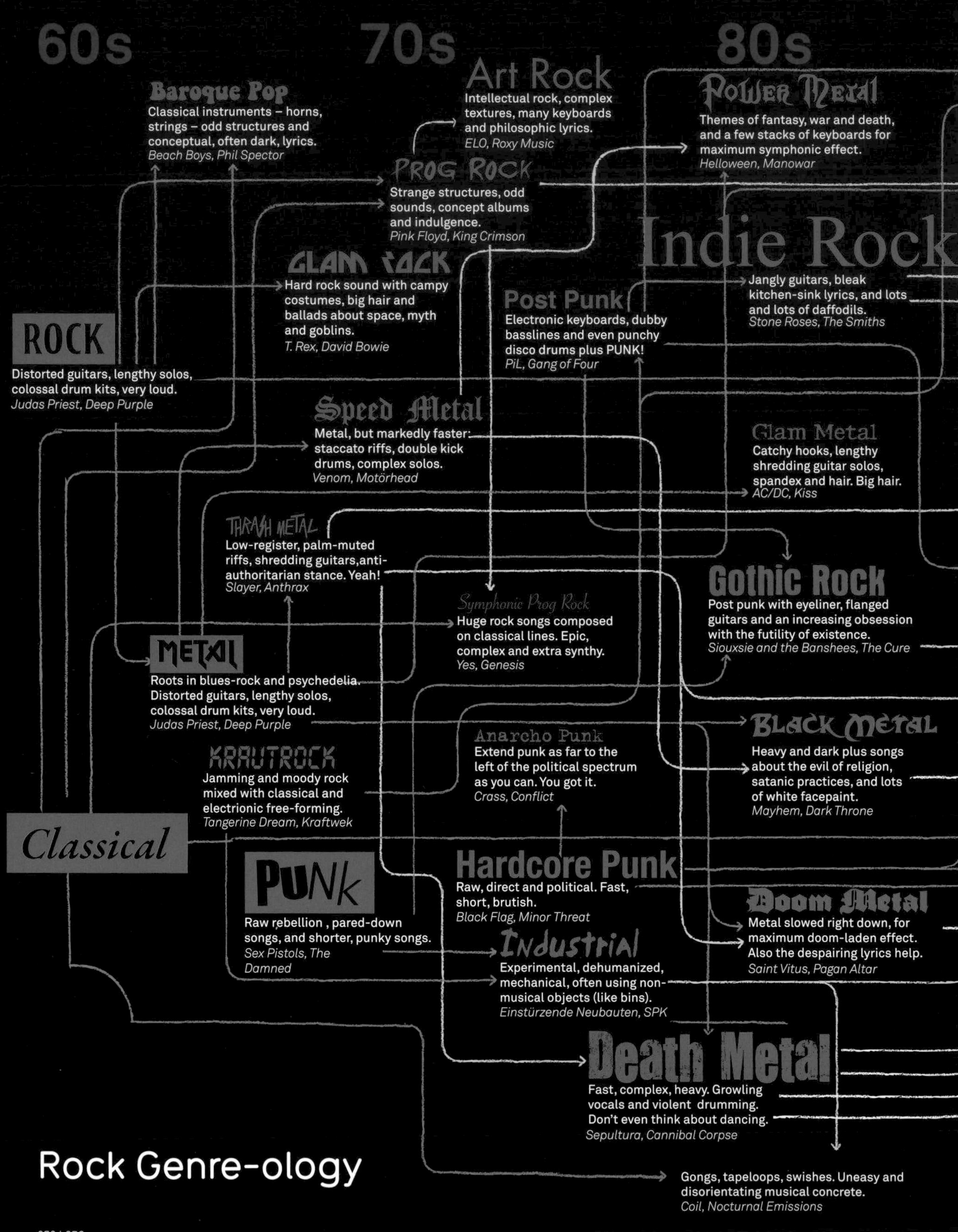
60s
70s
80s
Art Rock
Intellectual rock, complex textures, many keyboards and philosophic lyrics.
ELO, Roxy Music
Baroque Pop
Classical instruments – horns, strings – odd structures and conceptual, often dark, lyrics.
Beach Boys, Phil Spector
Power Metal
Themes of fantasy, war and death, and a few stacks of keyboards for maximum symphonic effect.
Helloween, Manowar
Prog Rock
Strange structures, odd sounds, concept albums and indulgence.
Pink Floyd, King Crimson
Indie Rock
Jangly guitars, bleak kitchen-sink lyrics, and lots and lots of daffodils.
Stone Roses, The Smiths
Glam Rock
Hard rock sound with campy costumes, big hair and ballads about space, myth and goblins.
T. Rex, David Bowie
Post Punk
Electronic keyboards, dubby basslines and even punchy disco drums plus PUNK!
PiL, Gang of Four
ROCK
Distorted guitars, lengthy solos, colossal drum kits, very loud.
Judas Priest, Deep Purple
Speed Metal
Metal, but markedly faster: staccato riffs, double kick drums, complex solos.
Venom, Motörhead
Glam Metal
Catchy hooks, lengthy shredding guitar solos, spandex and hair. Big hair.
AC/DC, Kiss
Thrash Metal
Low-register, palm-muted riffs, shredding guitars,anti-authoritarian stance. Yeah!
Slayer, Anthrax
Gothic Rock
Post punk with eyeliner, flanged guitars and an increasing obsession with the futility of existence.
Siouxsie and the Banshees, The Cure
Symphonic Prog Rock
Huge rock songs composed on classical lines. Epic, complex and extra synthy.
Yes, Genesis
METAL
Roots in blues-rock and psychedelia. Distorted guitars, lengthy solos, colossal drum kits, very loud.
Judas Priest, Deep Purple
Black Metal
Heavy and dark plus songs about the evil of religion, satanic practices, and lots of white facepaint.
Mayhem, Dark Throne
Anarcho Punk
Extend punk as far to the left of the political spectrum as you can. You got it.
Crass, Conflict
KRAUTROCK
Jamming and moody rock mixed with classical and electronic free-forming.
Tangerine Dream, Kraftwek
Classical
Hardcore Punk
Raw, direct and political. Fast, short, brutish.
Black Flag, Minor Threat
PUNK
Raw rebellion , pared-down songs, and shorter, punky songs.
Sex Pistols, The Damned
Doom Metal
Metal slowed right down, for maximum doom-laden effect. Also the despairing lyrics help.
Saint Vitus, Pagan Altar
Industrial
Experimental, dehumanized, mechanical, often using non-musical objects (like bins).
Einstürzende Neubauten, SPK
Death Metal
Fast, complex, heavy. Growling vocals and violent drumming. Don't even think about dancing.
Sepultura, Cannibal Corpse
Gongs, tapeloops, swishes. Uneasy and disorientating musical concrete.
Coil, Nocturnal Emissions

Rock Genre-ology

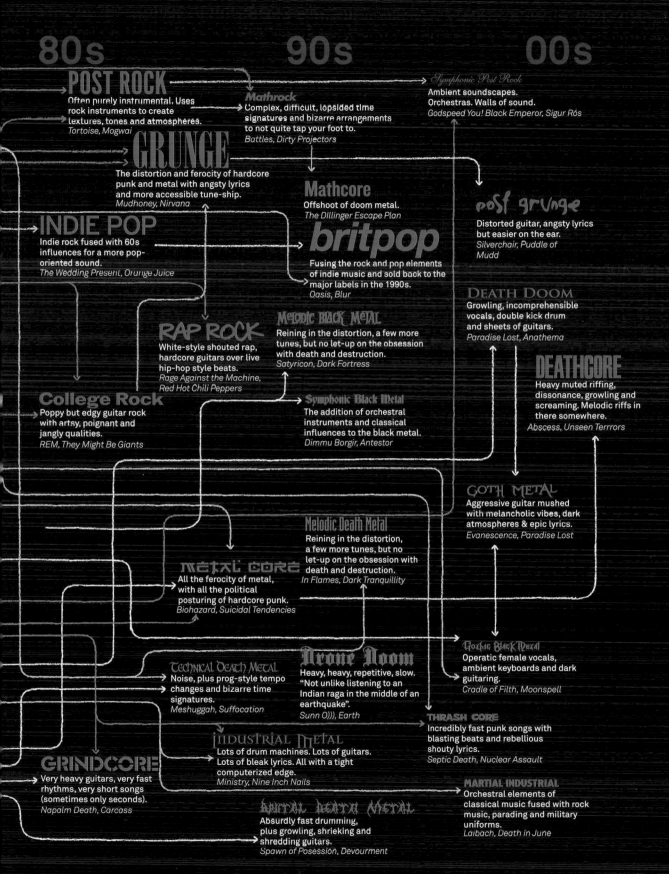

80s 90s 00s

POST ROCK
Often purely instrumental. Uses rock instruments to create textures, tones and atmospheres.
Tortoise, Mogwai

Mathrock
Complex, difficult, lopsided time signatures and bizarre arrangements to not quite tap your foot to.
Battles, Dirty Projectors

Symphonic Post Rock
Ambient soundscapes. Orchestras. Walls of sound.
Godspeed You! Black Emperor, Sigur Rós

GRUNGE
The distortion and ferocity of hardcore punk and metal with angsty lyrics and more accessible tune-ship.
Mudhoney, Nirvana

Mathcore
Offshoot of doom metal.
The Dillinger Escape Plan

post grunge
Distorted guitar, angsty lyrics but easier on the ear.
Silverchair, Puddle of Mudd

INDIE POP
Indie rock fused with 60s influences for a more pop-oriented sound.
The Wedding Present, Orange Juice

britpop
Fusing the rock and pop elements of indie music and sold back to the major labels in the 1990s.
Oasis, Blur

DEATH DOOM
Growling, incomprehensible vocals, double kick drum and sheets of guitars.
Paradise Lost, Anathema

Melodic Black Metal
Reining in the distortion, a few more tunes, but no let-up on the obsession with death and destruction.
Satyricon, Dark Fortress

RAP ROCK
White-style shouted rap, hardcore guitars over live hip-hop style beats.
Rage Against the Machine, Red Hot Chili Peppers

DEATHCORE
Heavy muted riffing, dissonance, growling and screaming. Melodic riffs in there somewhere.
Abscess, Unseen Terrrors

College Rock
Poppy but edgy guitar rock with artsy, poignant and jangly qualities.
REM, They Might Be Giants

Symphonic Black Metal
The addition of orchestral instruments and classical influences to the black metal.
Dimmu Borgir, Antestor

GOTH METAL
Aggressive guitar mushed with melancholic vibes, dark atmospheres & epic lyrics.
Evanescence, Paradise Lost

Melodic Death Metal
Reining in the distortion, a few more tunes, but no let-up on the obsession with death and destruction.
In Flames, Dark Tranquillity

METAL CORE
All the ferocity of metal, with all the political posturing of hardcore punk.
Biohazard, Suicidal Tendencies

Gothic Black Metal
Operatic female vocals, ambient keyboards and dark guitaring.
Cradle of Filth, Moonspell

Technical Death Metal
Noise, plus prog-style tempo changes and bizarre time signatures.
Meshuggah, Suffocation

Drone Doom
Heavy, heavy, repetitive, slow. "Not unlike listening to an Indian raga in the middle of an earthquake".
Sunn O))), Earth

THRASH CORE
Incredibly fast punk songs with blasting beats and rebellious shouty lyrics.
Septic Death, Nuclear Assault

Industrial Metal
Lots of drum machines. Lots of guitars. Lots of bleak lyrics. All with a tight computerized edge.
Ministry, Nine Inch Nails

GRINDCORE
Very heavy guitars, very fast rhythms, very short songs (sometimes only seconds).
Napalm Death, Carcass

MARTIAL INDUSTRIAL
Orchestral elements of classical music fused with rock music, parading and military uniforms.
Laibach, Death in June

Brutal Death Metal
Absurdly fast drumming, plus growling, shrieking and shredding guitars.
Spawn of Posession, Devourment

source: Wikipedia

Simple Part I

Think of the Children

% of children living in poverty

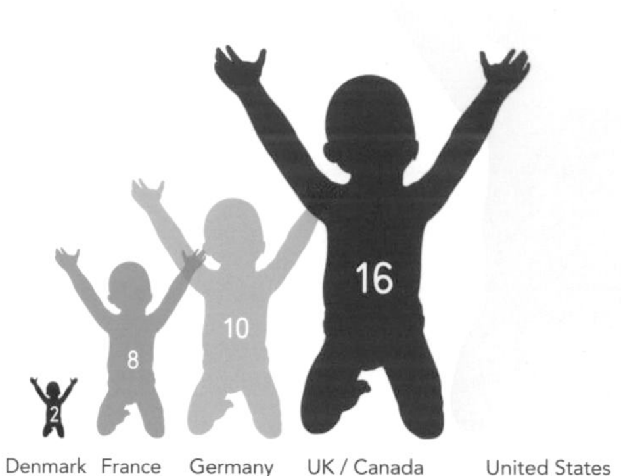
16
10
8
2
Denmark
France
Germany
UK / Canada
United States

source UNICEF 2007. Numbers rounded up.

Farty Animals

Annual methane emissions in equivalent CO_2

3500
370
230
320
73

source: UN Environmental Programme, theregister.co.uk

Who Reads the Most?

Amazon book stock as % of population size

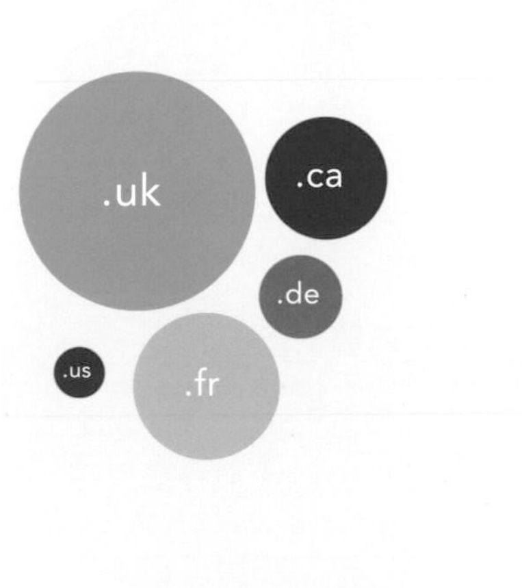
.uk
.ca
.de
.us
.fr

source: Data scraped from Amazon websites.

Wave of Generosity

% of promised tsunami aid money actually paid

Greece 100%
New Zealand
Iceland UK Norway
Japan 90%
Australia Canada 75%
Portugal Netherlands
Italy France 50%
USA 35%
Germany 26%

source: OECD

Celebrities with Issues

Number of celebs behind each cause

Mostly male celebs

Equal men & women

Mostly female celebs

weapons reduction
veterans
conservation
organ donation
addiction
physical challenges
sports
unemployment
fair trade
disaster relief
mental challenges
voter education
human rights
literacy
environment
homelessness
children
health
HIV
refugees
education
cancer
creative arts
depression & suicide
women
poverty
peace
family support
hunger
adoptions & orphans
rape & sexual abuse
animals
abuse
substance abuse
missing children
gay & lesbian support

idea: Richard Rogers @ govcom.org // source: looktothestars.org

How Rich?

Yearly earnings of world's wealthiest nations as combined earnings of US states

2007

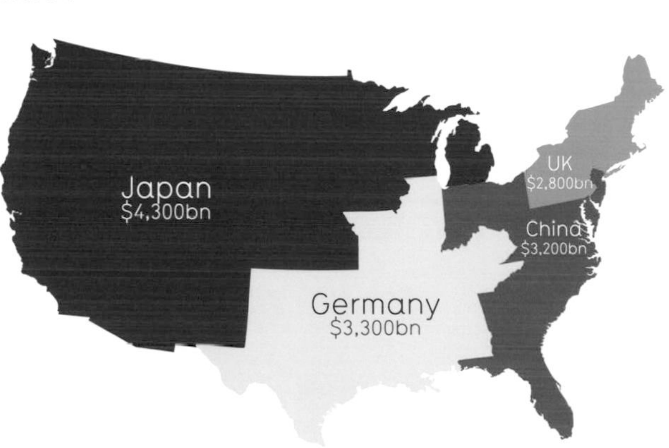
Japan
$4,300bn
UK
$2,800bn
China
$3,200bn
Germany
$3,300bn

2010

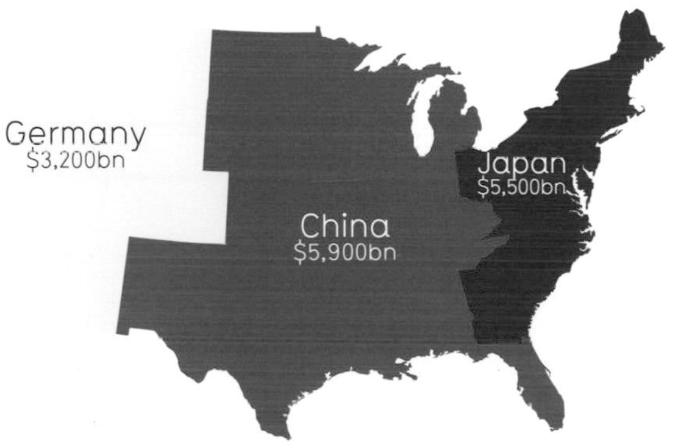
Germany
$3,200bn
Japan
$5,500bn
China
$5,900bn

source: WorldBank, ASecondHandConjecture.com

Sex Education

% virgin students by university subject

0% 50% 100%

Studio Art

Anthropology

Neuroscience

Art History

Computer Science

Spanish

English

French

Philosophy

History

Economics

Undecided

Psychology

International Relations

Biology

Political Science

Biochemistry

Mathematics

0% 50% 100%

source: MIT/Wellesley College magazine, Counterpoint (2001)

Godless Swedes

% of atheists, agnostics & non-believers

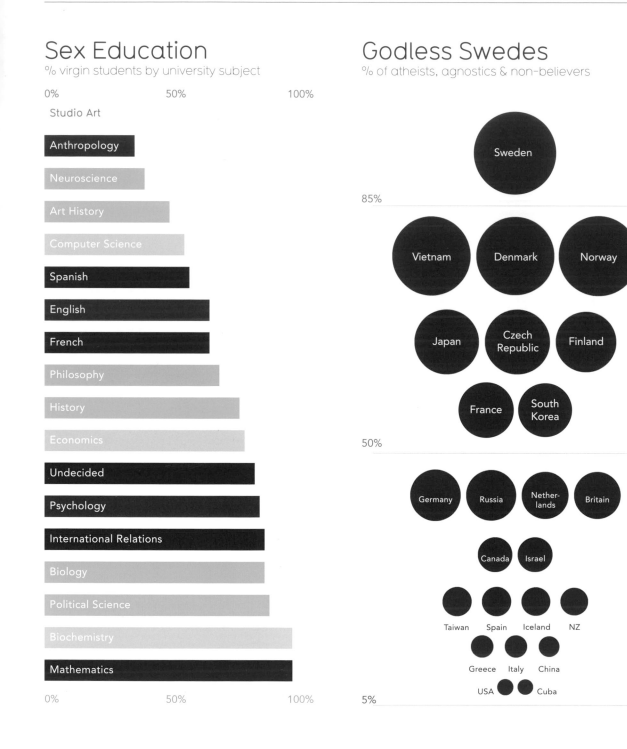

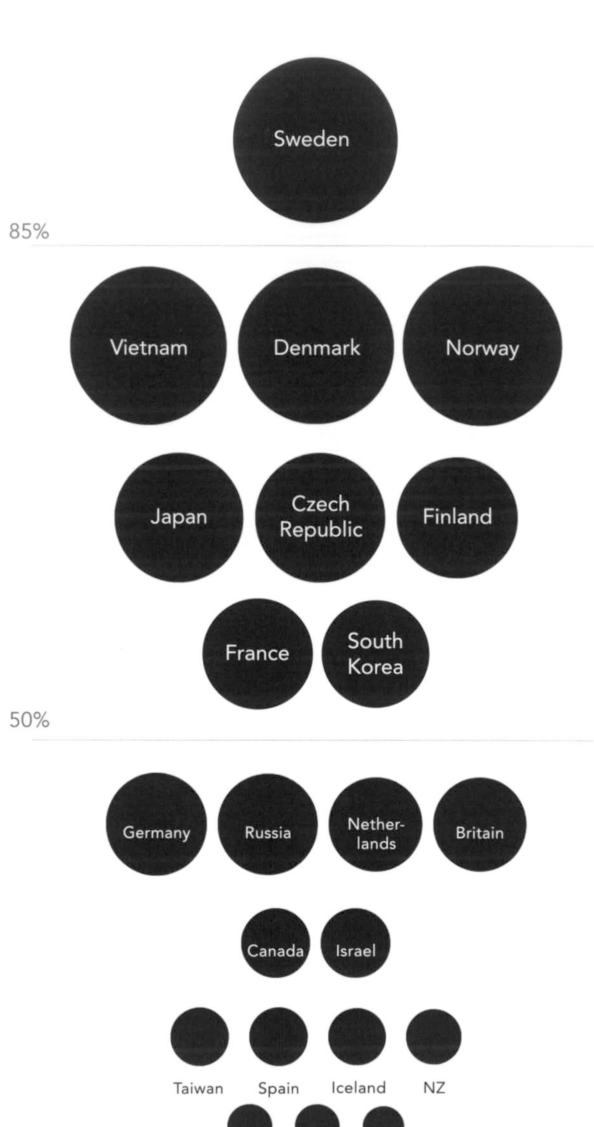
Sweden
85%
Vietnam
Denmark
Norway
Japan
Czech Republic
Finland
France
South Korea
50%
Germany
Russia
Nether-lands
Britain
Canada
Israel
Taiwan
Spain
Iceland
NZ
Greece
Italy
China
USA
Cuba
5%

source: Adherents.com

Net Increase

Internet traffic growth

Entire Internet per year
1993
Internet per second
2008
Internet per year, 2000
YouTube per month, 2008

source: Cisco

Left-Hand Path

Increased wealth of left-handed men

26%

Does not apply to left-handed women.

source: Lafayette College and Johns Hopkins University study

Goggle Box

The cognitive surplus...

200 billion hours
per year spent watching TV by US adults
100 million hours
to create
Wikipedia

source: Cognitive Surplus. Clay Shirky (Allen Lane, 2010)

Clear Cut

Drop in HIV transmission in circumcised males

55%

source: University of Melbourne, BBC News

Excuse Us

Reasons for divorce

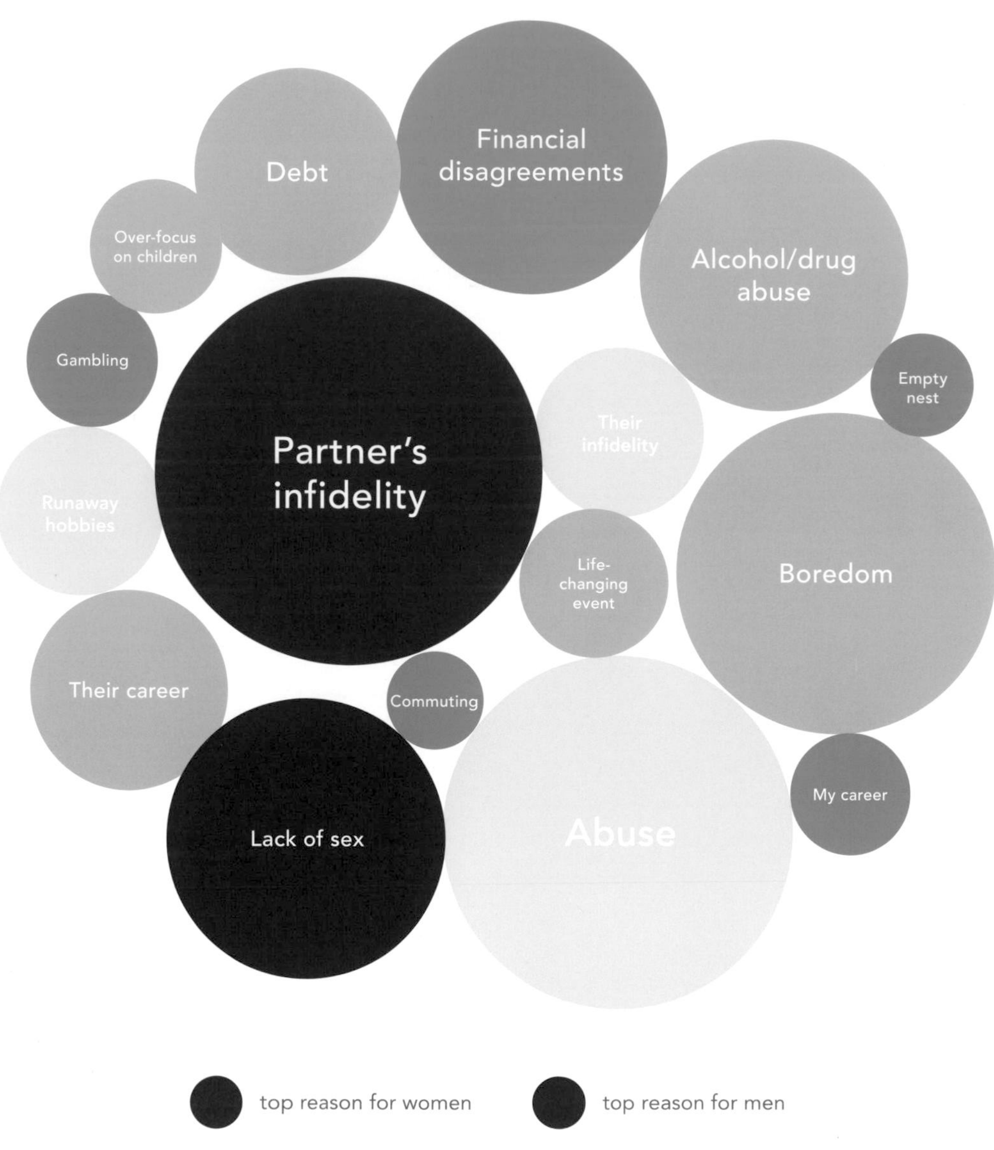

Debt
Financial disagreements
Over-focus on children
Alcohol/drug abuse
Gambling
Partner's infidelity
Their infidelity
Empty nest
Runaway hobbies
Life-changing event
Boredom
Their career
Commuting
Lack of sex
Abuse
My career
top reason for women
top reason for men

source: Insidedivorce.com

National Hypochondriacs Service

Top health searches

UK

Sciatica Shingles
IBS Thyroid Back pain
Pregnancy
Kidney Infection Ringworm
Chickenpox
Thrush Anaemia
Glandular Fever
Diabetes

source: NHS Direct

USA

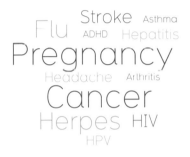

Stroke Asthma
Flu ADHD Hepatitis
Pregnancy
Headache Arthritis
Cancer
Herpes HIV
HPV

source: About.com

Germany

Cancer
Arthritis Stroke
Anorexia Flu Spots
Diarrhea Hemorrhoids
Diabetes
HIV MS
Hypertension

source: Google Insights

For Cod's Sake

Stocks of cod in the North Atlantic (100,000 tons)

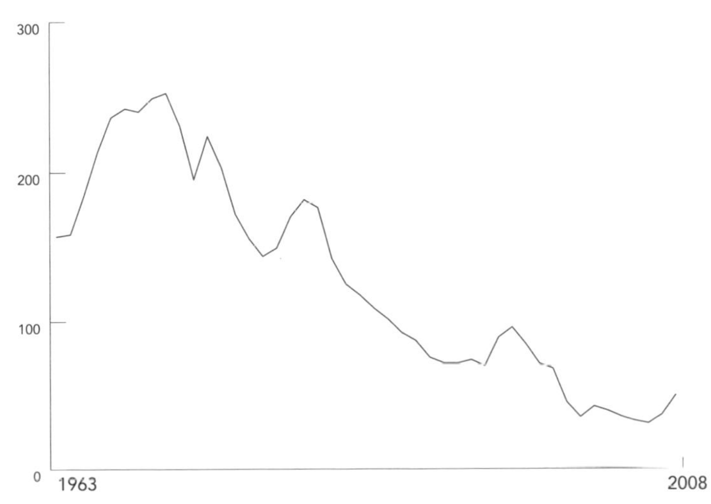

300
200
100
0
1963
2008

source: Fisheries Research Service

Ups and Downs

Cover vs coverage

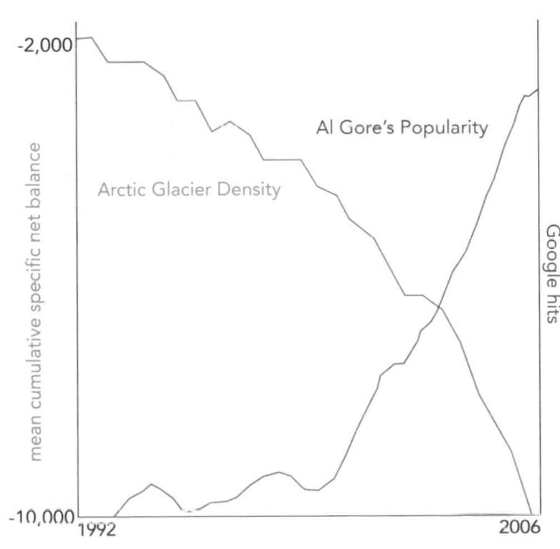

-2,000
-10,000
1992
2006
Al Gore's Popularity
Arctic Glacier Density
mean cumulative specific net balance
Google hits

source: Google Insights

What is Consciousness?

Make up your own mind

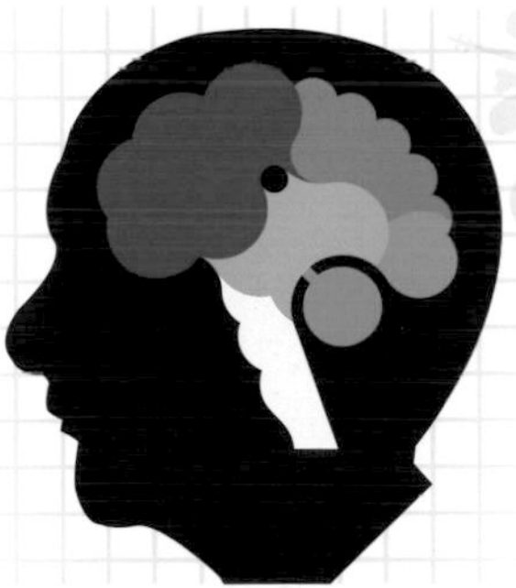

A field that exists in its own parallel "realm" of existence outside reality, so can't be seen.
(Substance Dualism)

A sensation that "grows" inevitably out of complicated brain states.
(Emergent Dualism)

A physical property of all matter, like electromagnetism, just not one scientists know about.
(Property Dualism)

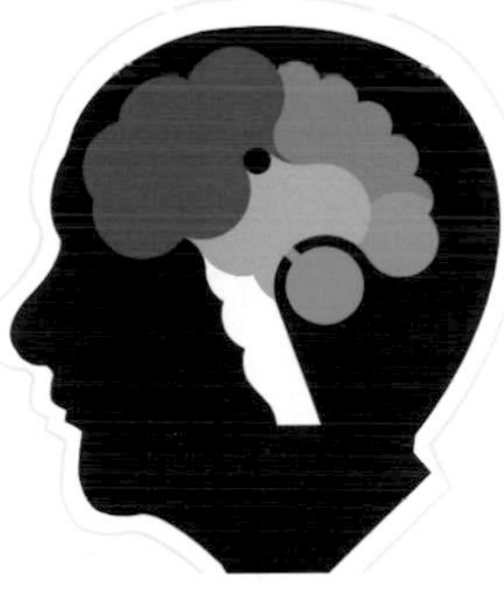

All matter has a psychic part. Consciousness is just the psychic part of our brain.
(Panpsychism)

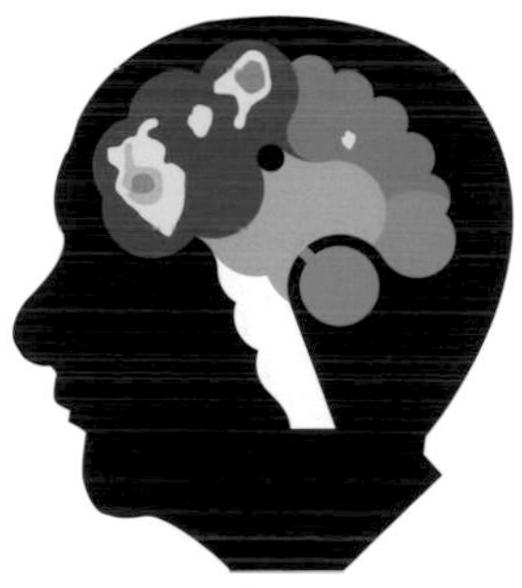

Mental states are simply physical events that we can see in brain scans.
(Identity Theory)

Consciousness and its states (belief, desire, pain) are simply functions the brain performs.
(Functionalism)

Literally just behaviour. When we behave in a certain way, we appear conscious.
(Behaviourism)

An accidental side-effect of complex physical processes in the brain.
(Epiphenomenalism)

Not sure. But quantum physics, over classical physics, can better explain it.
(Quantum Consciousness)

The sensation of your most significant thoughts being highlighted.
(Cognitivism)

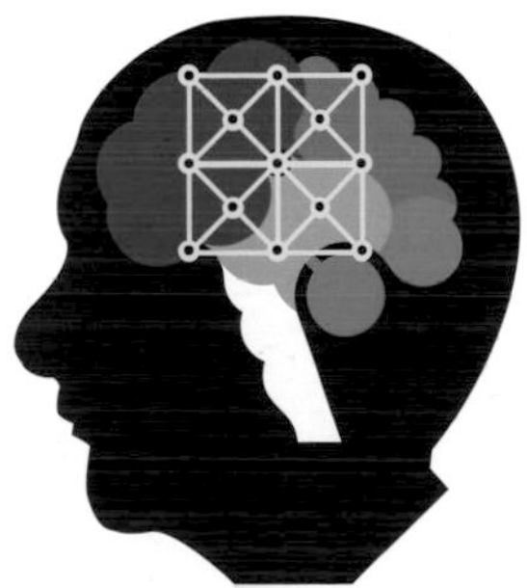

Consciousness is just higher-order thoughts (thoughts about other thoughts).
(Higher-Order Theory)

A continuous stream of ever-recurring phenomena, pinched like eddies into isolated minds.
(Buddhism)

source: Wikipedia

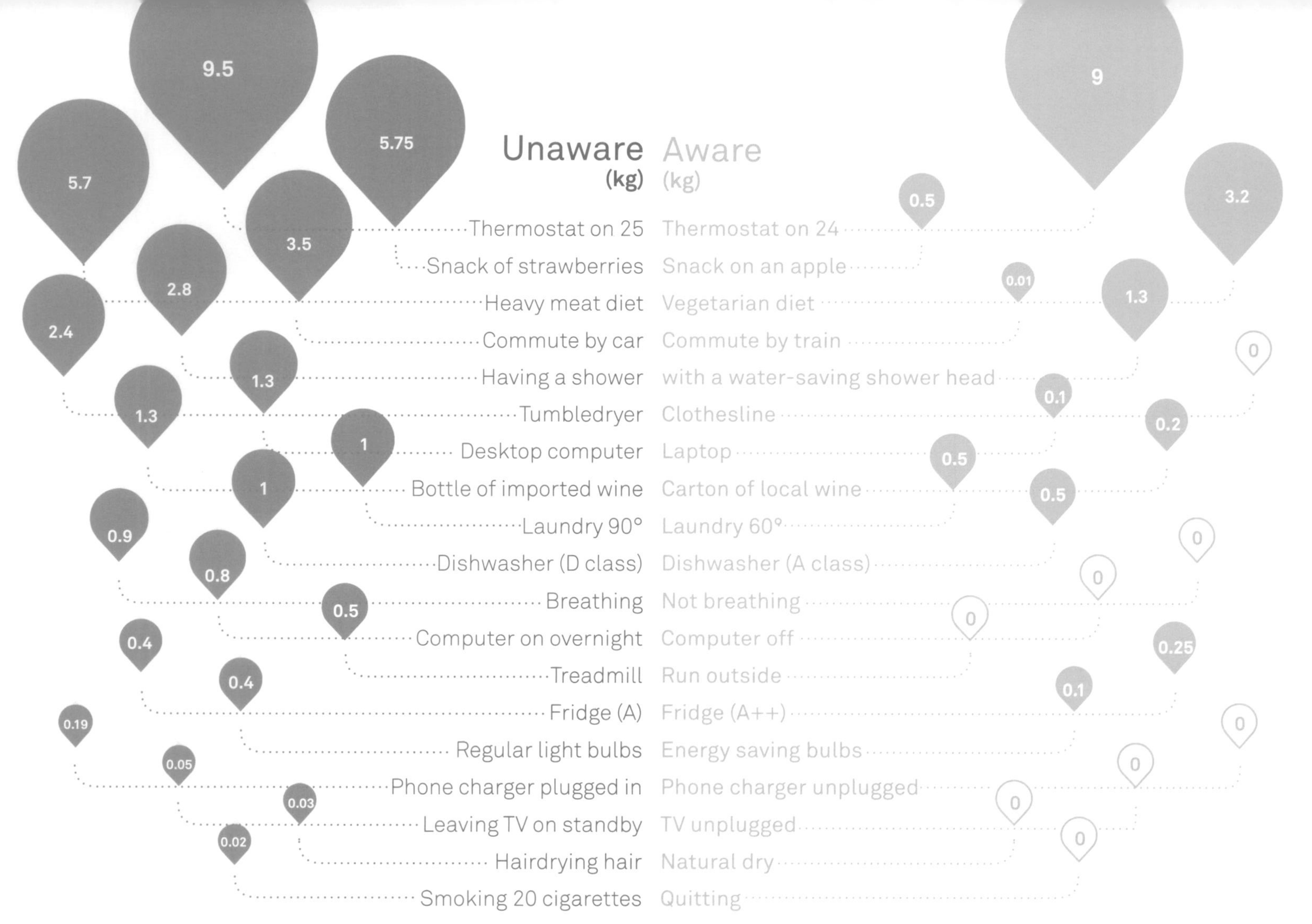

Unaware (kg)
Aware (kg)
Thermostat on 25
Thermostat on 24
Snack of strawberries
Snack on an apple
Heavy meat diet
Vegetarian diet
Commute by car
Commute by train
Having a shower
with a water-saving shower head
Tumbledryer
Clothesline
Desktop computer
Laptop
Bottle of imported wine
Carton of local wine
Laundry 90°
Laundry 60°
Dishwasher (D class)
Dishwasher (A class)
Breathing
Not breathing
Computer on overnight
Computer off
Treadmill
Run outside
Fridge (A)
Fridge (A++)
Regular light bulbs
Energy saving bulbs
Phone charger plugged in
Phone charger unplugged
Leaving TV on standby
TV unplugged
Hairdrying hair
Natural dry
Smoking 20 cigarettes
Quitting

Carbon Conscious

Tweak your day

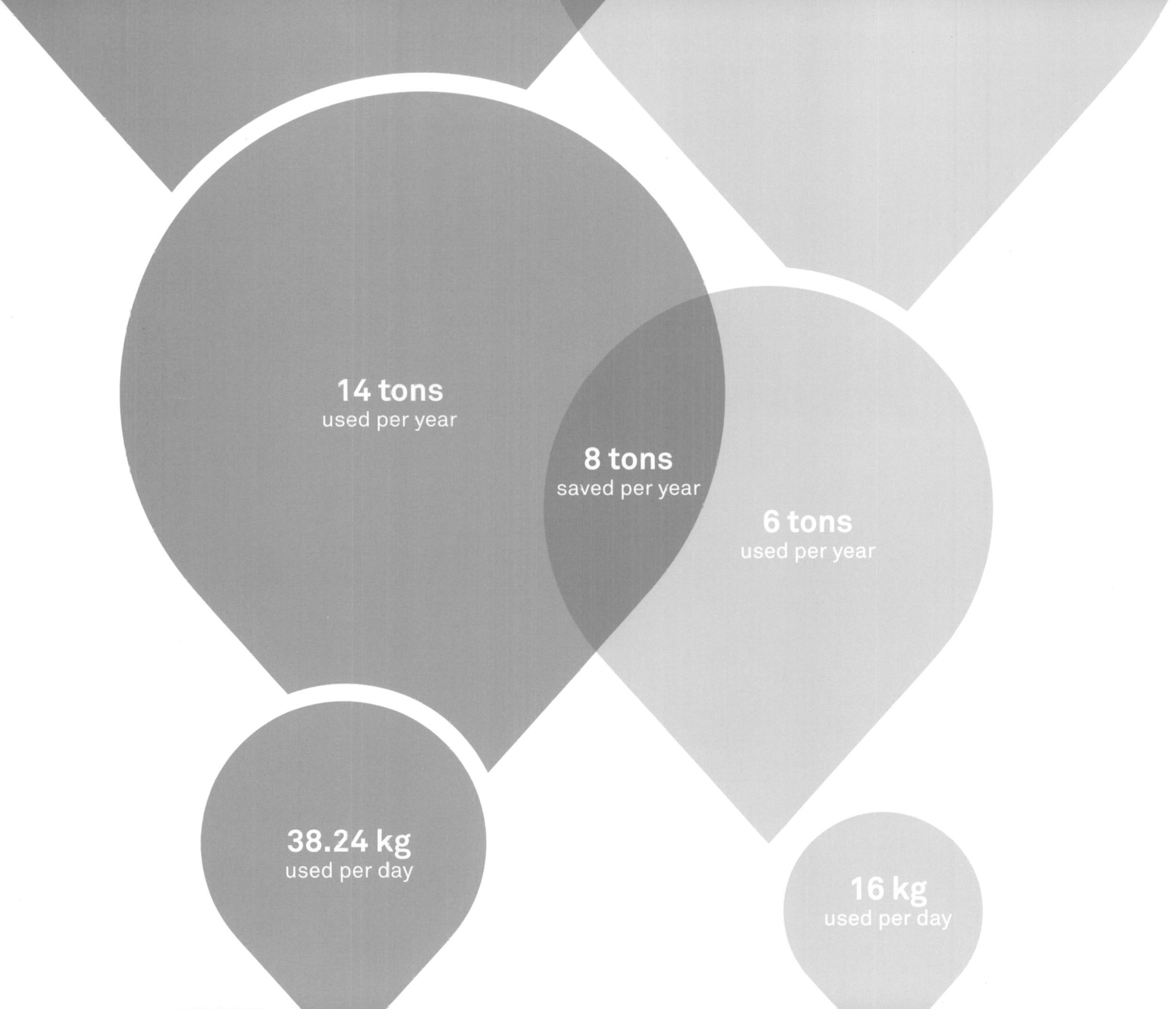
14 tons
used per year
8 tons
saved per year
6 tons
used per year
38.24 kg
used per day
16 kg
used per day

source: UNESCO, Environmental Protection Agency, Energy Information Administration

including everyone in the UK & USA
4,187,280,000 tons

including everyone in the UK & USA
1,752,000,000 tons
(Equivalent to Japan's annual CO_2 emissions)

including everyone in the UK
907,244,000 tons
used per year

527,644,000
tons saved

including everyone in the UK
379,600,000 tons
used per year

2,435,280,000 tons

saved

(equivalent to Russia & India's total combined CO_2 emissions per year)

Colours and Culture

The meanings of colours around the world

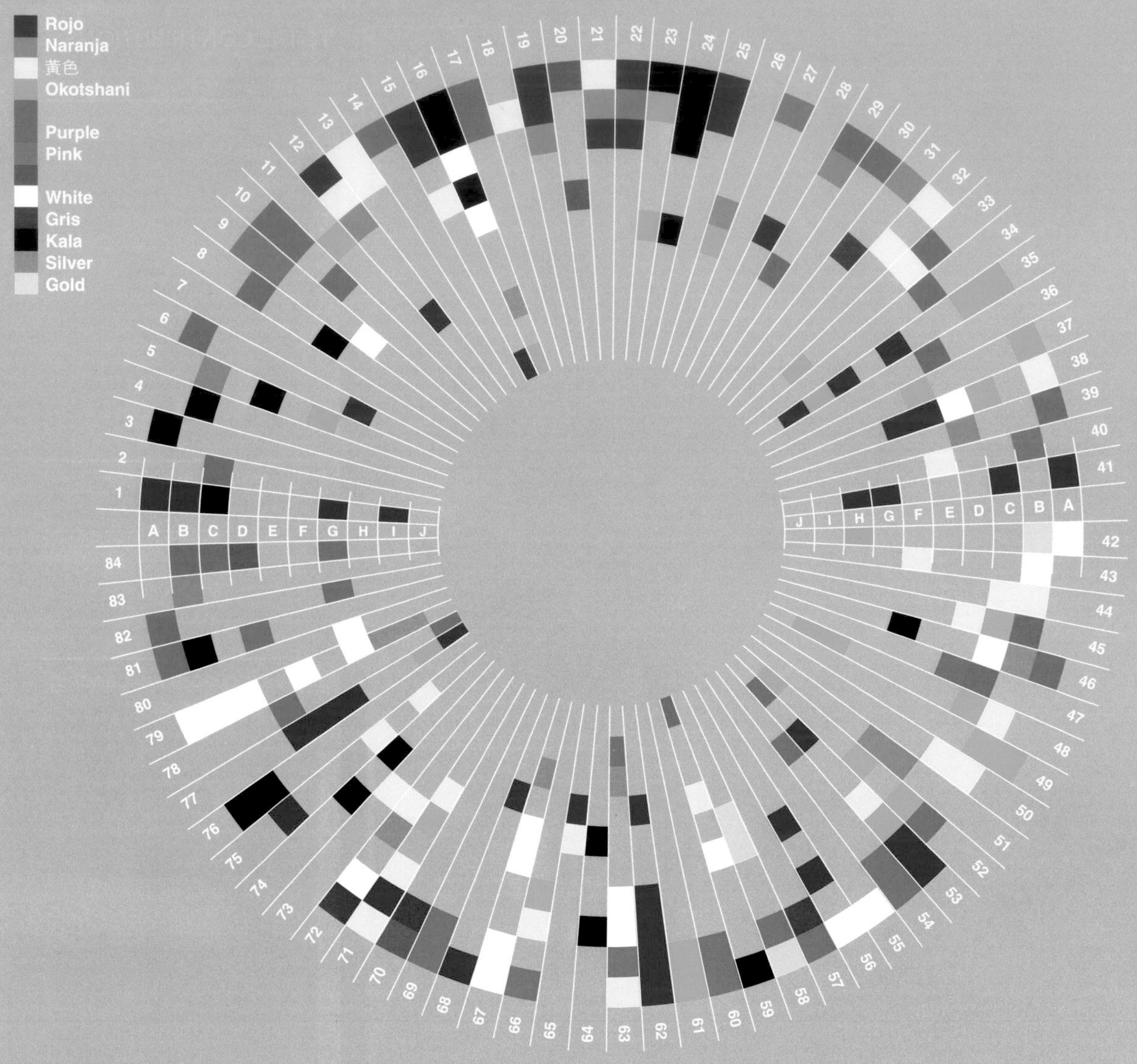

Rojo
Naranja
黄色
Okotshani
Purple
Pink
White
Gris
Kala
Silver
Gold
A B C D E F G H I J

A American
B Japanese
C Hindu
D Native American
E Chinese
F Asian
G Eastern European
H Muslim
I African
J South American

1 Anger
2 Art / Creativity
3 Authority
4 Bad Luck
5 Balance
6 Beauty
7 Calm
8 Celebration
9 Children
10 Cold
11 Compassion
12 Courage
13 Cowardice
14 Cruelty
15 Danger
16 Death
17 Decadence
18 Deceit
19 Desire
20 Earth
21 Energy
22 Eroticism
23 Eternity
24 Evil
25 Excitement
26 Family
27 Femininity
28 Fertility
29 Flamboyance
30 Freedom
31 Friendliness
32 Fun
33 God
34 Gods
35 Good Luck
36 Gratitude
37 Growth
38 Happiness
39 Healing
40 Healthiness
41 Heat
42 Heaven
43 Holiness
44 Illness
45 Insight
46 Intelligence
47 Intuition
48 Religion
49 Jealousy
50 Joy
51 Learning
52 Life
53 Love
54 Loyalty
55 Luxury
56 Marriage
57 Modesty
58 Money
59 Mourning
60 Mystery
61 Nature
62 Passion
63 Peace
64 Penance
65 Political Power
66 Personal Power
67 Purity
68 Radicalism
69 Rationality
70 Reliability
71 Repelling Evil
72 Respect
73 Royalty
74 Self-cultivation
75 Strength
76 Style
77 Success
78 Trouble
79 Truce
80 Trust
81 Unhappiness
82 Virtue
83 Warmth
84 Wisdom

source: Wikipedia, general web

Stages of You

Children grow in phases. Do adults too? If so, what are the stages? Some theories...

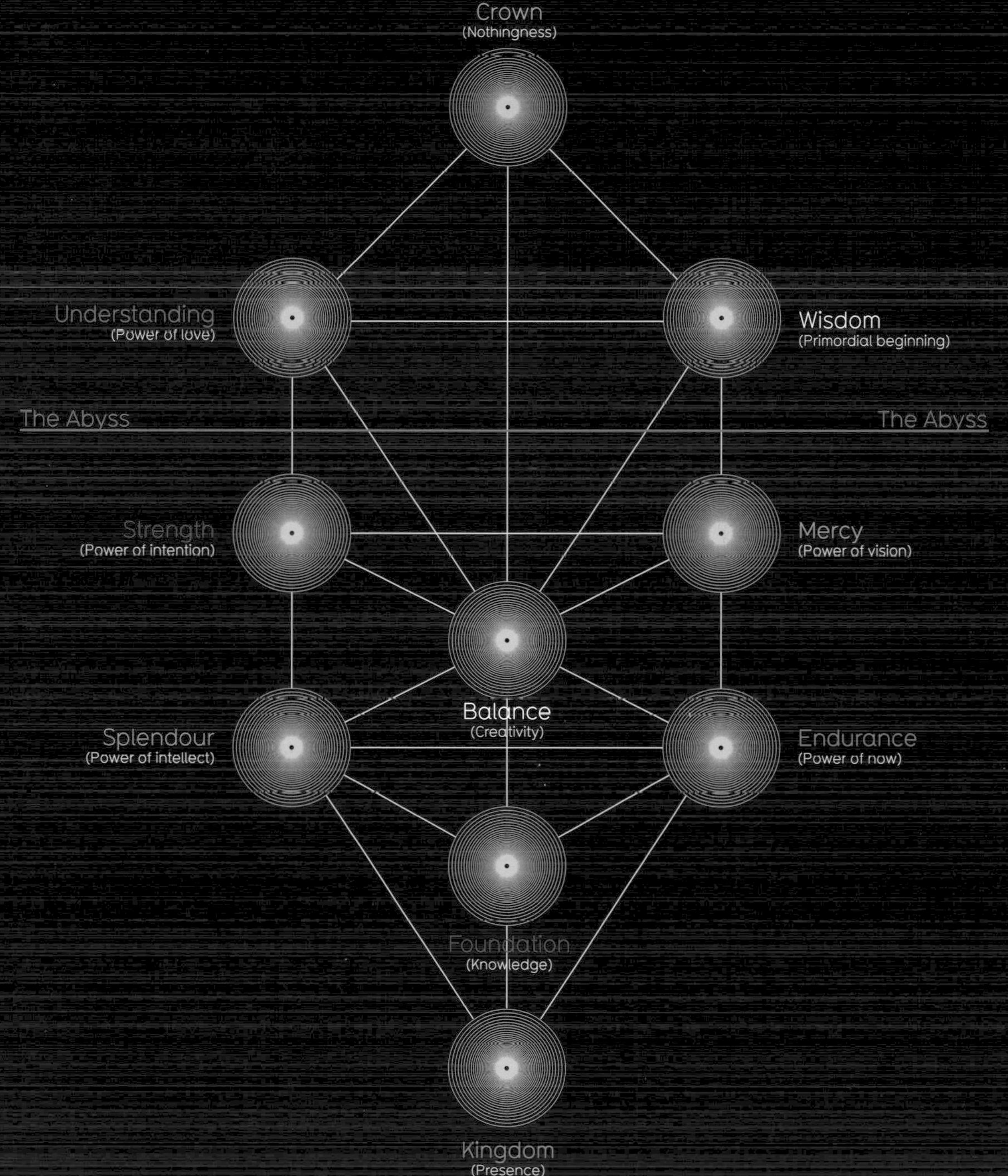

Crown
(Nothingness)
Understanding
(Power of love)
Wisdom
(Primordial beginning)
The Abyss
The Abyss
Strength
(Power of intention)
Mercy
(Power of vision)
Balance
(Creativity)
Splendour
(Power of intellect)
Endurance
(Power of now)
Foundation
(Knowledge)
Kingdom
(Presence)

The Tree of Life

In the Jewish Kabbalah, these are the ten stages through which the universe was created. They're also the ten qualities of God. As an adult grows, they ascend the tree and acquire these qualities for themselves.

CRITICS SAY: "Where's the evidence?"

source: Wikipedia

world

Sufism

In the mystical form of Islam, the soul or self (nafs) has seven degrees of development, each with increasing purity.

The Pure Self

Self is entirely transcended. No ego or separate self left. Only the Divine exists. Any sense of individuality or separateness is an illusion.

The Self Pleasing to God

Inner marriage of self and soul. All power to act comes from God. You can do nothing by yourself. You no longer fear anything nor ask for anything. Genuine inner unity and wholeness.

The Pleased Self

You are content with your lot, and pleased with even the difficulties and trials of life, realizing that these difficulties come from God. Very different from the usual way of experiencing the world (i.e. focused on seeking pleasure and avoiding pain).

The Contented Self

The struggles of the earlier stages are basically over. The self is at peace. Old desires and attachments still exist but are no longer binding. Grateful, trusting, and adoring. One accepts difficulties in the same way one accepts benefits. The ego-self begins to let go, allowing the individual to come more closely in contact with the Divine.

The Inspired Self

Beginning to taste the joys of spiritual experience. Genuine pleasure from prayer, meditation and other spiritual activities, motivated by compassion, service and morals. Though not free from desires and selfishness, their power is significantly reduced. Emotional maturity is dawning.

The Regretful Self

Insight dawns. The negative effects of a habitually self-centred approach to the world become apparent. Wants and desires still dominate. But now you can see your faults. Regret and a desire for change grow. Attempts to follow higher impulses follow – not always successfully.

The Commanding Self

A false personality created by parents, school and culture. Selfish, controlling and lacking compassion. Must be recognized and bypassed (not destroyed) to grow.

The Arc of Ascent

self

CRITICS SAY
"Says who?"

Source: Sufi (Laleh Bakhtair), Sufi.org, Wikipedia, Idries Shah

The Seven Chakras

In this Eastern system, you develop by mastering life-force energy expressed through certain energy centres or "chakras" (roughly centred on various glands and organs). Imbalances in these energy wheels create feelings of blockage and dissatisfaction.

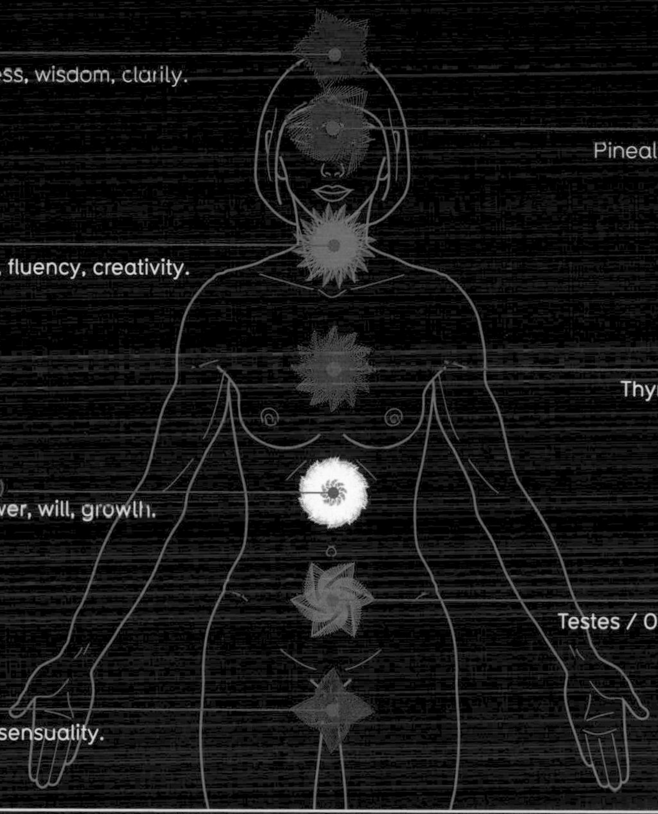

Crown (Sahasrara)
Pituitary gland. Awareness, wisdom, clarity.

Third Eye (Ajna)
Pineal gland. Intuition, clarity, thought.

Throat (Vishuddha)
Thyroid. Communication, fluency, creativity.

Heart (Anahata)
Thymus. Compassion, love, passion.

Solar Plexus (Manipura)
Islets of langerhans. Power, will, growth.

Sacral (Svadisthana)
Testes / Ovaries. Pleasure, desire, activity.

Base (muladhara)
Perineum. Stability, sex, sensuality.

CRITICS SAY
"There's no mystical energy-field controls my destiny."

Maslow's "Hierarchy of Needs"

Psychologist Abraham Maslow believed that adult growth occurs in seven stages. But only after certain needs are fulfilled in your life.

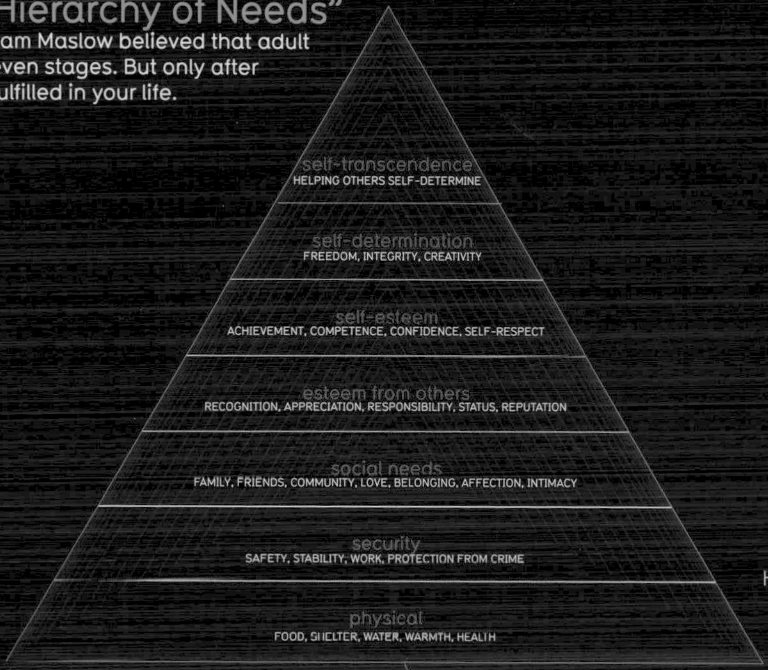

self-transcendence
HELPING OTHERS SELF-DETERMINE

self-determination
FREEDOM, INTEGRITY, CREATIVITY

self-esteem
ACHIEVEMENT, COMPETENCE, CONFIDENCE, SELF-RESPECT

esteem from others
RECOGNITION, APPRECIATION, RESPONSIBILITY, STATUS, REPUTATION

social needs
FAMILY, FRIENDS, COMMUNITY, LOVE, BELONGING, AFFECTION, INTIMACY

security
SAFETY, STABILITY, WORK, PROTECTION FROM CRIME

physical
FOOD, SHELTER, WATER, WARMTH, HEALTH

CRITICS SAY
"Little evidence. Fundamental human needs don't change over time and certainly can't be ranked in a hierarchy."

source: Wikipedia, Sufi.org, IdriesShah.com

Loevinger's Stages of Self-Development

Psychologist Jane Loevinger's system emphasizes the maturing of conscience. Social rules govern most people's personal decisions. But if differences appear between social rules and your behaviour, you must adapt to resolve the conflict, i.e. you have to grow.

	Opportunist	Diplomat	Expert
DEFINED BY	mistrust & manipulation	the group (tribe, family, nation)	knowledge
POSITIVES	energetic	dependable	ideas & solutions
SELF-DEFINITION	self-centred	self-in-group	self-autonomy
ACTION	whatever	obeying	doing
INTERESTS	domination, control	neatness, status, reputation	efficiency, improvemer perfection
THINKING	black & white	concrete	watertight
BEHAVIOUR	opportunistic	controlled	superior
WORLD VIEW	hostile, dangerous place	conformist, fundamentalist	rational, scientific
LOOKING FOR	rewards	acceptance	perfection
MORALITY	for self-interest only	given by the group	self-righteous
LANGUAGE HABITS	polarities: good/bad, fun/boring	superlatives, platitudes, clichés	"yes but..."
COMMON FLAWS	selfish	hostility to "outsiders"	selfish
FEAR OF	being overpowered	disapproval, rejection	loss of uniqueness
DEFENCES	blaming, distortion	suppression, projection, idealization	intellectualizing, hostil humour, blaming tools
SOCIALLY	two-faced, hostile	facilitator, socialite	seek to stand out from crowd
RELATIONSHIPS	exploitative, volatile	useful for status	useful or not?
WHEN OPPOSED	tantrums, harsh retaliation	meekly accept	argumentative, belittli opinionated

Achiever	Individualist	Strategist	Alchemist
independence	unconventionality	strength & autonomy	complexity, authenticity
conviction, fairness, enthusiasm	inspiring & spontaneous	insightful, principled, balanced	charismatic, authentic leaders
self-in-society	self as individual	self-determination	transparent self
perfecting	being & feeling	integrating	playing, reinventing
reasons, causes, goals, effectiveness	unique personal achievements	patterns, trends, processes, complexity	problems of language and meaning
rational, sceptical	holistic	visionary	intuitive
challenging, supportive	creative	highly collaborative, spontaneous	free
postmodern, scientific	paradoxical, no need to explain everything	multi-faceted, ambiguous	chaotic
root causes	uniqueness	authenticity	truths
self-chosen	non-judgemental, almost amoral	deeply principled, will sacrifice self for values	very high moral standards
ask lots of "why" questions	contrasting ideas, vivid language	complex, lyrical	fluid orators
exhaustion, over-extension, self-criticism	can appear aloof & unapproachable	impatient with theirs & others' development	feeling better than others
failure, loss of control	self-deception	not fulfilling their potential	fearless
rationalization, self-criticism	sublimation, spiritualization	suppression, humour, altruism	sublimation, humour
genuinely friendly	fun!	great communicators	can talk to anyone
diverse, intense & meaningful	intense & mutually rewarding	vital for intimacy & growth	deeply empathic
"we agree to differ"	respectful, differences are celebrated	tolerant, insightful, responsive	empathetic

CRITICS SAY: The "self" is a complex of developing parts, not governed by a single factor.

source: Susanne Cook-Greuter, Ego Development: Nine Levels of Increasing Embrace, Wikipedia

Spiral Dynamics

Measures how people think. The intensity with which you embrace or reject each coloured value system reveals how high you are up the development spiral. Can also be applied to societies and cultures.

Developed by Professor Clare Graves, Dr Don Beck and Chris Cowan

Yellow Autonomous

Behaviour Ecological thinking. **Embraces** Change and chaos. Self-directed. **Attitude** See the big picture. Life is learning. **Decision-making** Highly principled. Knowledge based. **Admires** The competent. **Seeks** integrity. **Loves** Natural systems, knowledge, multiplicity. **Wants** Self-knowledge. **Hides** Attachment. **Good side:** Free. Wise. Aware. **Bad side:** Overly intellectual, excessively sceptical, angst ridden.

Orange Achiever

Behaviour Strategic. Scientific thinking. Competes for success. Driven. Competitive. **Attitude** Goal orientated. Play to win. Survival of the fittest. **Decisions** Bottom line. Test options for best results. Consult experts. **Admires** The successful. **Seeks** Affluence. Prosperity. Rational truth. **Loves** Success, status. **Wants** Self-expression. **Hides** Lies **Good side:** Great communication and creativity. Risk taking. Optimistic. **Bad side:** Workaholic. Babbling. Fearful.

Red Egocentric

Behaviour Self-centred. **Attitude** Do what you want, regardless. Live for the moment. The world is a jungle. Might makes right. **Decisions based on** what gets respect, what feels good now. **Admires** The powerful. **Seeks** Power, glory and revenge. **Loves** Glitz, conquest, action. **Wants** Self-definition. **Hides** Shame. **Good side**: Spontaneous, purposeful. **Under pressure**: Dominating, blaming, aggressive. **Bad side**: Passive, sluggish, fearful.

Beige Instinctive

Behaviour Instinctive. Materialistic. Greedy. Fearful. **Attitude** Do what you can to stay alive. **Seeks** Food, water, warmth, security.

Turquoise Whole View

Behaviour Holistic intuitive thinking. **Attitude** Global. Harmonious. An ecology of perspectives. **Decision-making** Flow. Blending. Looking up and downstream. Long range. **Admires** Life! **Seeks** Interconnectedness. Peace in an incomprehensible world. **Loves** Information. Belonging. Doing.

Green Communitarian

Behaviour Consensus-seeking. Harmony within the group. Accepting. Dialogue. **Attitude** Everybody is equal. **Decision-making** Consensus. Collaborative. Accept everyone's input. **Admires** The charismatic. **Seeks** Inner peace with caring community. **Loves** Affection, good relationships, beneficial resolution. **Wants** Self-reflection. **Hides** Doubts. **Good side:** Listens well. Receptive. Perceptive, imaginative. **Bad side:** "Politically correct", inauthentic.

Blue Absolutist

Behaviour Authoritarian. Cautious. Careful. Fit in. Discipline. Faith. **Attitude** Only one right way. **Decision-making** based on obeying rules, following orders, doing "right". **Admires** The righteous. **Seeks** Peace of mind. **Loves** Everything in its right place. **Wants** Self-acceptance. **Hides** Grief. **Good side:** Balanced, compassionate. **Bad side:** Needy, possessive, jealous, bitter, critical.

Purple Tribal

Behaviour Impulsive. Honour the "old ways". **Attitude** Self-gratifying. **Decision-making** Based on custom and tradition. **Seeks** Safety, security. **Admires** The clan. **Hides** Guilt. **Good side:** Fluid with a healthy sexuality. **Bad side:** Overly emotional, obsessive, frigid, impotent, numb.

CRITICS SAY: "Says who? Exact characteristics for advance stages are unclear and speculative."

source: spiraldynamics.net, wikipedia

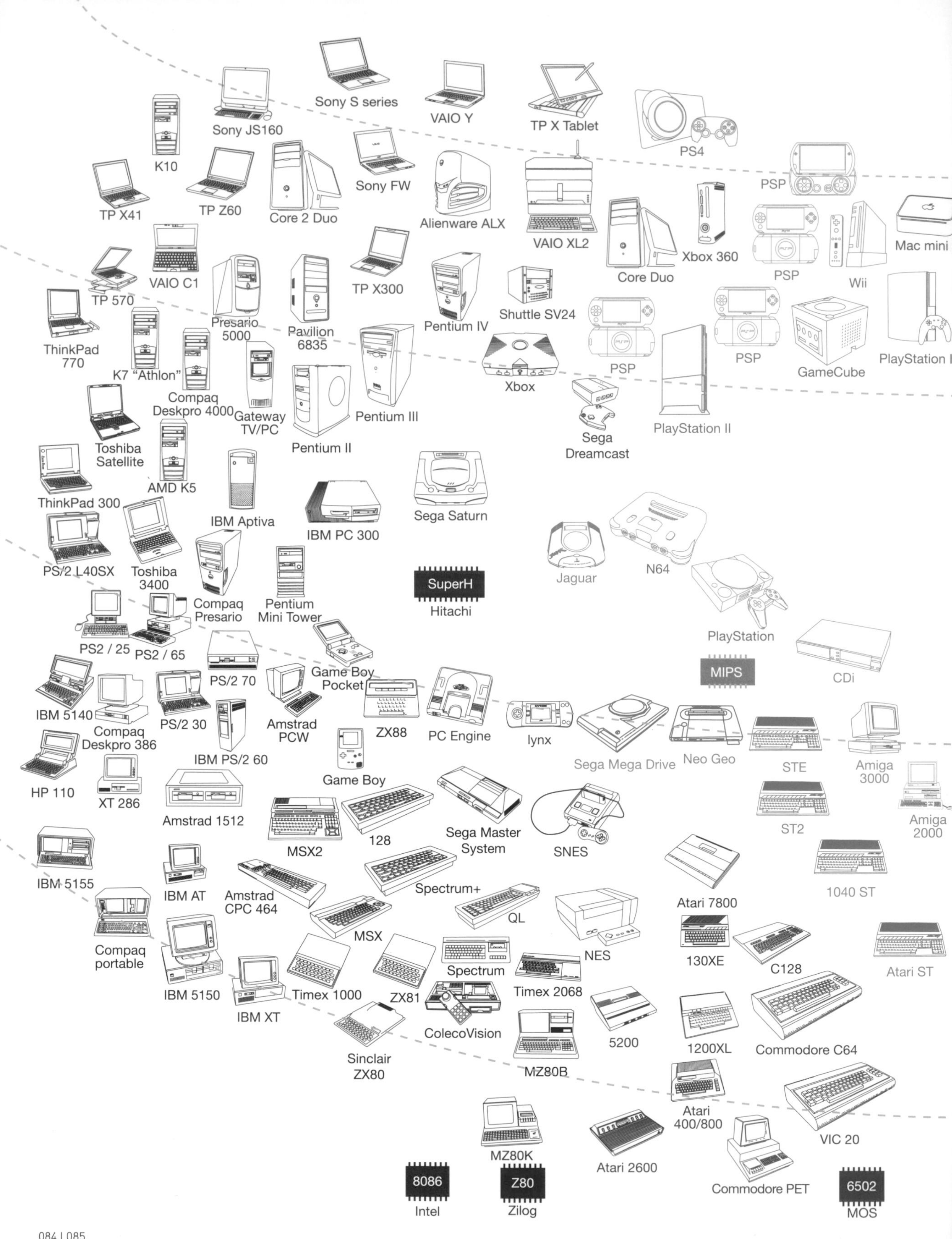

Sony S series
VAIO Y
TP X Tablet
PS4
Sony JS160
K10
PSP
Sony FW
TP X41
TP Z60
Core 2 Duo
Alienware ALX
VAIO XL2
Xbox 360
Mac mini 2
Core Duo
PSP
Wii
VAIO C1
TP X300
TP 570
Presario 5000
Pavilion 6835
Pentium IV
Shuttle SV24
ThinkPad 770
PSP
PSP
GameCube
PlayStation III
K7 "Athlon"
Xbox
Compaq Deskpro 4000
Gateway TV/PC
Pentium III
PlayStation II
Sega Dreamcast
Toshiba Satellite
Pentium II
AMD K5
ThinkPad 300
IBM Aptiva
IBM PC 300
Sega Saturn
PS/2 L40SX
Toshiba 3400
Jaguar
N64
SuperH
Hitachi
Compaq Presario
Pentium Mini Tower
PS2 / 25
PS2 / 65
PlayStation
PS/2 70
Game Boy Pocket
MIPS
CDi
IBM 5140
Compaq Deskpro 386
PS/2 30
Amstrad PCW
ZX88
PC Engine
lynx
IBM PS/2 60
Sega Mega Drive
Neo Geo
STE
Amiga 3000
HP 110
XT 286
Game Boy
Amstrad 1512
MSX2
128
Sega Master System
SNES
ST2
Amiga 2000
IBM 5155
IBM AT
Amstrad CPC 464
Spectrum+
QL
Atari 7800
1040 ST
MSX
NES
Compaq portable
130XE
C128
Atari ST
Spectrum
Timex 2068
IBM 5150
Timex 1000
ZX81
IBM XT
ColecoVision
5200
1200XL
Commodore C64
Sinclair ZX80
MZ80B
Atari 400/800
VIC 20
MZ80K
Atari 2600
Commodore PET
8086
Intel
Z80
Zilog
6502
MOS

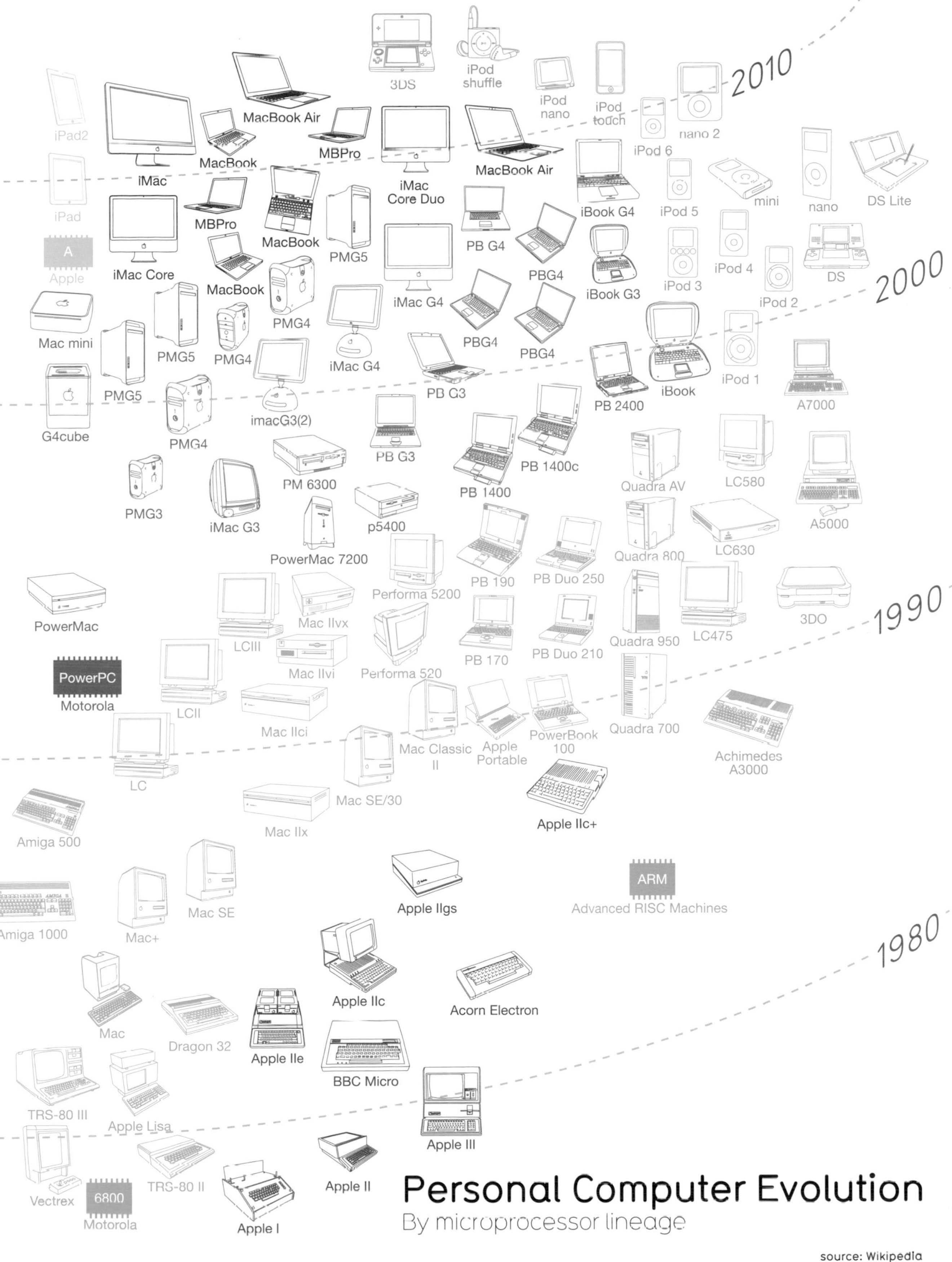
2010
2000
1990
1980
3DS
iPod shuffle
iPad2
MacBook Air
iPod nano
iPod touch
nano 2
iPod 6
iMac
MacBook
MBPro
iMac Core Duo
MacBook Air
iPad
MBPro
MacBook
PMG5
PB G4
iBook G4
iPod 5
mini
nano
DS Lite
A
Apple
iMac Core
MacBook
PMG4
iMac G4
PBG4
iBook G3
iPod 3
iPod 4
iPod 2
DS
Mac mini
PMG5
PMG4
iMac G4
PBG4
PBG4
iBook
iPod 1
A7000
G4cube
PMG5
imacG3(2)
PB G3
PB 2400
PMG4
PB G3
PB 1400c
PM 6300
PB 1400
Quadra AV
LC580
PMG3
iMac G3
p5400
A5000
PowerMac 7200
Quadra 800
LC630
Performa 5200
PB 190
PB Duo 250
PowerMac
Mac IIvx
LCIII
Quadra 950
LC475
3DO
PB 170
PB Duo 210
PowerPC
Motorola
Mac IIvi
Performa 520
LCII
Mac IIci
Mac Classic II
Apple Portable
PowerBook 100
Quadra 700
Achimedes A3000
LC
Mac SE/30
Amiga 500
Mac IIx
Apple IIc+
ARM
Advanced RISC Machines
Apple IIgs
Mac SE
Amiga 1000
Mac+
Apple IIc
Acorn Electron
Mac
Dragon 32
Apple IIe
BBC Micro
TRS-80 III
Apple Lisa
Apple III
Vectrex
6800
Motorola
TRS-80 II
Apple II
Apple I
Personal Computer Evolution
By microprocessor lineage
source: Wikipedia

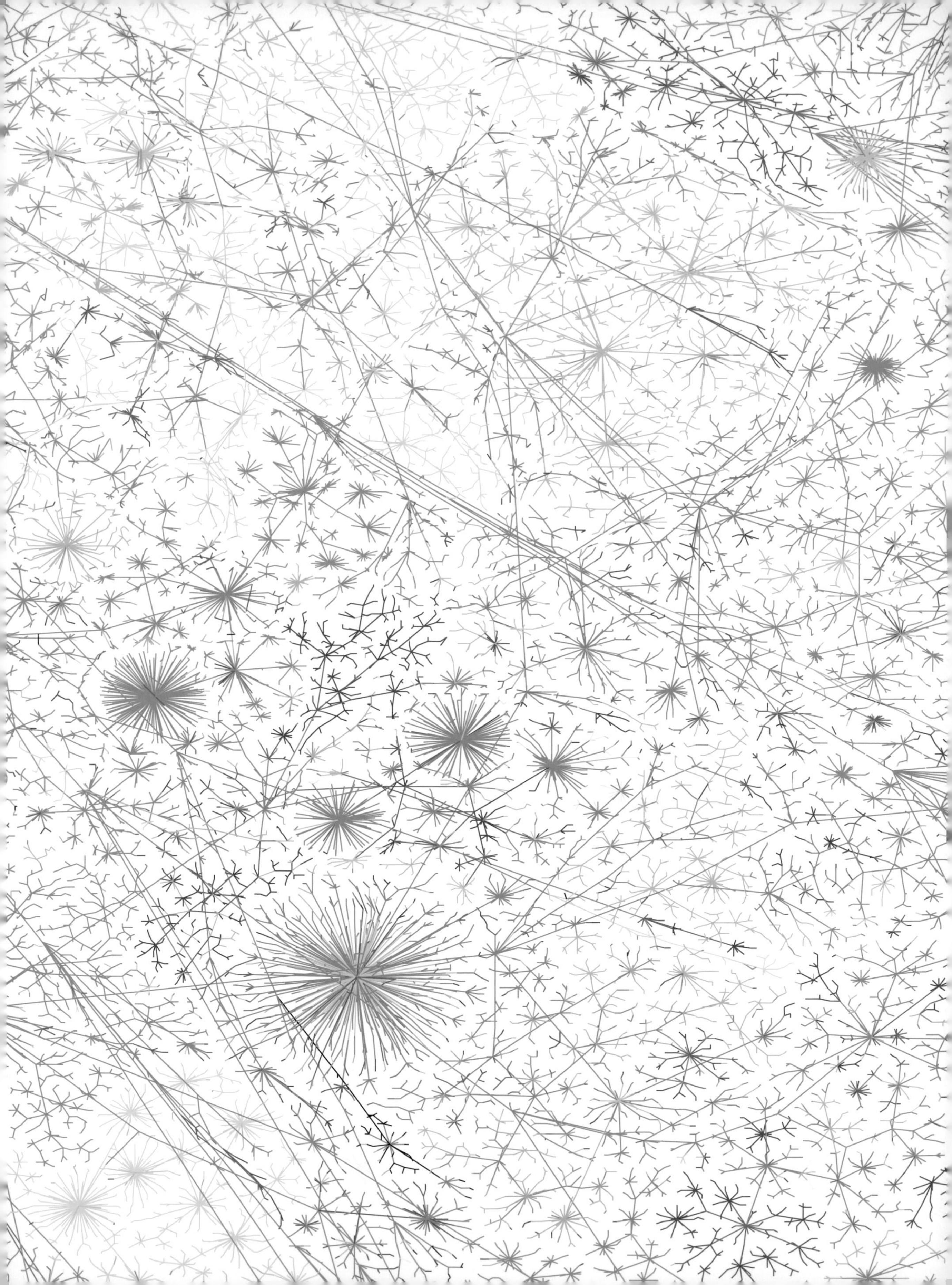

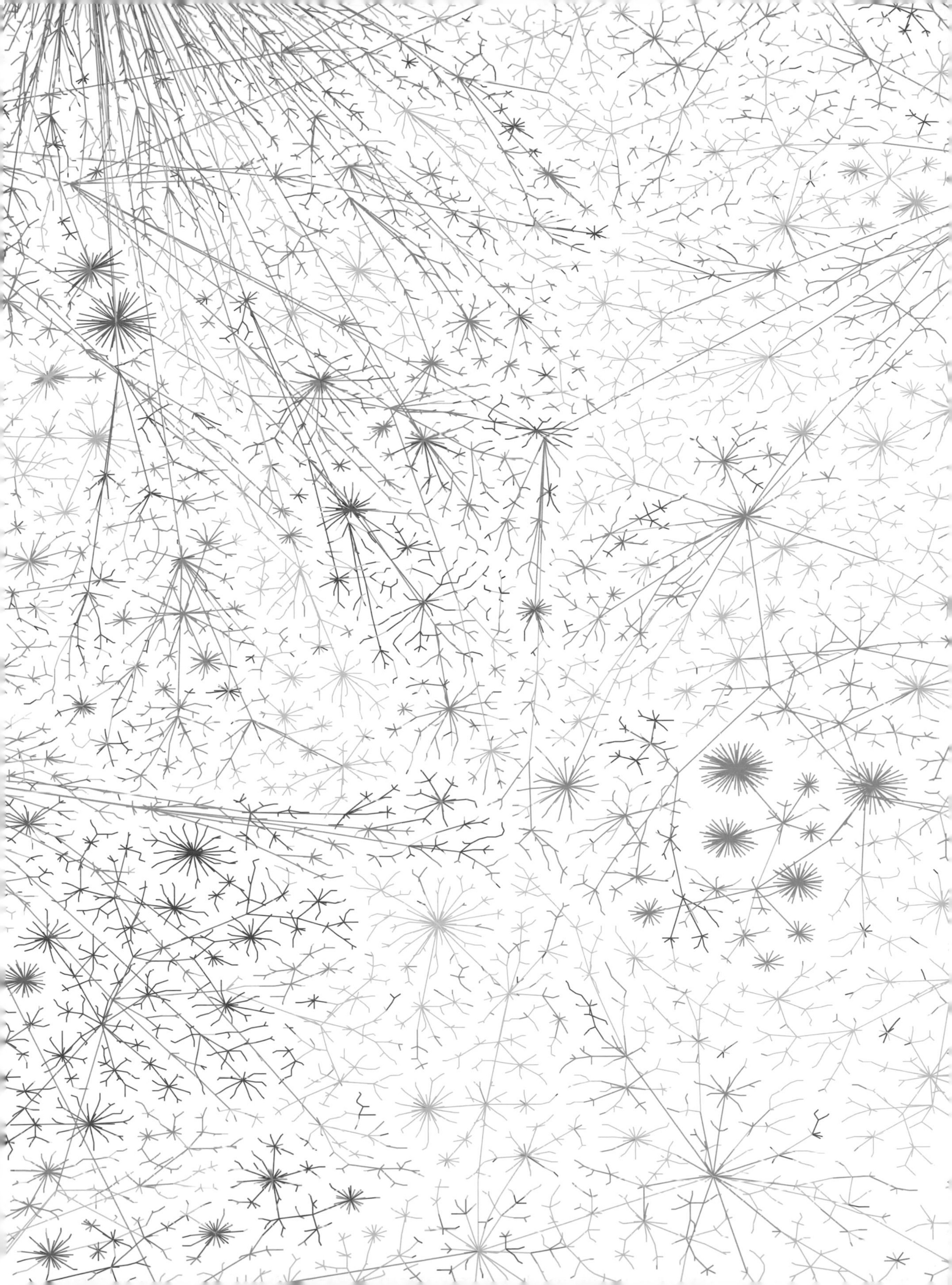

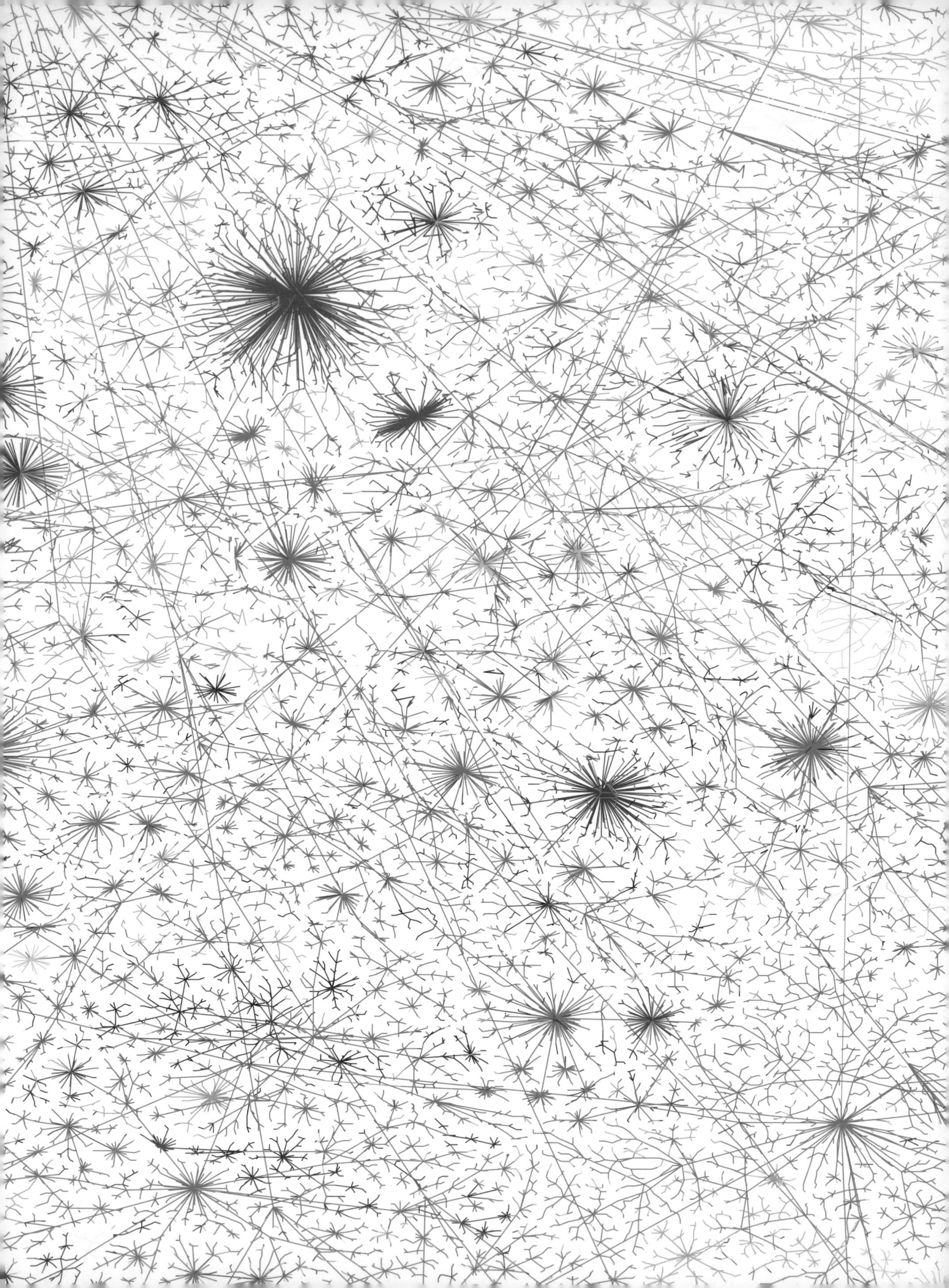

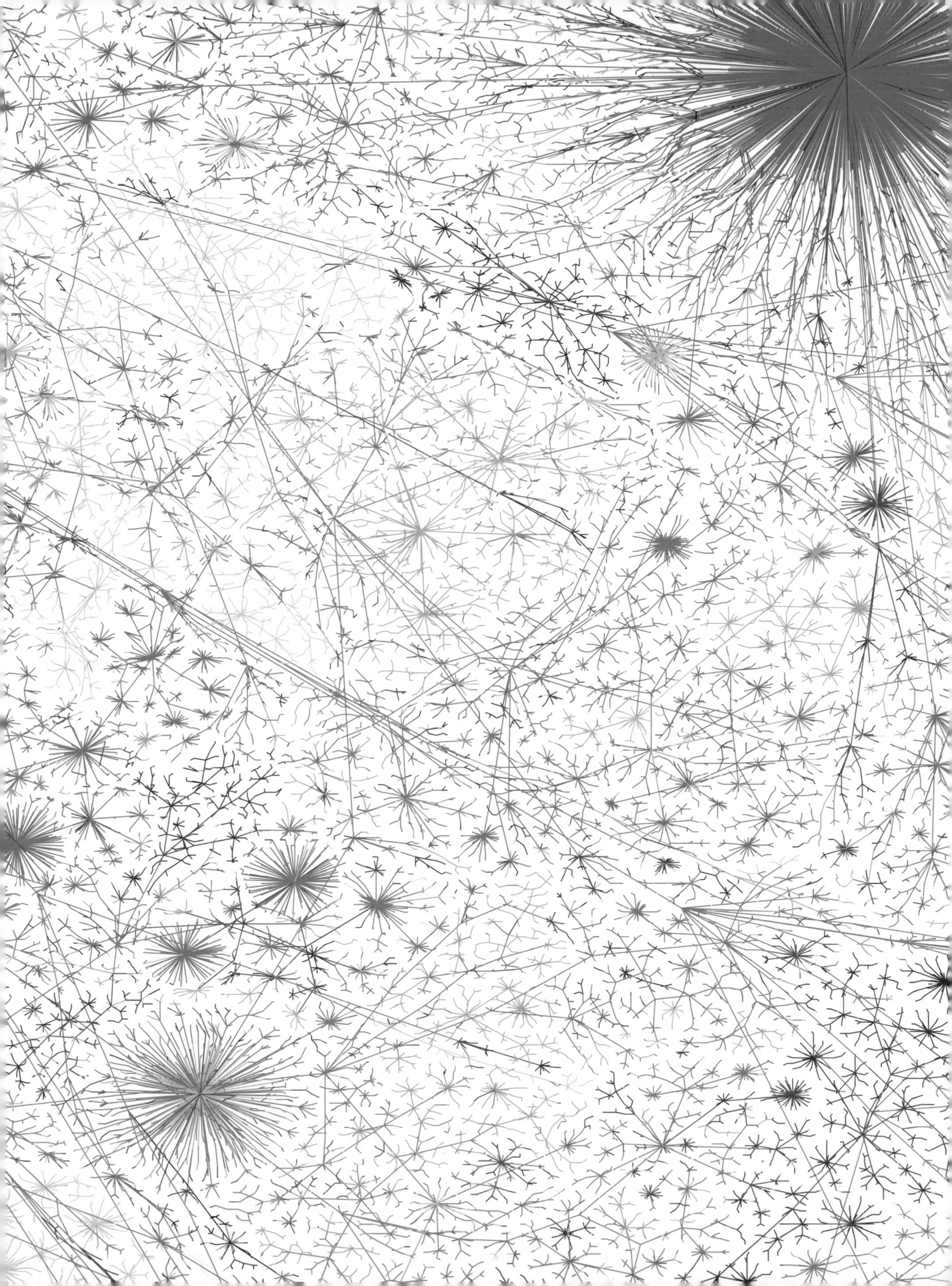

The One Machine

Map of the internet

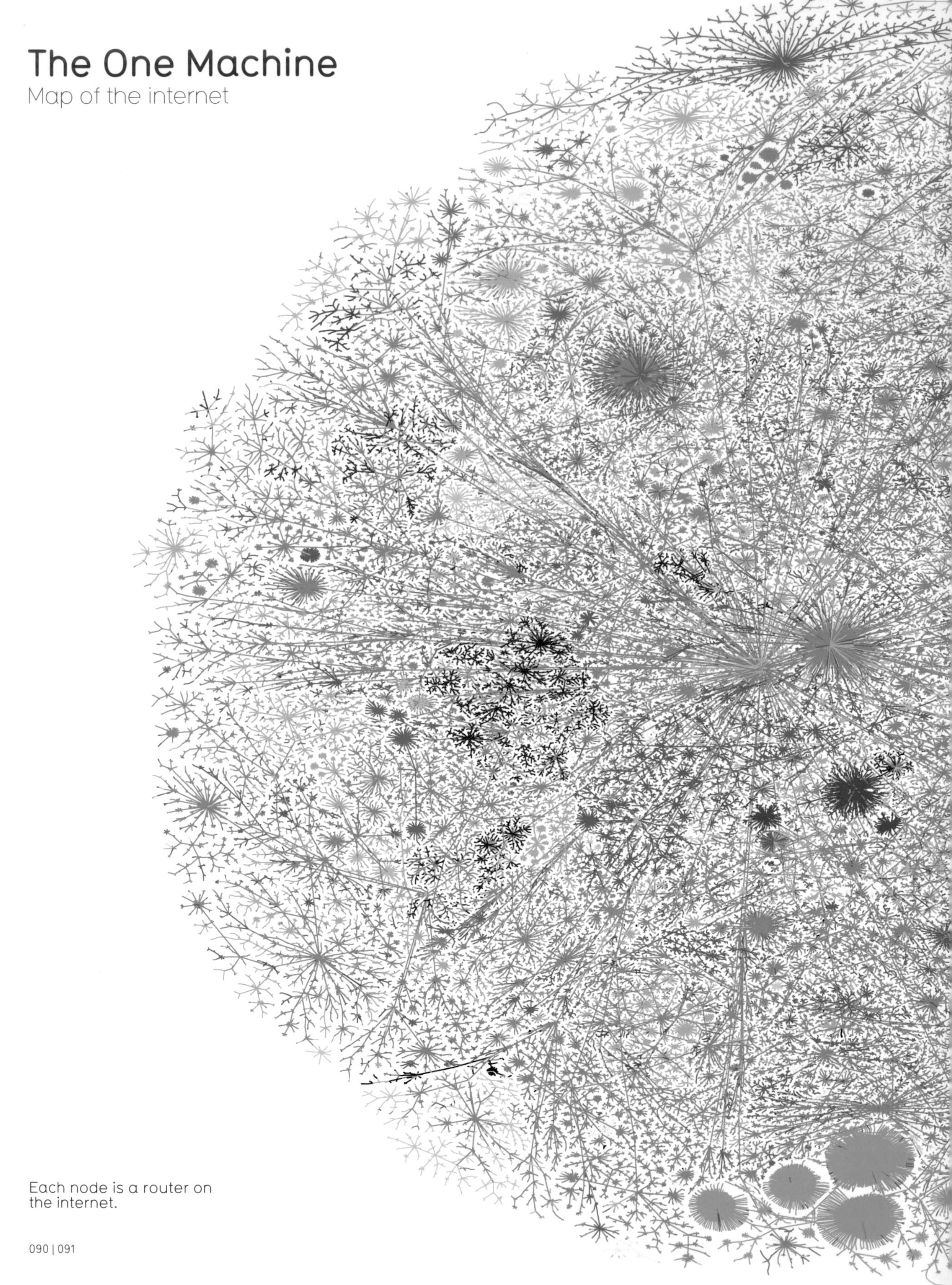

Each node is a router on the internet.

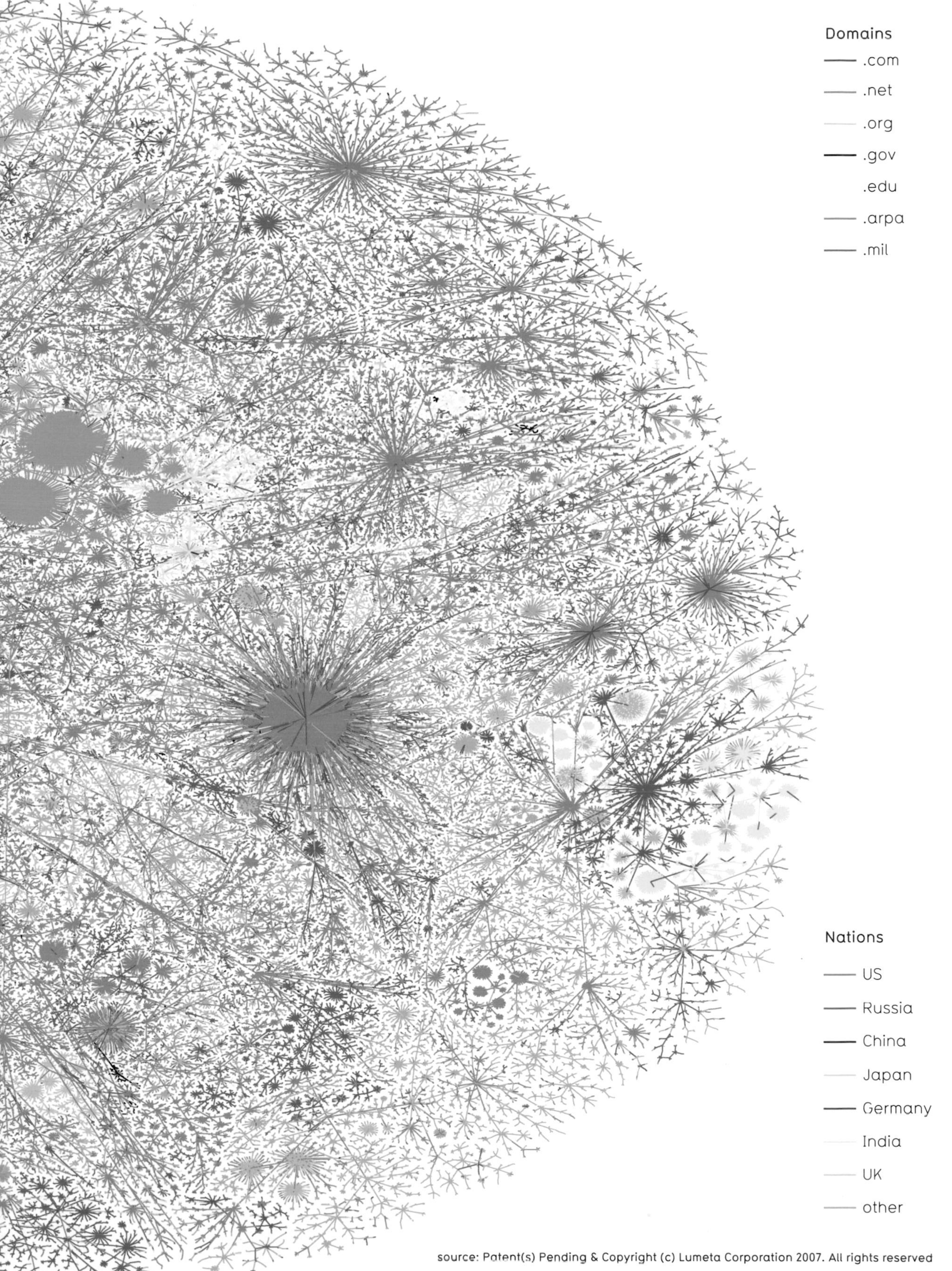

Domains
.com
.net
.org
.gov
.edu
.arpa
.mil
Nations
US
Russia
China
Japan
Germany
India
UK
other

source: Patent(s) Pending & Copyright (c) Lumeta Corporation 2007. All rights reserved

What Does China Censor Online?

Blocked keywords and websites

Falun Gong
A qigong-like spiritual practice violently supressed after followers protested against the government.

Gedhun Choekyi Nyima
2nd highest-ranking Tibetan spiritual leader after Dalai Lama. Arrested by the authorities in 1995. Not seen since.

Xinjiang
Northwest province, home to the Uyghur people and much ethnic tension.

June 4th
The usual name for the Tiananmen Square protests of 1989. (The word "Tiananmen" does not have the same association. It usually refers to the geographical place.)

01net.com 2ch.net 4chan.org 6park.com addicti
amnestyinternational.org antro.cl aol.com app
bbc.com bbspot.com bebo.com bild.de blogge
bundestag.de cbc.ca china.ch china.cn china.co
cnn.com collegehumor.com crailtap.com cyber
de.wikipedia.org delfi.lt democracy.com
drudgereport.com e-gold.com ebaumswor
ehrenselmundo.es el "brain wash" elpais.com
facebook.com fark "censorship jail" flickr.com fo
friendster.com ga movement" gamefaqs.com
globo.com goo "dalai" "democracy" ogle.ch
googl "democratic progressive party" "despotism
great "dissident" "eighty-nine" "buddha stretch
home Times" "eroticism" "evil" "exile" "falun" "
indym Nyima" "genocide" "gerontocracy" "hon
level.ro liberta"lun gong" "Ma Sanjia""Mein Ka
marca.es mc browser" "oppression" "persecuti
msn.com m Department""political dissident" "Pl
nhl.com through labor" "Shanghai clique" "Sha
arcade.com "student federation" "student move
purepwnage.co Chinese Students and Scholars"
sapo.pt seznam.cz Mothers" "Tiananmen Squar
stern.de studivz.de suchar.ne tagesscha indep
tibet.com traffic4u.nl tw.yahoo.com tumblr.com
usa.gov userfriendly.org vatican.va vg.n
whatreallyhappened.com whitehouse.com whit Z
wikipedia.org wordpress.com worldofwarcra
xanga.com yahoo.cn yahoo.co.jp yahoo.com a
yandex.ru yle.fi youtube.com ytmnd.com zh.
6park.com addictinggames.com aftonbla
amnestyinternational.org antro.cl aol.com app

nes.com amazon.com amnesty.com amnesty.org
as.com asahi.com barrapunto.com bbc.co.uk
(blogspot) boingboing.net bundesregierung.de
a.de china.org china "anti-communist" rin.com
.ca dagbladet.no "Beijing Spring" motion.com
antart.com digg.com "anti-society" isney.com
ebay.com ebay.de "blocking" com com
.es en.wikipedia.org "brutal torture" n espn.com
news.com free.fr "Chinese democracy tibet.org
spot.com gay "communist bandits" geenstijl.nl
.co.uk goog "democracy movement" google.de
gle.pl "dictatorship" cn greatfirewallofchina.org
ousand hands" "Epoch rg heise.de hi5.com
gong" "Gedhun Choekyi .com imdb.com index.hu
"Hui people riot" "human rights" org lemonde.fr
news blackout" "no-limit m mail.ru marca.com
Chinese Central Propaganda lip.com mitbbs.com
"Red Terror" "reeducation com news.bbc.co.uk
"sky burial" "Sino-Russian border" no.be penny-
"Independent Federation of prisonplanet.com
anmen incident" "Tiananmen a.it runescape.com
sacre" "Tibet Talk" "Tibetan sony.com spiegel.de
nce" "Voice of the People" n.com thoonsen.com
rground church" "Xinjiang g uol.com.br usa.com
endence" "yilishen" "yellow peril" wenxuecity.com
yang "Freedom Forum of pedia.com wikipedia.de
g University" "June 4th" .pl wretch.cc wwe.com
com.cn yahoo.com.hk yahoo.com.tw yahoo.fr
dia.org01net.com 163.com 2ch.net 4chan.org
amazon.com amnesty.com amnesty.org
as.com asahi.com barrapunto.com bbc.co.uk

Beijing Spring
Brief period of political liberalization in 1977. The public were allowed to criticise the regime. Lasted a year.

Communist Bandits
Derogatory term for communists used by the Taiwan National Party.

buddha stretches a thousand hands
A Falun Gong pose.

Ma Sanjia
Forced labour camp where Falun Gong followers were detained.

Shanwei
Refers to Dongzhou, a village where a series of protests against government plans ended in a number of villagers being shot.

Yilishen
A company which scammed more than one million Chinese investors by promising ants could be bought, bred and sold back at a profit. Revealed as a Ponzi scheme in 2007.

Websites are either completely blocked or have offending pages removed

source: ConceptDoppler.com, Wikipedia, GreatFirewallofChina.org (2008)

Water Towers

Daily total use
per person
4645 bottles
Direct use
Indirect use

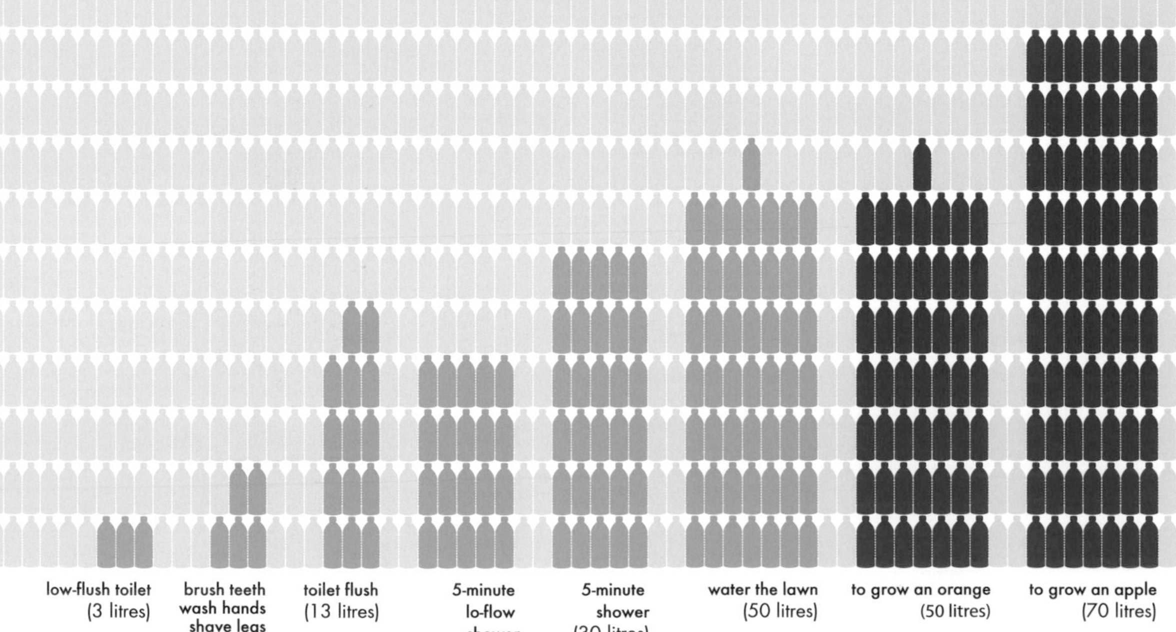
low-flush toilet
(3 litres)
brush teeth
wash hands
shave legs
(5 litres)
toilet flush
(13 litres)
5-minute
lo-flow
shower
(20 litres)
5-minute
shower
(30 litres)
water the lawn
(50 litres)
to grow an orange
(50 litres)
to grow an apple
(70 litres)

bath
(80 litres)
no bath
(0 litres)
3-star washing
machine
(92 litres)
energy star
washing machine
(44 litres)
to make one egg
(200 litres)
1-litre bottle
of water
(5 litres)

source: Wikipedia, Good Magazine

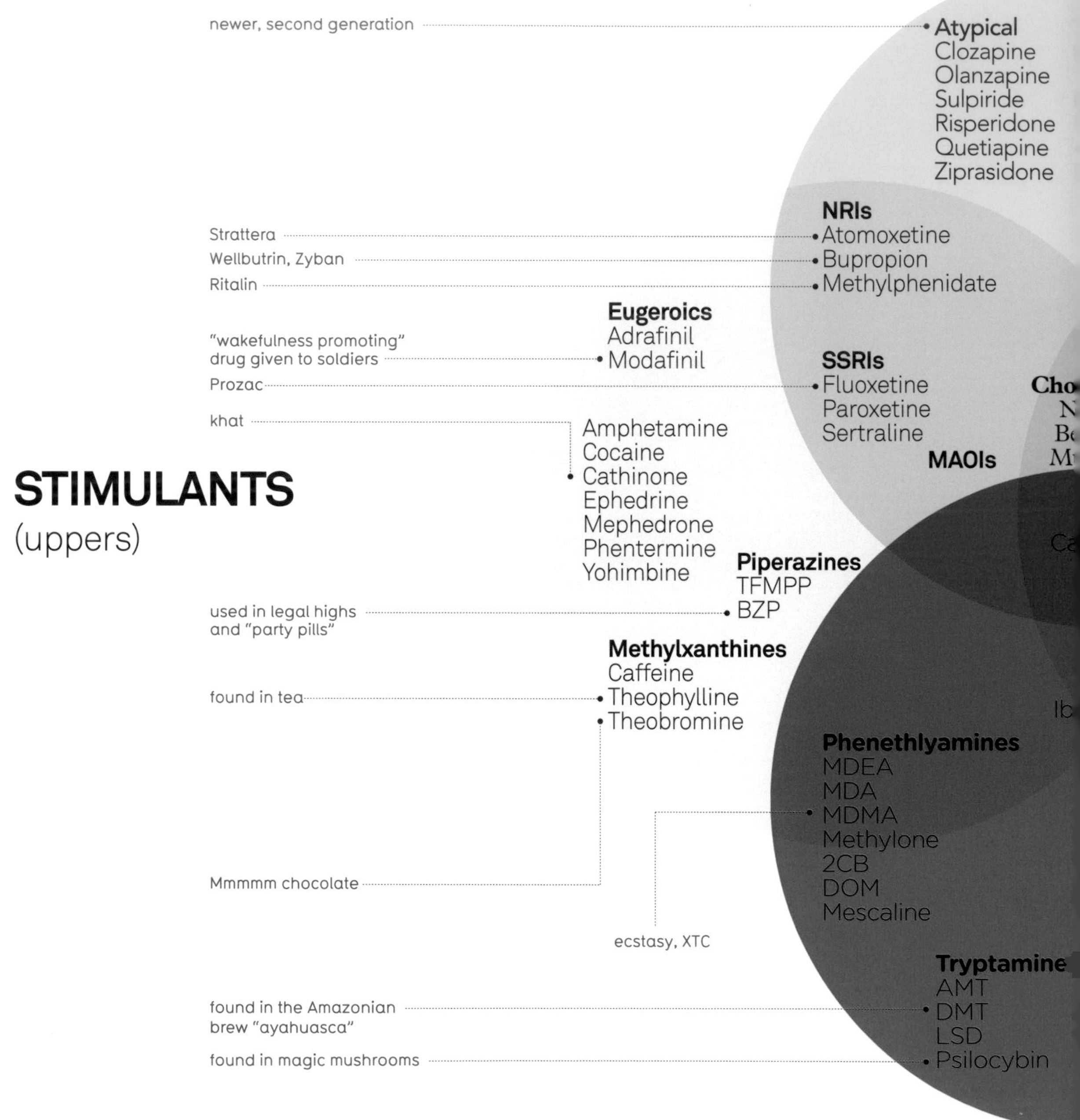
Anti-Ps
(tranc
newer, second generation
Atypical
Clozapine
Olanzapine
Sulpiride
Risperidone
Quetiapine
Ziprasidone
NRIs
Strattera
Atomoxetine
Wellbutrin, Zyban
Bupropion
Ritalin
Methylphenidate
Eugeroics
Adrafinil
"wakefulness promoting" drug given to soldiers
Modafinil
SSRIs
Prozac
Fluoxetine
Paroxetine
Sertraline
MAOIs
khat
Amphetamine
Cocaine
Cathinone
Ephedrine
Mephedrone
Phentermine
Yohimbine
STIMULANTS
(uppers)
Piperazines
TFMPP
used in legal highs and "party pills"
BZP
Methylxanthines
Caffeine
found in tea
Theophylline
Theobromine
Mmmmm chocolate
Phenethlyamines
MDEA
MDA
MDMA
Methylone
2CB
DOM
Mescaline
ecstasy, XTC
Tryptamine
AMT
found in the Amazonian brew "ayahuasca"
DMT
LSD
found in magic mushrooms
Psilocybin
Halluc

hotics

zers)

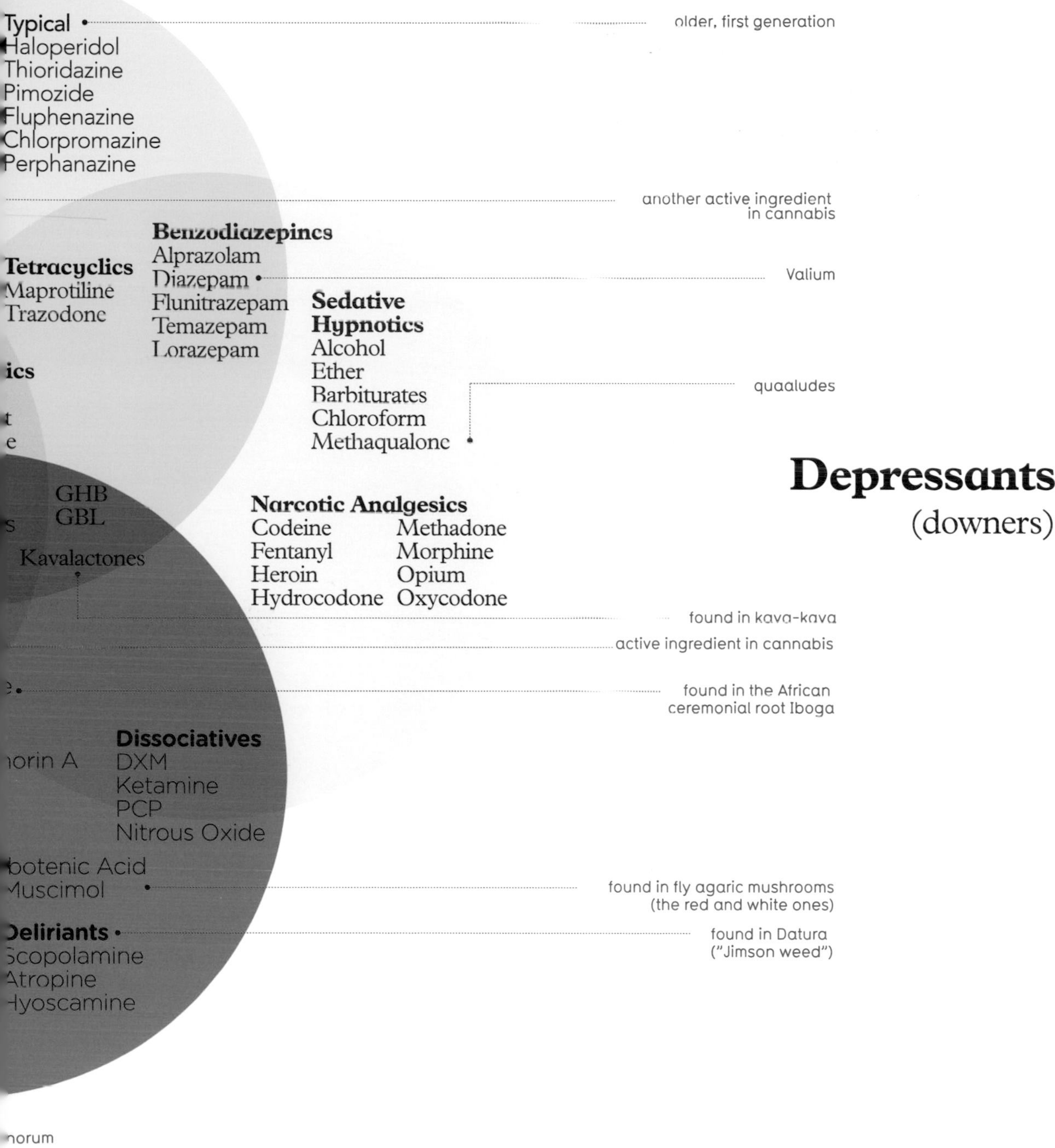

Typical
Haloperidol
Thioridazine
Pimozide
Fluphenazine
Chlorpromazine
Perphanazine
older, first generation
another active ingredient in cannabis
Benzodiazepines
Alprazolam
Diazepam
Flunitrazepam
Temazepam
Lorazepam
Valium
Tetracyclics
Maprotiline
Trazodone
Sedative Hypnotics
Alcohol
Ether
Barbiturates
Chloroform
Methaqualone
quaaludes
GHB
GBL
Kavalactones
Narcotic Analgesics
Codeine
Fentanyl
Heroin
Hydrocodone
Methadone
Morphine
Opium
Oxycodone
found in kava-kava
active ingredient in cannabis
found in the African ceremonial root Iboga
Dissociatives
DXM
Ketamine
PCP
Nitrous Oxide
botenic Acid
Muscimol
found in fly agaric mushrooms (the red and white ones)
Deliriants
Scopolamine
Atropine
Hyoscamine
found in Datura ("Jimson weed")
norum

Depressants

(downers)

gens

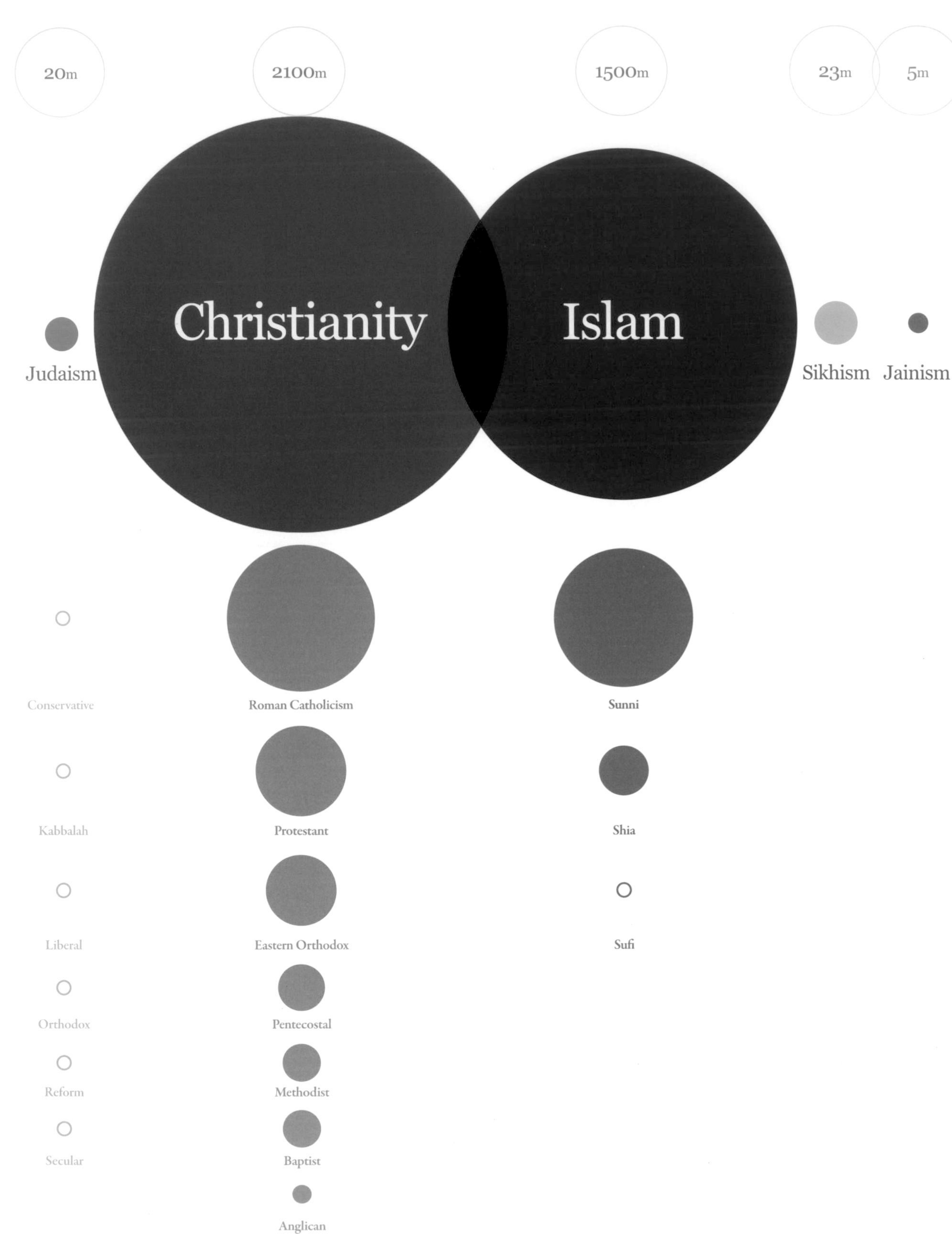
20m
2100m
1500m
23m
5m
Judaism
Christianity
Islam
Sikhism
Jainism
Conservative
Roman Catholicism
Sunni
Kabbalah
Protestant
Shia
Liberal
Eastern Orthodox
Sufi
Orthodox
Pentecostal
Reform
Methodist
Secular
Baptist
Anglican

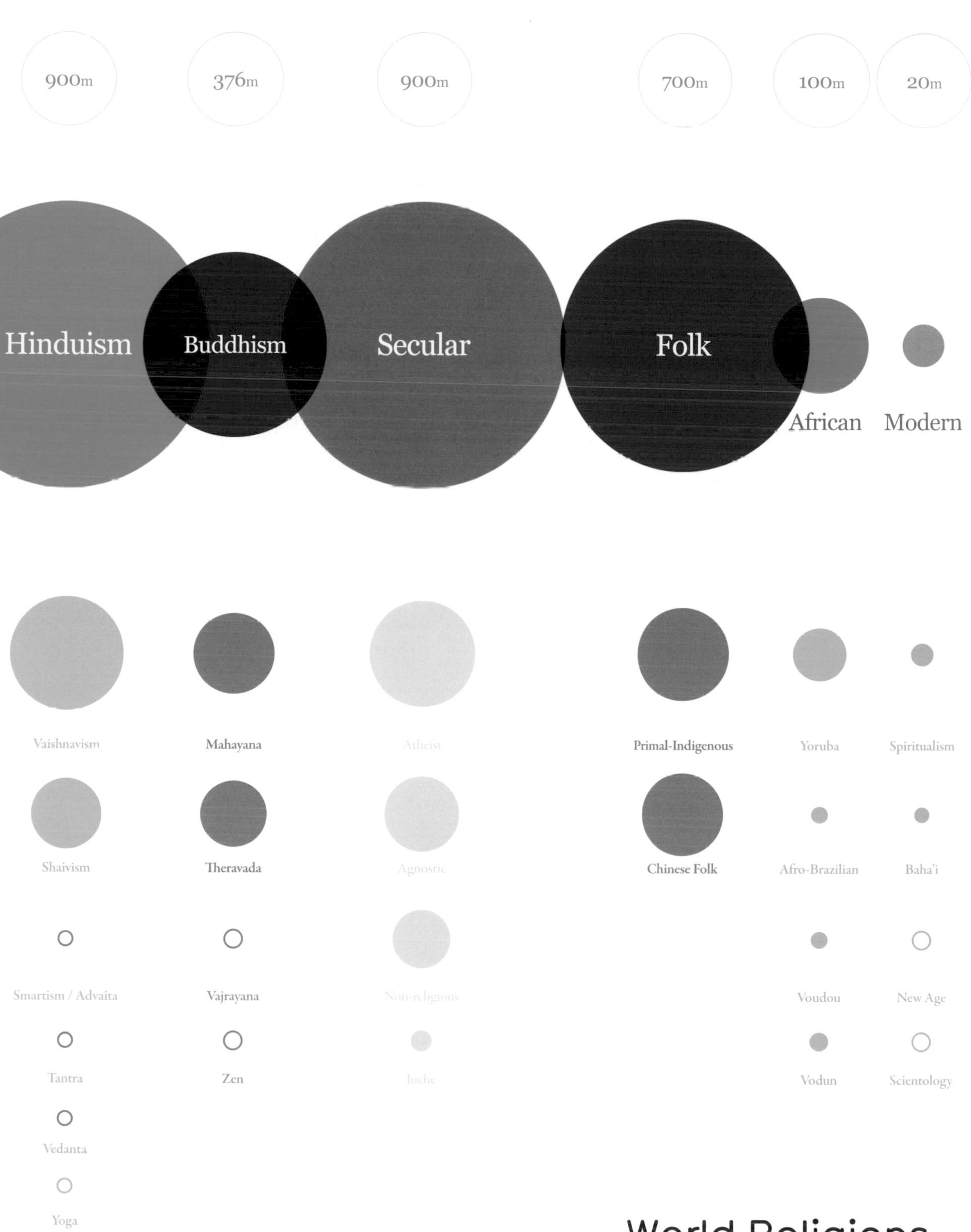
900m
376m
900m
700m
100m
20m
Hinduism
Buddhism
Secular
Folk
African
Modern
Vaishnavism
Mahayana
Atheist
Primal-Indigenous
Yoruba
Spiritualism
Shaivism
Theravada
Agnostic
Chinese Folk
Afro-Brazilian
Baha'i
Smartism / Advaita
Vajrayana
Non-religious
Voudou
New Age
Tantra
Zen
Juche
Vodun
Scientology
Vedanta
Yoga

Number of adherents

Adherents unknown

World Religions

By followers

source: Adherents.com

Moral Matrix

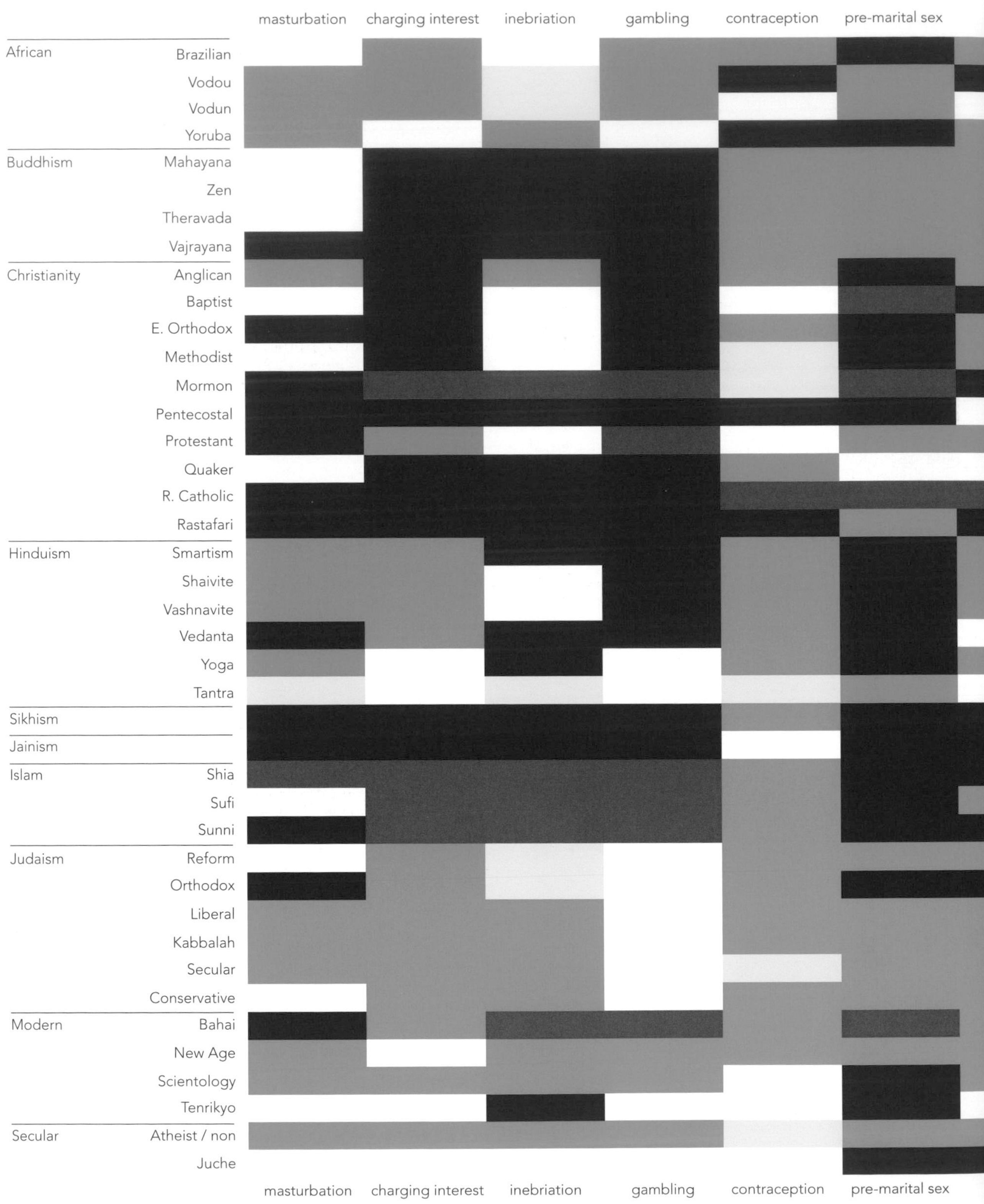

masturbation
charging interest
inebriation
gambling
contraception
pre-marital sex
African
Brazilian
Vodou
Vodun
Yoruba
Buddhism
Mahayana
Zen
Theravada
Vajrayana
Christianity
Anglican
Baptist
E. Orthodox
Methodist
Mormon
Pentecostal
Protestant
Quaker
R. Catholic
Rastafari
Hinduism
Smartism
Shaivite
Vashnavite
Vedanta
Yoga
Tantra
Sikhism
Jainism
Islam
Shia
Sufi
Sunni
Judaism
Reform
Orthodox
Liberal
Kabbalah
Secular
Conservative
Modern
Bahai
New Age
Scientology
Tenrikyo
Secular
Atheist / non
Juche
masturbation
charging interest
inebriation
gambling
contraception
pre-marital sex

yes
no
condemned
blessed
neutral or don't know
adultery
married clergy
female clergy
being gay
gay sex
gay clergy
gay marriage
abortion
adultery
married clergy
female clergy
being gay
gay sex
gay clergy
gay marriage
abortion

source: Wikipedia, Adherents.com

The Carbon Dioxide Cycle

Yearly man-made vs natural carbon emissions in gigatons (g)

CO_2 in atmo

emitted absorbed

9g a year + **550g** already in the atmosphere

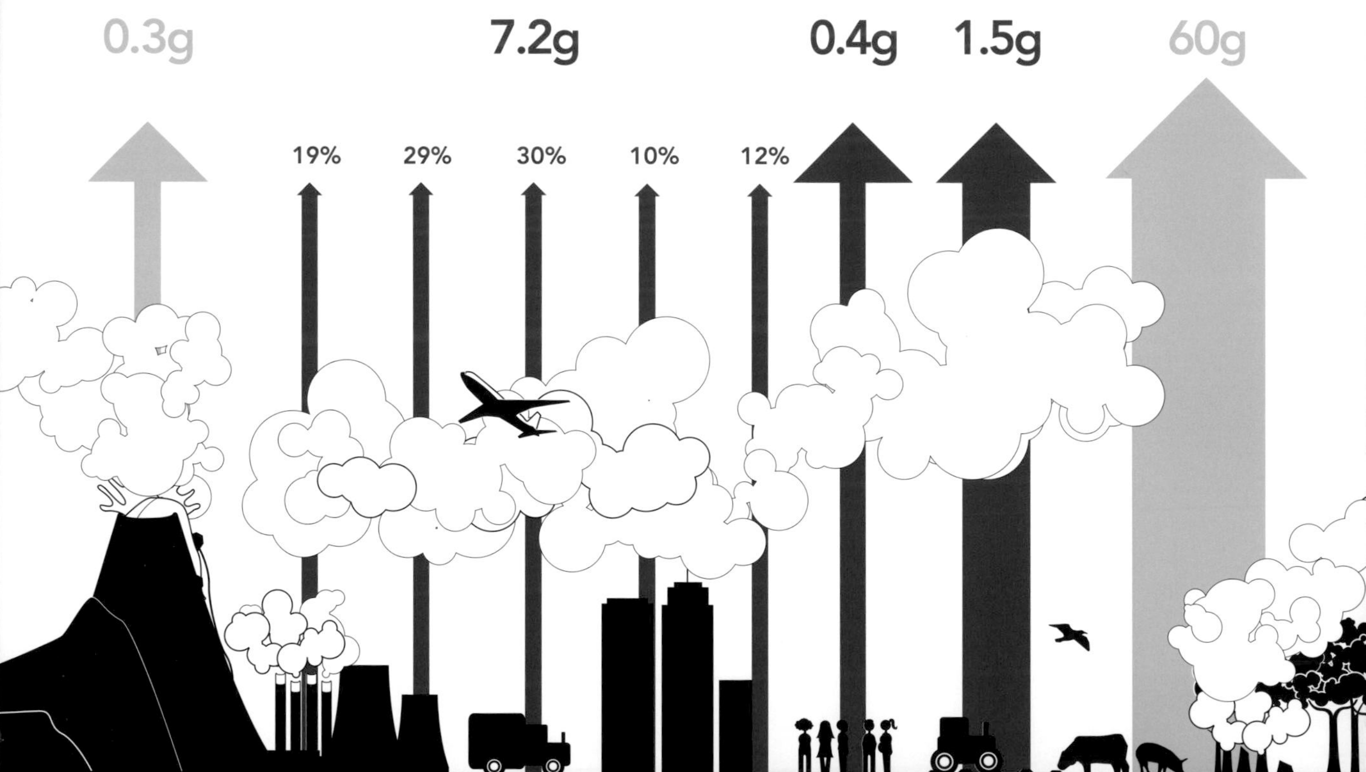
0.3g
7.2g
0.4g
1.5g
60g
19%
29%
30%
10%
12%
industry
energy
transport
residential
other
deforestation
volcanoes
fossil fuels
people
animals
forest fires

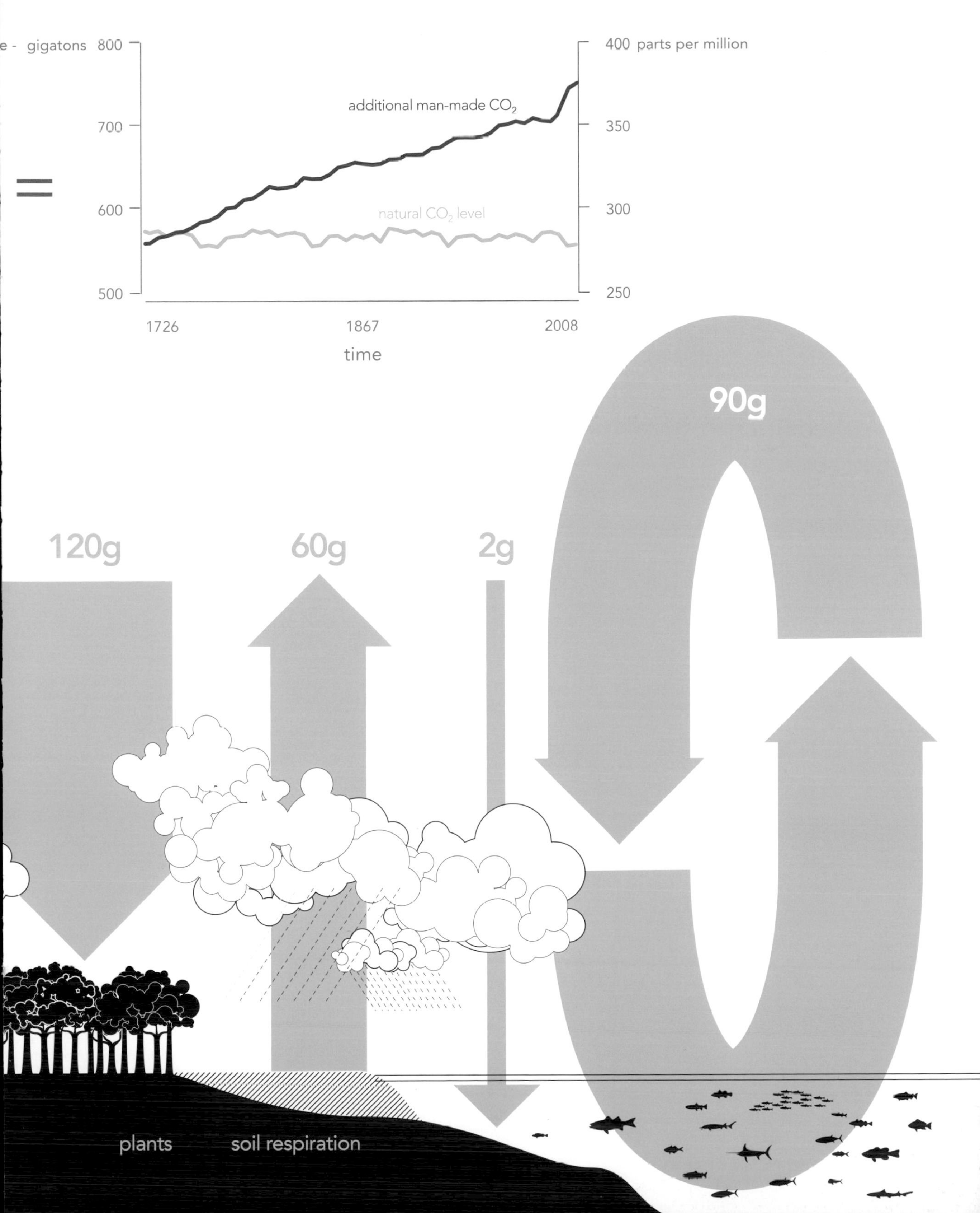

e - gigatons
800
700
600
500
400 parts per million
350
300
250
additional man-made CO_2
natural CO_2 level
1726
1867
2008
time
=
90g
120g
60g
2g
plants
soil respiration
source: UNESCO Scope , IPCC 2007, Wikipedia, Realclimate.org

1250 MB/s

same bandwidth as a computer network

125 MB/s

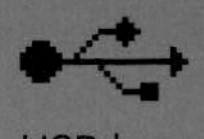

USB key

Low Resolution

Amount of sensory information reaching the brain per second

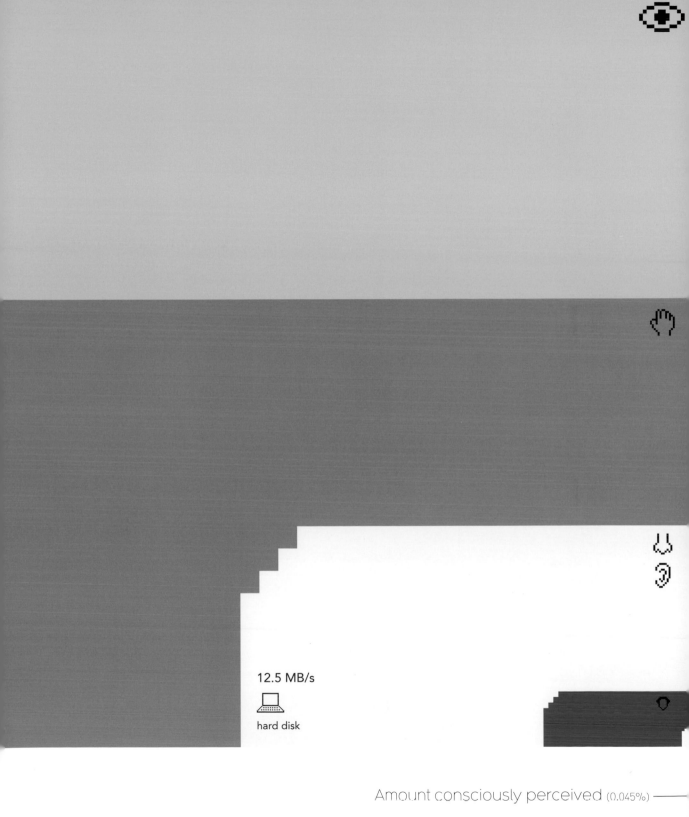
12.5 MB/s
hard disk

Amount consciously perceived (0.045%)

source: Tor Nørretranders, The User Illusion: Cutting Consciousness Down to Size

Taste Buds

Complementary tastes

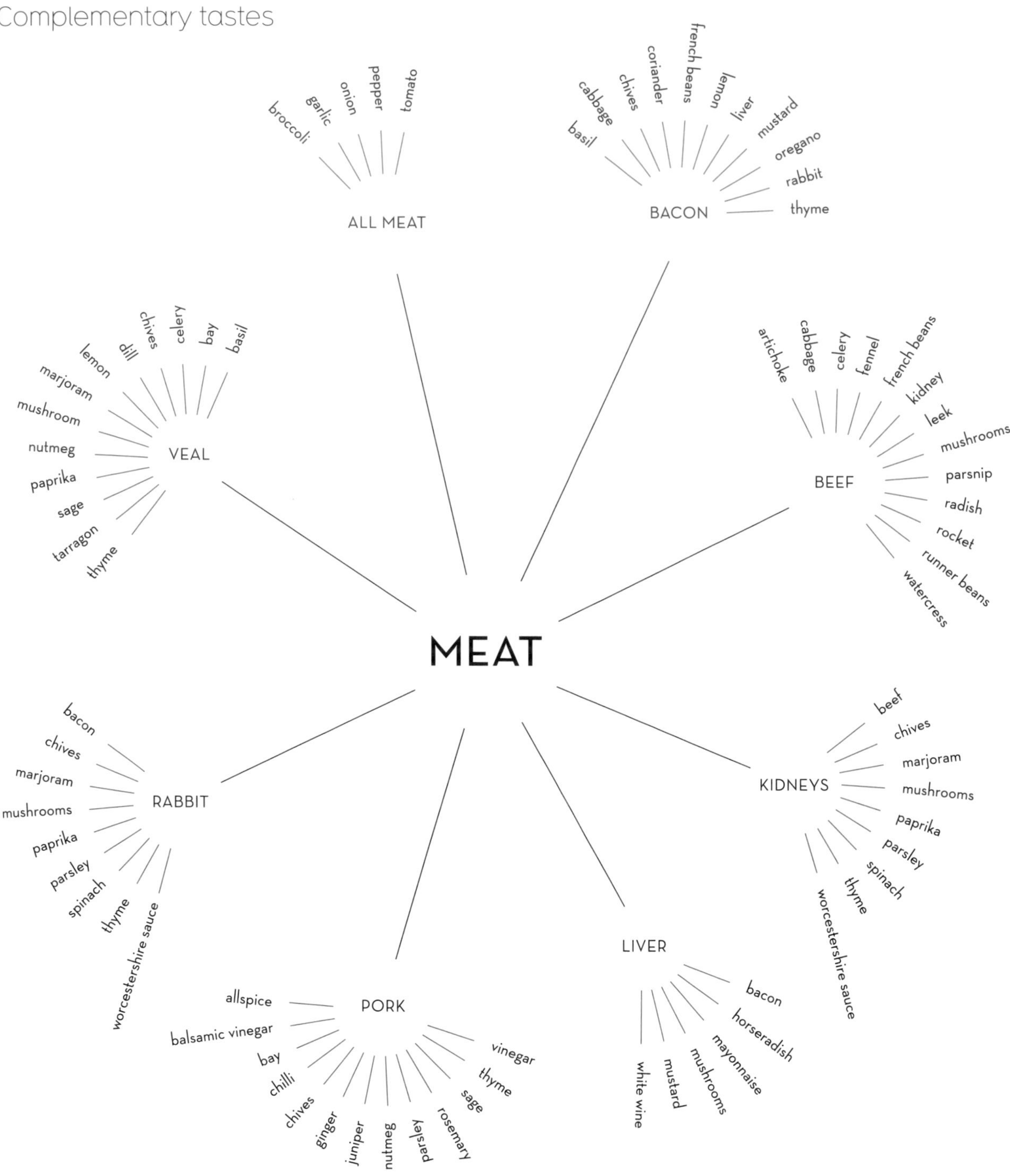

MEAT
ALL MEAT
broccoli
garlic
onion
pepper
tomato
BACON
basil
cabbage
chives
coriander
french beans
lemon
liver
mustard
oregano
rabbit
thyme
VEAL
lemon
dill
chives
celery
bay
basil
marjoram
mushroom
nutmeg
paprika
sage
tarragon
thyme
BEEF
artichoke
cabbage
celery
fennel
french beans
kidney
leek
mushrooms
parsnip
radish
rocket
runner beans
watercress
RABBIT
bacon
chives
marjoram
mushrooms
paprika
parsley
spinach
thyme
worcestershire sauce
KIDNEYS
beef
chives
marjoram
mushrooms
paprika
parsley
spinach
thyme
worcestershire sauce
PORK
allspice
balsamic vinegar
bay
chilli
chives
ginger
juniper
nutmeg
parsley
rosemary
sage
thyme
vinegar
LIVER
bacon
horseradish
mayonnaise
mushrooms
mustard
white wine

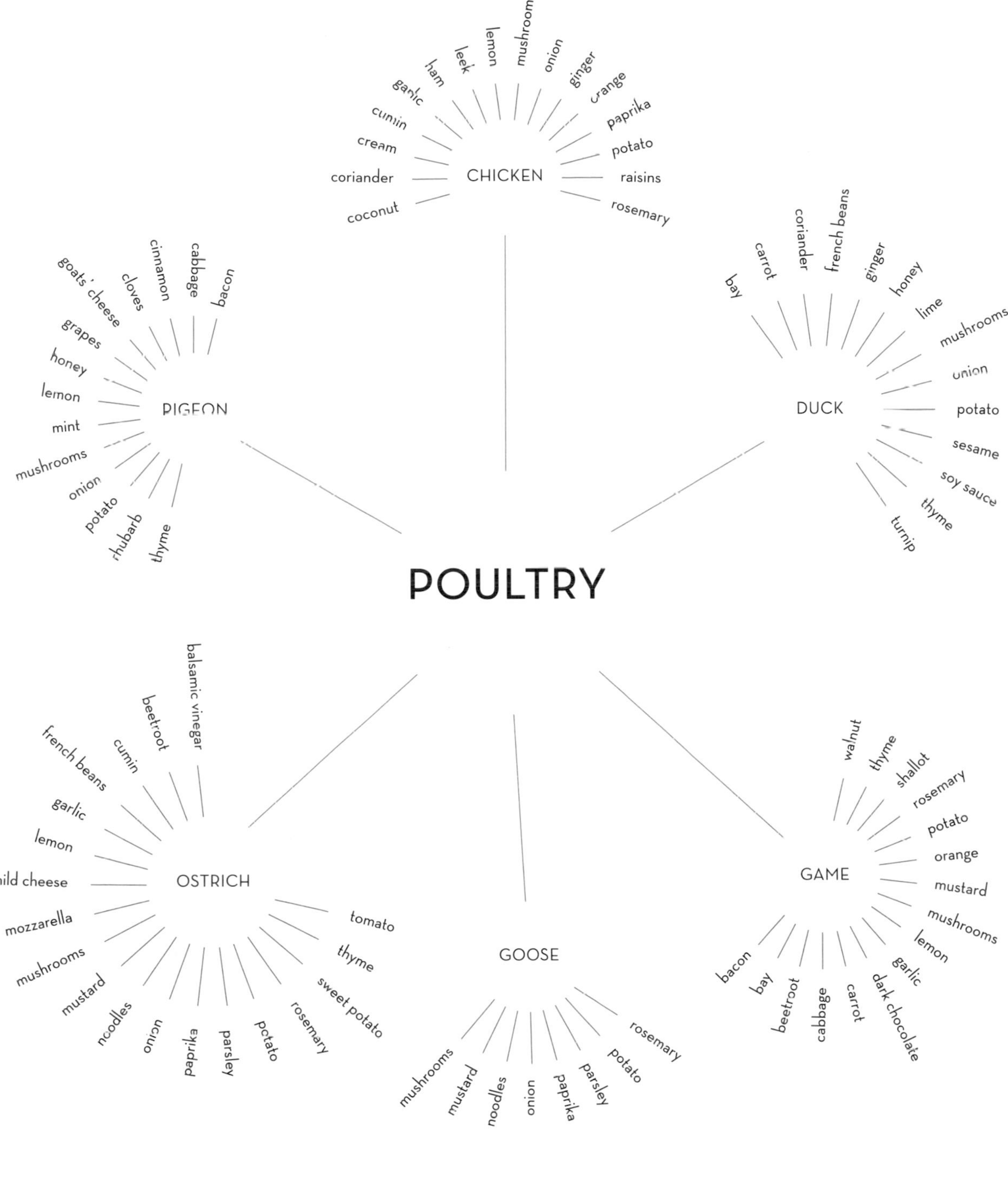

POULTRY
CHICKEN
coconut
coriander
cream
cumin
garlic
ham
leek
lemon
mushrooms
onion
ginger
orange
paprika
potato
raisins
rosemary
DUCK
bay
carrot
coriander
french beans
ginger
honey
lime
mushrooms
onion
potato
sesame
soy sauce
thyme
turnip
PIGEON
goats' cheese
cloves
cinnamon
cabbage
bacon
grapes
honey
lemon
mint
mushrooms
onion
potato
rhubarb
thyme
OSTRICH
balsamic vinegar
beetroot
cumin
french beans
garlic
lemon
mild cheese
mozzarella
mushrooms
mustard
noodles
onion
paprika
parsley
potato
rosemary
sweet potato
thyme
tomato
GOOSE
mushrooms
mustard
noodles
onion
paprika
parsley
potato
rosemary
GAME
walnut
thyme
shallot
rosemary
potato
orange
mustard
mushrooms
lemon
garlic
dark chocolate
carrot
cabbage
beetroot
bay
bacon

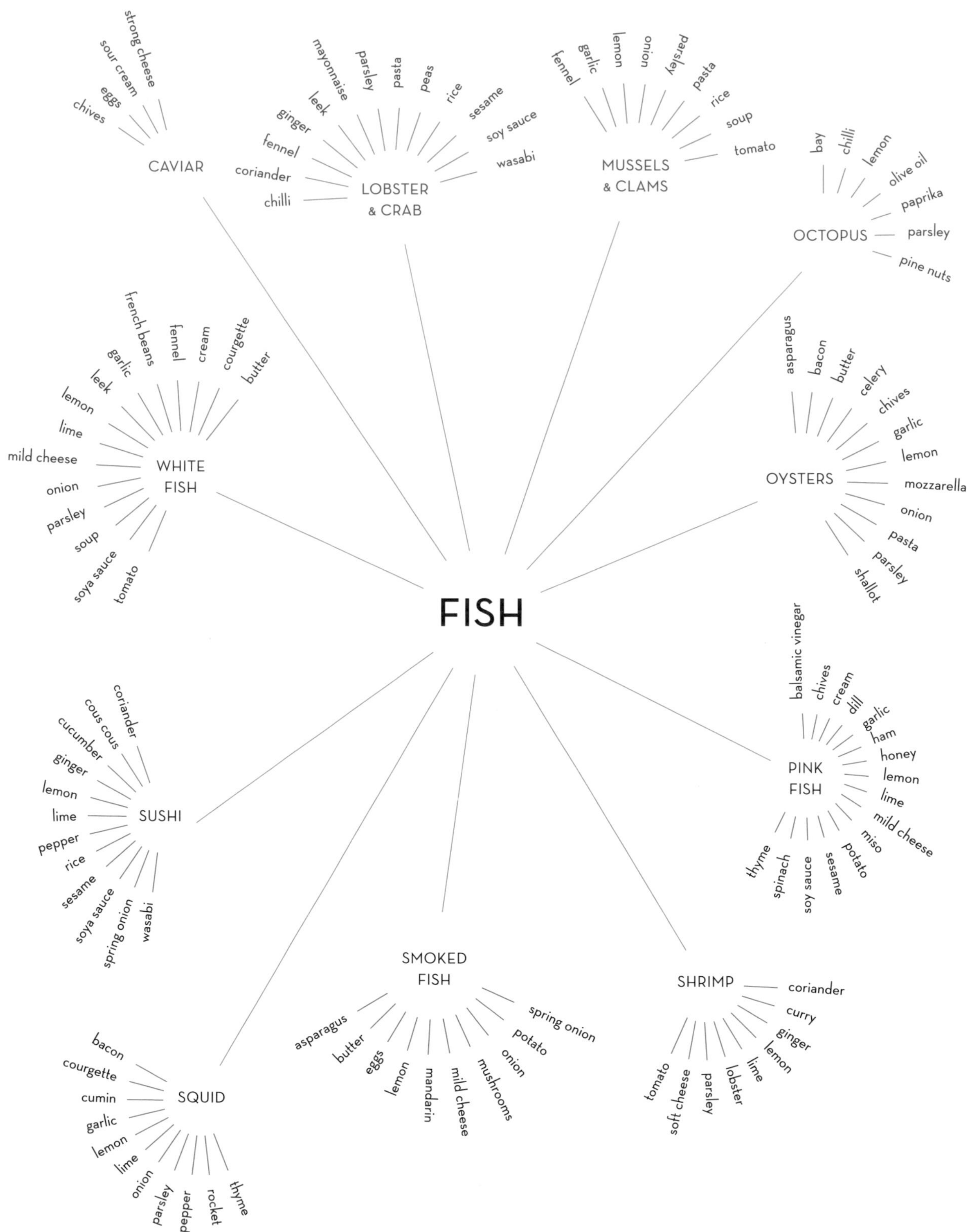

FISH
CAVIAR
chives
eggs
sour cream
strong cheese
LOBSTER & CRAB
chilli
coriander
fennel
ginger
leek
mayonnaise
parsley
pasta
peas
rice
sesame
soy sauce
wasabi
MUSSELS & CLAMS
fennel
garlic
lemon
onion
parsley
pasta
rice
soup
tomato
OCTOPUS
bay
chilli
lemon
olive oil
paprika
parsley
pine nuts
WHITE FISH
butter
courgette
cream
fennel
french beans
garlic
leek
lemon
lime
mild cheese
onion
parsley
soup
soya sauce
tomato
OYSTERS
asparagus
bacon
butter
celery
chives
garlic
lemon
mozzarella
onion
pasta
parsley
shallot
PINK FISH
balsamic vinegar
chives
cream
dill
garlic
ham
honey
lemon
lime
mild cheese
miso
potato
sesame
soy sauce
spinach
thyme
SUSHI
coriander
cous cous
cucumber
ginger
lemon
lime
pepper
rice
sesame
soya sauce
spring onion
wasabi
SMOKED FISH
asparagus
butter
eggs
lemon
mandarin
mild cheese
mushrooms
onion
potato
spring onion
SHRIMP
coriander
curry
ginger
lemon
lime
lobster
parsley
soft cheese
tomato
SQUID
bacon
courgette
cumin
garlic
lemon
lime
onion
parsley
pepper
rocket
thyme

GREENS & SALAD

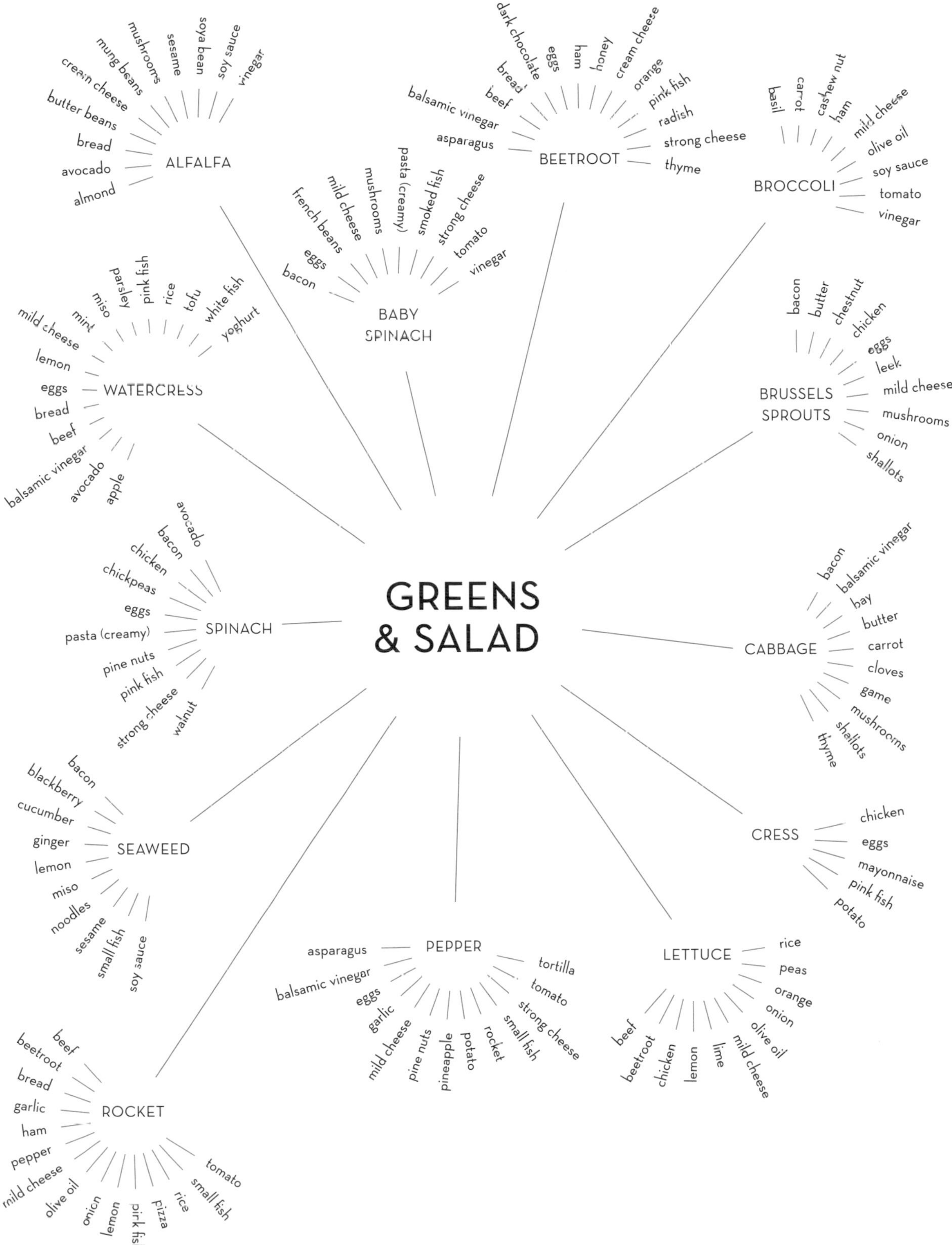

GREENS & SALAD
ALFALFA
almond
avocado
bread
butter beans
cream cheese
mung beans
mushrooms
sesame
soya bean
soy sauce
vinegar
BABY SPINACH
bacon
eggs
french beans
mild cheese
mushrooms
pasta (creamy)
smoked fish
strong cheese
tomato
vinegar
BEETROOT
asparagus
balsamic vinegar
beef
bread
dark chocolate
eggs
ham
honey
cream cheese
orange
pink fish
radish
strong cheese
thyme
BROCCOLI
basil
carrot
cashew nut
ham
mild cheese
olive oil
soy sauce
tomato
vinegar
WATERCRESS
apple
avocado
balsamic vinegar
beef
bread
eggs
lemon
mild cheese
mint
miso
parsley
pink fish
rice
tofu
white fish
yoghurt
BRUSSELS SPROUTS
bacon
butter
chestnut
chicken
eggs
leek
mild cheese
mushrooms
onion
shallots
SPINACH
avocado
bacon
chicken
chickpeas
eggs
pasta (creamy)
pine nuts
pink fish
strong cheese
walnut
CABBAGE
bacon
balsamic vinegar
bay
butter
carrot
cloves
game
mushrooms
shallots
thyme
SEAWEED
bacon
blackberry
cucumber
ginger
lemon
miso
noodles
sesame
small fish
soy sauce
CRESS
chicken
eggs
mayonnaise
pink fish
potato
PEPPER
asparagus
balsamic vinegar
eggs
garlic
mild cheese
pine nuts
pineapple
potato
rocket
small fish
strong cheese
tomato
tortilla
LETTUCE
beef
beetroot
chicken
lemon
lime
mild cheese
olive oil
onion
orange
peas
rice
ROCKET
beef
beetroot
bread
garlic
ham
pepper
mild cheese
olive oil
onion
lemon
pink fish
pizza
rice
small fish
tomato

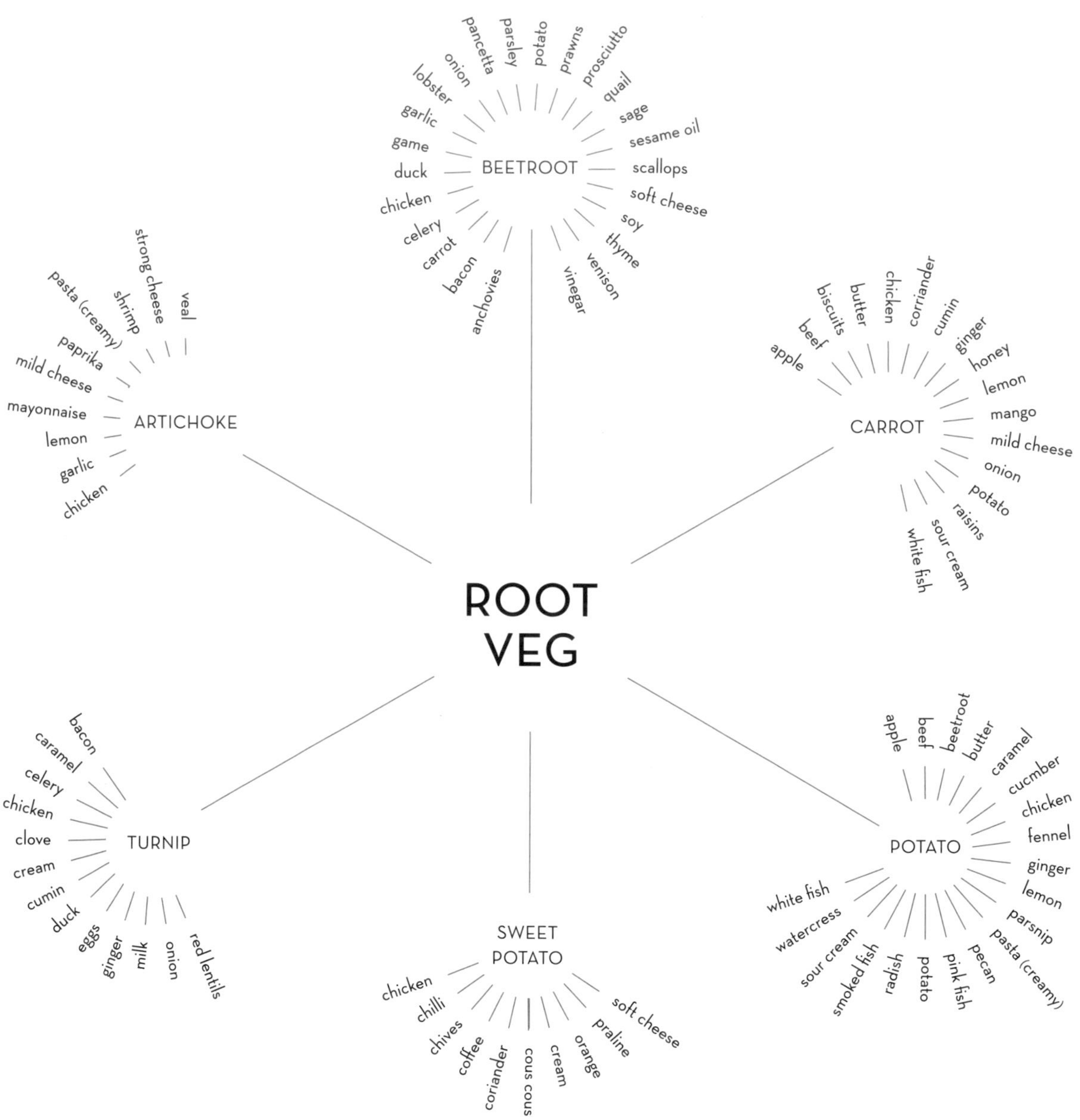
ROOT VEG
BEETROOT
pancetta
parsley
potato
prawns
prosciutto
quail
sage
sesame oil
scallops
soft cheese
soy
thyme
venison
vinegar
anchovies
bacon
carrot
celery
chicken
duck
game
garlic
lobster
onion
CARROT
chicken
corriander
cumin
ginger
honey
lemon
mango
mild cheese
onion
potato
raisins
sour cream
white fish
apple
beef
biscuits
butter
ARTICHOKE
strong cheese
veal
shrimp
pasta (creamy)
paprika
mild cheese
mayonnaise
lemon
garlic
chicken
TURNIP
bacon
caramel
celery
chicken
clove
cream
cumin
duck
eggs
ginger
milk
onion
red lentils
SWEET POTATO
chicken
chilli
chives
coffee
coriander
cous cous
cream
orange
praline
soft cheese
POTATO
apple
beef
beetroot
butter
caramel
cucmber
chicken
fennel
ginger
lemon
parsnip
pasta (creamy)
pecan
pink fish
potato
radish
smoked fish
sour cream
watercress
white fish

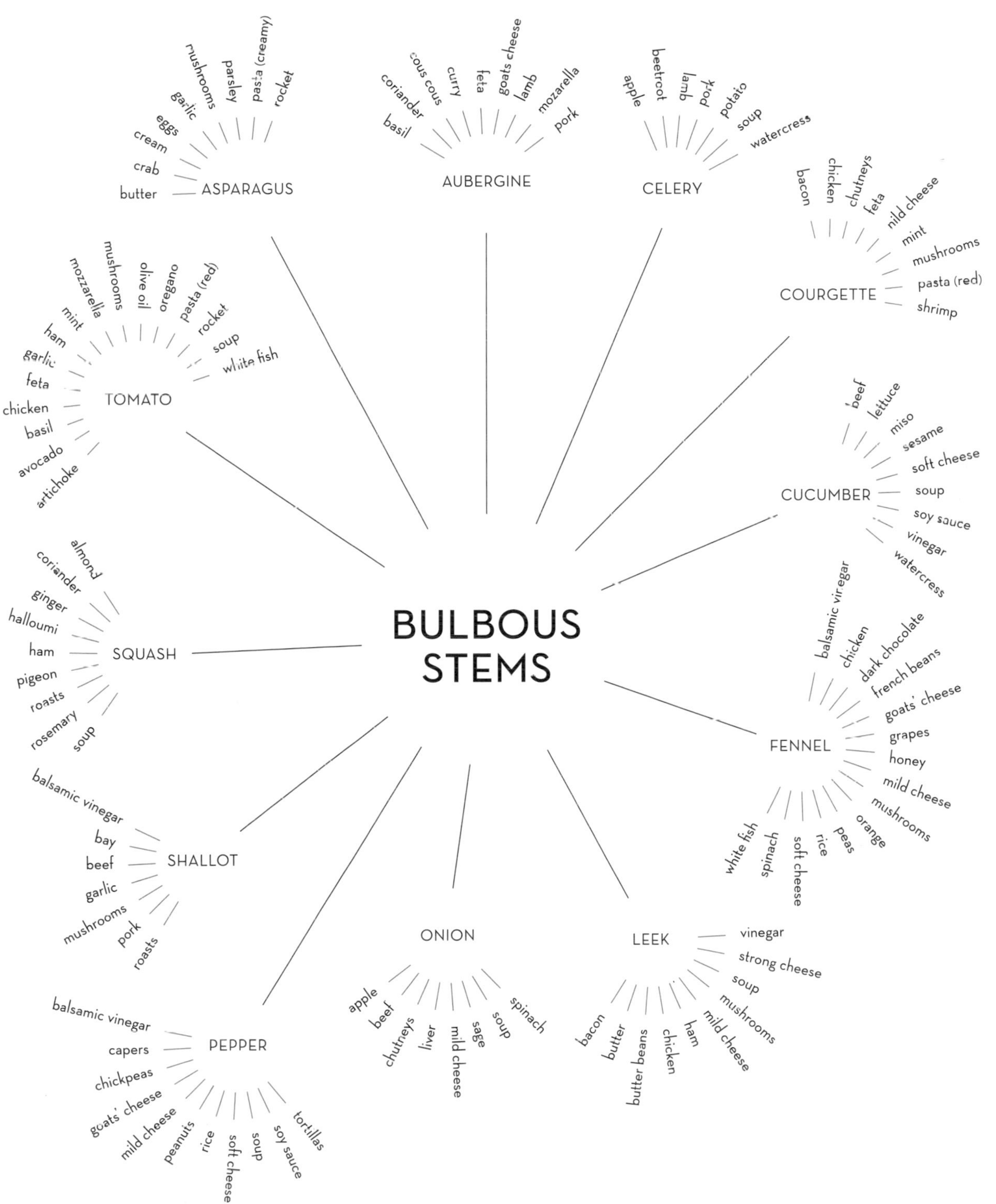

BULBOUS STEMS
ASPARAGUS
butter
crab
cream
eggs
garlic
mushrooms
parsley
pasta (creamy)
rocket
AUBERGINE
basil
coriander
cous cous
curry
feta
goats cheese
lamb
mozarella
pork
CELERY
apple
beetroot
lamb
pork
potato
soup
watercress
COURGETTE
bacon
chicken
chutneys
feta
mild cheese
mint
mushrooms
pasta (red)
shrimp
CUCUMBER
beef
lettuce
miso
sesame
soft cheese
soup
soy sauce
vinegar
watercress
FENNEL
balsamic vinegar
chicken
dark chocolate
french beans
goats' cheese
grapes
honey
mild cheese
mushrooms
orange
peas
rice
soft cheese
spinach
white fish
LEEK
vinegar
strong cheese
soup
mushrooms
mild cheese
ham
chicken
butter beans
butter
bacon
ONION
apple
beef
chutneys
liver
mild cheese
sage
soup
spinach
PEPPER
balsamic vinegar
capers
chickpeas
goats' cheese
mild cheese
peanuts
rice
soft cheese
soup
soy sauce
tortillas
SHALLOT
balsamic vinegar
bay
beef
garlic
mushrooms
pork
roasts
SQUASH
almond
coriander
ginger
halloumi
ham
pigeon
roasts
rosemary
soup
TOMATO
artichoke
avocado
basil
chicken
feta
garlic
ham
mint
mozzarella
mushrooms
olive oil
oregano
pasta (red)
rocket
soup
white fish

source: general internet and bbc.co.uk/food

Sunlight

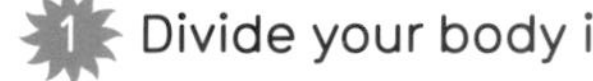

TWO MAIN TYPES OF ULTRAVIOLET

UVA	UVB	UVC
Ages your skin	Burns your skin	UVC blocked by atmosphere

% REACHING GROUND

95% 5%

RELATED SKIN CANCER

Carcinoma (nasty)

Melanoma (deadly)

SUNSCREEN PROTECTION

STAR SYSTEM

UVA

SUN FACTOR (SPF)

12

How much sunscreen?

1 Divide your body into eleven zones

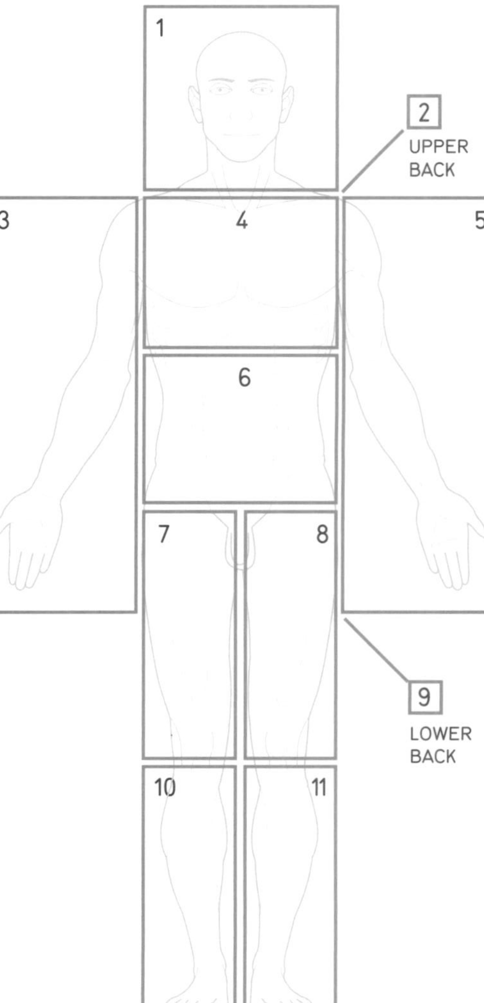
1
2
UPPER BACK
3
4
5
6
7
8
9
LOWER BACK
10
11

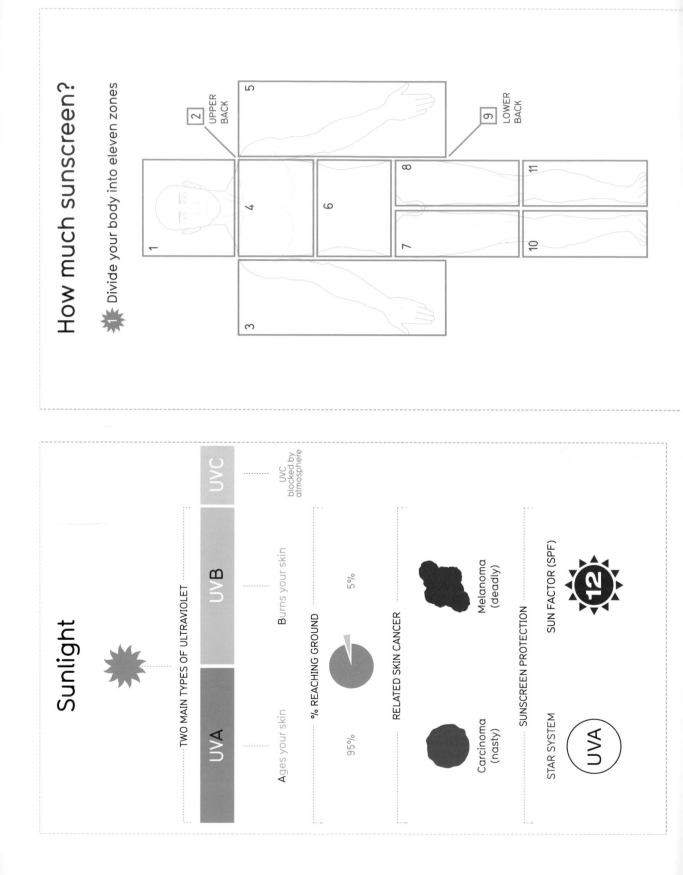

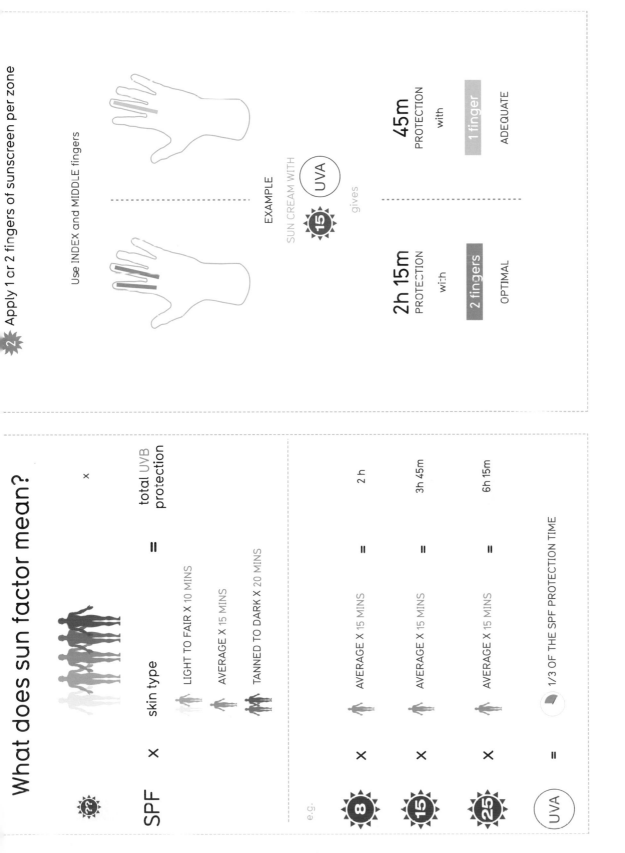

What does sun factor mean?

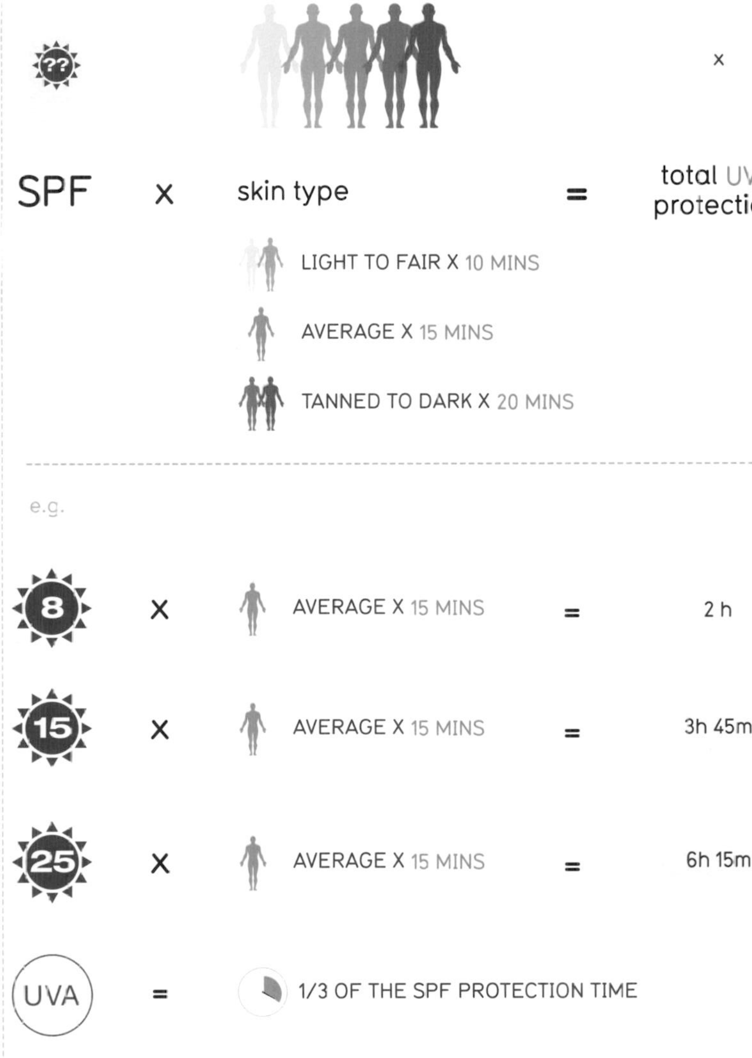

??
x
SPF × skin type = total UVB protection
LIGHT TO FAIR X 10 MINS
AVERAGE X 15 MINS
TANNED TO DARK X 20 MINS
e.g.
8 × AVERAGE X 15 MINS = 2 h
15 × AVERAGE X 15 MINS = 3h 45m
25 × AVERAGE X 15 MINS = 6h 15m
UVA = 1/3 OF THE SPF PROTECTION TIME

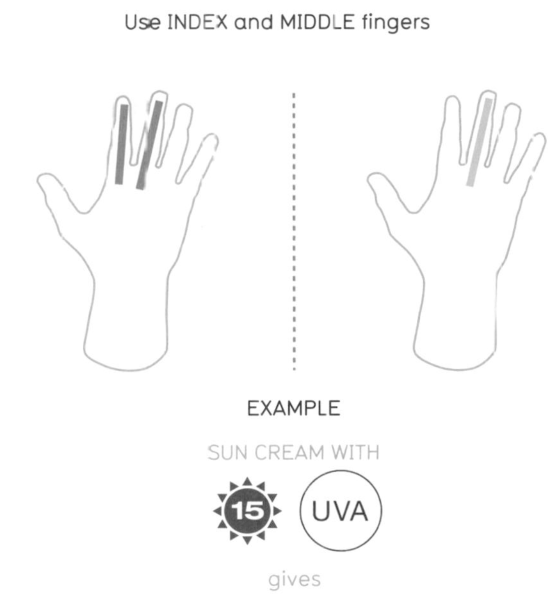

2 Apply 1 or 2 fingers of sunscreen per zone
Use INDEX and MIDDLE fingers
EXAMPLE
SUN CREAM WITH
15 UVA
gives
2h 15m PROTECTION with 2 fingers OPTIMAL
45m PROTECTION with 1 finger ADEQUATE

The Sunscreen Smokescreen

How often?

Previous wisdom

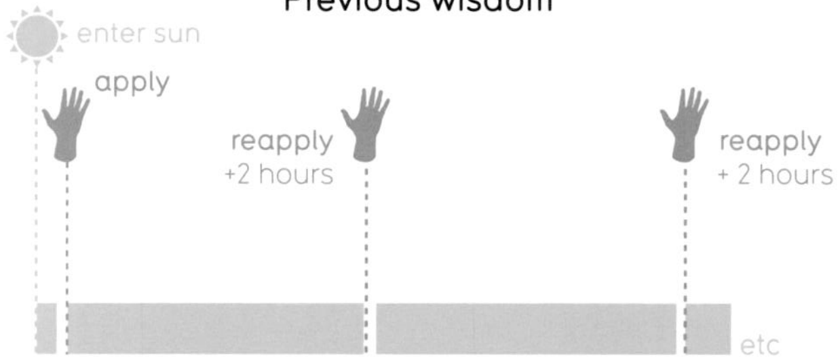

enter sun
apply
reapply
+2 hours
reapply
+ 2 hours
etc

Current wisdom

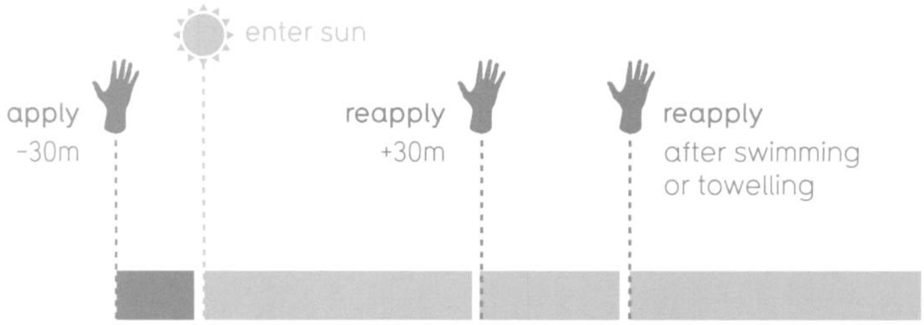

apply
-30m
enter sun
reapply
+30m
reapply
after swimming
or towelling

Intuitive wisdom

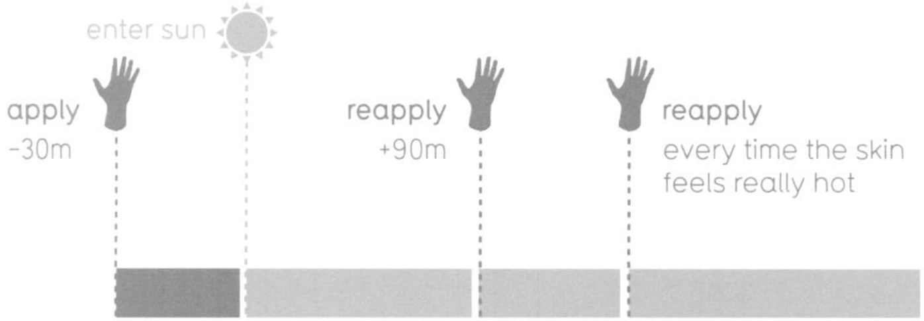

apply
-30m
enter sun
reapply
+90m
reapply
every time the skin
feels really hot

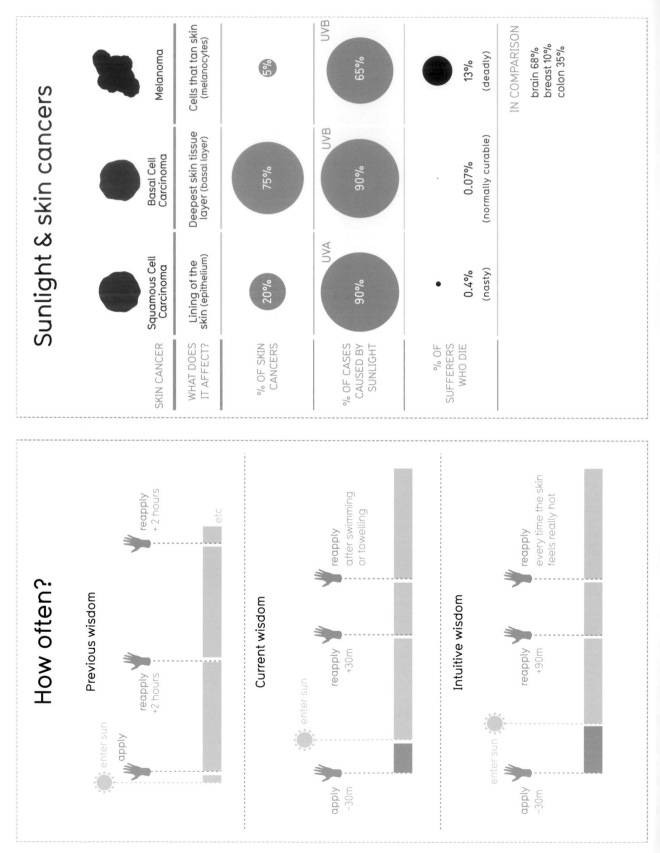

Sunlight & skin cancers

SKIN CANCER	Squamous Cell Carcinoma	Basal Cell Carcinoma	Melanoma
WHAT DOES IT AFFECT?	Lining of the skin (epithelium)	Deepest skin tissue layer (basal layer)	Cells that tan skin (melanocytes)
% OF SKIN CANCERS	20%	75%	5%
% OF CASES CAUSED BY SUNLIGHT	UVA 90%	UVB 90%	UVB 65%
% OF SUFFERERS WHO DIE	0.4% (nasty)	0.07% (normally curable)	13% (deadly)

IN COMPARISON

brain 68%
breast 10%
colon 35%

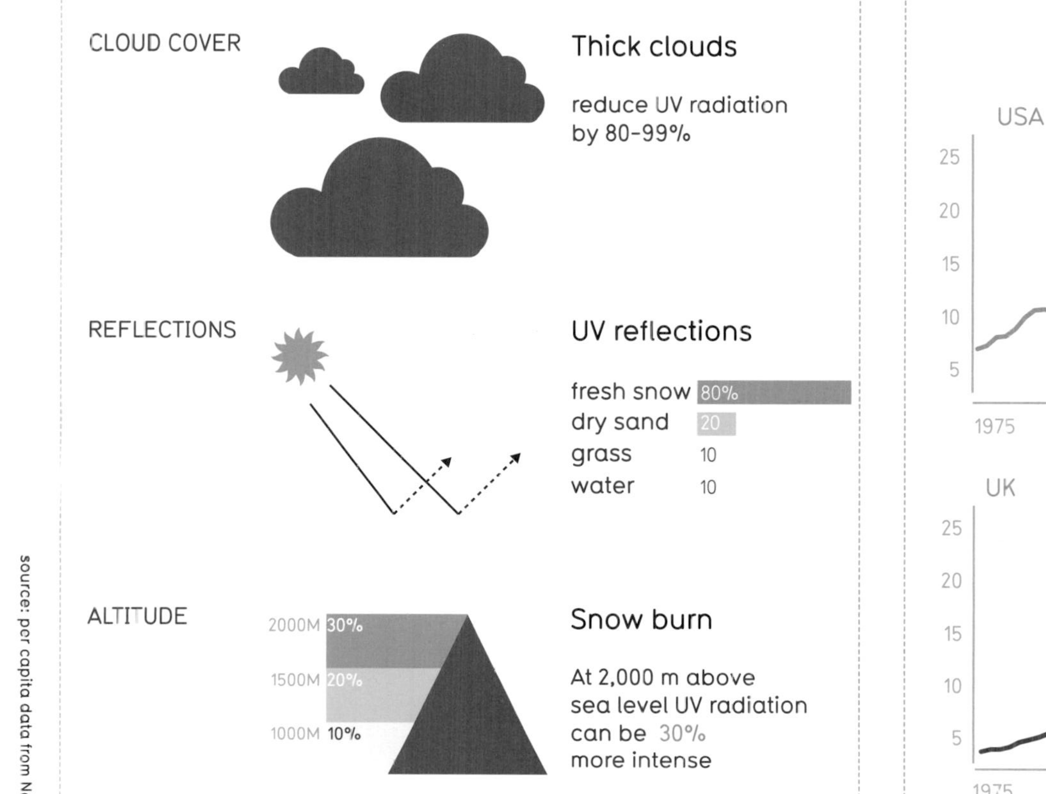
What if it's cloudy?
CLOUD COVER
Thick clouds
reduce UV radiation by 80–99%
REFLECTIONS
UV reflections
fresh snow 80%
dry sand 20
grass 10
water 10
ALTITUDE
2000M 30%
1500M 20%
1000M 10%
Snow burn
At 2,000 m above sea level UV radiation can be 30% more intense

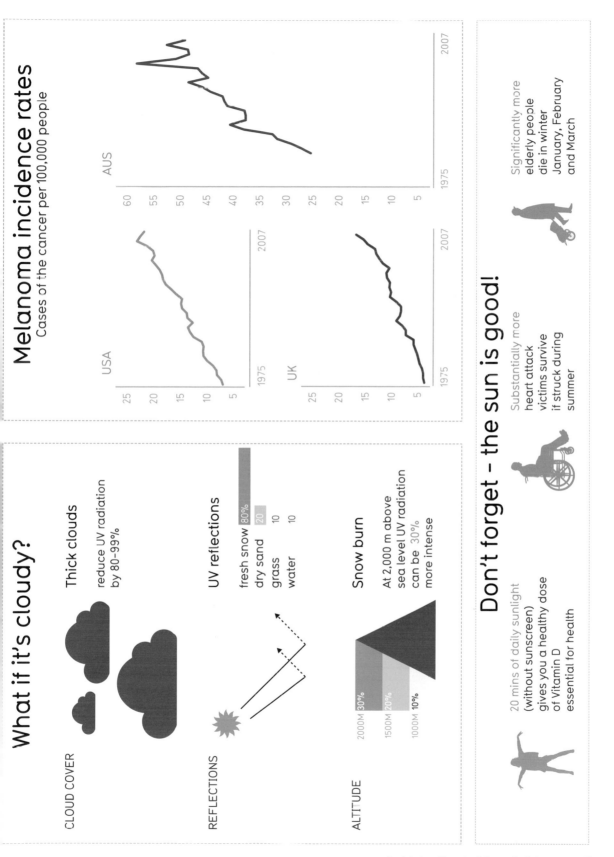

Melanoma incidence rates

Cases of the cancer per 100,000 people

USA
25 20 15 10 5
1975 2007

UK
25 20 15 10 5
1975 2007

AUS
60 55 50 45 40 35 30 25 20 15 10 5
1975 2007

Don't forget – the sun is good!

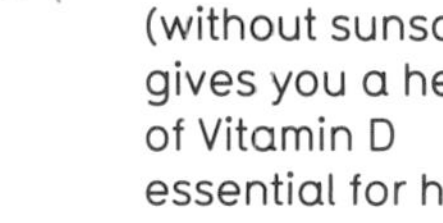

20 mins of daily sunlight (without sunscreen) gives you a healthy dose of Vitamin D essential for health

Substantially more heart attack victims survive if struck during summer

Significantly more elderly people die in winter January, February and March

source: per capita data from Newscientist.com, Unstats.un.org, NationMaster.com

The Poison
1 Lime juice
1 Orange liqueur
1 Tequila
Margarita
1 Vermouth
7 Gin
Martini
Angostura
1 Sweet Vermouth
4 Whisky
Manhattan
8 White rum
1 Lime juice
1 Sugar syrup
1 Orange liqueur
1 Dark rum
Mai Tai
Lime juice
1 Cranberry juice
1 Orange liqueur
1.5 Vodka
Cosmopolitan
12 Vodka
12 Kahlua
8 Single cream
White Russian
1 Sugar syrup
6 Lemon juice
6 Vodka
6 Gin
6 White rum
Long Island Iced Tea
Mint leaves
12 White rum
2 Sugar
1 Lime juice
12 Club soda
Mojito
1 Galliano
2 Vodka
6 Orange juice
.75 Sugar syrup
1.5 Bourbon
1.5 Lemon juice
2 Lime juice
1 Sugar syrup
8 White rum
White pepper
Worcester sauce
Tabasco
1 Lemon juice
40 Tomato juice
12 Vodka

The Remedy

Hangover cures from around the world

pepper
Egg yolk
1 Lemon juice
1Worcester s.
Traditional
Egg yolk
1 Worcester sauce
American
Beer
Dutch
Sour pickle juice
Polish
Coffee
Italian
salt
Strong coffee
French
Water
1 Salt
2 Sugar
Isotonic
Water
1 Honey
1 Cider vinegar
Icelandic
10 Cow's stomach
5 Root veg soup
2 Cream
1 Vinegar
Romanian
Strong green tea
Chinese
Baked beans
Egg
Bacon
Sausage
British
diarrhoea medicine
Water
Medical
Mustard berries
Juniper berries
Pickled herring
Germanic
Ginger ale
1 Lime juice
6 Brandy
6 Gin
Hedonistic

source: Google

Salad Dressings

All in proportion

12 Oil
4 Vinegar
1 Mustard

Vinaigrette

6 Buttermilk
8 Cottage cheese
2 Chives
1 Garlic
1 Parmesan

Ranch

8 Oil
4 Cider vinegar
4 Honey
1 Garlic

Honey

Worcester sauce
8 Sour cream
16 Mayonnaise
8 Parsley
4 Basil
Chives
3 Vinegar
3 Onion
1 Garlic

Creamy Herb

Mayonnaise
Garlic
Mustard
4 Oil
1 White wine vinegar

Creamy Garlic

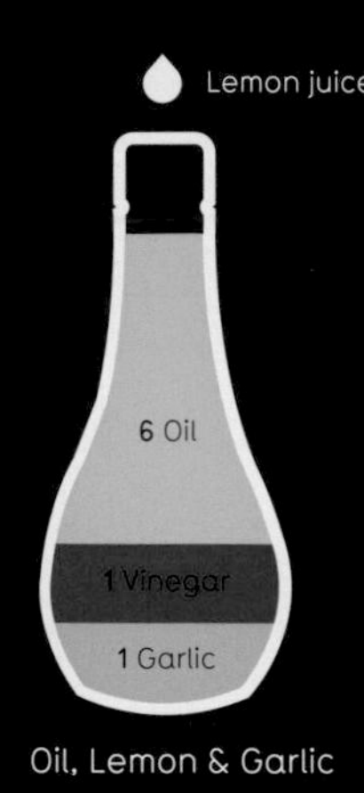

Lemon juice
6 Oil
1 Vinegar
1 Garlic

Oil, Lemon & Garlic

Worcester sauce
Garlic
Sugar
16 Oil
1 White wine vinegar
2 Black olives
1 Egg

Thousand Island

Lemon juice
16 Yoghurt
1 Mustard
Parsley, chives

Lemon, Herb & Yoghurt

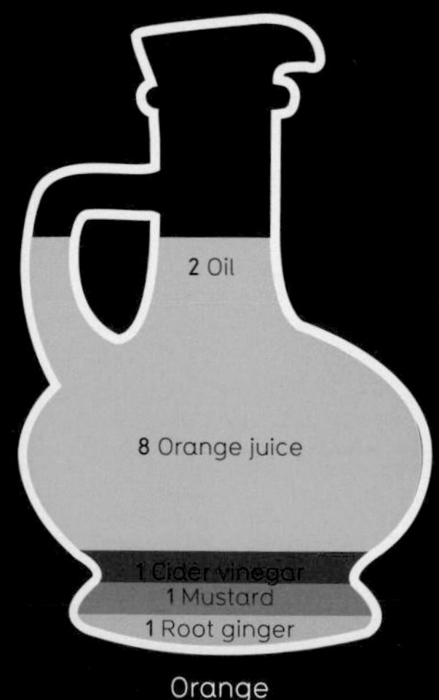

2 Oil
8 Orange juice
1 Cider vinegar
1 Mustard
1 Root ginger

Orange

6 Oil
2 Lemon juice

Oil & Lemon

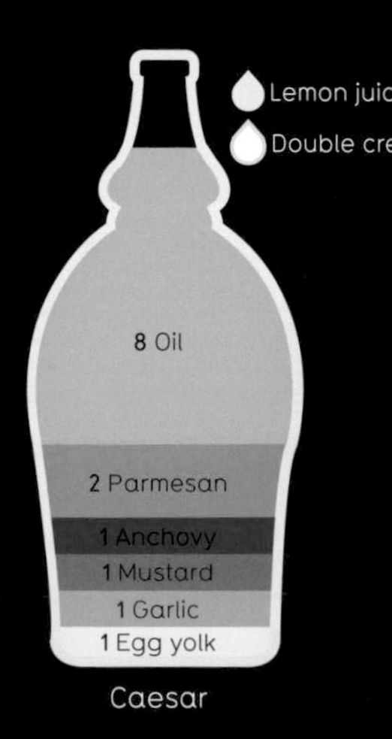

Lemon juice
Double cream
8 Oil
2 Parmesan
1 Anchovy
1 Mustard
1 Garlic
1 Egg yolk

Caesar

Lime juice
Soy sauce
4 Oil
1 Curry powder

Curry

source: Google

Not Nice

Food colourings linked to unpleasant health effects

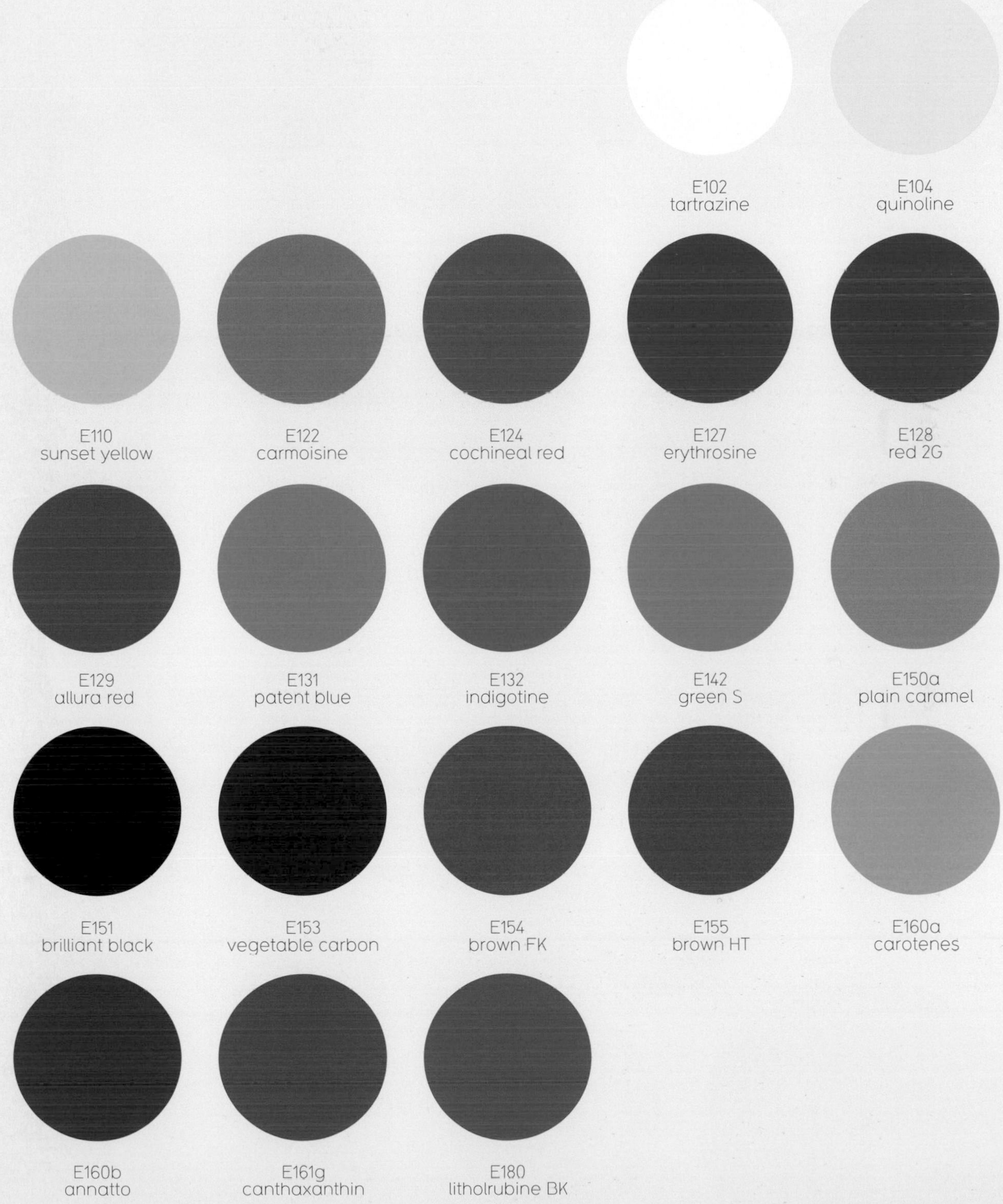
E102
tartrazine
E104
quinoline
E110
sunset yellow
E122
carmoisine
E124
cochineal red
E127
erythrosine
E128
red 2G
E129
allura red
E131
patent blue
E132
indigotine
E142
green S
E150a
plain caramel
E151
brilliant black
E153
vegetable carbon
E154
brown FK
E155
brown HT
E160a
carotenes
E160b
annatto
E161g
canthaxanthin
E180
litholrubine BK

source: Centre for Science in the Public Interest, Cspinet.org

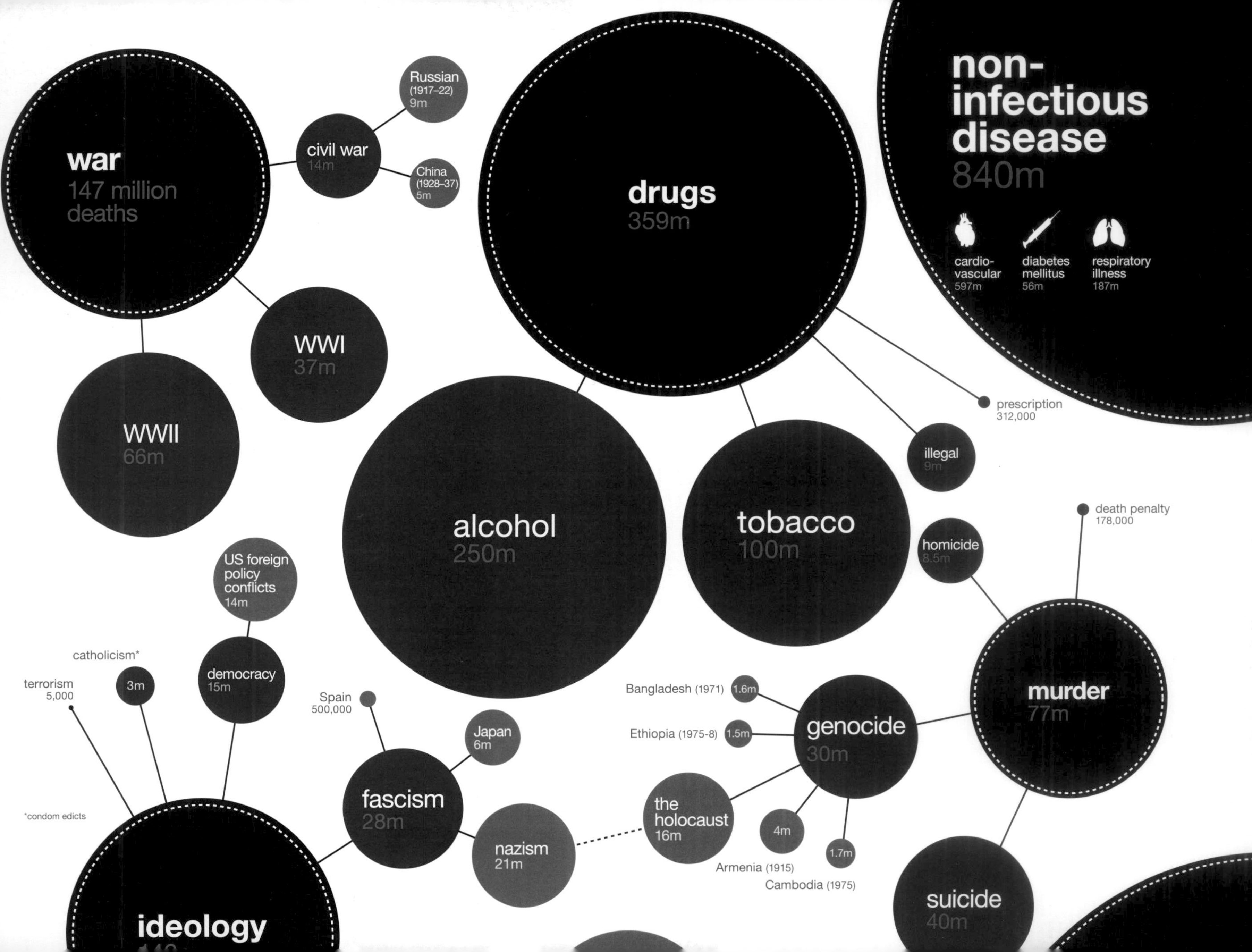

war
147 million deaths
civil war
14m
Russian (1917–22) 9m
China (1928–37) 5m
WWI
37m
WWII
66m
drugs
359m
alcohol
250m
tobacco
100m
illegal
9m
prescription
312,000
non-infectious disease
840m
cardio-vascular
597m
diabetes mellitus
56m
respiratory illness
187m
death penalty
178,000
homicide
8.5m
murder
77m
suicide
40m
genocide
30m
Bangladesh (1971) 1.6m
Ethiopia (1975-8) 1.5m
the holocaust
16m
4m
Armenia (1915)
1.7m
Cambodia (1975)
US foreign policy conflicts
14m
democracy
15m
catholicism*
3m
terrorism
5,000
*condom edicts
Spain
500,000
Japan
6m
fascism
28m
nazism
21m
ideology

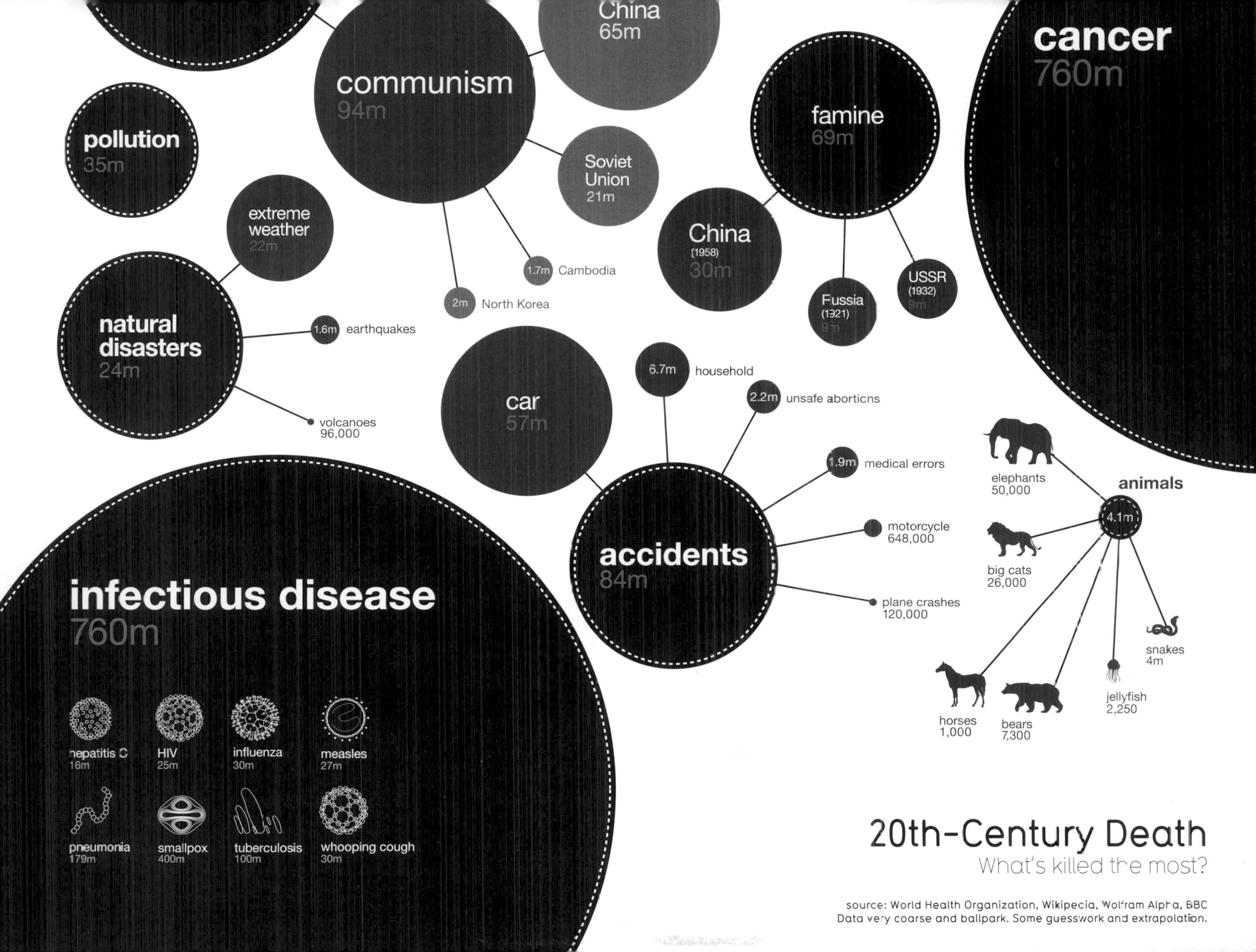

communism
94m
China
65m
Soviet Union
21m
1.7m Cambodia
2m North Korea
pollution
35m
extreme weather
22m
natural disasters
24m
1.6m earthquakes
volcanoes
96,000
famine
69m
China
(1958)
30m
Fussia
(1321)
9m
USSR
(1932)
9m
cancer
760m
car
57m
accidents
84m
6.7m household
2.2m unsafe aborticns
1.9m medical errors
motorcycle
648,000
plane crashes
120,000
animals
4.1m
elephants
50,000
big cats
26,000
horses
1,000
bears
7,300
jellyfish
2,250
snakes
4m
infectious disease
760m
nepatitis C
16m
HIV
25m
influenza
30m
measles
27m
pneumonia
179m
smallpox
400m
tuberculosis
100m
whooping cough
30m
20th-Century Death
What's killed tre most?
source: World Health Organization, Wikipecia, Wolfram Alpha, BBC
Data very coarse and ballpark. Some guesswork and extrapolation.

THE GLOBAL WARMING SCEPTICS

We don't believe there is any credible evidence that mankind's activities are the cause of global warming if that's even happening at all. There's only circumstantial evidence of a link between carbon dioxide levels and rising global temperatures.

THE SCIENTIFIC CONSENSUS

The earth's climate is rapidly warming. The cause is a thickening layer of carbon dioxide pollution, caused by humanity's activities. It traps heat in the atmosphere, creating a "greenhouse effect" that heats the earth. A rise in global temperatures of 3 to 9 degrees will cause devastation.

Rising CO_2 levels are not always linked with rising temperatures

Because of extreme weather, Arctic temperature is often a dramatic barometer of global climate. But the temperatures there match poorly with human CO_2 emissions.

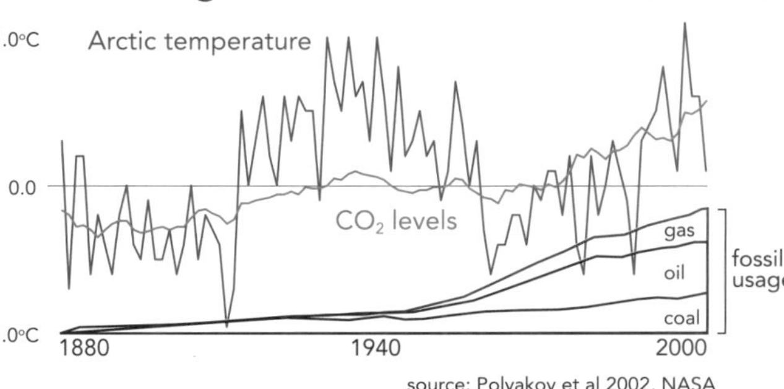

1.0°C
Arctic temperature
0.0
CO_2 levels
gas
oil
coal
fossil fuel usage
-1.0°C
1880
1940
2000

source: Polvakov et al 2002. NASA

A single graph for a single small area is not enough evidence

You can't draw conclusions about the warming of the whole planet just by looking at a small area. It's like comparing apples and pears. It's impossible to tell what caused the warming of the Arctic in the 1930. Or whether it's the same mechanism that's causing global warming today.

In the past, CO_2 rises have occured after temperature rises

Recognize this from *An Inconvenient Truth*? Al Gore famously showed that temperature and CO_2 are clearly linked back over 400,000 years. But if you zoom in....

Global temperatures

CO_2 levels

400 350 300 250 200 150 100 50 0

thousands of years ago

source: Vostok ice core, Petit et al 2002

800 years

...you see that CO_2 levels rise 800 years after the temperature does. This massive lag proves that CO_2 can't cause global warming!

We don't claim CO_2 caused temperature rises in the past

We say, because of its greenhouse effect, CO_2 makes natural temperature rises worse. Much worse in fact.

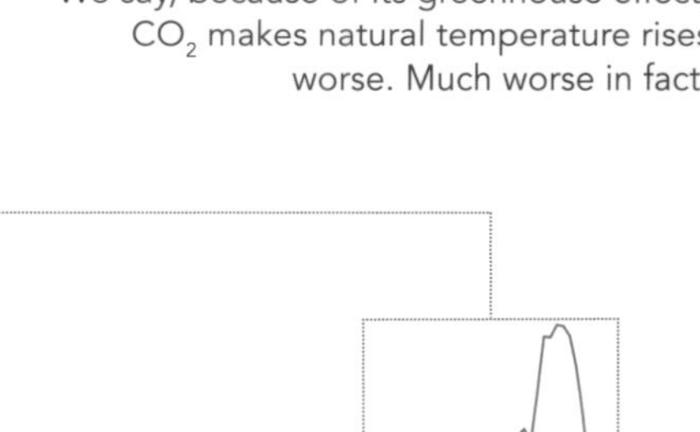

50,000 years

Historically, global warming cycles last 5000 years. The 800-year lag only shows that CO_2 did not cause the first 16% of warming. The other 4200 years were likely to have been caused by a CO_2 greenhouse effect.

We don't even have accurate temperature records

90% of temperature recording stations are on land. 70% of the world's surface is ocean. Cities and towns heat the atmosphere around land-based weather stations enough to distort the record of historical temperatures. It's called the urban heat island effect. And it's why we can't trust temperature records.

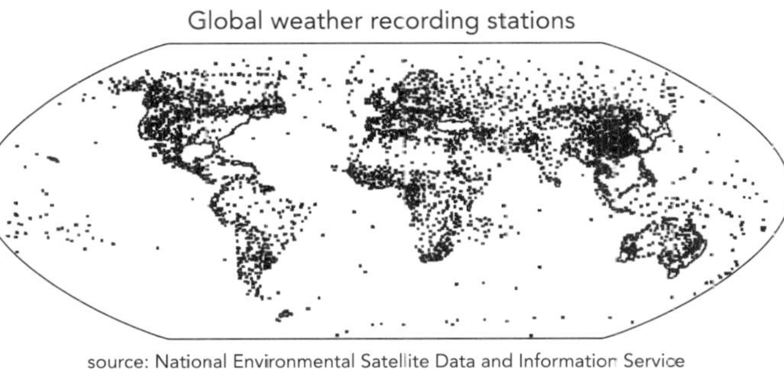
Global weather recording stations
source: National Environmental Satellite Data and Information Service

We do have accurate temperature records

Distortion of temperature records is a very real phenomenon. But it's one climate scientists are well aware of. Detailed filters are used to remove the effect from the records.

It was actually hotter in medieval times than today

Between AD 800 and 1300 was a Medieval Warm Period where temperatures were very high. Grapes were grown in England. The Vikings colonized Greenland. This occurred centuries before we began pumping CO_2 into the atmosphere. More proof that CO_2 and temperature are not linked. Because of this – and to make 20th-century warming look unique – UN scientists constantly play down this medieval period in their data.

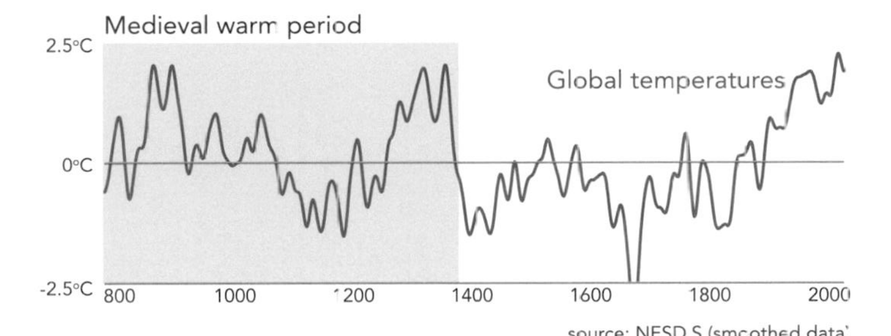
Medieval warm period
Global temperatures
2.5°C
0°C
-2.5°C
800
1000
1200
1400
1600
1800
2000
source: NESDIS (smoothed data)

It was hotter in some areas of the world and not in others

This was likely a local warming, rather than a global warming, equivalent to warming today. Ice cores show us that there were periods of both cold and warmth at the time. And there's no evidence it affected the southern hemisphere at all.

The records also show that the earth may have been slightly cooler (by 0.03 degrees Celsius) during the 'medieval warm period' than today.

The famous "hockey stick" temperature graph has been discredited

Made famous by Al Gore, the "hockey stick" graph shows that 20th-century temperatures are showing an alarming rise. But the hockey stick appears or disappears depending on the statistical methods employed. So unreliable has it become that the UN's International Panel On Climate Change dropped it from their 2007 report.

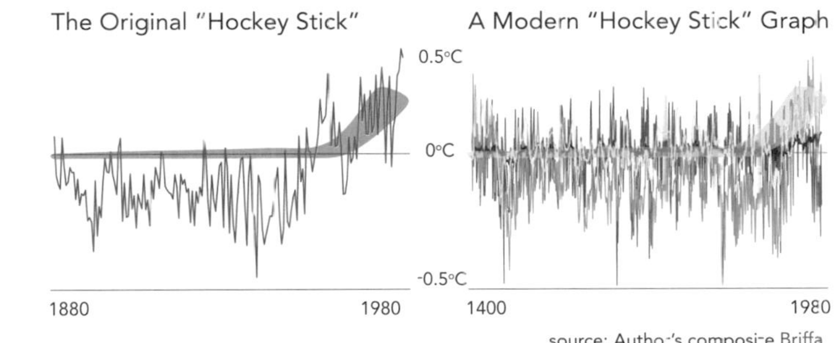
The Original "Hockey Stick"
A Modern "Hockey Stick" Graph
0.5°C
0°C
-0.5°C
1880
1980
1400
1980
source: Author's composite Briffa Anmann & Wahl Mann 2003 Mann 1998

Reworked, enhanced versions still show the "hockey stick" shape

The hockey stick is 8 years old. There are dozens of other newer, more detailed temperature reconstructions. Each one is different due to different methods and data. But they all show similar striking patterns: the 20th century is the warmest of the entire record. And that warming is most dramatic after 1920 (when industrial activity started releasing CO_2 into the atmosphere).

THE GLOBAL WARMING SCEPTICS

THE SCIENTIFIC CONSENSUS

Ice core data is unreliable

A lot of our temperature records come from measuring the gases trapped in ice cores. These are segments of deep ice unmelted for hundreds of thousands of years. The trapped air inside acts as "photographs" of the contents of the atmosphere going back millennia. But ice-cores are not "closed systems" that preserve ancient air perfectly. Air can get in and out. Water can also absorb the gases, changing the result. And deep ice is under huge amounts of pressure. Enough to squeeze gas out. All in all this adds up to make ice cores unreliable.

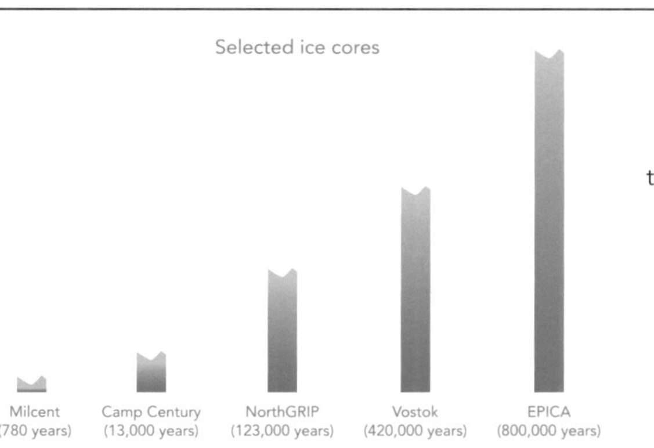
Selected ice cores
Milcent (780 years)
Camp Century (13,000 years)
NorthGRIP (123,000 years)
Vostok (420,000 years)
EPICA (800,000 years)

Ice records are reliable

Ice core data is taken from many different samples to reduce errors. Also, other evidence (temperature records, tree rings, etc) back these readings up. All these results combined make the records very reliable.

The predictions of future global warming don't depend on ice cores. But ice cores do show that the climate is sensitive to changes in cycles and that CO_2 has a strong influence.

Overall, CO_2 levels from different ice cores are remarkably similar.

When the evidence doesn't fit, the scientists edit the evidence

Ice core data from Siple in the Arctic shows the concentrations of CO_2 in the atmosphere in 1890 to be 328 parts per million. However, according to the consensus, that level was not reached until 1973. So the rise in CO_2 levels happens 83 years too early.

To fix it, scientists moved the graph 83 years to the right to make the data exactly fit.

CO_2 levels ice at Siple (Arctic)

the original data
328 ppm
the adjusted data

350
300
250

1744
1878
1891
1953
2000

Source: Neftel 1985, Friedli 1986

Scientists correct their results when new evidence comes to light

No other ice core data in the world shows CO_2 levels rising above 290 parts per million in the last 650,000 years. It's possible it might have happened for a year or a day. But consistently, no.

Some areas of ice are more porous than others. At Siple, the more recent shallow ice was quite porous. So new air was able to circulate quite far down. That affected the record.

We detected and compensated for this. That's why the data has been shifted.

CO_2 stays in the atmosphere for only 5 to 10 years, not the 50–200 years stated by UN scientists

The ocean absorbs the CO_2 so it can't accumulate to dangerous levels in the atmosphere. In fact, the oceans are so vast they can absorb 50 times as much CO_2 as there is in the atmosphere – more than all the fossil fuels on the planet!

Conclusion: humans can't have been emitting CO_2 fast enough to account for all the extra CO_2 in the atmosphere.

CO_2 absorption by the oceans

CO2
atmos
shallow ocean
"fertilizer" for plankton
dissolved as carbonic acid
5-10 years
deep ocean
dead plankton
shells, bones
50-200 years

When you take the entire complex ocean-climate system into account 50–200 years is more accurate

CO_2 is absorbed in 5 to 10 years by the *shallow* ocean. Not the deep ocean. It takes 50–200 years for CO_2 to be mixed into the deep ocean where it stays. CO_2 in the shallow ocean, however, is prone to escaping back into the atmosphere. So CO_2 absorbed by the ocean often comes straight back out again.

Also the more carbon the ocean absorbs, the less it's able to absorb. It becomes saturated. It's a very complex process. But if you take the entire ocean-climate system, full absorption of atmospheric CO_2 takes around 50,000 years.

SCEPTICAL CONCLUSION

Man-made CO_2 cannot be driving climate change

Whatever affects global temperatures and causes global warming is not CO_2. Whatever the cause, it works like this: the cause affects the climate balance, then the temperature changes accordingly. The oceans then adjust over a period of decades and centuries. Then the balance of CO_2 in the atmosphere increases.

So the global panic about CO_2 causing global warming is baseless and fear-mongering. The UN's reports on the matter are biased, unscientific and alarmist.

CONSENSUS CONCLUSION

Man-made CO_2 is driving climate change this time

We don't claim that greenhouse gases are the major cause of the ice ages and warming cycles. What drives climate change has long been believed to be the variation in the earth's orbit around the sun over thousands of years.

In a normal warming cycle, the sun heats the earth, the earth gets hotter. The oceans warm up, releasing huge amounts of CO_2. This creates a greenhouse effect that makes warming much, much more intense.

That's why humanity's release of CO_2 is so perilous. We're out of step with the natural cycle. And we haven't even got to the stage where the oceans warm up.

source: Solomon, Lawrence, The Deniers (Richard Vigilante Books, 2008), RealClimate.org

Behind Every Great Man...

Dictators' wives

Wife	Nadezhda Alliluyeva	Eva Braun	Yang Kaihui	Imelda Marcos	Mirjana (Mira) Markovic
Husband	Stalin	Hitler	Mao	Marcos	Milosevic
Pre-marital occupation	clerk	assistant and model	communist!	beauty queen	professor of sociology
How they met	her father sheltered Stalin in 1911 after he escaped from Siberian exile	she was assistant to his personal photographer	her father was Mao's teacher	whirlwind courtship during "holy week"	at school, she borrowed his card to rent *Antigone* from the library. Oh yeah?
Years of marriage	13	about 40 minutes	8	35	32
Children	2		3	4	2
Rumoured quality of marriage	strained and violent	changeable	troubled	good	very good
Political power rating	none	1	none	5	4
Key governmental roles	none	none	prominent female member of party	Governor of Manila, Ambassador plenipotentiary	puppet-master, leader of "Yugoslav United Left"
Style rating	none	4	4	5	5
Nickname	none	The Rolleiflex Girl	none	The Steel Butterfly	The Red Witch
Notable talents	none – super dull	photography, athletics	very intelligent	none	politics
Trademark/idiosyncrasy	left-handed	nude sunbathing	feminist	very ostentatious and flamboyant	would berate her husband in front of state officials, wore only black Versace
Obsessions and pathologies	suicide	lots of make-up	good communists don't covet material things	shoes, clothes, paintings	media products, plastic surgeons, rich friends
Most salacious rumour	she was Stalin's daughter	she was pregnant when she died OR she didn't sleep in the same room as Hitler	said she would have killed herself when she and Mao divorced if she didn't have kids	sent a plane to pick up white sand from Australia for her beach resort	ordered the murder of Ivan Stambolic, a rival to her husband. Had at least four officials killed after they disagreed with her. Disappeared a journalist who criticized her.
Reason for death	officially "appendicitis" – really, shot	suicide – bit into a cyanide capsule	publicly executed by the Nationalists	still alive	still alive

Grace Marufu
Mugabe
secretary
worked as his secretary then became his mistress
13
good
none
Dis Grace
shopping (once spent £75,000 on a shopping spree in Paris)
spending - called one of the £500,000 palaces she had built, "Gracelands"
hates journalists
uses the Reserve Bank of Zimbabwe as her own bank account. Spent over $10m and transferred huge funds to build luxury properties in Malaysia
still alive
Khieu Ponnary
Pol Pot
teacher
at university. She came from a privileged background. He did not
23
good at start, terrible when she flipped
President of the Democratic Kampuchea Women's Association
Old Virgin
inspiring young communists
paranoia
Communist ideologies, PARANOIA
Pol Pot couldn't bear to look at her when she became ill and avoided her
natural causes
Jiang Qing
Mao
actress
at the Chinese Communist HQ. She "joined the revolution"
39
bad
key member of the politburo & infamous "gang of four"
Madame Mao
photography, seduction
sexy and chic, in the gossip columns
hypochondriac, insomnia, hyper-sensitive, paranoid
entertained her prison jailors by being their dinner (and bed) companion
allegedly hanged herself
Carmen Polo
Franco
none
family connections
52
good
key advisor and censor of the press
La Señora
being glamorous
always accompanied her husband EVERYWHERE
completely isolated herself in her old age
smuggled 300 million pesetas worth of gold, jewellery & medals
old age
Sajida Talfah
Hussein
teacher
arranged marriage (her father is his uncle)
43
crazy – many family feuds
none
none
paranoia
none
paranoid
none
no one knows where she is...
He Zizhen
Mao
communist!
introduced by a classmate of her elder brother
7
bad
none
none
none
excellent markswoman
none
nervous breakdown/ insomnia
none
old age

source: Wikipedia

Bubble chart

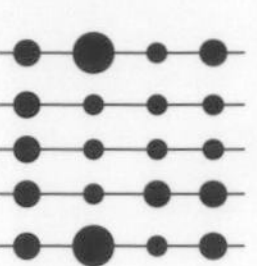

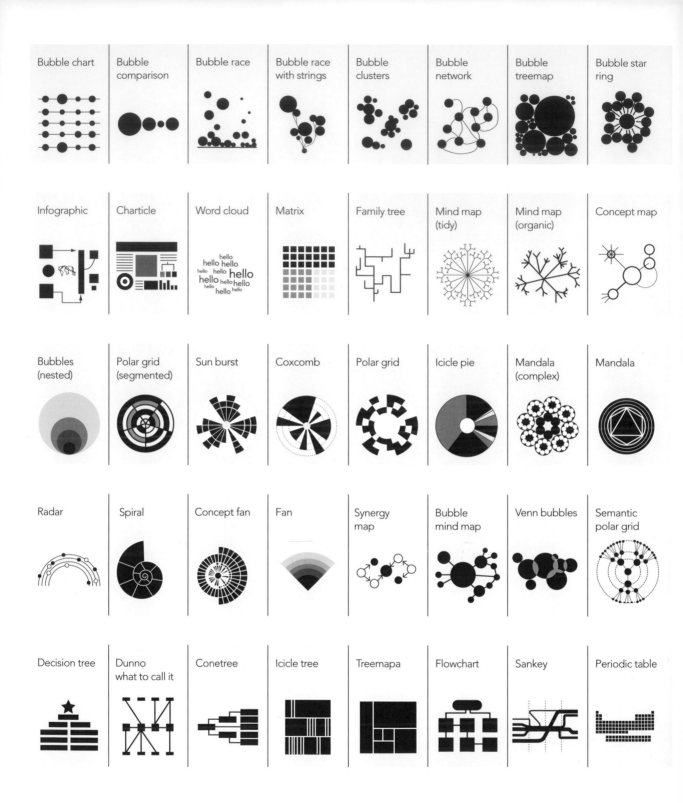

Bubble comparison

Bubble race

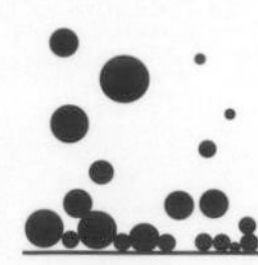

Bubble race with strings

Bubble clusters

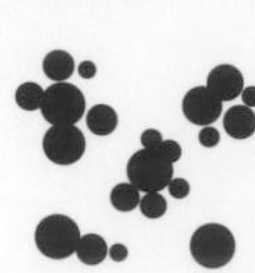

Bubble network

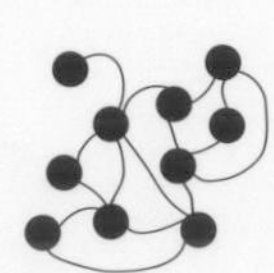

Bubble treemap

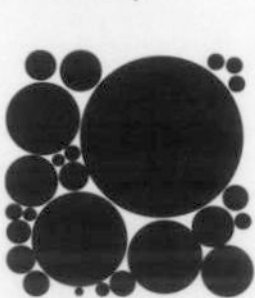

Bubble star ring

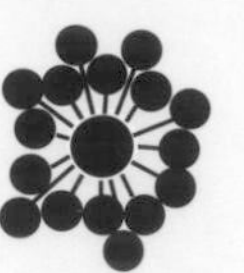

Infographic

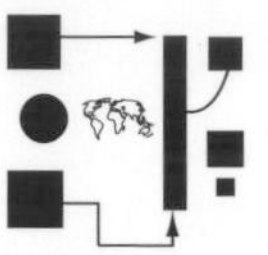

Charticle

Word cloud

hello
hello hello
hello hello hello
hello hello hello
hello hello hello

Matrix

Family tree

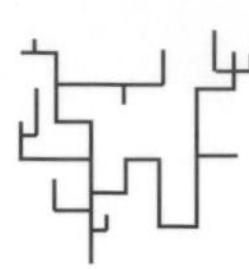

Mind map (tidy)

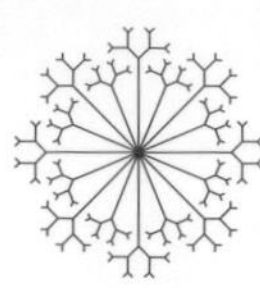

Mind map (organic)

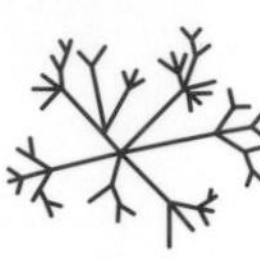

Concept map

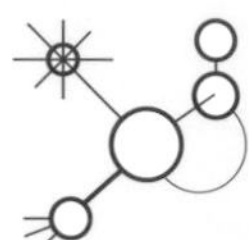

Bubbles (nested)

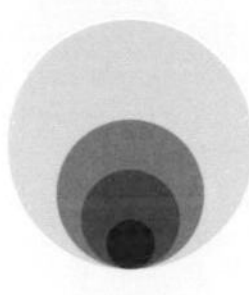

Polar grid (segmented)

Sun burst

Coxcomb

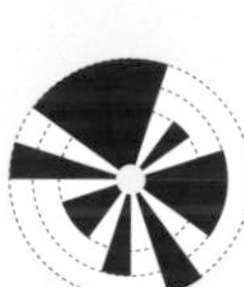

Polar grid

Icicle pie

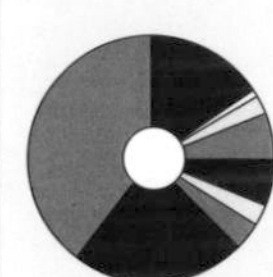

Mandala (complex)

Mandala

Radar

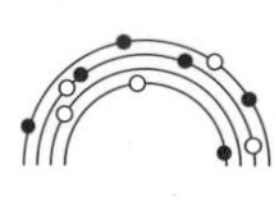

Spiral

Concept fan

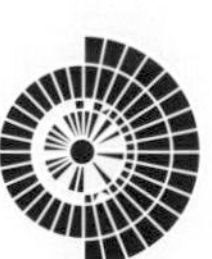

Fan

Synergy map

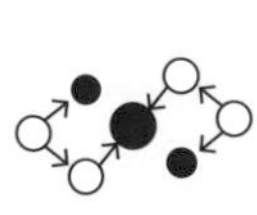

Bubble mind map

Venn bubbles

Semantic polar grid

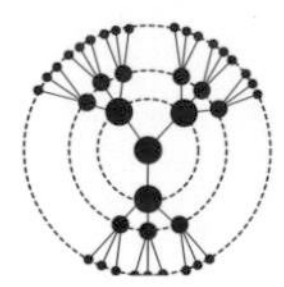

Decision tree

Dunno what to call it

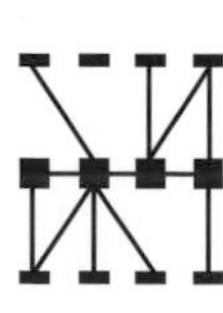

Conetree

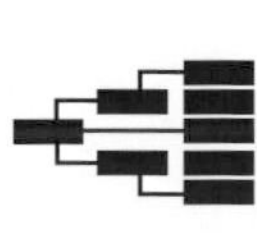

Icicle tree

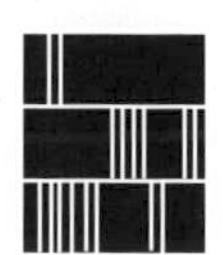

Treemapa

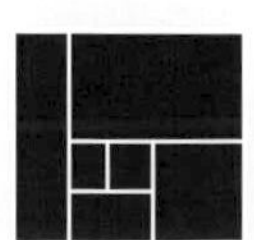

Flowchart

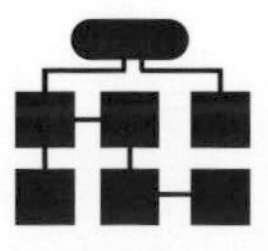

Sankey

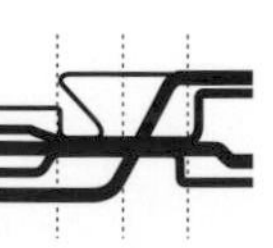

Periodic table

Types of Information Visualization

source: Edward Tufte, visual-literacy.org

Pass the...

A table of condiments that periodically go bad

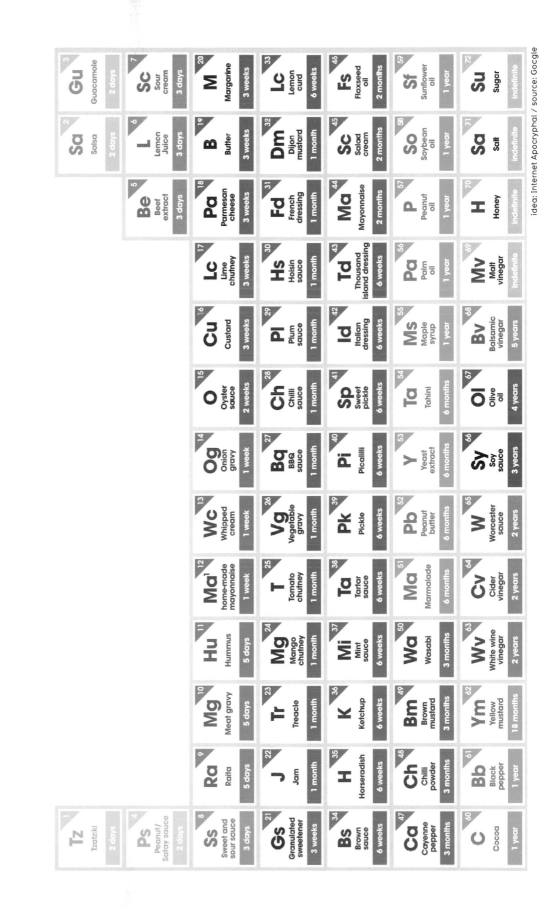

1 Tz Tzatziki 2 days											2 Sa Salsa 2 days	3 Gu Guacamole 2 days
4 Ps Peanut/ Satay sauce 2 days										5 Be Beef extract 3 days	6 L Lemon Juice 3 days	7 Sc Sour cream 3 days
8 Ss Sweet and sour sauce 3 days	9 Ra Raita 5 days	10 Mg Meat gravy 5 days	11 Hu Hummus 5 days	12 Ma[1] home-made mayonnaise 1 week	13 Wc Whipped cream 1 week	14 Og Onion gravy 1 week	15 O Oyster sauce 2 weeks	16 Cu Custard 3 weeks	17 Lc Lime chutney 3 weeks	18 Pa Parmesan cheese 3 weeks	19 B Butter 3 weeks	20 M Margarine 3 weeks
21 Gs Granulated sweetener 3 weeks	22 J Jam 1 month	23 Tr Treacle 1 month	24 Mg Mango chutney 1 month	25 T Tomato chutney 1 month	26 Vg Vegetable gravy 1 month	27 Bq BBQ sauce 1 month	28 Ch Chilli sauce 1 month	29 Pl Plum sauce 1 month	30 Hs Hoisin sauce 1 month	31 Fd French dressing 1 month	32 Dm Dijon mustard 1 month	33 Lc Lemon curd 6 weeks
34 Bs Brown sauce 6 weeks	35 H Horseradish 6 weeks	36 K Ketchup 6 weeks	37 Mi Mint sauce 6 weeks	38 Ta Tartar sauce 6 weeks	39 Pk Pickle 6 weeks	40 Pi Picalilli 6 weeks	41 Sp Sweet pickle 6 weeks	42 Id Italian dressing 6 weeks	43 Td Thousand island dressing 6 weeks	44 Ma Mayonnaise 2 months	45 Sc Salad cream 2 months	46 Fs Flaxseed oil 2 months
47 Ca Cayenne pepper 3 months	48 Ch Chilli powder 3 months	49 Bm Brown mustard 3 months	50 Wa Wasabi 3 months	51 Ma Marmalade 6 months	52 Pb Peanut butter 6 months	53 Y Yeast extract 6 months	54 Ta Tahini 6 months	55 Ms Maple syrup 1 year	56 Pa Palm oil 1 year	57 P Peanut oil 1 year	58 So Soybean oil 1 year	59 Sf Sunflower oil 1 year
60 C Cocoa 1 year	61 Bb Black pepper 1 year	62 Ym Yellow mustard 18 months	63 Wv White wine vinegar 2 years	64 Cv Cider vinegar 2 years	65 W Worcester sauce 2 years	66 Sy Soy sauce 3 years	67 Ol Olive oil 4 years	68 Bv Balsamic vinegar 5 years	69 Mv Malt vinegar indefinite	70 H Honey indefinite	71 Sa Salt indefinite	72 Su Sugar indefinite

idea: Internet Apocryphal / source: Google

NATURE vs NURTURE

Your genes control everything. Hair colour. Behaviour. Intelligence. Personality. Sure, environment has a role, but it's your genes that rule you.

You learn pretty much everything you do. From standing and walking to talking and socializing. Your environment and your choices make you who you are...

Most behaviour is genetic. Genes for speech, empathy and even altruism all evolved when we lived as hunter-gatherers on the ancient grasslands of Africa.

The evidence for that ancient lifestyle is complete guesswork.

The proof is in the brain. It has evolved "modules" for all human abilities, even for religious experience!

Nah. Those "structures" could simply be projections of human interpretation on the brain. Behaviour isn't genetically evolved. We learn it.

Oh yeah? Animal breeders know it takes only a few generations of controlled mating to influence behaviours like fierceness or tameness in dogs.

Dogs, maybe. But complex human behaviour like musical ability or humour? C'mon. These are learnt. In fact, learning, we now know, changes the physical structure of the brain! So much for genes.

Genes change the brain too. And at a more fundamental level, before your so-called "choices" come in. Try "deciding" to override a genetic expression. You can't! Hah!

Most genetic expression, from traits to behaviours, are triggered by your environment. Nurture comes first!

Okay then, what about behavioural problems such as depression, mental illness and autism? They're all highly inheritable.

Yeah, it's fashionable to say that, yes. But, even after years of study, researchers have failed to turn up a

Ahhhhh but behavioural disorders like autism are highly inheritable. In identical twins, if one twin is autistic, the other has a 60% chance of being autistic. In non-identical twins the chance is only 5%. That goes for intelligence too.

In autism, maybe. But you can't then stretch it to all behaviour and certainly not intelligence. Intelligent parents *teach* their kids to be intelligent.

But don't intelligent parents also provide the genes for high IQ? Twins separated at birth are often remarkably similar in IQ and personality, even when they haven't met. This proves there are genetic influences for everything. Even taste in music!

Yeah, but if it was all genes, you'd expect identical twins to be 100% the same. Figures for IQ may be high. But it's way less, to non-existent, for other traits like personality.

But identical twins reared apart become more alike, even when they haven't met. That means that genes must shape our personalities.

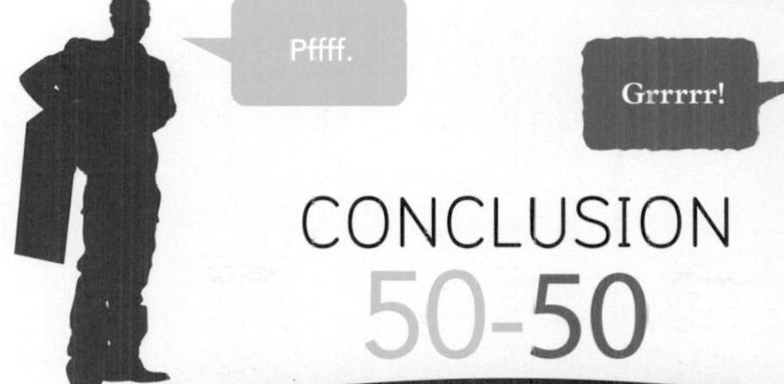

Hmmmmmm. Many studies of twins are flawed and biased. Often they just compare identical twins reared apart after birth. They don't use "controls" of unrelated people with the same background as the twins to check that age, gender, ethnicity and cultural environment are not also influencing personality. The whole field is biased.

Pffff.

Grrrrr!

CONCLUSION 50-50

Both nature and nurture each contribute (in arguable proportions) to who we are. They also "speak the same language". That is, they both change the structure of the brain. In summary, humans are dynamic creative organisms. Learning and experience amplify the effect of genes or behaviour.

source: Skeptic.com

Postmodernism

Postmodernism is pretty much a buzz word now. Anything – and everything – can be described as postmodern now. The design of a building. The samples used in a record. The layout of a page. The collective mood of a generation. Cultural or political fragmentation. The rise of blogging and crowd-wisdom. Anything that starts with the word "meta". But what does it mean?

In art, where it all began, it's a style of sorts. Ironic and parodying. Very playful and very knowing. Knowing of history, culture, and often knowing of itself. Postmodern art and entertainment is often self-conscious. It calls attention to itself as a piece of art, or a production, or something constructed. A character who knows they are a character in a novel, for example. Or even the appearance of an author in their own book. (Like me, David, writing this. Hello.)

Overall, postmodern art says there's no difference between refined and popular culture, "high" or "low" brow. It rejects genres and hierarchies. Instead, it embraces complexity, contradiction, ambiguity, diversity, interconnectedness, and criss-crossing referentiality.

The idea is: let's not pretend that art can make meaning or is even meaningful. Let's just play with nonsense.

All of this springs from the discovery of a new relationship to truth. In a postmodern perspective, truth is a not single thing "out there" to be discovered. Instead truth must be assembled or constructed. Sometimes, it's constructed visibly, from many different components (i.e. scientists gathering results of multiple studies). Other times, it happens invisibly by society, or by cultural mechanisms and other processes that can't be easily seen by the individual.

So when someone "speaks the truth", what they are saying is actually an assemblage of their schooling, their cultural background, and the thoughts and opinions they've absorbed from their environment. In a way, you could say that their culture is speaking through them.

For that reason, it becomes more accurate and safer, in postmodern times, to assemble truth with the help of other people, rather than just decide it independently.

A clear example of this is the scientific method. Any scientist can do an experiment and declare a discovery about the world. But teams of other scientists must verify or "peer-review" that truth before it's safe to accept it. The truth here has been assembled by many people.

All the time, though, there is an understanding that even this final "truth" may well just be temporary or convenient, a place-holder to be changed or binned later on. (Well, that *should* be the case. Even scientific discoveries have a tendency to harden into dogma.)

If you accept this key postmodern insight, then immediately it becomes impossible for any individual to have a superior belief. There's no such thing as "absolute truth". No one "knows" the truth. Or can have a better truth than someone else. If an individual – or a group, organization or government – does claims to have truth and declares that truth to you, they are likely to be attempting to overpower and control you.

Confusingly, these kinds of entities are known as "Modernist". Modernity is all about order and rationality. The more ordered a society is, Modernists believe, the better it functions. If "order" is superior, then anything that promotes "disorder" has to be wrong. Taken to an extreme, that means anything different from the norm – ideas, beliefs, people – must be excluded. Or even destroyed. In the history of Western culture this has usually meant anyone non-white, non-male, non-heterosexual and non-rational.

This is one reason why tension still erupts between holders of "absolute truth" (say the Church) and postmodern secular societies. Or between an entity like an undemocratic government which seeks to control its populace and the internet, a truly postmodern piece of technology. This is because postmodernity has a powerful weapon that can very easily and very quickly corrode Modernist structures built on "old-fashioned" absolute truth: *deconstruction*.

If all truth is constructed, then deconstruction becomes useful. Really useful. If you deconstruct something, its meanings, intentions and agendas separate and rise to the surface very quickly – and everything quickly unravels.

Take a novel, for example. You can deconstruct the structure of the text, and the personality of the characters. Then you can deconstruct the author's life story, their psychological background, and their culture and see how that influenced the text. If you keep going, you can start on the structure of human language and thought. Beyond that, a vast layer of human symbols. Beyond that ... well, you can just keep going...

Belief systems and modernist structures protect themselves from threats like deconstruction with "grand narratives". These are compelling stories to explain and justify why a certain belief system exists. They work to gloss over and mask the contradictions, instabilities and general "scariness" inherent in nature and human life.

Liberate the entire working class. Peace on Earth. There is one true God. Hollywood is one big happy family. History is progress. One day we will know everything. These are all grand narratives.

All modern societies – even those based on science – depend on these myths. Postmodernism rejects them on principle. Instead it goes for "mini-narratives", stories that explain small local events – all with an awareness that any situation, no matter how small, reflects in some way the global pattern of things. Think global, act local, basically.

So a postmodern society, unglossed-over by a grand narrative, must embrace the values of postmodernity as its key values. That means that complexity, diversity, contradiction, ambiguity, and interconnectedness all become central. In social terms that means a lack of obvious hierarchies (equal rights for all), embracing diversity (multi-culturalism), and that all voices should be heard (consensus). Interconnectedness is reflected in our technology and communications. In the 21st century anything that cannot be stored by a computer ceases to be knowledge.

That's the goal, anyway. There are pitfalls. Runaway postmodernism creates a grey goo of no-meaning. Infinite consensus creates paralysis. Over-connection leads to saturation. Too much diversity leads to disconnection. Complexity to confusion.

So in the midst of all this confusion and noise and diversity, without a grand narrative, who are you? Postmodern personal values are not moral but instead values of participation, self-expression, creativity. The focus of spirituality shifts from security in absolute given truth to a search for significance in a chaotic world. The idea that there is anything stable or permanent disappears. The floor drops away. And you are left there, playing with nonsense.

source: constructed from Wikipedia, an essay by Mary Klages, University of Colorado, Wisegeek.com

Death Spiral

You're going to go one way. Which way?

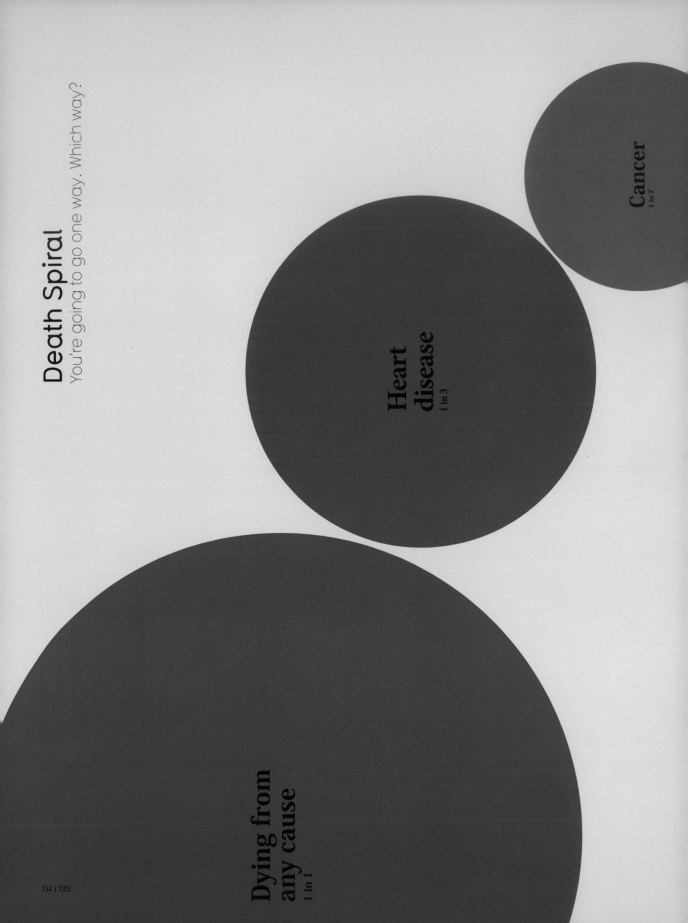

Dying from any cause
1 in 1

Heart disease
1 in 3

Cancer
1 in 7

Stroke
1 in 23

Bus/train accident
1 in 77

Ageing sun engulfs Earth

Medical error (hospital)
1 in 300

Assault by firearm
1 in 325

House fire
1 in 1431

Diabetes
1 in 4096

Freak lawnmower accident
1 in 5300

Passive smoking
1 in 7895

Electrocution (home)
1 in 9308

Suicide
1 in 9380

Assault
1 in 16,421

Hernia
1 in 16,742

Murder
1 in 18,000

Drug overdose
1 in 18,125

Car accident
1 in 18,585

Flu
1 in 19,415

Falling down
1 in 20,666

Skin cancer
1 in 29,500

Power-line accident
1 in 40,103

Super volcano
Destroys climate

Tsunami (coastal dweller)
1 in 50,000

Walking down the street
1 in 52,000

Food poisoning
1 in 55,600

Avalanche
1 in 78,535

Accidental drowning
1 in 79,065

Fire
1 in 81,524

Choking
1 in 97,000

Explosion
1 in 107,787

Magnetic Field Reversal
Earth fried by cosmic radiation

Dog attack
1 in 147,717

Act of nature
1 in 225,107

Runaway climate change
Earth cooked

Falling off a boat
1 in 400,900

Freezing
1 in 469,000

Asteroid impact
1 in 500,000

Bicycle accident
1 in 578,000

Terrorist attack (overseas)
1 in 650,000

Drowning in the bath
1 in 685,000

Choking on your own vomit
1 in 740,000

Heat stroke
1 in 950,000

Fireworks accident
1 in 1,000,000

Asteroid collision
Seismic shock wave destroys us

Falling out of bed
1 in 72,000,000

Falling off a ladder
1 in 2,300,000

Lightning
1 in 2,320,000

Flood
We all drown

Legal execution
1 in 3,441,325

Ozone layer destruction
UV radiation kills all life

Nuclear accident
1 in 10,000,000

Global nuclear war
That was our planet, you mani

Plane crash
1 in 11,000,000

Bee sting
1 in 15,000,000

Bubonic plague
1 in 30,000,000

Super virus
Super ill

Ignition of nightwear
1 in 30,589,556

Galactic magnetic cloud collapses
Crushing the planet

Wandering black hole
Tears planet apart

Mountain lion attack
1 in 32,000,000

Freak solar flare
Fries us all

Grey goo
Runaway nanotech eats us

Blogging
1 in 35,000,000

Mad Cow Disease
1 in 40,000,000

Amusement park accident
1 in 72,300,000

SARS
1 in 100,000,000

Gamma ray burst
Nearby dying star irradiates us

Cybernetic revolution
All hail our new robotic overlords

Hadron Collider accident
Oops! Scientists create a black hole

Alien invasion
All hail our new extraterrestrial overlords

Falling coconut
1 in 250,000,000

Omega Point
Storage capacity of universe hit

New Ice Age
Planet freezes

Shark attack
1 in 578,000,000

Meteor landing on your house
1 in 182, 139,00,000

Biblical apocalypse
Jesus returns for Judgement Day

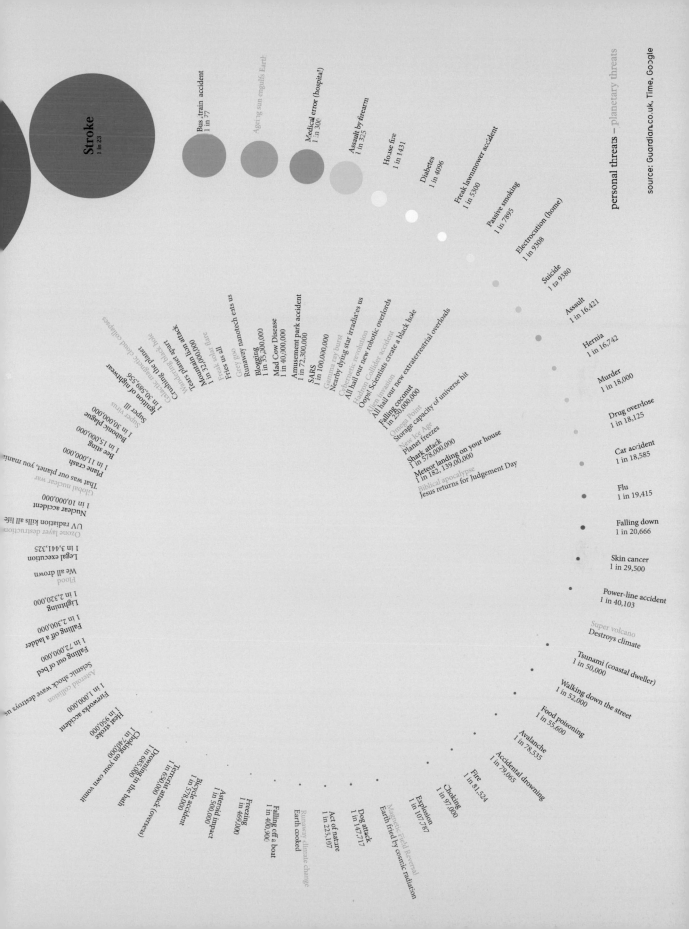

personal threats – planetary threats

source: Guardian.co.uk, Time, Google

Google Insights

The intensity of certain search terms compared

Beer vs Wine

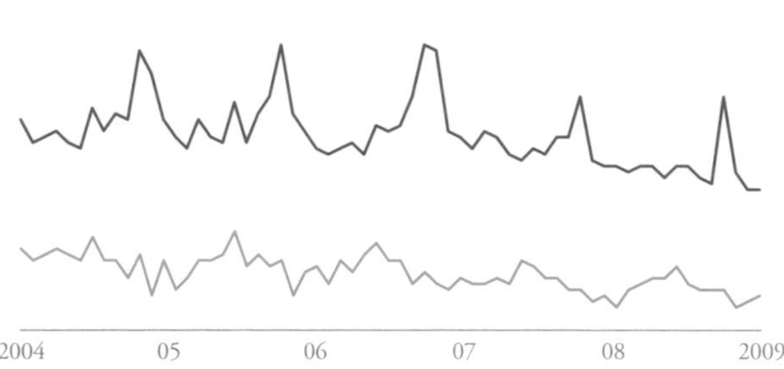
2004
05
06
07
08
2009

Lipstick vs Recession

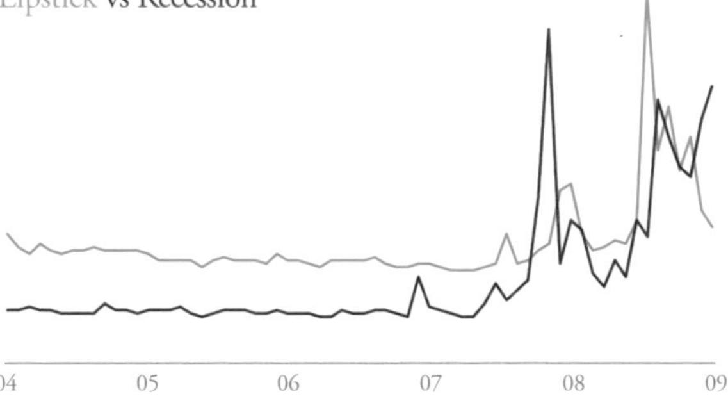
04
05
06
07
08
09

Microsoft vs Apple

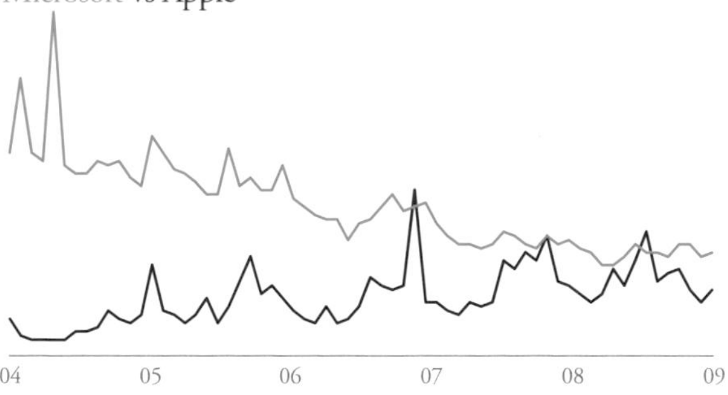
04
05
06
07
08
09

Cornflakes vs Muesli vs Porridge

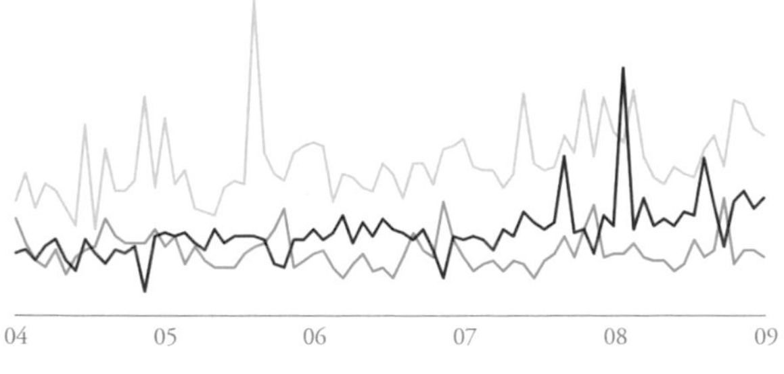
04
05
06
07
08
09

Tea vs Coffee

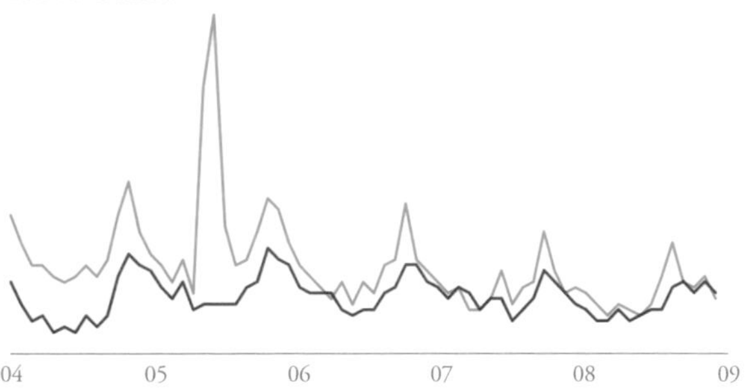
04
05
06
07
08
09

Marriage vs Divorce

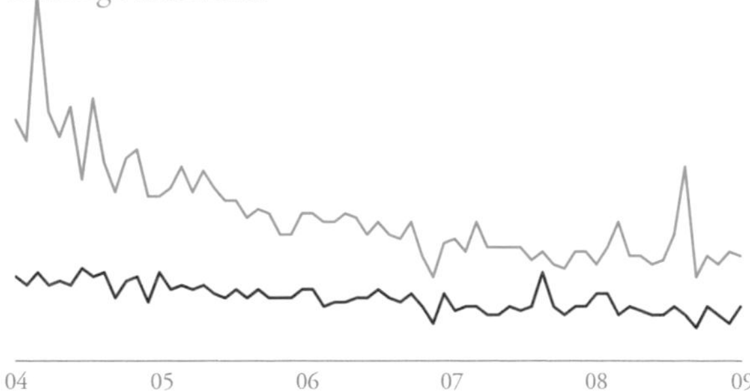
04
05
06
07
08
09

MySpace vs Facebook

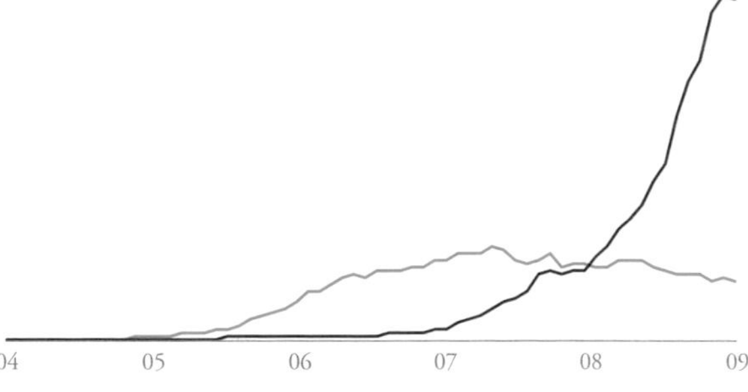
04
05
06
07
08
09

Cornflakes vs Muesli vs Porridge vs Toast

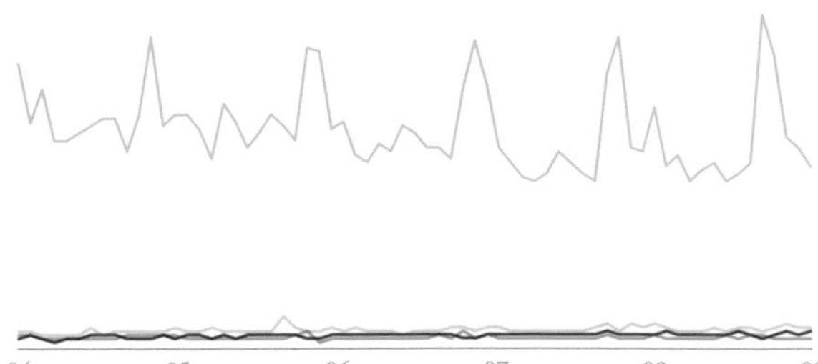
04
05
06
07
08
09

What's Better than Sex?

PTO for the answer

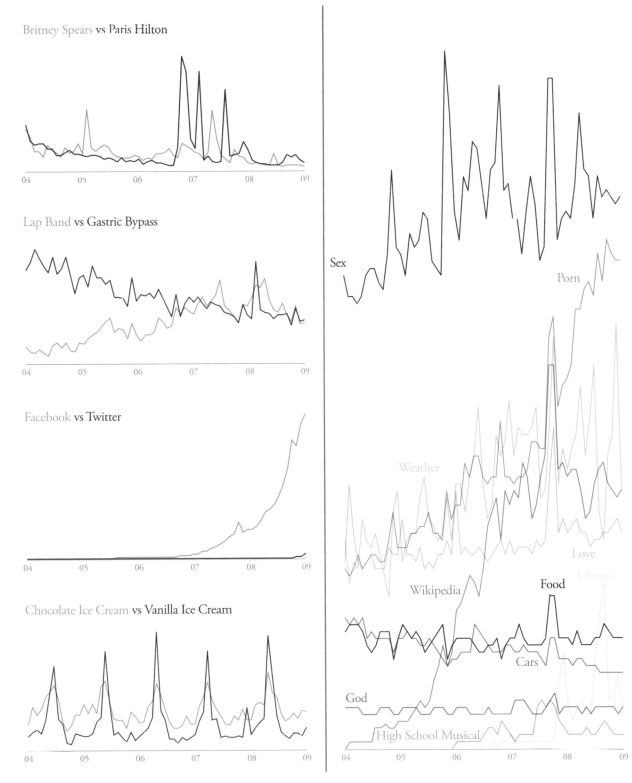

Britney Spears vs Paris Hilton

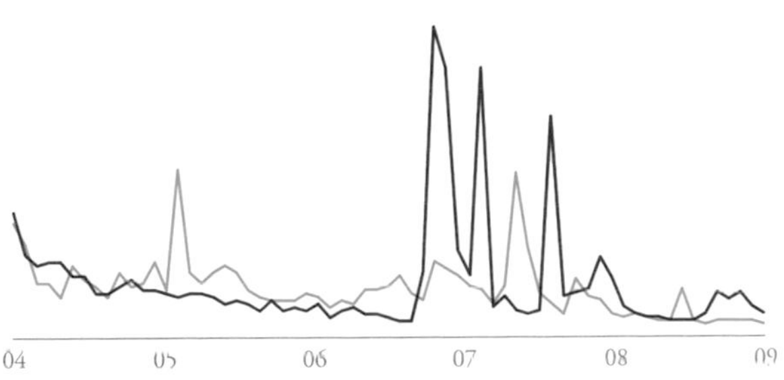
04
05
06
07
08
09

Lap Band vs Gastric Bypass

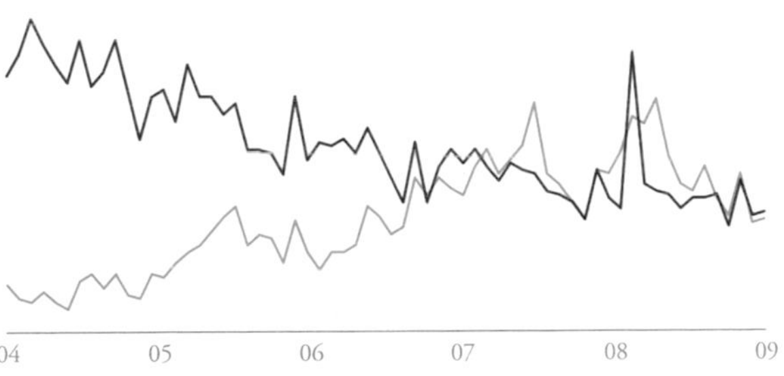
04
05
06
07
08
09

Facebook vs Twitter

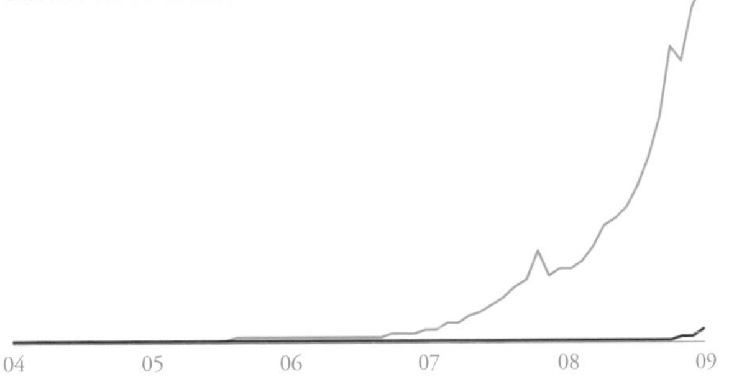
04
05
06
07
08
09

Chocolate Ice Cream vs Vanilla Ice Cream

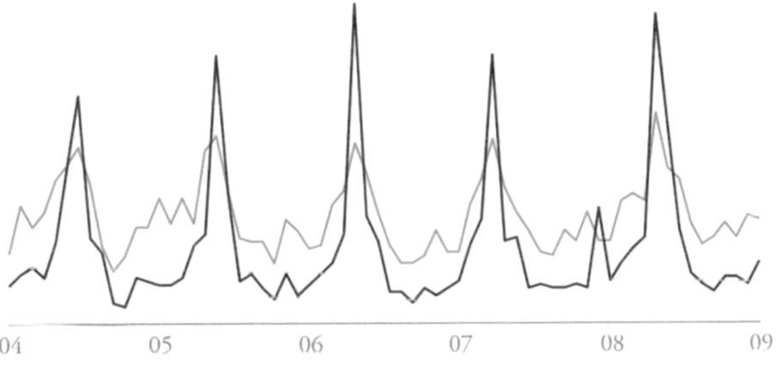
04
05
06
07
08
09

Sex

Porn

Weather

Love

Obama

Wikipedia

Food

Cars

God

High School Musical

04 05 06 07 08 09

source: Google Insights

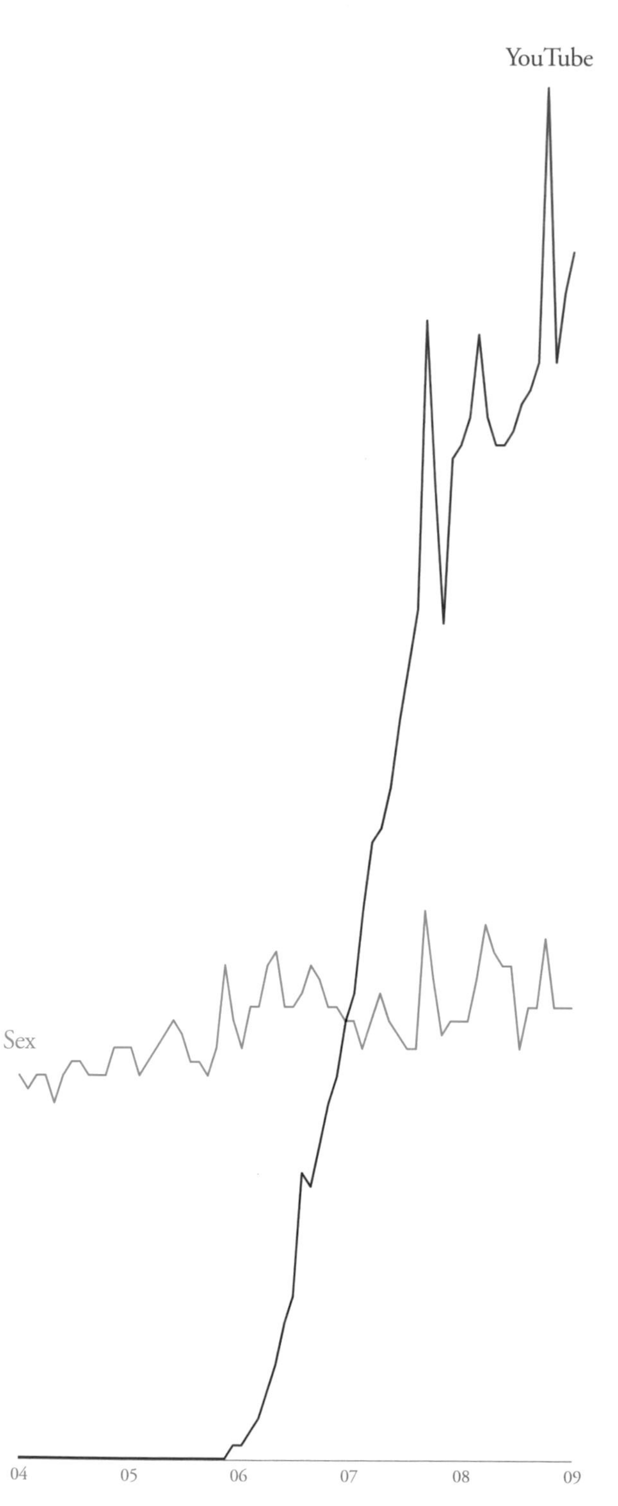
YouTube
Sex
04
05
06
07
08
09

Kyoto Targets

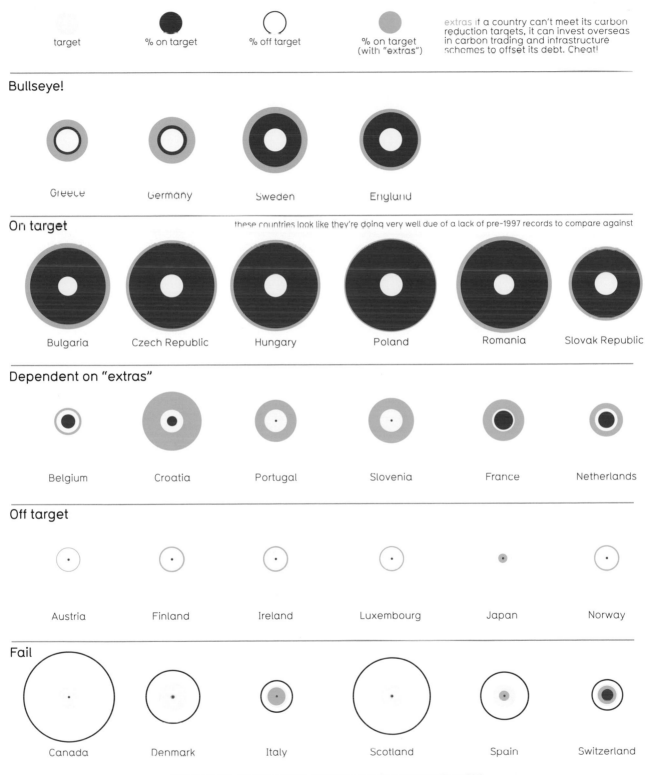

target

% on target

% off target

% on target (with "extras")

extras if a country can't meet its carbon reduction targets, it can invest overseas in carbon trading and infrastructure schemes to offset its debt. Cheat!

Bullseye!

Greece

Germany

Sweden

England

On target

these countries look like they're doing very well due of a lack of pre-1997 records to compare against

Bulgaria

Czech Republic

Hungary

Poland

Romania

Slovak Republic

Dependent on "extras"

Belgium

Croatia

Portugal

Slovenia

France

Netherlands

Off target

Austria

Finland

Ireland

Luxembourg

Japan

Norway

Fail

Canada

Denmark

Italy

Scotland

Spain

Switzerland

Despite Kyoto, the EU's carbon emmissions has increased by 1% by 2012

source: European Environment Agency

The Varieties of Romantic Relationship

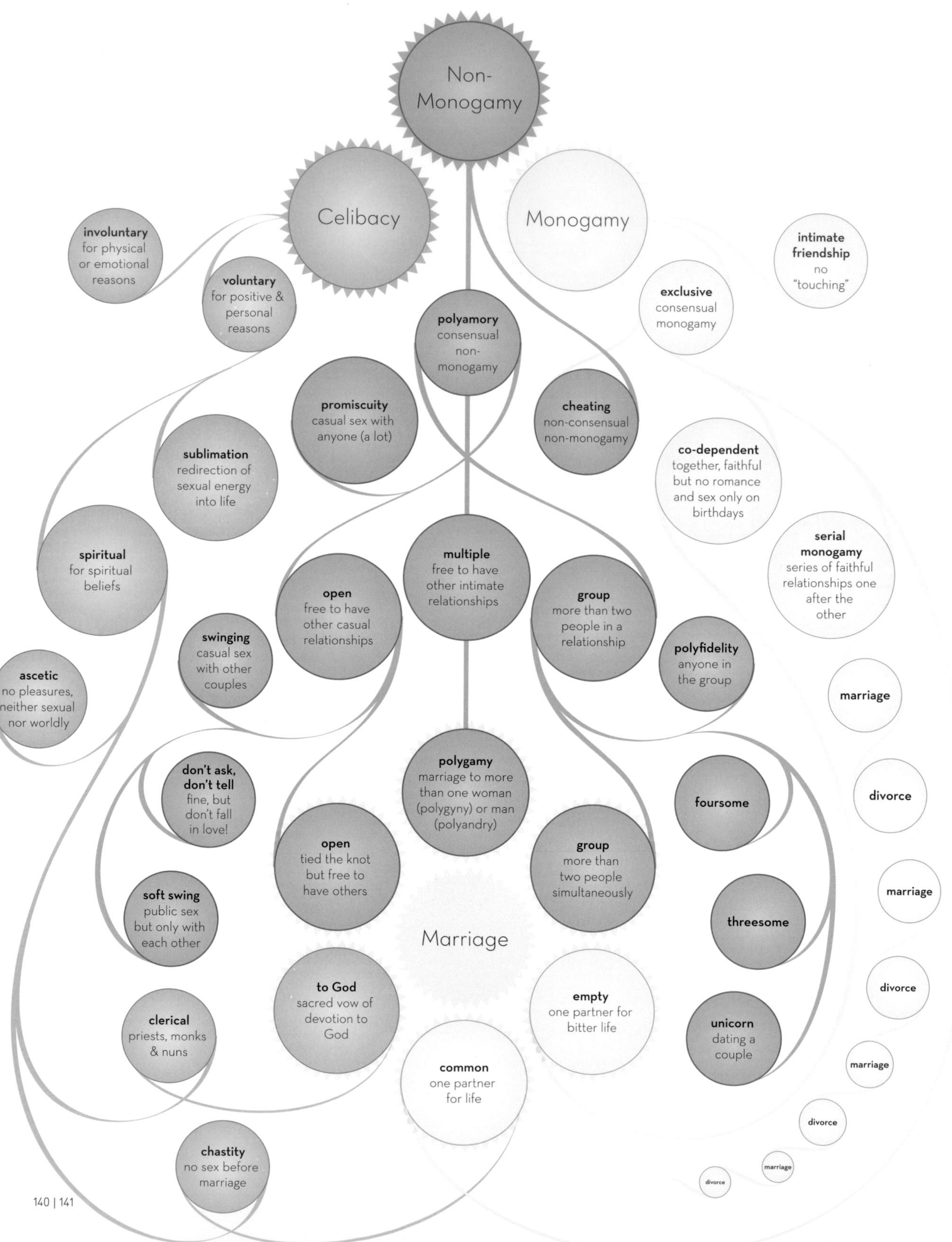
Non-Monogamy
Celibacy
Monogamy
involuntary for physical or emotional reasons
voluntary for positive & personal reasons
intimate friendship no "touching"
exclusive consensual monogamy
polyamory consensual non-monogamy
promiscuity casual sex with anyone (a lot)
cheating non-consensual non-monogamy
sublimation redirection of sexual energy into life
co-dependent together, faithful but no romance and sex only on birthdays
spiritual for spiritual beliefs
multiple free to have other intimate relationships
serial monogamy series of faithful relationships one after the other
open free to have other casual relationships
group more than two people in a relationship
swinging casual sex with other couples
polyfidelity anyone in the group
ascetic no pleasures, neither sexual nor worldly
marriage
don't ask, don't tell fine, but don't fall in love!
polygamy marriage to more than one woman (polygyny) or man (polyandry)
foursome
divorce
open tied the knot but free to have others
group more than two people simultaneously
marriage
soft swing public sex but only with each other
threesome
Marriage
to God sacred vow of devotion to God
empty one partner for bitter life
divorce
clerical priests, monks & nuns
unicorn dating a couple
marriage
common one partner for life
divorce
chastity no sex before marriage
marriage
divorce

The Evolution of Marriage in the West

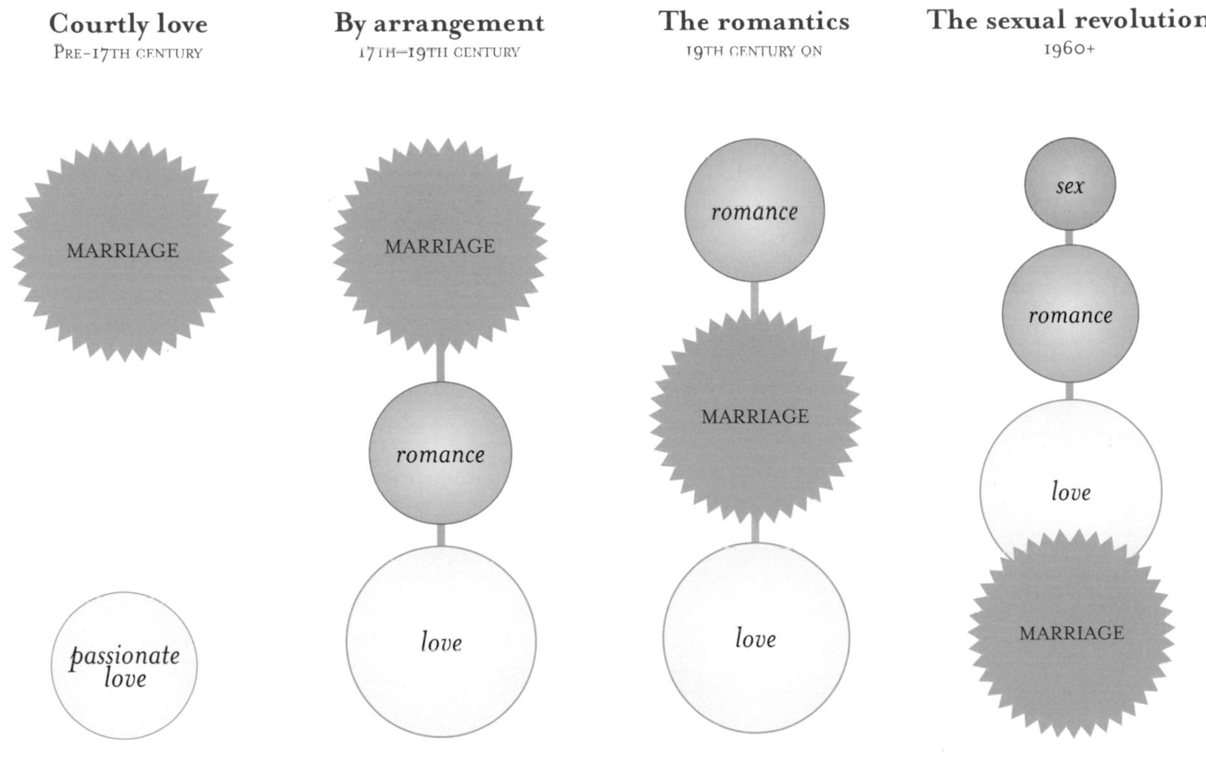

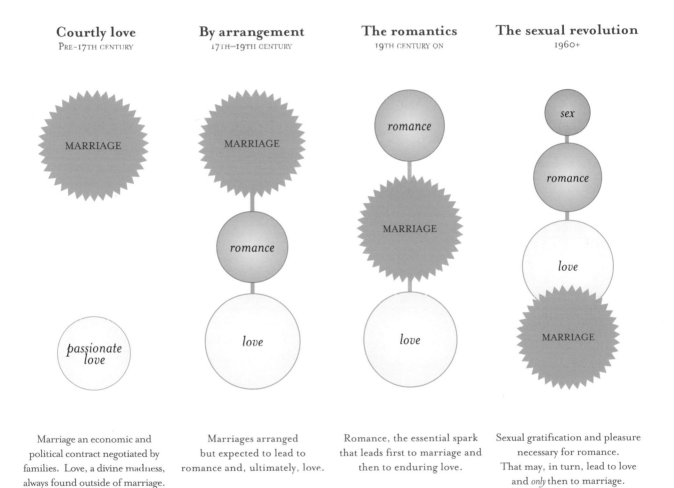

Courtly love
Pre-17th century
By arrangement
17th–19th century
The romantics
19th century on
The sexual revolution
1960+
MARRIAGE
passionate love
MARRIAGE
romance
love
romance
MARRIAGE
love
sex
romance
love
MARRIAGE

Marriage an economic and political contract negotiated by families. Love, a divine madness, always found outside of marriage.

Marriages arranged but expected to lead to romance and, ultimately, love.

Romance, the essential spark that leads first to marriage and then to enduring love.

Sexual gratification and pleasure necessary for romance. That may, in turn, lead to love and *only* then to marriage.

source: Wikipedia

30 Years Makes a Difference

LAKE CHAD

THE ARAL SEA

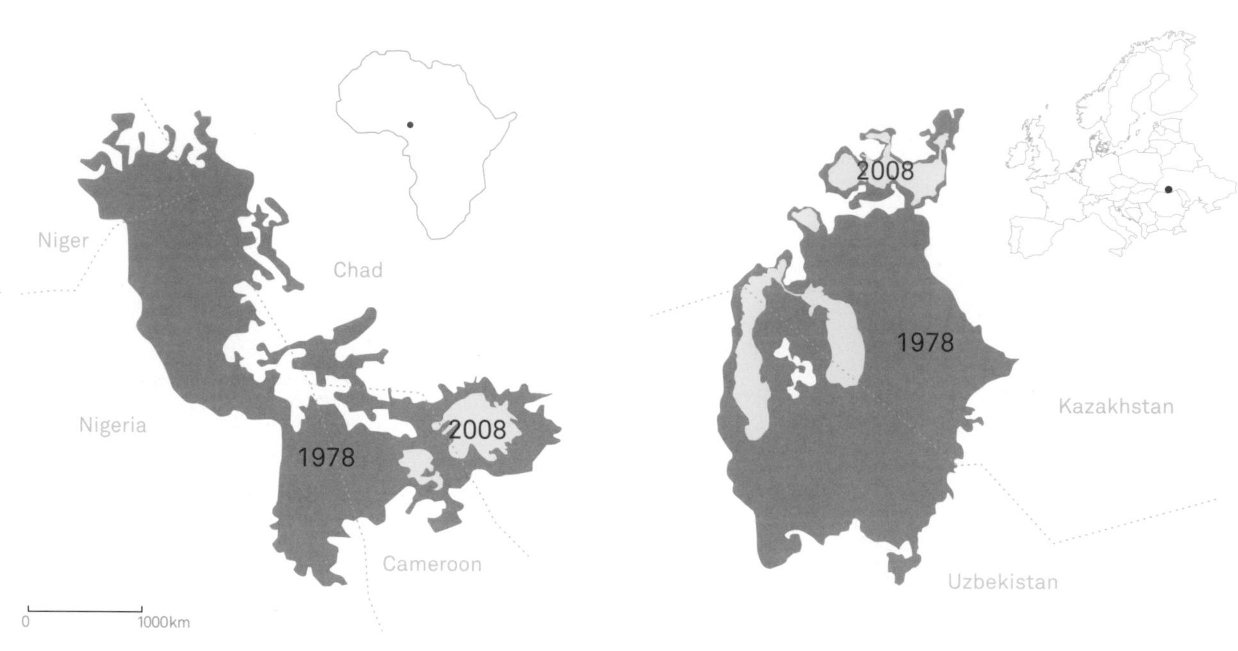
Niger
Chad
Nigeria
1978
2008
Cameroon
0
1000km
2008
1978
Kazakhstan
Uzbekistan

OZONE HOLE

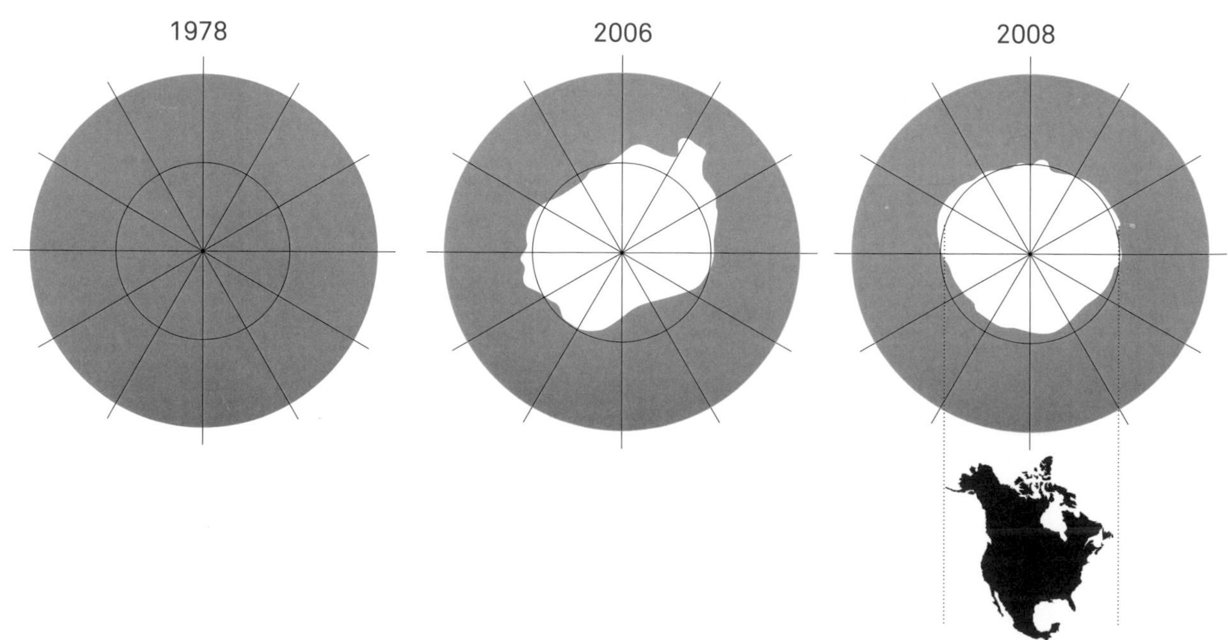
1978
2006
2008

NORTH POLAR ICE CAP

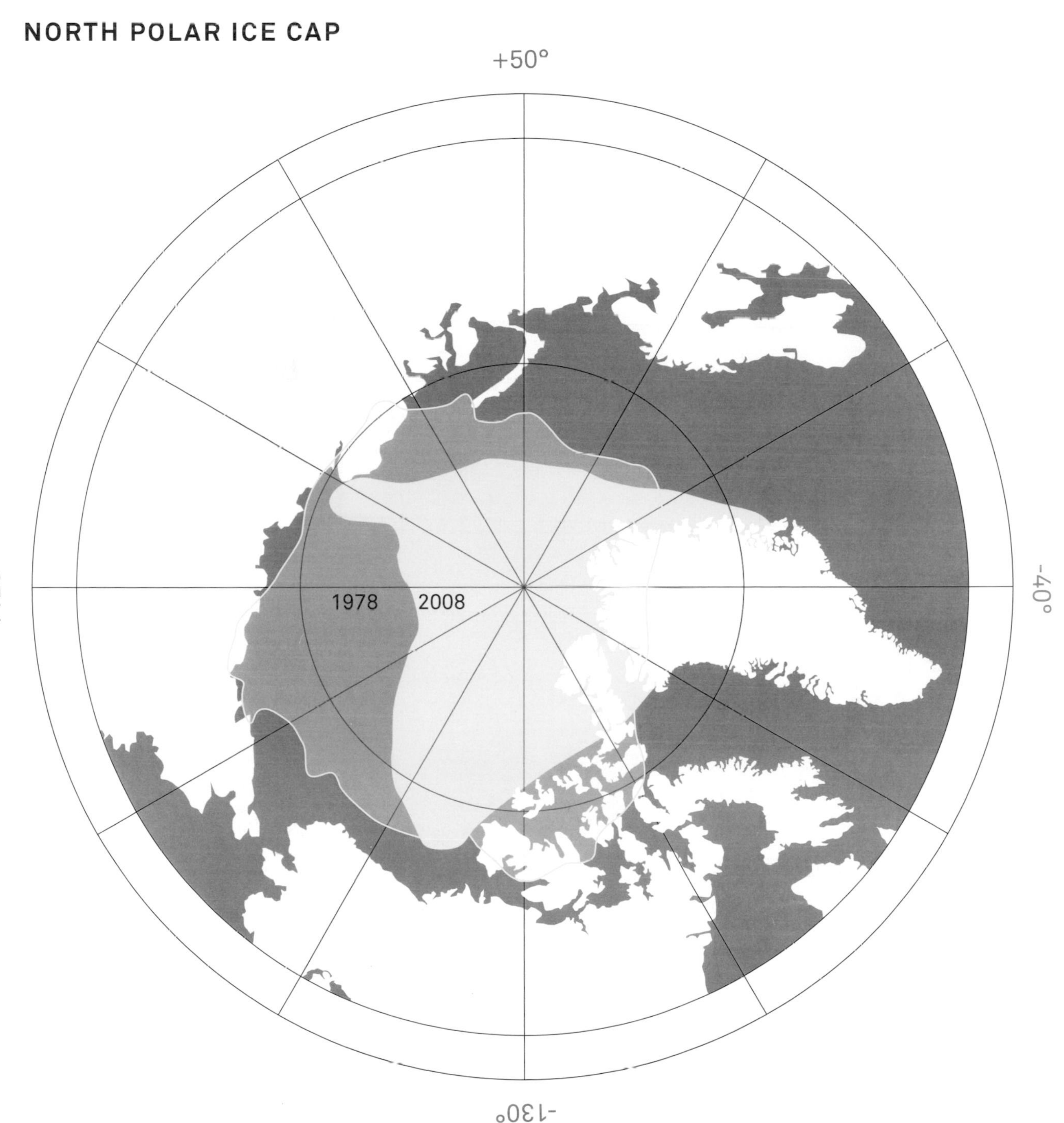
+50°
+120
-40°
-130°
1978
2008

source: NASA

AQUARIUS
CAPRICORN
SAGITTARIUS
SCORPIO
FEB 20 - MAR
PISCES
JAN 21 - FEB 19
AQUARIUS
DEC 23 - JAN 20
CA'CORN
NOV 23 - DEC 22
S'TTARIUS
OCT 24 - NOV 22
SCORPIO
SEP 24 - OCT
LIBRA

Horoscoped

Most common words

TAURUS
GEMINI
CANCER
LEO
AR 21 - APR 20
ARIES
APR 21 - MAY 21
TAURUS
MAY 22 - JUN 21
GEMINI
JUN 22 - JUL 23
CANCER
JUL 24 - AUG 23
LEO
UG 24 - SEP 23
VIRGO
nothing everything stop easy interested remember either lot open life plan keep comes moment needs else making sure friend maybe family worrying change usual enjoy already feel best matter help better nice situation ready love mind energy eyes
issues important able matter love change help fun energy sure others talk plans life maybe news mind keep relationships certainly party situation hard friends feel ready best listen mood easy better taking idea making comes stay
situation family home moment friends surprised mind maybe love care life feel change mood ready usual news world head sure keep plans else making energy turn best able better
away taking best charm share secret comes far help expect energy life hard waiting fun matter sure mind help past comes far everything keep exactly moment love world looking lot better ready needs turn care relationships plans matter feel able
situation others oh comes friends world far change help feel life plans exactly care energy ready love problem sure fun easy everything better mind busy whatever hard moment
plans best friends fun change perfect moment energy turn feel life comes takes world exactly love sure keep everything situation matter ready totally along
red words unique to each star sign
source: 60,000 scraped star sign predictions

Better than Bacon

The real centre of the Hollywood universe

A study of over 1 million films and actors at the website oracleofbacon.org has revealed a series of actors who are way better connectors for the game Six Degrees of Kevin Bacon than Mr Bacon himself.

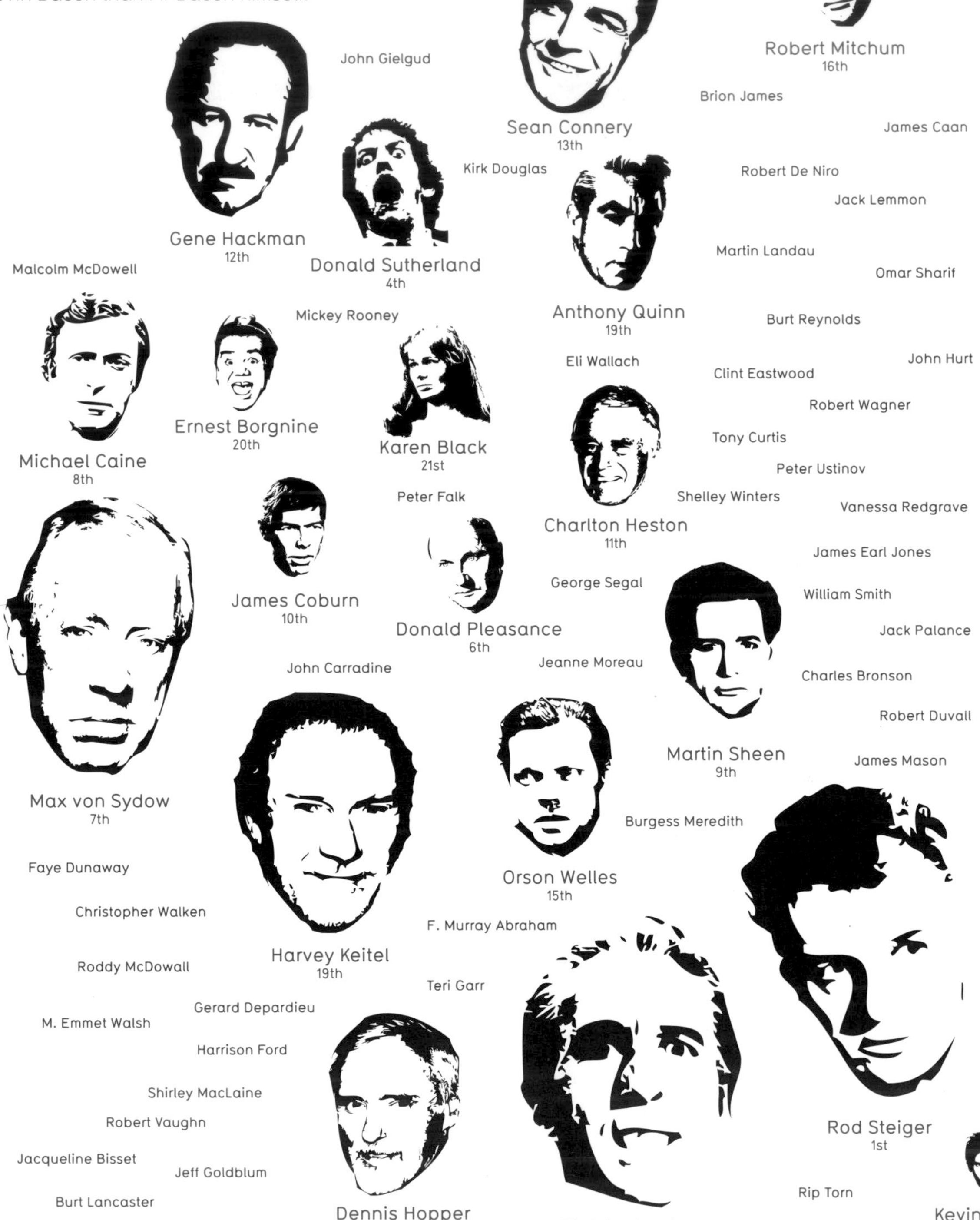

Robert Mitchum
16th
John Gielgud
Brion James
Sean Connery
13th
James Caan
Kirk Douglas
Robert De Niro
Jack Lemmon
Gene Hackman
12th
Donald Sutherland
4th
Martin Landau
Malcolm McDowell
Omar Sharif
Anthony Quinn
19th
Mickey Rooney
Burt Reynolds
Eli Wallach
John Hurt
Clint Eastwood
Robert Wagner
Ernest Borgnine
20th
Tony Curtis
Karen Black
21st
Michael Caine
8th
Peter Ustinov
Peter Falk
Shelley Winters
Vanessa Redgrave
Charlton Heston
11th
James Earl Jones
George Segal
William Smith
James Coburn
10th
Donald Pleasance
6th
Jack Palance
Jeanne Moreau
John Carradine
Charles Bronson
Robert Duvall
Martin Sheen
9th
James Mason
Max von Sydow
7th
Burgess Meredith
Faye Dunaway
Orson Welles
15th
Christopher Walken
F. Murray Abraham
Harvey Keitel
19th
Roddy McDowall
Teri Garr
Gerard Depardieu
M. Emmet Walsh
Harrison Ford
Shirley MacLaine
Robert Vaughn
Rod Steiger
1st
Jacqueline Bisset
Jeff Goldblum
Rip Torn
Burt Lancaster
Dennis Hopper
3rd
Christopher Lee
2nd
Kevin Bacon
1094th
Paul Newman

source: OracleofBacon.org

Calculating the Chances

Five-year cancer survival rates

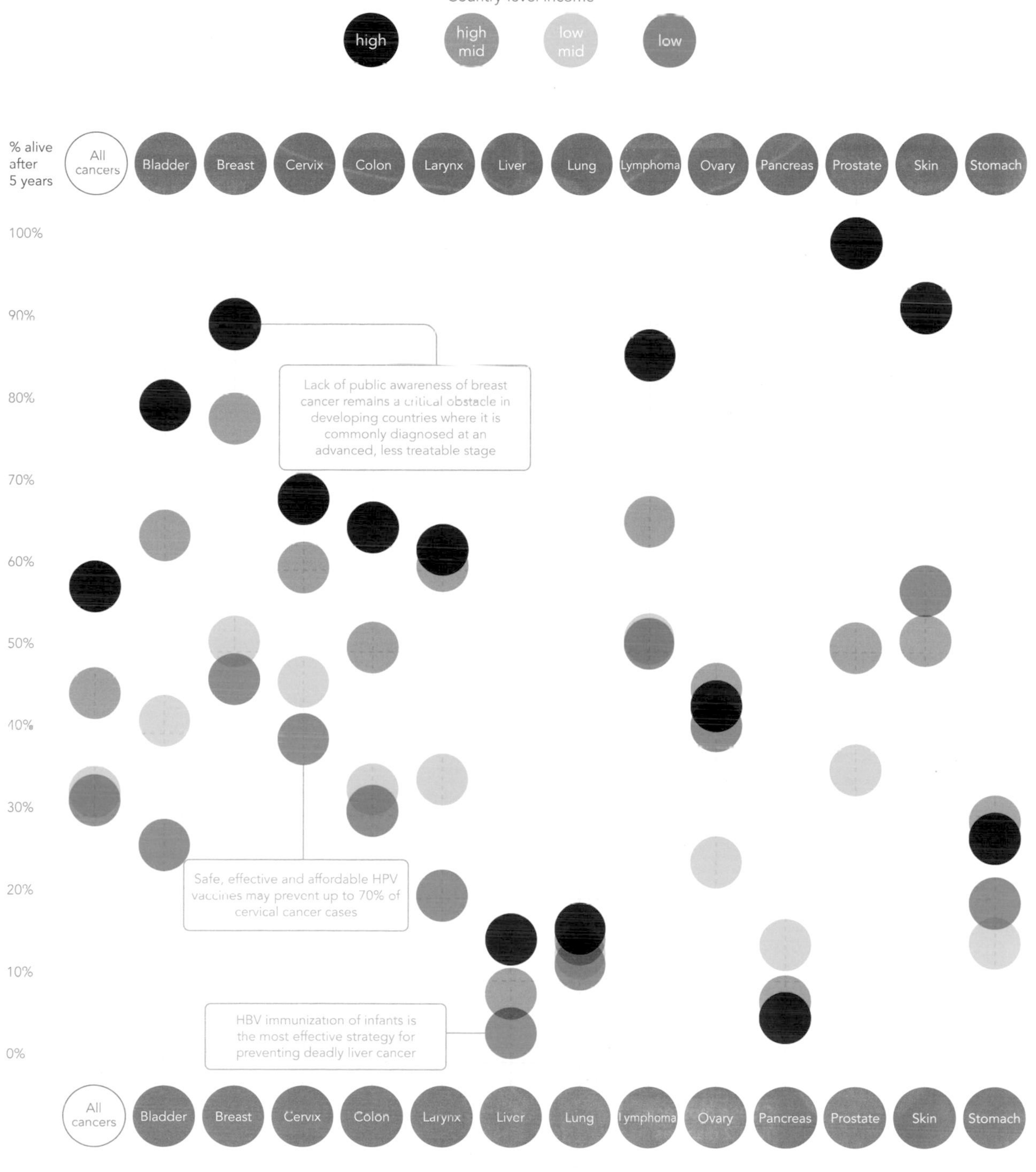

Country-level income
high
high mid
low mid
low
% alive after 5 years
All cancers
Bladder
Breast
Cervix
Colon
Larynx
Liver
Lung
Lymphoma
Ovary
Pancreas
Prostate
Skin
Stomach
100%
90%
80%
70%
60%
50%
40%
30%
20%
10%
0%
Lack of public awareness of breast cancer remains a critical obstacle in developing countries where it is commonly diagnosed at an advanced, less treatable stage
Safe, effective and affordable HPV vaccines may prevent up to 70% of cervical cancer cases
HBV immunization of infants is the most effective strategy for preventing deadly liver cancer

note: lack of colour spot means missing data // data: bit.ly/cancerburden
source: International Agency for Research on Cancer, UK Office for National Statistics, National Cancer Institute

Some Things You Can't Avoid

Characteristics and behaviours that increase the likelihood of certain ailments

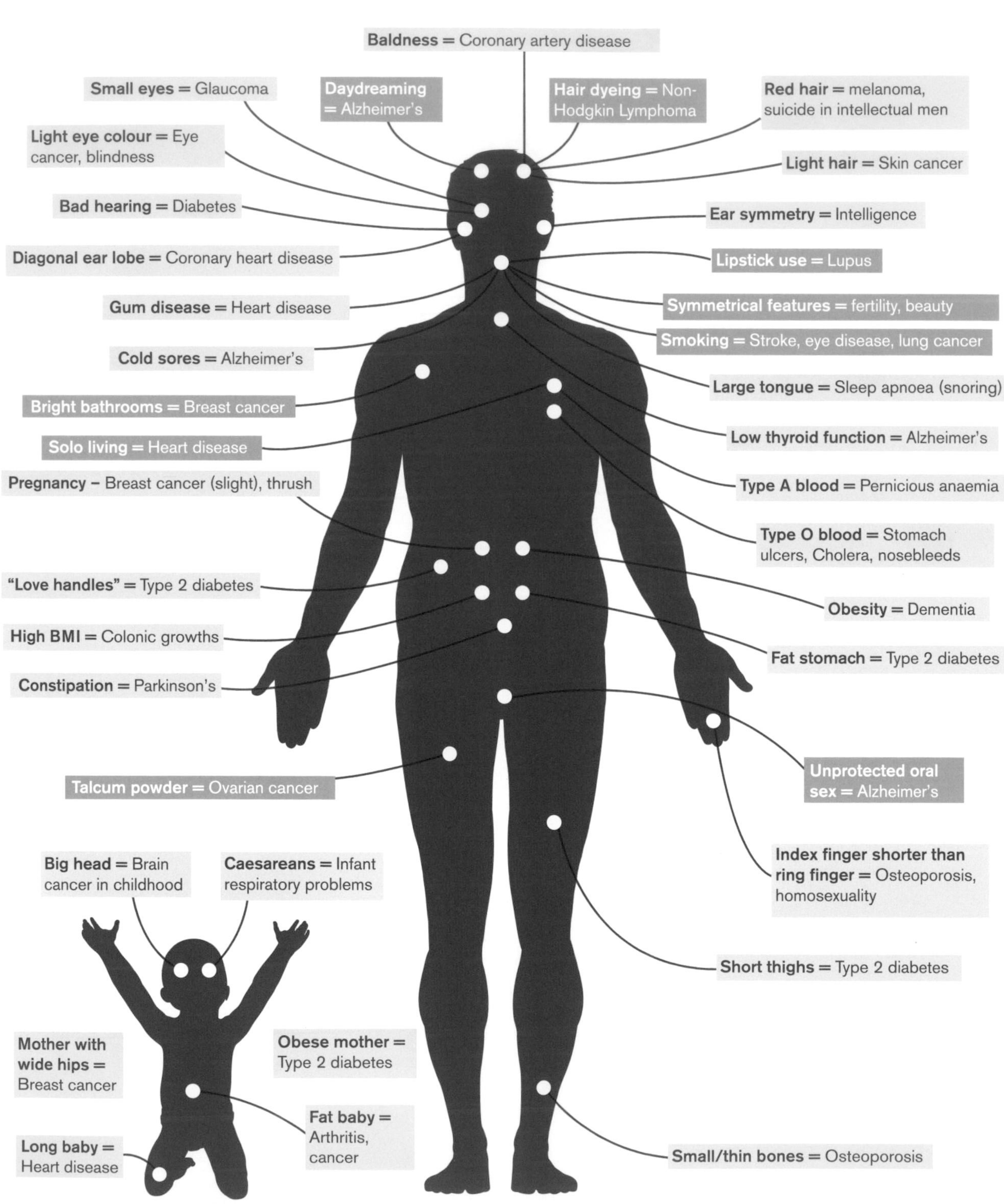

Baldness = Coronary artery disease
Small eyes = Glaucoma
Daydreaming = Alzheimer's
Hair dyeing = Non-Hodgkin Lymphoma
Red hair = melanoma, suicide in intellectual men
Light eye colour = Eye cancer, blindness
Light hair = Skin cancer
Bad hearing = Diabetes
Ear symmetry = Intelligence
Diagonal ear lobe = Coronary heart disease
Lipstick use = Lupus
Gum disease = Heart disease
Symmetrical features = fertility, beauty
Smoking = Stroke, eye disease, lung cancer
Cold sores = Alzheimer's
Large tongue = Sleep apnoea (snoring)
Bright bathrooms = Breast cancer
Low thyroid function = Alzheimer's
Solo living = Heart disease
Type A blood = Pernicious anaemia
Pregnancy – Breast cancer (slight), thrush
Type O blood = Stomach ulcers, Cholera, nosebleeds
"Love handles" = Type 2 diabetes
Obesity = Dementia
High BMI = Colonic growths
Fat stomach = Type 2 diabetes
Constipation = Parkinson's
Unprotected oral sex = Alzheimer's
Talcum powder = Ovarian cancer
Index finger shorter than ring finger = Osteoporosis, homosexuality
Big head = Brain cancer in childhood
Caesareans = Infant respiratory problems
Short thighs = Type 2 diabetes
Mother with wide hips = Breast cancer
Obese mother = Type 2 diabetes
Fat baby = Arthritis, cancer
Long baby = Heart disease
Small/thin bones = Osteoporosis

Or decrease the likelihood

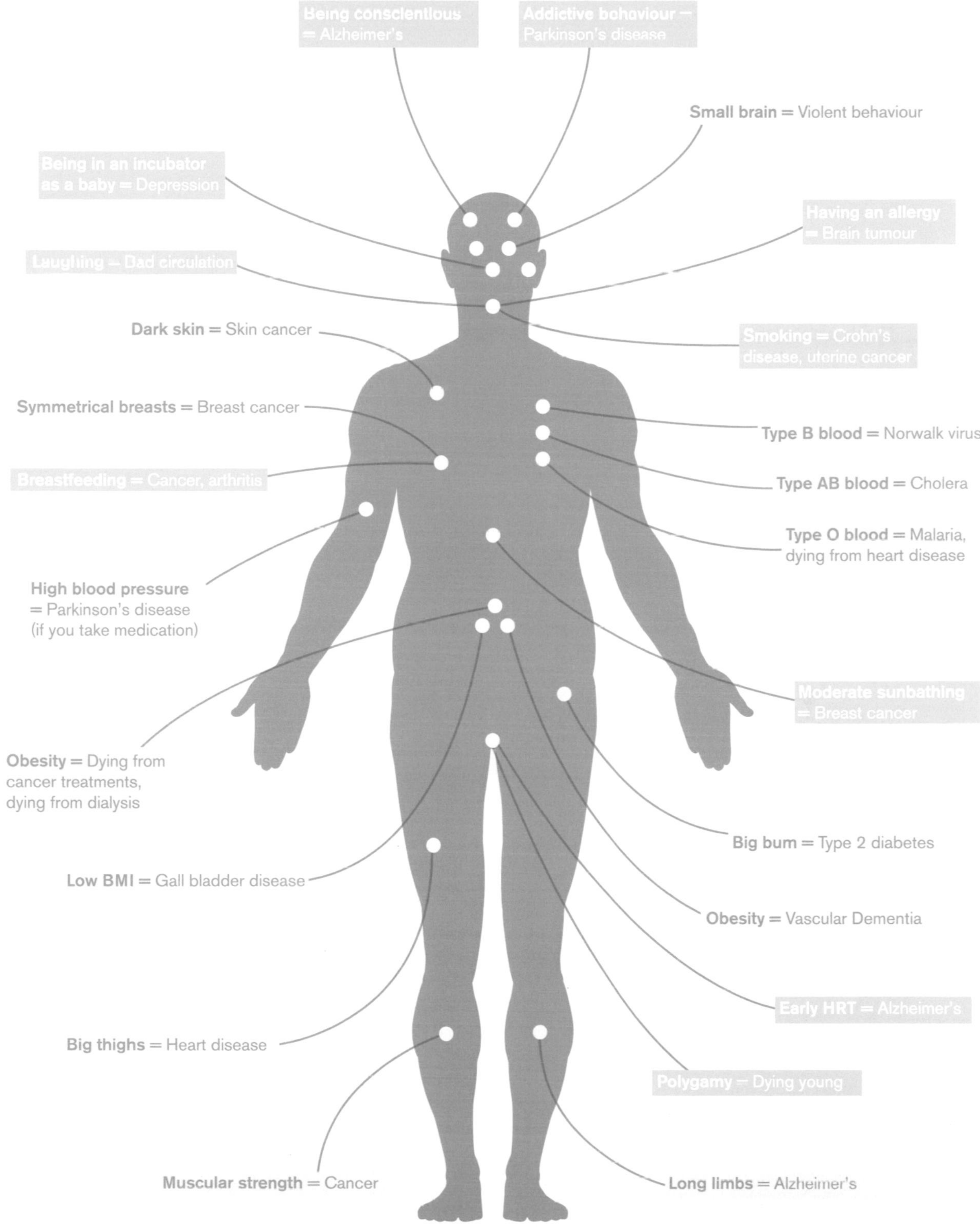

Being conscientious = Alzheimer's
Addictive behaviour = Parkinson's disease
Small brain = Violent behaviour
Being in an incubator as a baby = Depression
Having an allergy = Brain tumour
Laughing = Bad circulation
Dark skin = Skin cancer
Smoking = Crohn's disease, uterine cancer
Symmetrical breasts = Breast cancer
Type B blood = Norwalk virus
Breastfeeding = Cancer, arthritis
Type AB blood = Cholera
Type O blood = Malaria, dying from heart disease
High blood pressure = Parkinson's disease (if you take medication)
Moderate sunbathing = Breast cancer
Obesity = Dying from cancer treatments, dying from dialysis
Big bum = Type 2 diabetes
Low BMI = Gall bladder disease
Obesity = Vascular Dementia
Early HRT = Alzheimer's
Big thighs = Heart disease
Polygamy = Dying young
Muscular strength = Cancer
Long limbs = Alzheimer's

source: PubMed, Medscape.com, HealthDay, biomedicine.org, eupedia.com, Reuters, yale.edu, NHSdirect.nhs.uk

By Descent

Decreased risk – increased risk

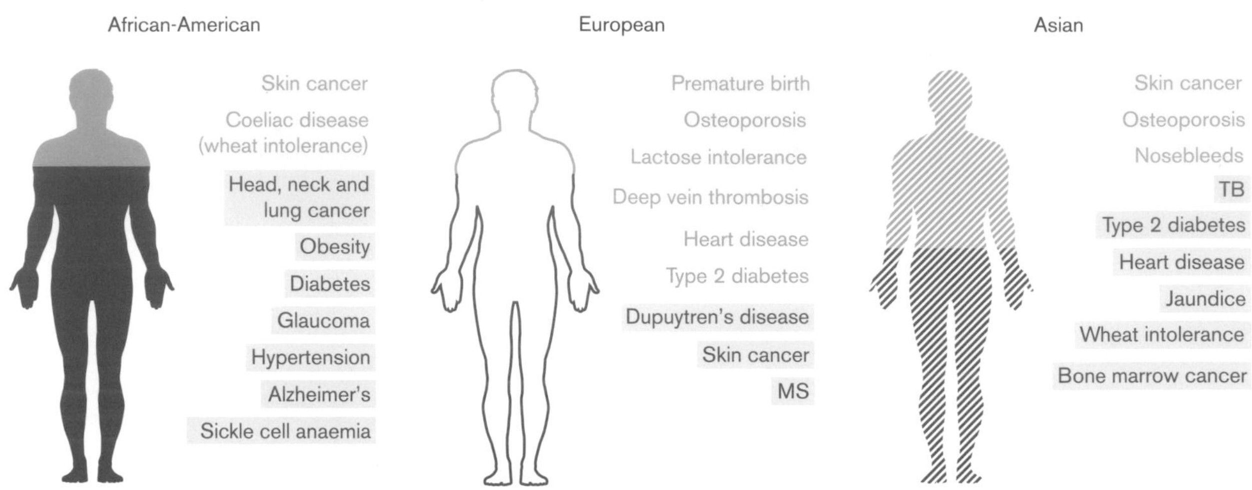
African-American
Skin cancer
Coeliac disease (wheat intolerance)
Head, neck and lung cancer
Obesity
Diabetes
Glaucoma
Hypertension
Alzheimer's
Sickle cell anaemia
European
Premature birth
Osteoporosis
Lactose intolerance
Deep vein thrombosis
Heart disease
Type 2 diabetes
Dupuytren's disease
Skin cancer
MS
Asian
Skin cancer
Osteoporosis
Nosebleeds
TB
Type 2 diabetes
Heart disease
Jaundice
Wheat intolerance
Bone marrow cancer

By Gender

Decreased risk – increased risk

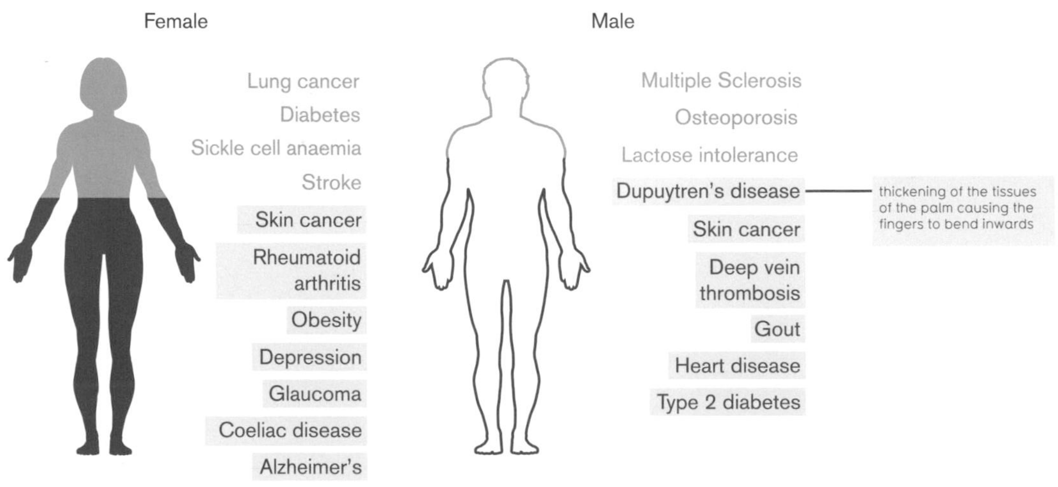
Female
Lung cancer
Diabetes
Sickle cell anaemia
Stroke
Skin cancer
Rheumatoid arthritis
Obesity
Depression
Glaucoma
Coeliac disease
Alzheimer's
Male
Multiple Sclerosis
Osteoporosis
Lactose intolerance
Dupuytren's disease
thickening of the tissues of the palm causing the fingers to bend inwards
Skin cancer
Deep vein thrombosis
Gout
Heart disease
Type 2 diabetes

source: PubMed, Medscape.com, HealthDay, biomedicine.org, eupedia.com, Reuters, yale.edu, NHSdirect.nhs.uk

Body By

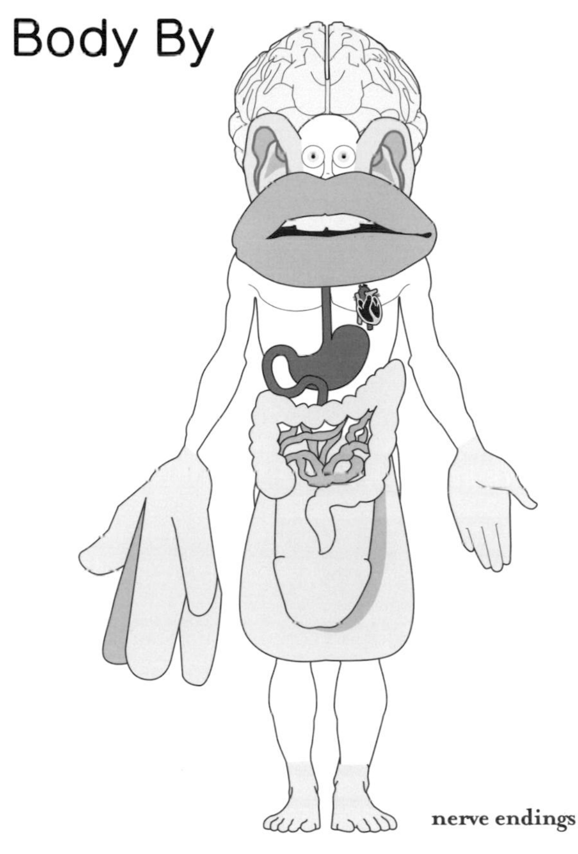
nerve endings

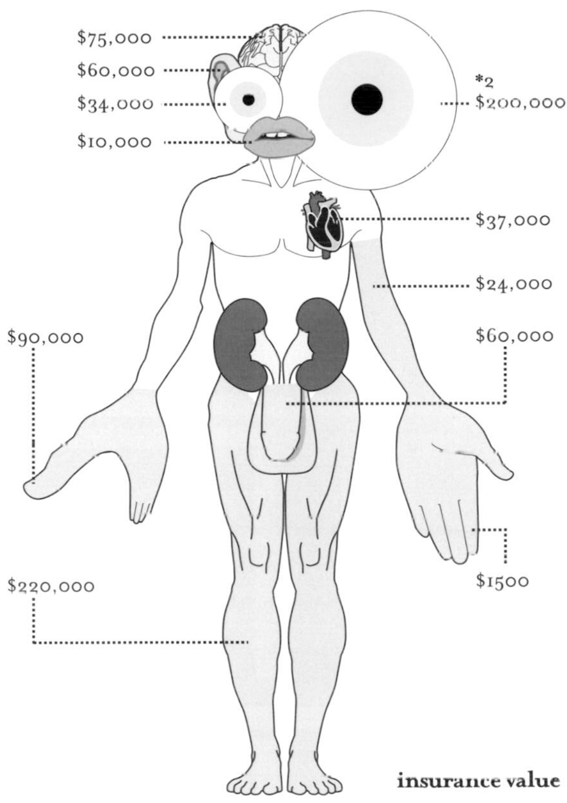
$75,000
$60,000
$34,000
$10,000
*2
$200,000
$37,000
$24,000
$90,000
$60,000
$220,000
$1500
insurance value

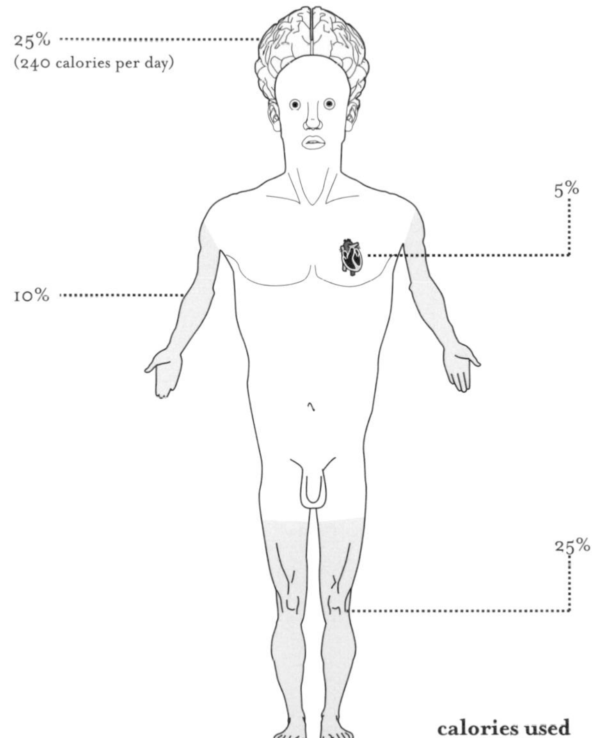
25%
(240 calories per day)
5%
10%
25%
calories used

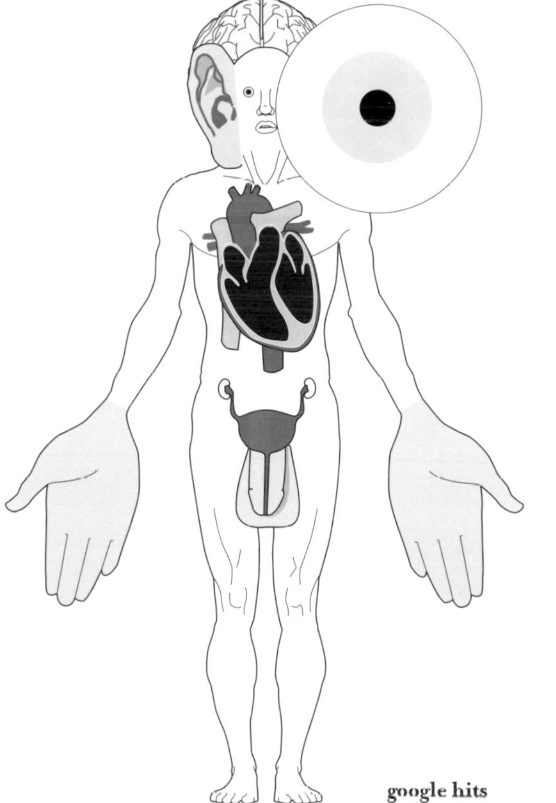
google hits

source: Google, Wikipedia

Microbes Most Dangerous

By survival time outside the body

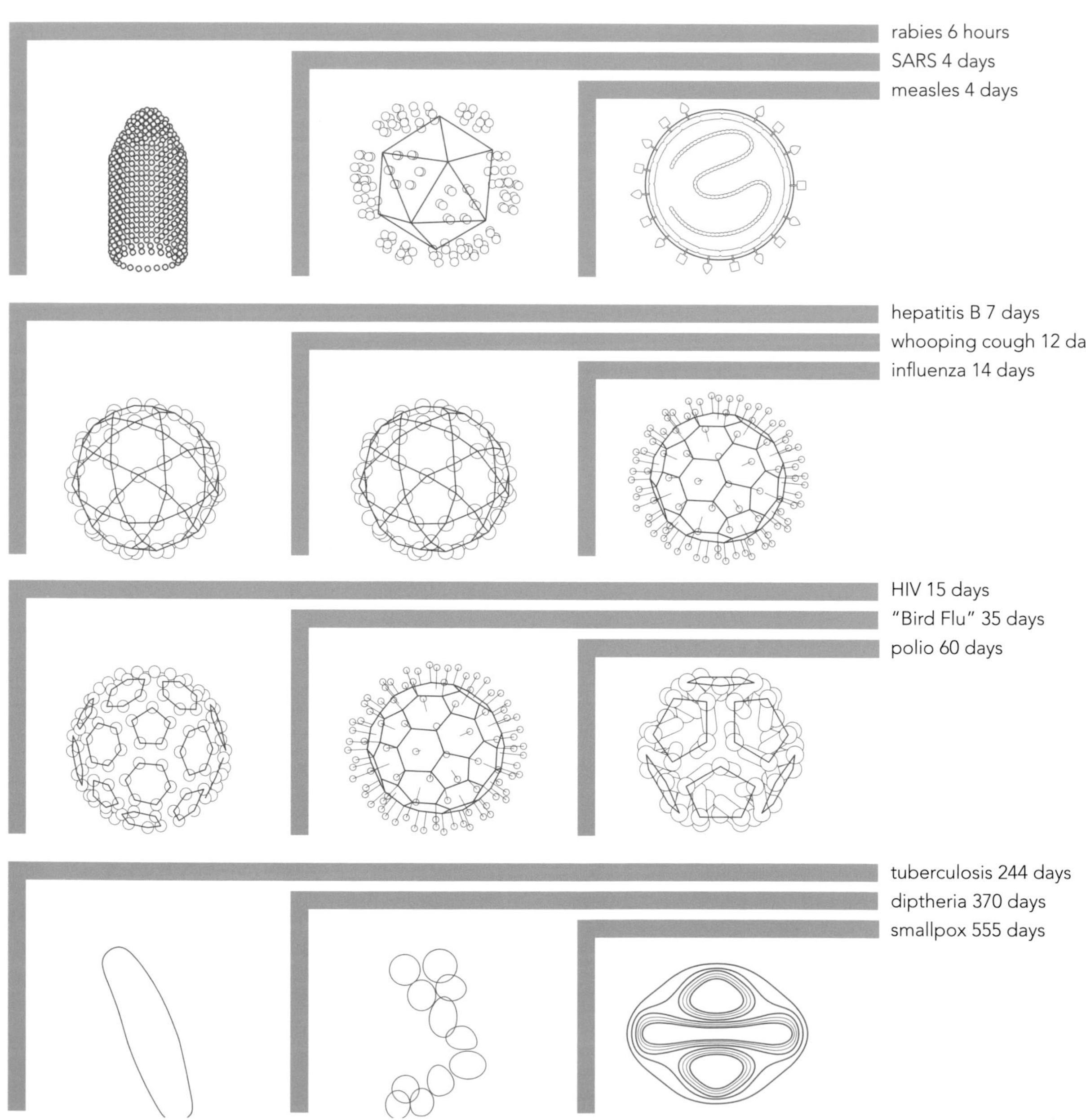

rabies 6 hours
SARS 4 days
measles 4 days
hepatitis B 7 days
whooping cough 12 days
influenza 14 days
HIV 15 days
"Bird Flu" 35 days
polio 60 days
tuberculosis 244 days
diptheria 370 days
smallpox 555 days

source: Centre For Disease Control & Prevention, NewScientist.com. Design inspired by Geigy

Cosmetic Ingredients

Shampoo. Suntan lotion. Soap. Cleanser. Lipstick.

CHLORHEXIDINE DIGLUCONATE, 1,4-DIOXANE, ACETATE, ACETONE, ACETYLATED LANOLIN ALCOHOL, ACRYLATES COPOLYMER, ACRYLATES / OCTYLPROPENAMIDE COPOLYMOR, ALCOHOL DENAT, ALCOHOL SD-40, ALGAE/SEAWEED EXTRACT, ALLANTOIN, ALPHA HYDROXY ACID, ALPHA LIPOIC ACID, ALPHA-ISOMETHYL IONONE, AMMONIUM LAURETH SULFATE, AMMONIUM LAURYL SULPHATE, ANIGOZANTHOS FLAVIDUS (BLOODWORT), ARACHIDYL PROPIONATE, ASCORBIC ACID, ASCORBYL PALMITATE, BEESWAX, BENZALKONIUM CHLORIDE, BENZOIC ACID, BENZOYL PEROXIDE, BENZYL SALICYLATE, BETA HYDROXY ACID (SALICYLIC ACID), BORIC ACID, BUTYL METHOXYDIBENZOYLMETHANE, BUTYLATED HYDROXYANISOLE, BUTYLENE GLYCOL DICAPRYLATE/DICRAPATE, BUTYLPARABEN, BUTYLPHENYL METHYLPROPIONAL, C12-15 ALKYL BENZOATE, CAFFEINE, CAMPHOR, CARBOMERS (934, 940, 941, 980, 981), CARICA PAPAYA (PAPAYA), CARMINE, CARNAUBA WAX, CAVIAR (ROE EXTRACT), CELLULOSE, CERAMIDES, CETALKONIUM CHLORIDE, CETEARETH, CETEARYL ALCOHOL, CHAMOMILLA RECUTITA (CHAMOMILE), CL 14700 (E125), CL 191140 (YELLOW 5 ALUMINIUM LAKE), CITRONELLOL, COCAMIDE MEA, COCAMIDOPROPYL BETAINE, COLLAGEN, COUMARIN, CYCLIC (HYDROXY) ACID, CYCLOMETHICONE, D&C RED NO. 6 BARIUM LAKE, DIETHANOLAMINE (DEA), DIETHYLHEXYL BUTAMIDO TRIAZONE, DIEMETHICONE, DIOCTYL SODIUM SULFOSUCCINATE, DISODIUM COCOAMPHODIACETATE, DISODIUM LAURYL PHENYL ETHER DISULFONATE, DMDM HYDANTOIN, EDTA, ELASTIN, ELLAGIC ACID, ETHYL ALCOHOL (ETHANOL), ETHYLPARABEN, EUGENOL, FD&C YELLOW NO. 5 ALUMINUM LAKE, GLYCERIN, GLYCERYL STEARATE, GLYCINE, GLYCOGEN, GLYCOL STEARATE, GLYCOLIC ACID, GRAPE SEED EXTRACT, GREEN TEA EXTRACT (CAMELLIA SINENSIS), HEXYL CINNAMAL, HYALURONIC ACID, HYDROGEN PEROXIDE, HYDROLYZED COLLAGEN, HYDROQUINONE, HYDROXYLSOHEXYL 3-CYCLOHEXENE CARBOXALDEHYDE, ISOPROPYL ALCOHOL, ISOPROPYL ISOSTEARATE, ISOPROPYL IANOLATE, ISOPROPYL MYRISTATE, ISOPROPYL PALMITATE, ISOSTEARAMIDOPROPYL ETHYLDIMONIUM ETHOSULFATE, ISOSTEARIC ACID KAOLINE (CHINA CLAY), KOJIC ACID, L-ERGOTHIONEINE, LACTIC ACID, LAMINARIA DIGITATA (HORSEHAIR KELP), LANOLIN, LECITHIN, LICORICE EXTRACT (BHT), LIGHT MINERAL OIL, LIMONENE, LINALOOL, LINOLEAMIDOPROPYL, LINOLEIC ACID, LYSINE, METHYLISOTHIAZOLINONE, METHYLPARABEN, MINERAL OIL, MYRISTYL MYRISTATE, MYRTRIMONIUM BROMIDE, OCTOCRYLENE, OCTYL METHOXYCINNAMATE, OCTYL PALMITATE, OCTYLDODECANOL, OLEYL ALCOHOL, OXYBENZONE (BENZOPHENONE-3), PABA (PARA-AMINOBENZOIC ACID), PADIMATE O, PANTHENOL, PARABEN, PARAFFIN, PARFUM, PC-DIMONIUM CHLORIDE PHOSPHATE, PEG-40 CASTOR OIL, PETROLATUM, PHENOXYETHANOL, PHENYL TRIMETHICONE, PHENYLBENZIMIDAZOLE SULFONIC ACID, PHTHALATES, POLY HYDROXY ACID, POLYBUTENE, PROLINE, PROPYLENE GLYCOL, PROPYLPARABEN, QUATERNIUM-15, RESVERATROL, RETINOL (ALSO VITAMIN A), RETINYL PALMITATE, RETINAL PALMITATE POLYPEPTIDE, ROSE HIPS, SALYCYLIC ACID, SILICONE (DIMETHYL SILICONE), SILICA, SILK POWDER, SILK PROTEINS, SODIUM ACRYLATES/C10-30 ALKYL ACRYLATE CROSSPOLYMER, SODIUM BICARBONATE, SODIUM BORATE, SODIUM CETEARYL SULFATE, SODIUM CHLORIDE, SODIUM FLUORIDE, SODIUM HYALURONATE, SODIUM LAUREL SULFATE, SODIUM LAURETH SULFATE, SODIUM LAURYL SULFATE, SODIUM METHACRYLATE, SORBIC ACID, SORBITOL (MINERAL OIL), STEARIC ACID, SULFUR, TALC, TAPIOCA STARCH, TARTARIC ACID, TITANIUM DIOXIDE, TOCOPHERYL ACETATE, TRICLOSAN, TRIDECETH-12, TRIMETHOXYCAPRYLYLSILANE, TRISODIUM EDTA, TYROSINE, VITAMIN A (RETINOL), VITAMIN B, VITAMIN C (CITRIC ACID), VITAMIN D, VITAMIN E (TOCOPHEROL), WATER, WHITE PETROLATUM, WHITE WAX, XANTHAN GUM

GOOD FINE OKAY NASTY TOXIC DEADLY

source: CosmeticDatabase.com, Environmental Working Group

Things That'll Give You Cancer

Source: the media

abortion

acrylamide

agent orange

alcohol aldrin alfatoxin — Nut mould. Nasty.

asphalt fumes atrazine

meat benzene benzadine

betacarotene betel nuts birth — High doses in smokers linked to lung cancer

bread breasts bus stations cadmium

captan carbon tetrachloride careers — Fungicide

foods chewing gum Chinese food Chinese herbal — Vinyl acetate in gum

chlordane chlorinated camphene

chloroform cholesterol chromium coaltar

curry cyclamates dairy products DDT deodorants deplete

diesel exhaust diet soda dimethylsulphate

epichlorhydrin ethilenedibromide ethnic beliefs — Safe

facebook fat fibre fluoridation flying formaldehyde — Lack of real contact alters our biology apparently

gingerbread global warming gluteraldehyde granite grilled

supplements heliobacter pylori hepatitis B

bone mass HRT hydrazine hydrogen peroxide incense — In poorly ventilated spaces

laxatives lead left-handedness Lindane Listerine low — Higher risk of breast cancer

mammograms manganese menopause methylbromide — Minimal risk

mixed spices mobile phones moisturizers mould MTBE — No link. Now proven.

breast feeding not having a twin nuclear power

juice oxygenated gasoline oyster sauce ozone — Contains carcinogens

PCBs peanuts pesticides pet birds plastic — When mouldy

PVC radio masts radon railway sleepers — Itís the creosote. Donít lick.

sausage dye selenium semi conductor plants

soy sauce statins stress strontium styrene

sunscreen talc testosterone tetrachloroethylene

tooth fillings toothpaste tooth whitening — Probably okay

underarm-shaving unvented stoves

vegetables vinyl bromide

vitamins vitreous fibres wallpaper

well water wifi wine

x-rays

no risk maybe a risk **definite risk**

acrylonitril
air pollution alar ... Pesticide & fruit spray
arsenic **asbestos**
AZT babyfood **barbecued**
benzopyrene **beryllium**
control pills bottled water bracken ... Only if contaminated
calcium channel blockers cannabis ... Linked to testicular cancer but also has anti-tumour effects
for women car fumes casual sex celery **charred**
supplements chinese medicine chips chloramphenicol ... Antibiotic
chlorinated water **chlorodiphenyl**
coffee **coke ovens** cooked foods crackers creosote ... May help combat cancer
uranium depression **dichloryacetylene dieldrin**
dinitrotouluene **dioxane** **dioxin** dogs ... unproven links to breast cancer
ethyleacrilate ethylene **ethylenedichloride** Ex-Lax
free radicals french fries fruit frying **gasoline** genes
meat **Gulf war** **hair dye** hamburgers health ... Linked to many cancers
virus hexachlorbutadiene hexachlorethane high
infertility jewellery **Kepone** **kissing** lack of exercise ... Kissing disease (infectious mononucleosis)
cholesterol low fibre diet magnetic fields **malonaldehyde**
methylenechloride microwave ovens milk hormones
nickel night lighting **nightshifts** **nitrates not** ... Probable cause of cancer
plants Nutrasweet **oestrogen** olestra olive oil orange
ozone depletion papaya **passive smoking**
IV bags polio vaccine power lines proteins Prozac
redmeat Roundup saccharin salmon salt sausage ... Most red meat linked to bowel cancer
shaving shellfish sick buildings smoked fish ... Air quality
sulphuric acid **sunbeds** **sunlight**
tight bras toast toasters **tobacco**
train stations **trichloroethylene** tritium
uranium **UV radiation**
vinyl chloride vinyl toys
weight gain welding fumes
winter **wood dust** work

source: UK and US media reports [via numberwatch.co.uk], Wikipedia

Types of Coffee

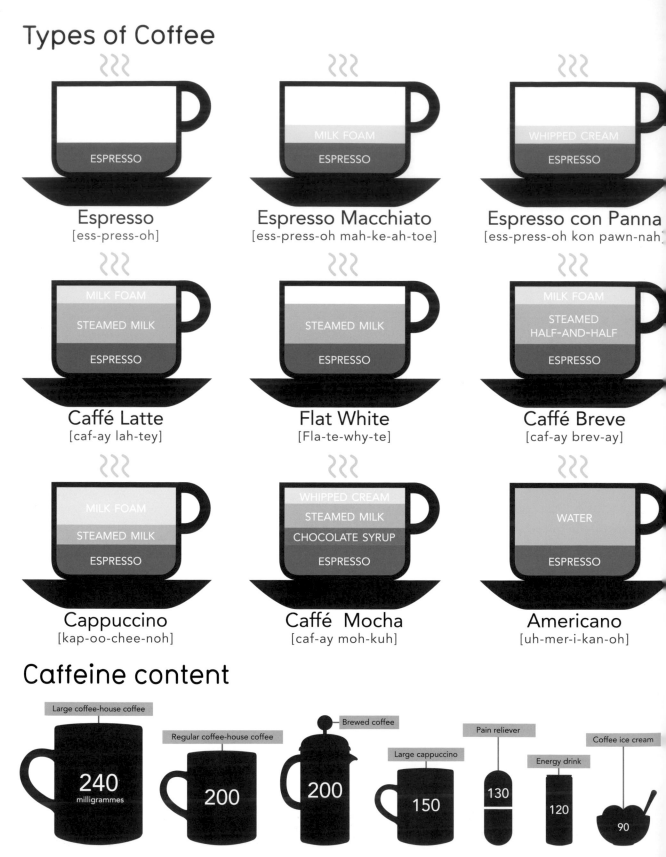

ESPRESSO

Espresso
[ess-press-oh]

MILK FOAM
ESPRESSO

Espresso Macchiato
[ess-press-oh mah-ke-ah-toe]

WHIPPED CREAM
ESPRESSO

Espresso con Panna
[ess-press-oh kon pawn-nah]

MILK FOAM
STEAMED MILK
ESPRESSO

Caffé Latte
[caf-ay lah-tey]

STEAMED MILK
ESPRESSO

Flat White
[Fla-te-why-te]

MILK FOAM
STEAMED HALF-AND-HALF
ESPRESSO

Caffé Breve
[caf-ay brev-ay]

MILK FOAM
STEAMED MILK
ESPRESSO

Cappuccino
[kap-oo-chee-noh]

WHIPPED CREAM
STEAMED MILK
CHOCOLATE SYRUP
ESPRESSO

Caffé Mocha
[caf-ay moh-kuh]

WATER
ESPRESSO

Americano
[uh-mer-i-kan-oh]

Caffeine content

Large coffee-house coffee
240
milligrammes
Regular coffee-house coffee
200
Brewed coffee
200
Large cappuccino
150
Pain reliever
130
Energy drink
120
Coffee ice cream
90

COLD MILK FOAM
ICE
ESPRESSO

Freddo
[fred-oh]

MILK FOAM
CHOCOLATE POWDER
ESPRESSO

Marocchino
[mar-oh-cheen-oh]

ESPRESSO

Stretto
[stret-toh]

CONCENTRATED
ESPRESSO

Ristretto
[wrist-tret-oh]

WHIPPED CREAM
WHISKEY
WATER
ESPRESSO

Irish
[eye-rish]

WHIPPED CREAM
FROZEN ESPRESSO

Granita con Panna
[gran-ee-ta-kon-pan-na]

BRANDY
ESPRESSO

Corretto
[kor-ret-oh]

STEAMED MILK
ESPRESSO

Con Leche
[kon-letch-eh]

WATER
INSTANT COFFEE

Crappa
[krap-aaahhh!]

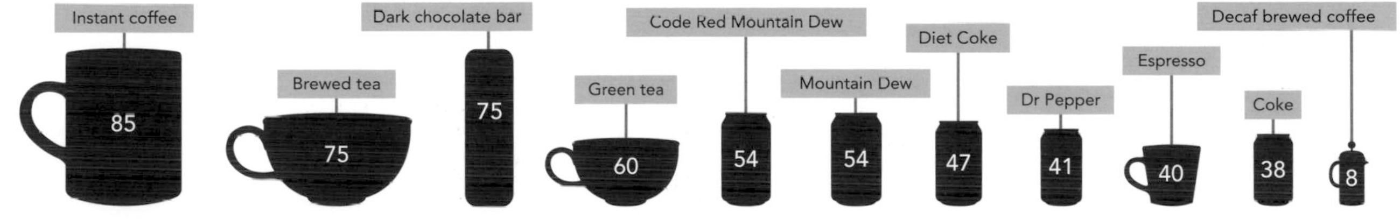
Instant coffee
85
Brewed tea
75
Dark chocolate bar
75
Green tea
60
Code Red Mountain Dew
54
Mountain Dew
54
Diet Coke
47
Dr Pepper
41
Espresso
40
Coke
38
Decaf brewed coffee
8

idea: Lokesh Dhakar @ lokeshdhakar.com

Tons of Carbon

Emissions per year

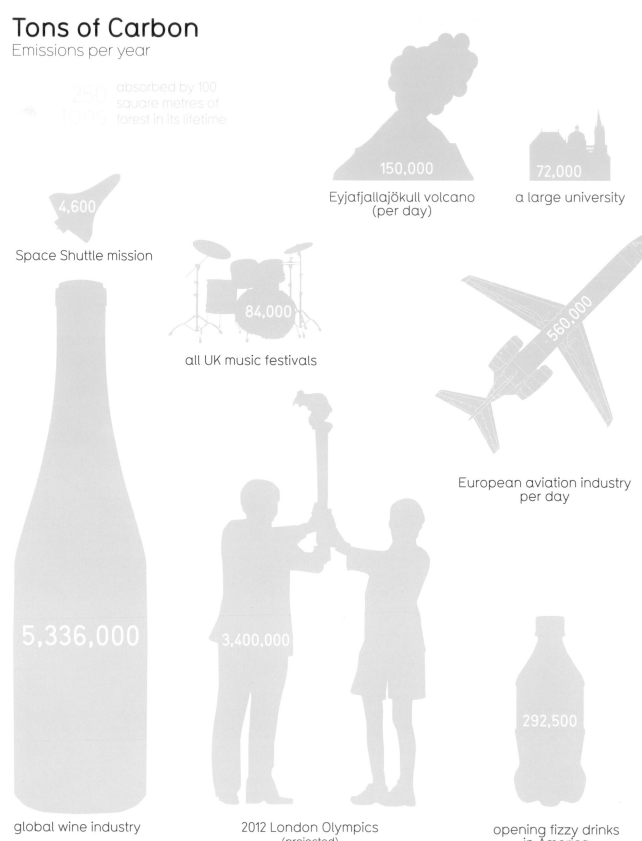

250 TONS absorbed by 100 square metres of forest in its lifetime

150,000

Eyjafjallajökull volcano (per day)

72,000

a large university

4,600

Space Shuttle mission

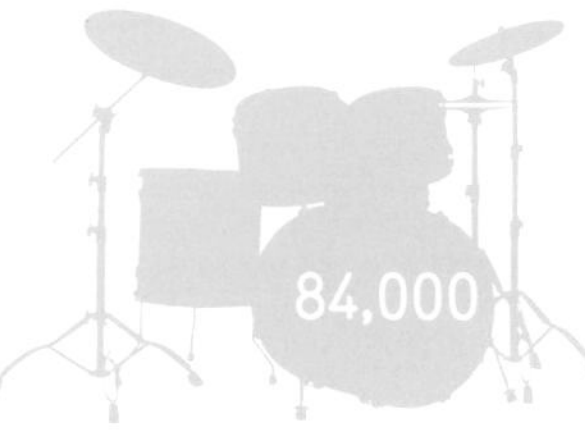
84,000

all UK music festivals

560,000

European aviation industry per day

5,336,000

global wine industry

3,400,000

2012 London Olympics
(projected)

292,500

opening fizzy drinks in America

Megatons of Carbon

Emissions per year

global aviation industry

300,000,000

the internet

300,000,000

all volcanic activity

1,210,000,000

862,000,000

the United Kingdom

3,073,400,000

250,000,000

global mobile phone use

global aviation industry adjusted for high-altitude CO_2 release

all measurements in tons

Articles of War

Most edited Wikipedia pages

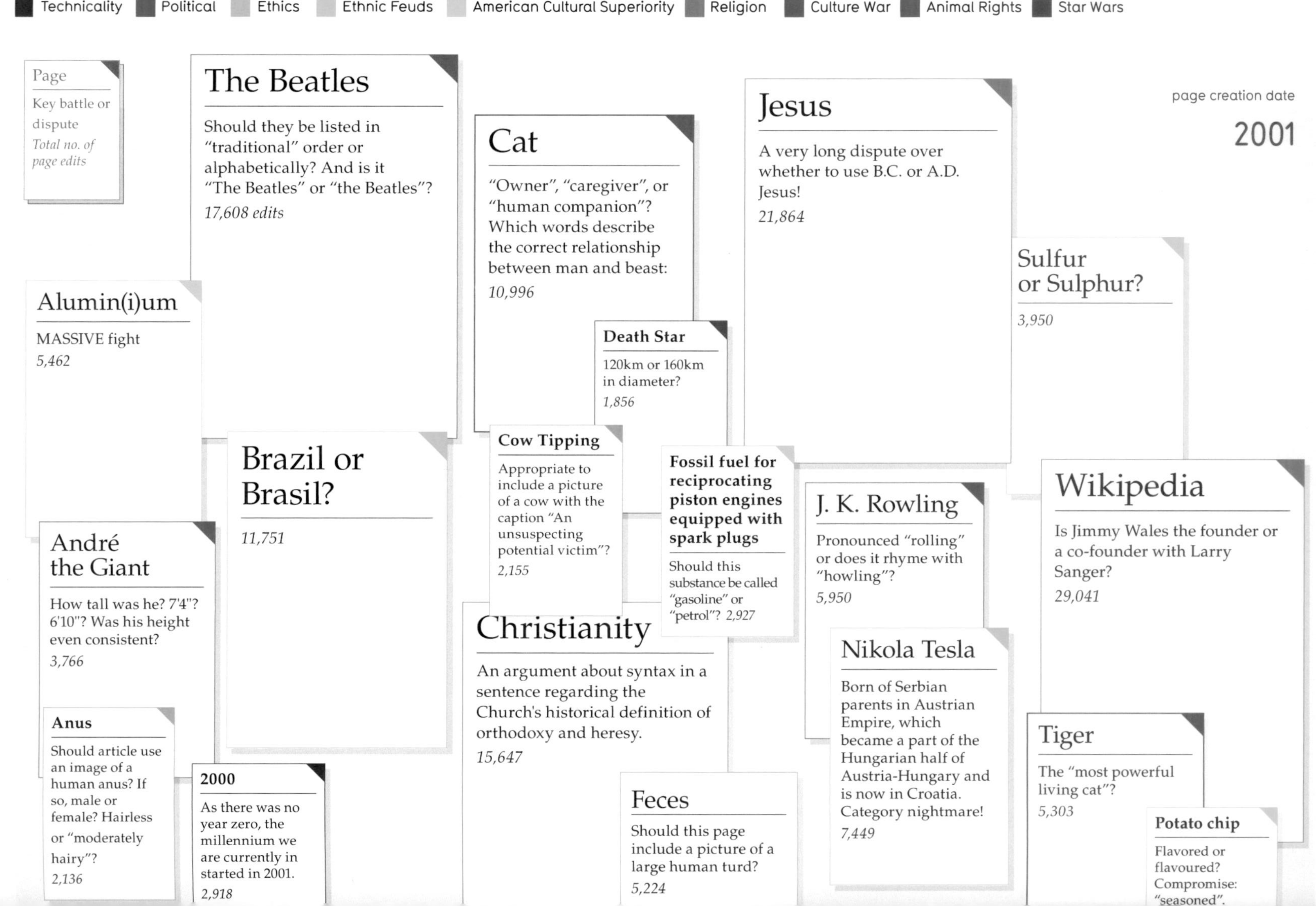

Technicality
Political
Ethics
Ethnic Feuds
American Cultural Superiority
Religion
Culture War
Animal Rights
Star Wars
Page
Key battle or dispute
Total no. of page edits
page creation date
2001
The Beatles
Should they be listed in "traditional" order or alphabetically? And is it "The Beatles" or "the Beatles"?
17,608 edits
Cat
"Owner", "caregiver", or "human companion"? Which words describe the correct relationship between man and beast:
10,996
Jesus
A very long dispute over whether to use B.C. or A.D. Jesus!
21,864
Sulfur or Sulphur?
3,950
Alumin(i)um
MASSIVE fight
5,462
Death Star
120km or 160km in diameter?
1,856
Brazil or Brasil?
11,751
Cow Tipping
Appropriate to include a picture of a cow with the caption "An unsuspecting potential victim"?
2,155
Fossil fuel for reciprocating piston engines equipped with spark plugs
Should this substance be called "gasoline" or "petrol"? 2,927
J. K. Rowling
Pronounced "rolling" or does it rhyme with "howling"?
5,950
Wikipedia
Is Jimmy Wales the founder or a co-founder with Larry Sanger?
29,041
André the Giant
How tall was he? 7'4"? 6'10"? Was his height even consistent?
3,766
Christianity
An argument about syntax in a sentence regarding the Church's historical definition of orthodoxy and heresy.
15,647
Nikola Tesla
Born of Serbian parents in Austrian Empire, which became a part of the Hungarian half of Austria-Hungary and is now in Croatia. Category nightmare!
7,449
Anus
Should article use an image of a human anus? If so, male or female? Hairless or "moderately hairy"?
2,136
2000
As there was no year zero, the millennium we are currently in started in 2001.
2,918
Feces
Should this page include a picture of a large human turd?
5,224
Tiger
The "most powerful living cat"?
5,303
Potato chip
Flavored or flavoured? Compromise: "seasoned".

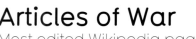

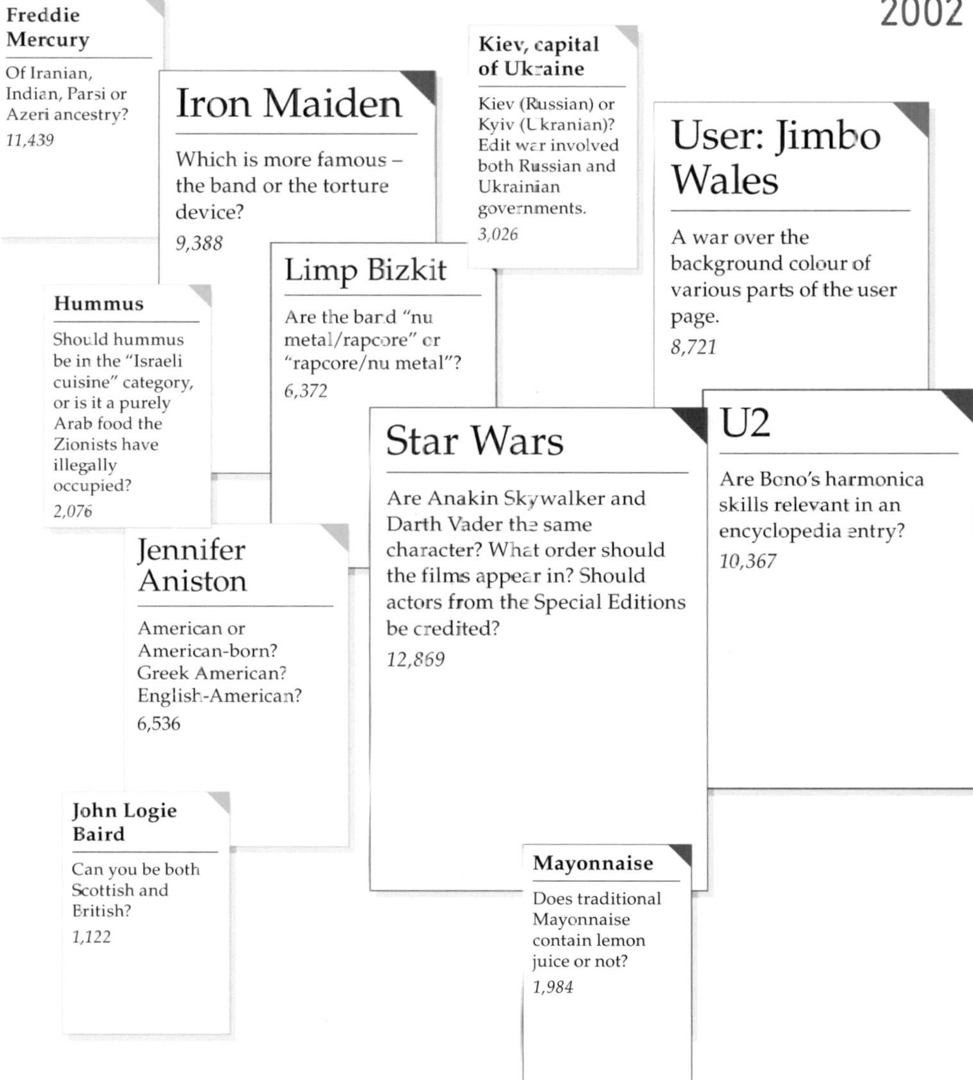

2002
Freddie Mercury
Of Iranian, Indian, Parsi or Azeri ancestry?
11,439
Iron Maiden
Which is more famous – the band or the torture device?
9,388
Kiev, capital of Ukraine
Kiev (Russian) or Kyiv (Ukranian)? Edit war involved both Russian and Ukrainian governments.
3,026
User: Jimbo Wales
A war over the background colour of various parts of the user page.
8,721
Hummus
Should hummus be in the "Israeli cuisine" category, or is it a purely Arab food the Zionists have illegally occupied?
2,076
Limp Bizkit
Are the band "nu metal/rapcore" or "rapcore/nu metal"?
6,372
Star Wars
Are Anakin Skywalker and Darth Vader the same character? What order should the films appear in? Should actors from the Special Editions be credited?
12,869
U2
Are Bono's harmonica skills relevant in an encyclopedia entry?
10,367
Jennifer Aniston
American or American-born? Greek American? English-American?
6,536
John Logie Baird
Can you be both Scottish and British?
1,122
Mayonnaise
Does traditional Mayonnaise contain lemon juice or not?
1,984

Arachnophobia

Appropriate to include a huge picture of a tarantula on a page about fear of spiders?

640

source: Wikipedia

Articles of War

Most edited Wikipedia pages

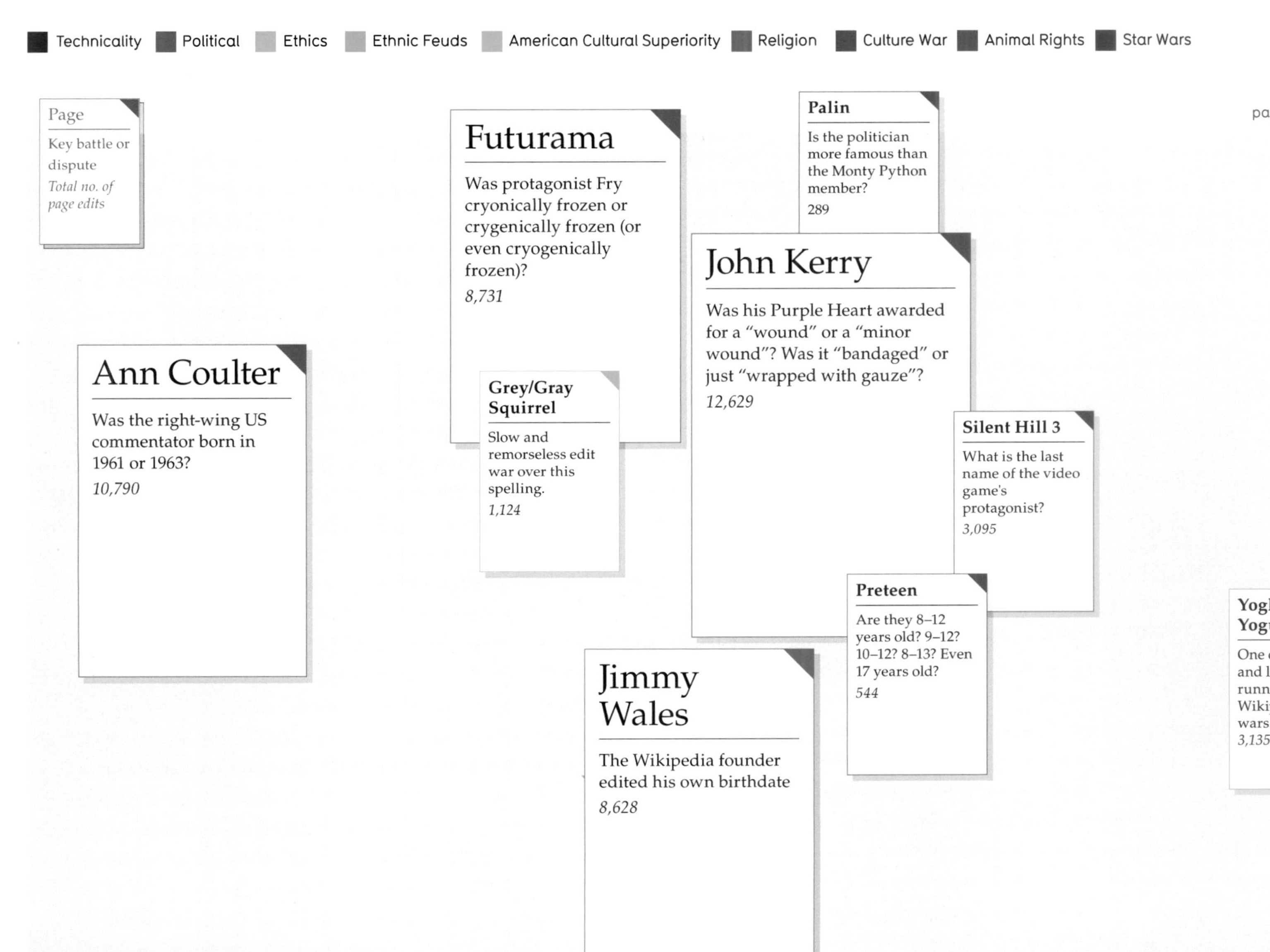
Technicality
Political
Ethics
Ethnic Feuds
American Cultural Superiority
Religion
Culture War
Animal Rights
Star Wars
Page
Key battle or dispute
Total no. of page edits
page creation date
2003
Ann Coulter
Was the right-wing US commentator born in 1961 or 1963?
10,790
Futurama
Was protagonist Fry cryonically frozen or crygenically frozen (or even cryogenically frozen)?
8,731
Grey/Gray Squirrel
Slow and remorseless edit war over this spelling.
1,124
Palin
Is the politician more famous than the Monty Python member?
289
John Kerry
Was his Purple Heart awarded for a "wound" or a "minor wound"? Was it "bandaged" or just "wrapped with gauze"?
12,629
Jimmy Wales
The Wikipedia founder edited his own birthdate
8,628
Silent Hill 3
What is the last name of the video game's protagonist?
3,095
Preteen
Are they 8–12 years old? 9–12? 10–12? 8–13? Even 17 years old?
544
Yoghurt or Yogurt?
One of the biggest and longest-running Wikipedia edit wars. Seriously.
3,135

2004+

2006 Atlantic Hurricane Season

Tropical Storm Zeta formed on 30 December, 2005 and lasted until 6 January, 2006. Which hurricane season does this count as?

3,254

Cute

Is it NPOV (Neutral Point of View) to say an animal is "cute"?

21

Grace Kelly and Cher

Gay icons?

2,282

Angels & Airwaves is/are a band

British English requires "are" as the band comprises multiple people. American English requires "is", as the band is a singular entity. FIGHT!

8,055

Clover (Creature)

Cloverfield, Clover, The Cloverfield creature, or Clover (creature)?

1,654

Compact Disc

Is a tradename and so should be capitalized. HOWEVER the logo says "Compact disc".

3,888

House MD

Should we mention the show's lack of Asian diversity?

8,423

Sega Genesis & Sega Mega Drive

What's the proper name for the article when both names are used? Surely something can't be two things at the same time? An eight-month debate.

3,670

Money (Pink Floyd song)

What exactly is this song's time signature? 7/8, 7/4 or even 21/8?

573

Pwned

What does this piece of geek slang actually mean? Who invented it? How do you pronounce it?

26

Street Fighter character articles

Drawn-out edit wars over the correct heights and weights of fictional characters

2,147

Wii

"Wii", "Nintendo Wii" or "the Wii"? Should "wee" link here or to the article on urine?

20,077

US Election 2008

Is Stephen Colbert considered a serious candidate? If so, was it Stephen Colbert (comedian) or Stephen Colbert (character)?

14,957

Pregnancy

The picture of a nude pregnant women in this article provoked an enormous debate – and even the intervention of Wikipedia founder, Jimmy Wales.

5,671

source: Wikipedia

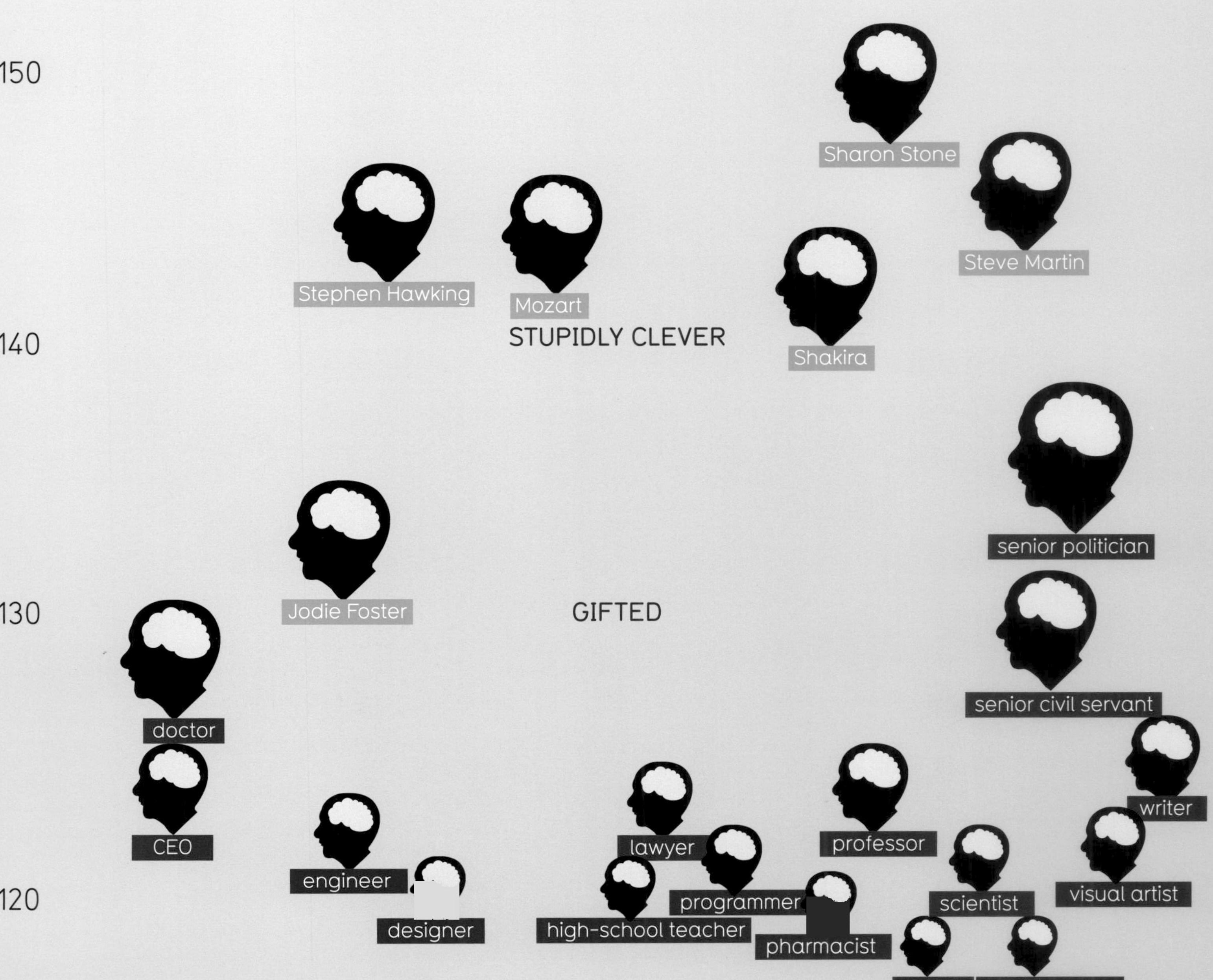
150
140
130
120
Sharon Stone
Steve Martin
Stephen Hawking
Mozart
STUPIDLY CLEVER
Shakira
senior politician
Jodie Foster
GIFTED
senior civil servant
doctor
CEO
engineer
designer
lawyer
high-school teacher
programmer
pharmacist
professor
scientist
priest
social worker
writer
visual artist

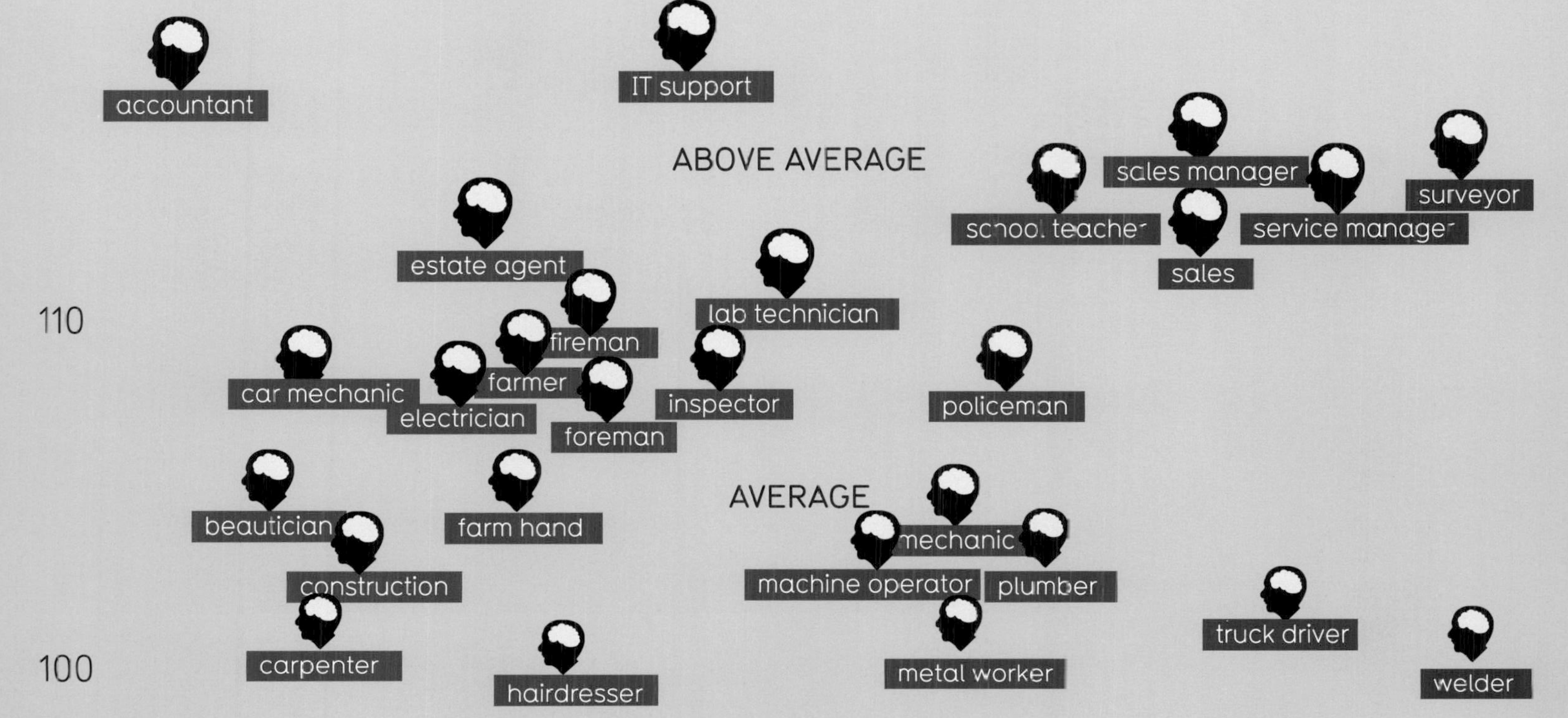
accountant
IT support
ABOVE AVERAGE
sales manager
surveyor
school teacher
service manager
sales
estate agent
110
lab technician
fireman
car mechanic
farmer
electrician
inspector
policeman
foreman
beautician
farm hand
AVERAGE
mechanic
construction
machine operator
plumber
truck driver
100
carpenter
hairdresser
metal worker
welder

Who Clever are You?

Average IQs of different callings

source: University of Wisconsin Henmon–Nelson IQ Distributions 1992–94 via Hauser, Robert M (2002)

The Buzz vs The Bulge

Caffeine vs Calories

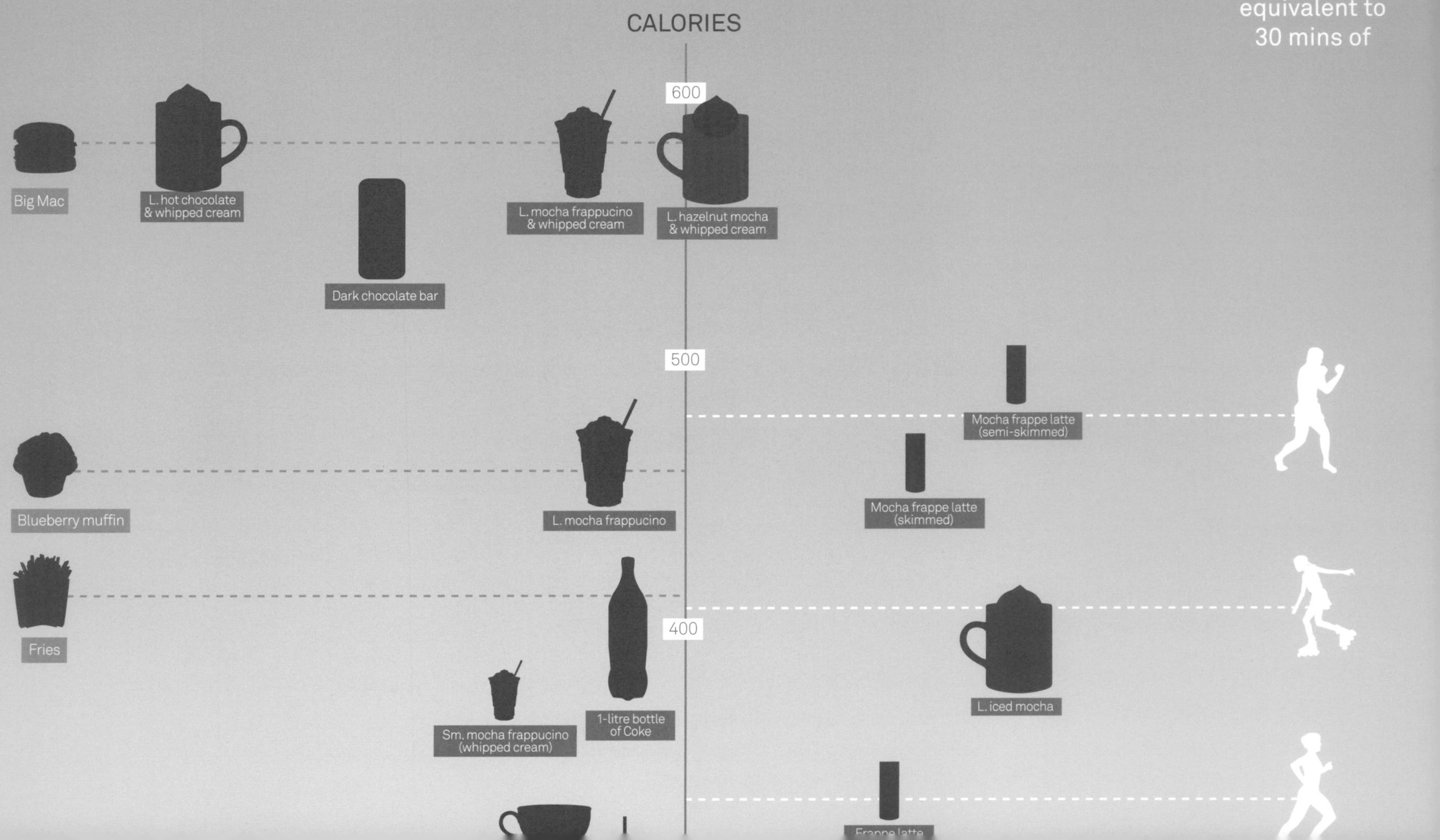

CALORIES
600
500
400
equivalent to
30 mins of
Big Mac
L. hot chocolate
& whipped cream
Dark chocolate bar
L. mocha frappucino
& whipped cream
L. hazelnut mocha
& whipped cream
Blueberry muffin
L. mocha frappucino
Mocha frappe latte
(skimmed)
Mocha frappe latte
(semi-skimmed)
Fries
1-litre bottle
of Coke
Sm. mocha frappucino
(whipped cream)
L. iced mocha

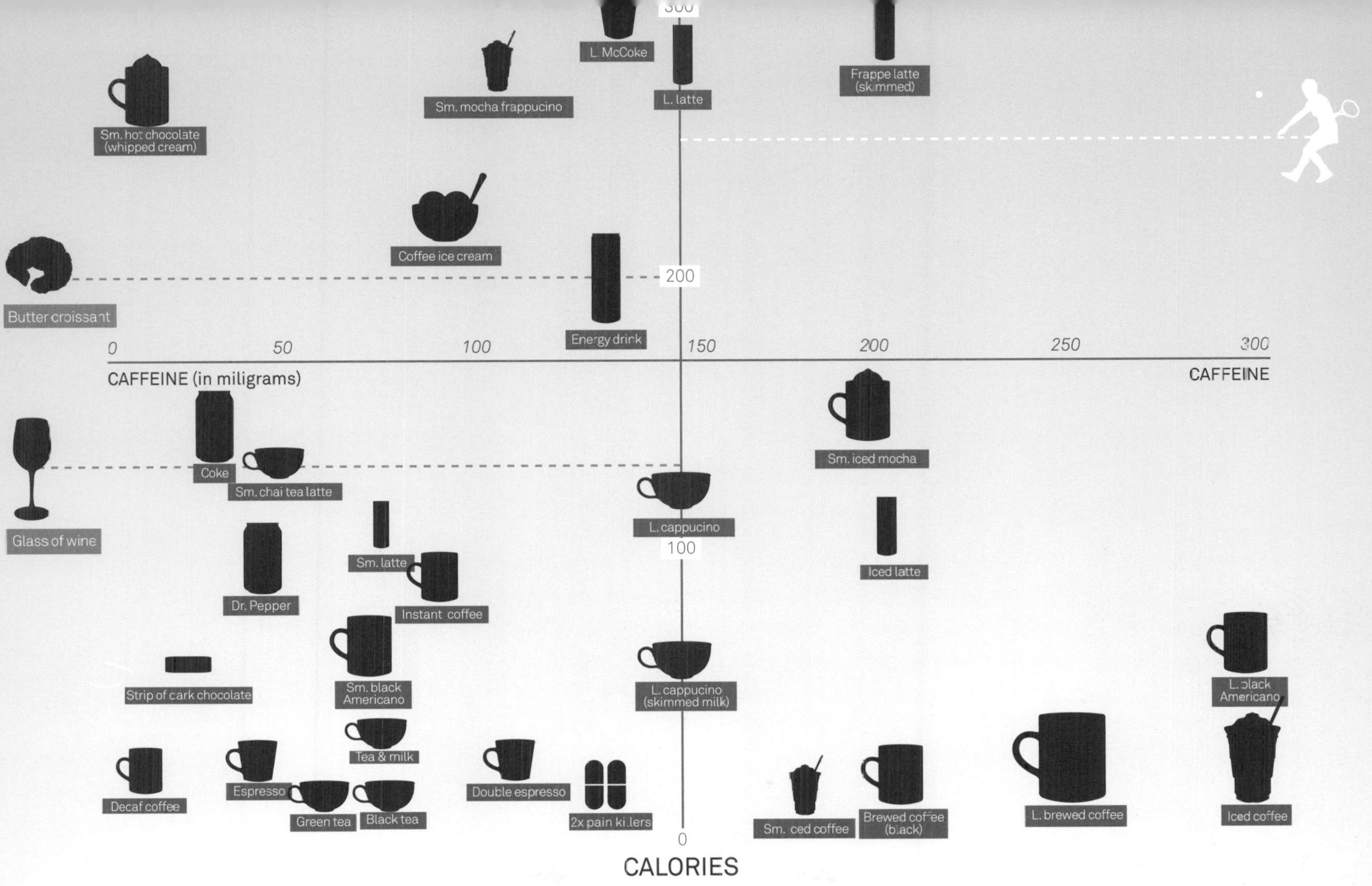

300
L. McCoke
Sm. mocha frappucino
L. latte
Frappe latte (skimmed)
Sm. hot chocolate (whipped cream)
Coffee ice cream
200
Butter croissant
Energy drink
0
50
100
150
200
250
300
CAFFEINE (in miligrams)
CAFFEINE
Sm. iced mocha
Coke
Sm. chai tea latte
Glass of wine
L. cappucino
100
Iced latte
Sm. latte
Dr. Pepper
Instant coffee
Strip of dark chocolate
Sm. black Americano
L. cappucino (skimmed milk)
L. black Americano
Tea & milk
Decaf coffee
Espresso
Green tea
Black tea
Double espresso
2x pain killers
Sm. iced coffee
Brewed coffee (black)
L. brewed coffee
Iced coffee
0
CALORIES

Source: Guardian Data Store, Starbucks.co.uk, Calorie-Counter.com

	MORNING	AFTERNOON
ATKINS	omelette, tomato	salmon, salad
LOW G.I.	porridge, skim milk, oj	carrot & barley soup
WEIGHT WATCHERS	porridge & raisins, brown sugar	small burger, salad, apple
ZONE	grapes, rye toast, fruit, peanut butter	
CABBAGE SOUP	fruit	cabbage soup
DETOX	oats, yoghurt, fruit	tzatziki, veg cruditès
JUICE DIET	carrot & apple	carrot & veg juice
CALORIE COUNTING	4 tbsp branflakes, skim milk, apple	mozzarella, tomato & avocado salad, french bread
MEDITERRANEAN	toast, yoghurt, blueberries, almonds	chickpea salad
WEIGHT GAIN	6 x cream cheese bagels, yoghurt, oj	pitta bread, tuna, lentil soup, apple juice
SUNLIGHT	sunlight	sunlight
SCARSDALE	grapefruit, toast, black coffee	assorted cold cuts, stewed tomatoes

EVENING	SNACKAGE	WATER
grilled chicken, veg	chocolate shake, granola bar	x 8
wholewheat pasta bake	yoghurt, raspberries	x 8
tuna steak, olive sauce, assorted veg, french bread	fat-free yoghurt	x 8
grapes, rye bread, olive oil, peanut butter		x 8
cabbage soup	fruit	x 8
potato & bean casserole	yoghurt, fruit	x 8
veg juice		x 8
roast pork	hummus, crudités	x 8
spinach frittata	hummus, crisp bread	x 8
spaghetti, salami, bread, milk	bread & jam, ice cream	x 8
vitamin D	oxygen	x 8
shellfish, salad, veg	hummus	x 8

Calories In

Average load

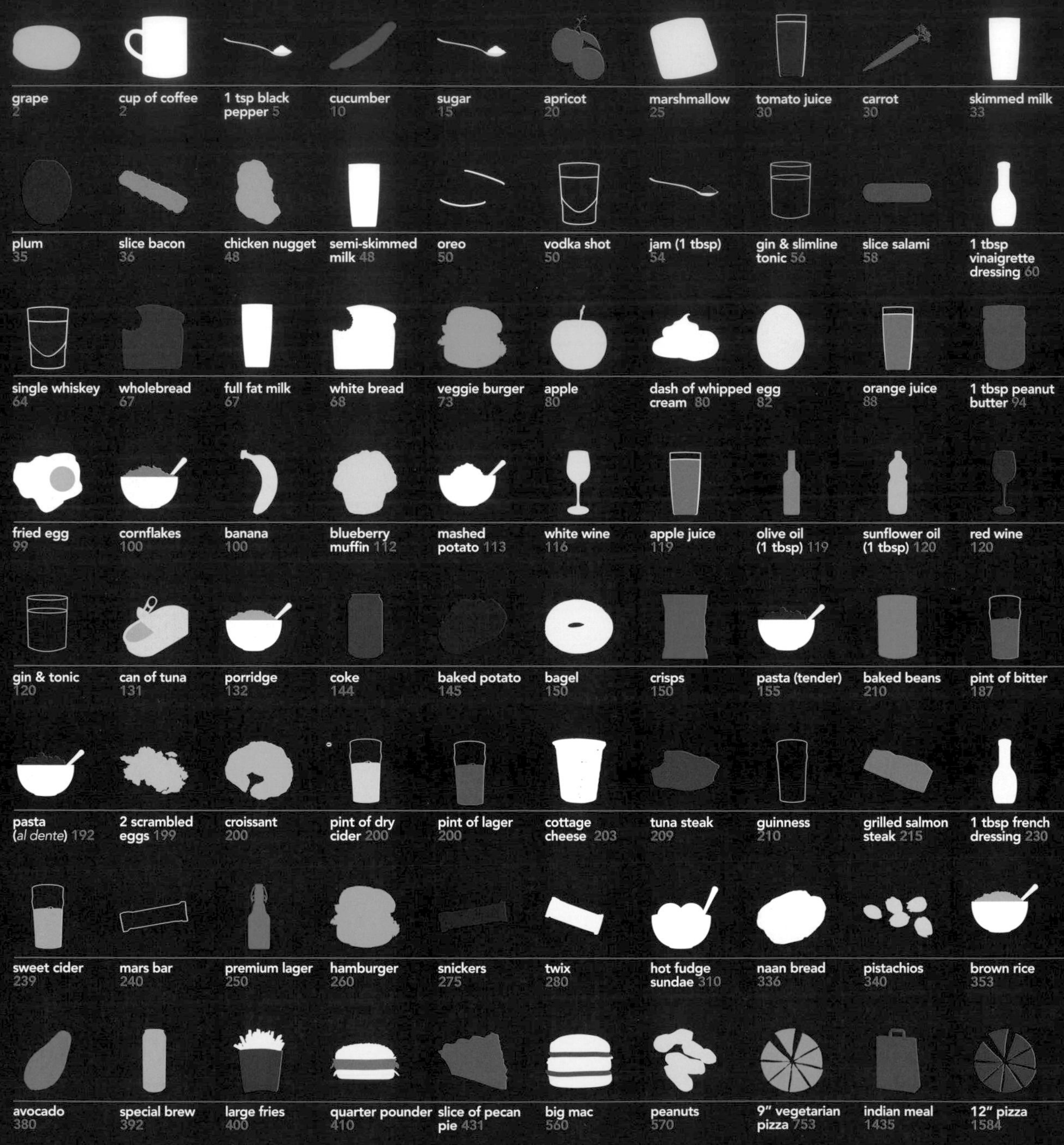
grape 2
cup of coffee 2
1 tsp black pepper 5
cucumber 10
sugar 15
apricot 20
marshmallow 25
tomato juice 30
carrot 30
skimmed milk 33
plum 35
slice bacon 36
chicken nugget 48
semi-skimmed milk 48
oreo 50
vodka shot 50
jam (1 tbsp) 54
gin & slimline tonic 56
slice salami 58
1 tbsp vinaigrette dressing 60
single whiskey 64
wholebread 67
full fat milk 67
white bread 68
veggie burger 73
apple 80
dash of whipped cream 80
egg 82
orange juice 88
1 tbsp peanut butter 94
fried egg 99
cornflakes 100
banana 100
blueberry muffin 112
mashed potato 113
white wine 116
apple juice 119
olive oil (1 tbsp) 119
sunflower oil (1 tbsp) 120
red wine 120
gin & tonic 120
can of tuna 131
porridge 132
coke 144
baked potato 145
bagel 150
crisps 150
pasta (tender) 155
baked beans 210
pint of bitter 187
pasta (al dente) 192
2 scrambled eggs 199
croissant 200
pint of dry cider 200
pint of lager 200
cottage cheese 203
tuna steak 209
guinness 210
grilled salmon steak 215
1 tbsp french dressing 230
sweet cider 239
mars bar 240
premium lager 250
hamburger 260
snickers 275
twix 280
hot fudge sundae 310
naan bread 336
pistachios 340
brown rice 353
avocado 380
special brew 392
large fries 400
quarter pounder 410
slice of pecan pie 431
big mac 560
peanuts 570
9" vegetarian pizza 753
indian meal 1435
12" pizza 1584

Calories Out

Average burn for 30 minutes of...

praying
36
lying down
36
meditating
36
sex (light)
36
queueing
40
knitting
43
toilet
44
reading
48
sex (moderate)
48
socializing
55
sex (vigorous)
57
desk work
66
pallbearing
68
brushing teeth
74
milking a cow
88
camping
92
baseball
93
darts
93
decorating
103
sailing
110
walking
110
frisbee
110
surfing
110
bowling
110
fishing
110
curling
118
juggling
148
horseriding
148
cricket
166
gardening
166
tai chi
166
golf
166
dancing
166
badminton
166
hopscotch
185
skateboarding
195
punching a bag
222
wheelchair
240
swimming laps
258
rowing
258
cycling
208
aerobics
258
tennis
258
skiing
258
football
265
running
295
push ups
sit ups 295
climbing
295
circuit training
295
basketball
295
american
football 310
yoga
310
martial arts
369
rugby
443
squash
443
roller-blading
443
boxing
443

source: cross-referenced from various dieting websites

Types of Facial Hair

A little hair says a lot about a man

Major
Al-Assad, Hafez
Syria (ruled 1971-2000)
Killed: 25,000

Traditional
Al-Bashir, Omar
Sudan (1989-)
Killed: 400,000

Painter's Brush
Kai-Shek, Chiang
China (1928-31)
Killed: 30,000

Pyramid
Franco, Francisco
Spain (1939-75)
Killed: 30,000

Freestyle
King Abdullah
Saudi Arabia (2005-)
Killed: -

Chevron
Lenin, Vladimir Ilyich
Russia (1917-24)
Killed: 30,000

Handlebar
Stalin, Joseph
Soviet Union (1924-53)
Killed: 23,000,000

Natural Full
Castro, Fidel
Cuba (1976-2008)
Killed: 30,000

Horseshoe
Habre, Hissene
Chad (1982-90)
Killed: 40,000

Toothbrush
Hitler, Adolf
Germany (1933-45)
Killed: 58,000,000

Walrus
Hussein, Saddam
Iraq (1979-2003)
Killed: 6,000,000

Zappa
Mengitsu, Haile Maiam
Ethiopa (1987-91)
Killed: 150,000

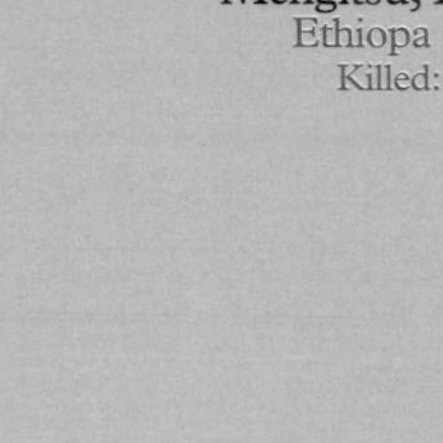

Fu Manchu
Temujin, Genghis Khan
Mongolia (1205-27)
Killed: millions

Nu Geek
McCandless
UK (1971)
Killed: 0

source: Wikipedia and general web

Exxon Valdez
oil spill
28,000 km²

Deepwater Horizon
oil spill
5,750 km²

Amazon rainforest
depletion yearly
6,400 km²

Forest loss
Indonesia yearly
5,900 km²

Arable land dest
2010 Russian hea
114,500 km²

Haiti earthquake
2010
13,000 km²

Chile earthquake
2010
300,000 km²

New Zealand earthquake
2011
5,800 km²

Japan e
2011
140,000 k

earthquake areas experiencing at least "strong" shaking

Thailand floods 2
60,000 km²

Scale of Devastation

Square kilometres

y

Wildfires during 2010 Russian heat wave

8,800 km²

Chernobyl exclusion zone

1,300 km²

United Kingdom surface area

242,000 km²

ıke

Pakistan floods 2010

114,500 km²

Australia floods 2010

850,000 km²

Sources: USGS, ScienceDirect, Wikipedia

Amphibian Extinction Rates

Canaries in a coal mine?

Normal rate

1x

1990s

200x

Chrytid fungus

Habitat Loss

UV-Radiation

Insecticides

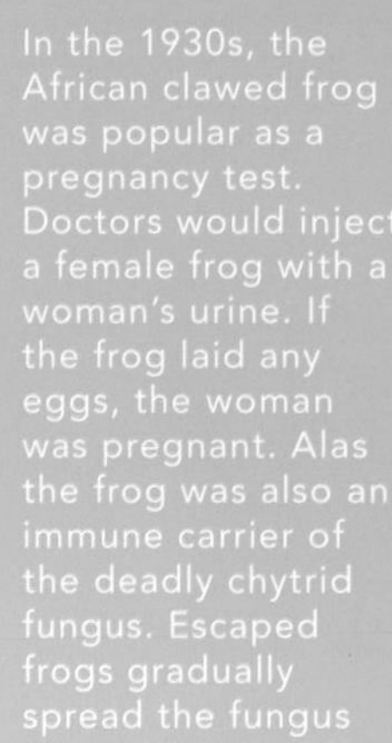

In the 1930s, the African clawed frog was popular as a pregnancy test. Doctors would inject a female frog with a woman's urine. If the frog laid any eggs, the woman was pregnant. Alas the frog was also an immune carrier of the deadly chytrid fungus. Escaped frogs gradually spread the fungus around the world.

Even a tiny amount of malathion, the most common insecticide in the US, can lead to a devastating chain reaction that destroys bottom-dwelling algae, the primary food of tadpoles. Malathion, together with the pesticide Atrazine, are considered key factors in the loss of entire populations of amphibians.

Today

25,400x

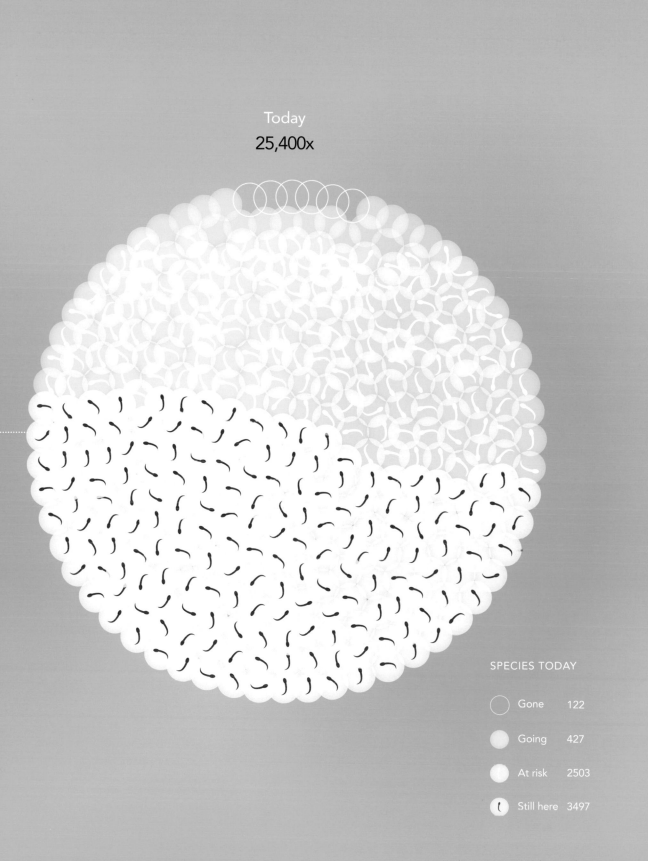

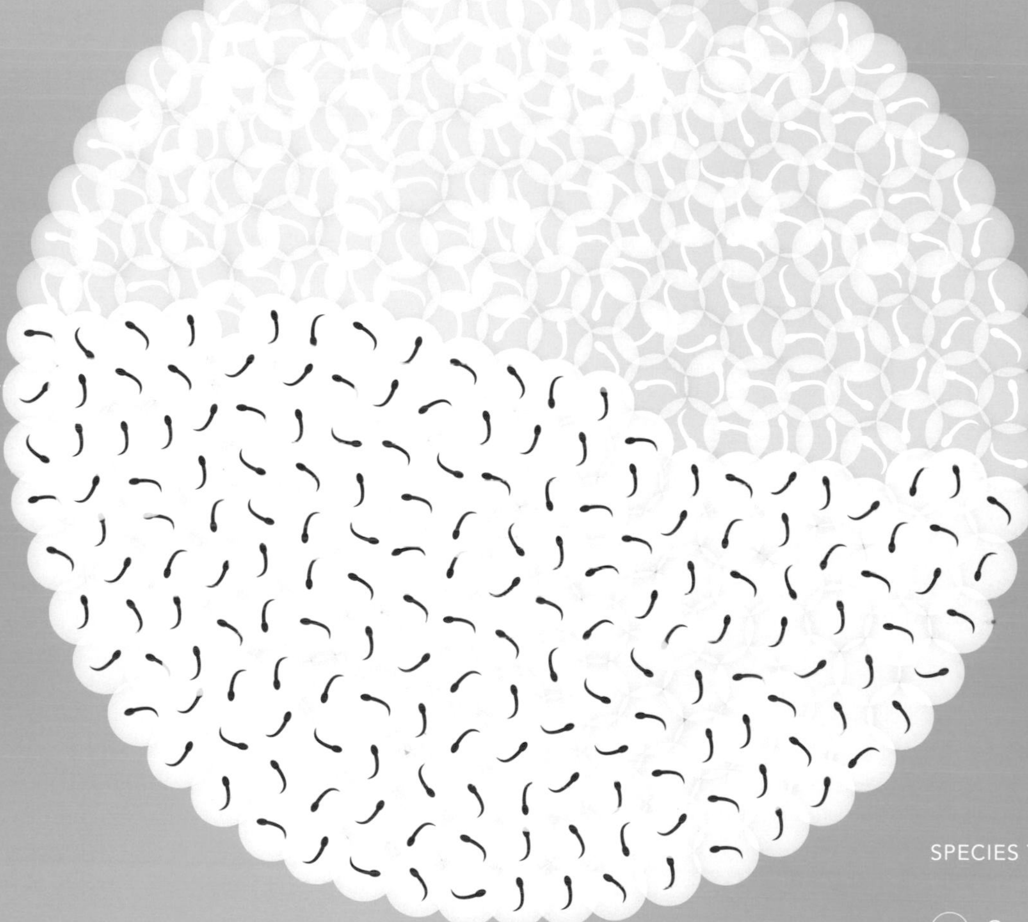

SPECIES TODAY

Gone 122

Going 427

At risk 2503

Still here 3497

source: National Academy of Sciences, Discovery.com

Motive

Searches for the phrase "we broke up because..."

he couldn't keep his hands to himself • "we're at different stages in our lives" • she was cheating with women • he wanted to experience the whole college thing • he said he needed space • he's a complete idiot with

I don't clip my toenails enough

• I was cheating on him so he made-out the guy I was cheating on him with • of Drugs • of Def Jam • of her partying ways • his parents don't like me • his girlfriend got suspicious • her husband needs oral sex • I didn't love her • i too much control him • of all of the time he spent on his attempts to break into film-making • we had different life goals • of religious reasons – he refused to worship me • of my drinking – I binge drink • he has a small pee-pee and wouldn't buy me any jewellery • I smothered her • we didn't have anything in common and everything was completely physical • of parental disapproval • he pressured me into having sex • I have a high-pitched voice! •

she just realized I'm a better friend

I wasn't comfortable telling her who I really am • we fell out of love • he couldn't keep his hands to himself • he is traumatized by his former relationship and can't reach his feelings for anything or anyone. • We, well, my family has money • i moved. i want him back more than i can say • I basically caught him in bed with one of his co-workers • he liked another guy. Yes, a guy • he was short and kind of looked like a giant mole that stood upright • of one of those arguments • she was way too hurt by my lack of effort to call her • I "bug" him • I was overprotective? • he lied too much & went crazy & punched a hole in the wall • he made out with my friend • i realized me being insecure due to the hurtful past experiences, was not going to enable us to take our level • he said i wasnt

he doesn't have "love" for me

relationship to the next treating him right. and i wasnt • of time and dist. • I was a complete arsehole to her • of this election • i asked "are we ok?" caused she seemed a little weird lately and she said next time you ask that again we are thru • we fought a lot and several red flags kept showing up • I felt that he deserved better than me. • I needed help. I have abandonment, insecurity, and anxiety issues • she wants to find herself as an individual • she likes to deal with her problems alone and not to really share them • he thinks his career won't match up to mine • I realized that I had been gradually developing strong feelings for one of her close friends • He belonged to a different religion and wanted me to convert • not because I got somebody pregnant • she hurt me on Valentines night • we love each other? • we had never been with anyone else and we felt it was too serious for our age To Treat Him Bad •

of artistic differences

• We Were On A Break And I Started i lied about my age • I can't make him stay with me • He's in love with his mother • I'm "immature" & like to party too much...... ummm hello I'm twenty-one!!!! • I couldn't have a tree • she didn't want to change her FB status • of the stock market • I'm passive • I wouldn't submit to his views on what a wife should be • we couldn't agree on a sex position together • he only saw me as a weekend fling • he has a fatal flaw, as caring, romantic, and intuitive as he is, he has a horrid temper... • I felt that he wasn't present in the relationship. I felt alone while seeing him • he was gay • I feel that I hurt her too much and I feel she deserves better • i told simple lies (small lies that i didnt have to tell) • im too "clingy" • he cheated on me twice and

he told people I was crazy

it was a year ago • I was jealous that he swiped her ass with her credit card, and not mine • she was too flirty • she just realized I'm a better friend. • he always ignored me and got mad over any little thing. He was extremely jealous • he messed around with my worse enemy • the sex was bad • his fear of commitment?!? • he is not financially stable • I am dangerous • no reason

source: searches for "we broke up because..." on Facebook, Twitter & Google. Apologies for heterosexual bias

Timing

Most common break-up times, according to Facebook status updates

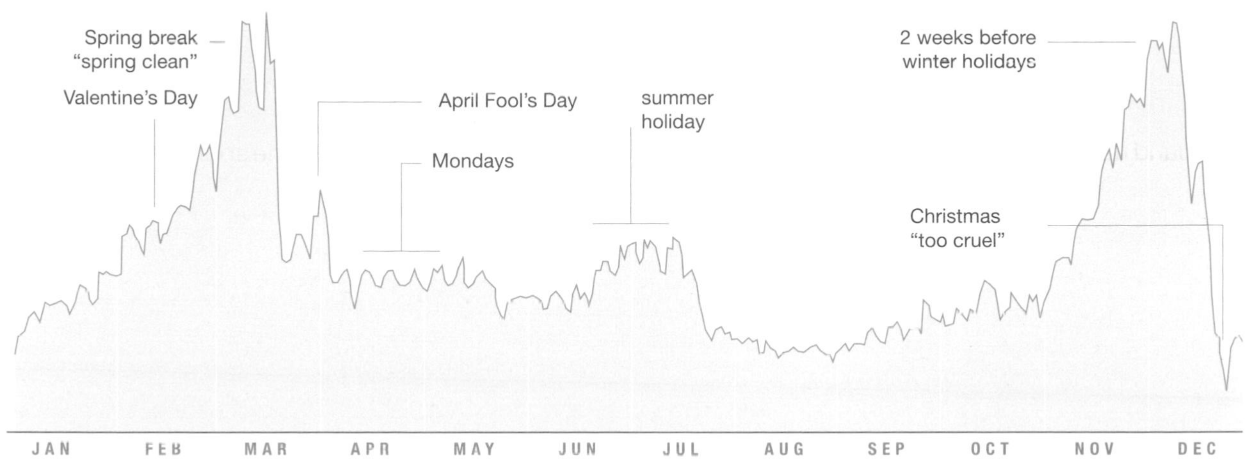
Spring break
"spring clean"
Valentine's Day
April Fool's Day
Mondays
summer
holiday
2 weeks before
winter holidays
Christmas
"too cruel"
JAN
FEB
MAR
APR
MAY
JUN
JUL
AUG
SEP
OCT
NOV
DEC

source: Facebook lexicon

Delivery

Most common methods of break-up

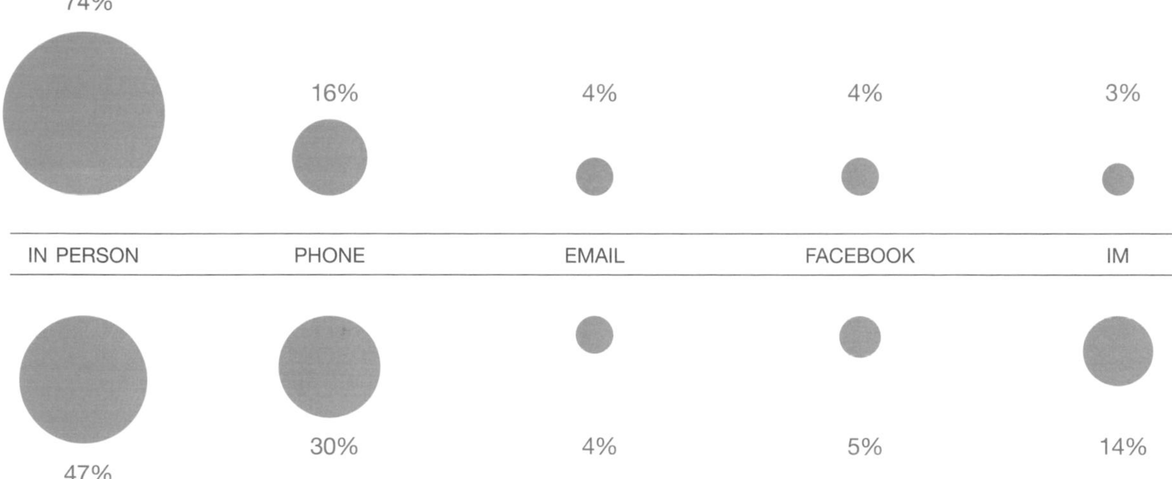
Those born before 1975
74%
16%
4%
4%
3%
IN PERSON
PHONE
EMAIL
FACEBOOK
IM
47%
30%
4%
5%
14%
Those born after 1984

source: survey of 10,000 Twitter users

Good News

It's all we could find. Sorry.

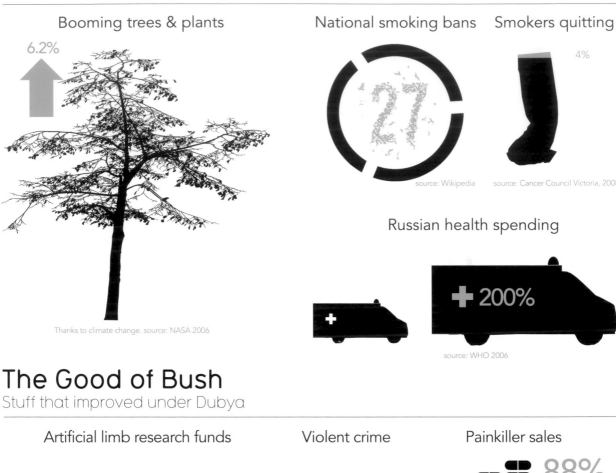

Booming trees & plants

6.2%

Thanks to climate change. source: NASA 2006

National smoking bans

27

source: Wikipedia

Smokers quitting

4%

source: Cancer Council Victoria, 2008

Russian health spending

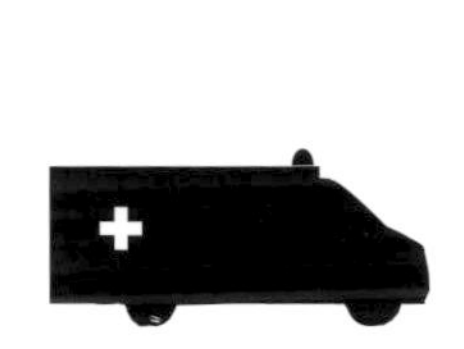

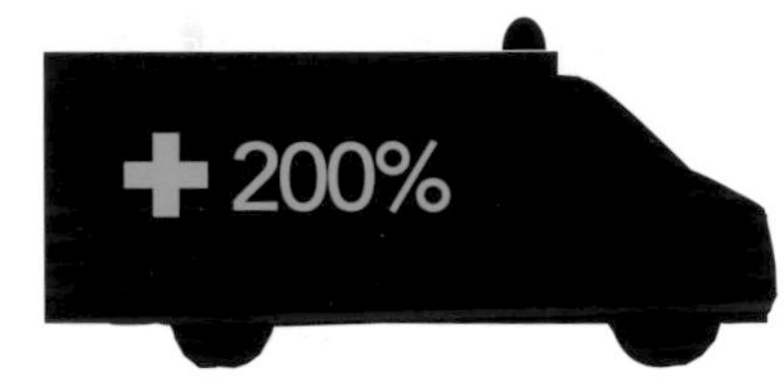

+ 200%

source: WHO 2006

The Good of Bush

Stuff that improved under Dubya

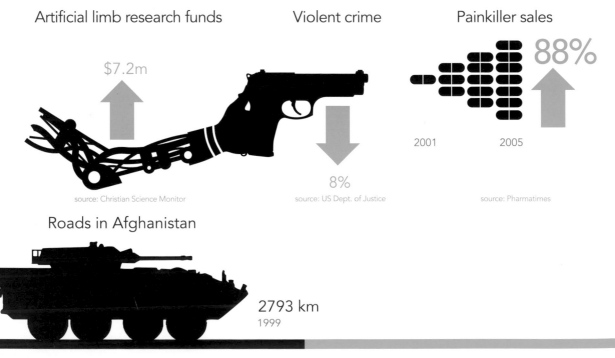

Artificial limb research funds

Violent crime

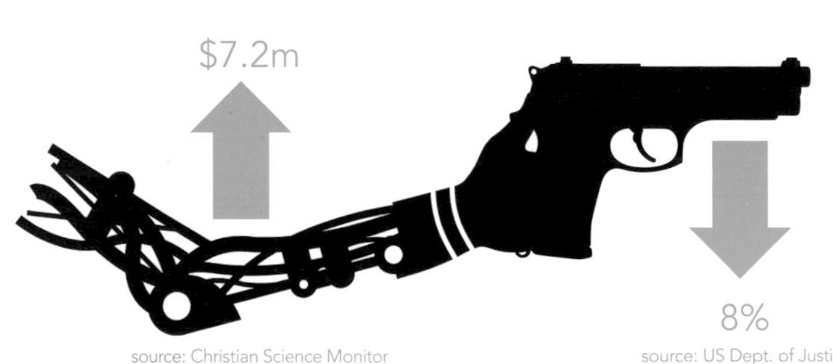

$7.2m
8%

source: Christian Science Monitor

source: US Dept. of Justice

Painkiller sales

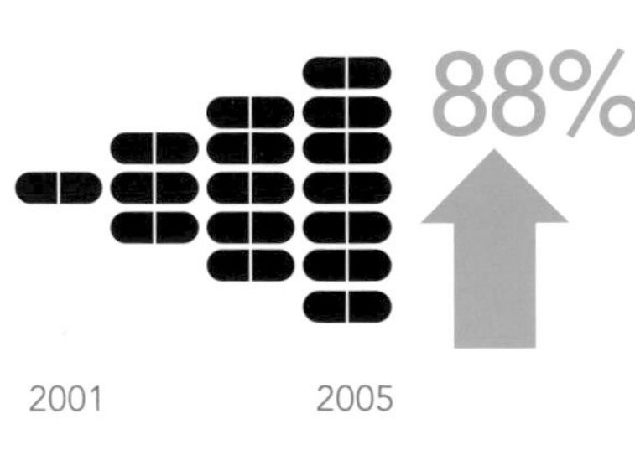

88%
2001
2005

source: Pharmatimes

Roads in Afghanistan

2793 km

1999

Mobile phones & cancer

SAFE

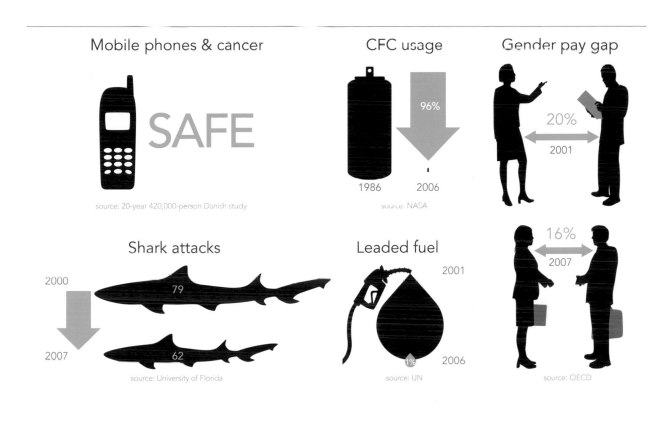

source: 20-year 420,000-person Danish study

CFC usage

96%

1986 2006

source: NASA

Gender pay gap

20%

2001

16%

2007

source: OECD

Shark attacks

2000

79

2007

62

source: University of Florida

Leaded fuel

2001

1%

2006

source: UN

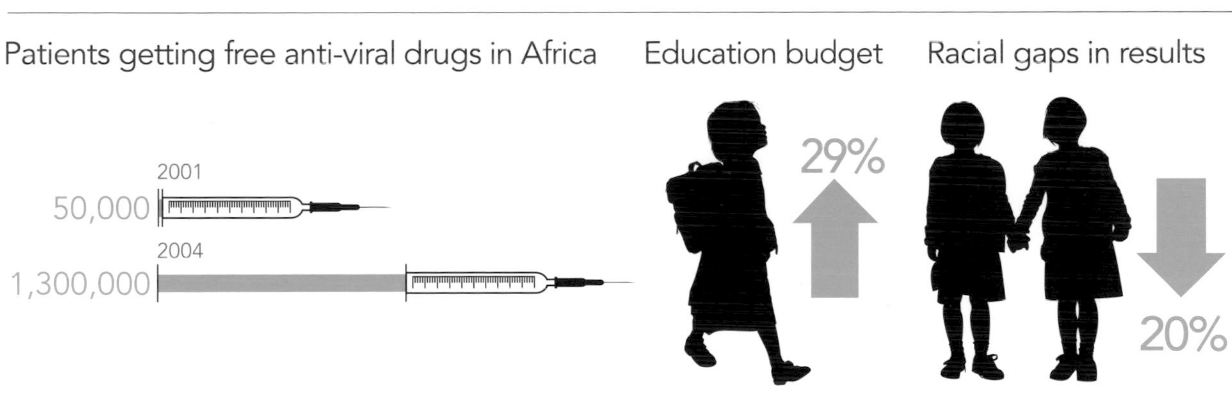

Patients getting free anti-viral drugs in Africa
2001
50,000
2004
1,300,000
Education budget
29%
Racial gaps in results
20%

source: Independent newspaper

source: US Dept. of Education

12350 km

2008

source: USAID

Immortality

Biographies of the famously long-lived examined for clues to longevity

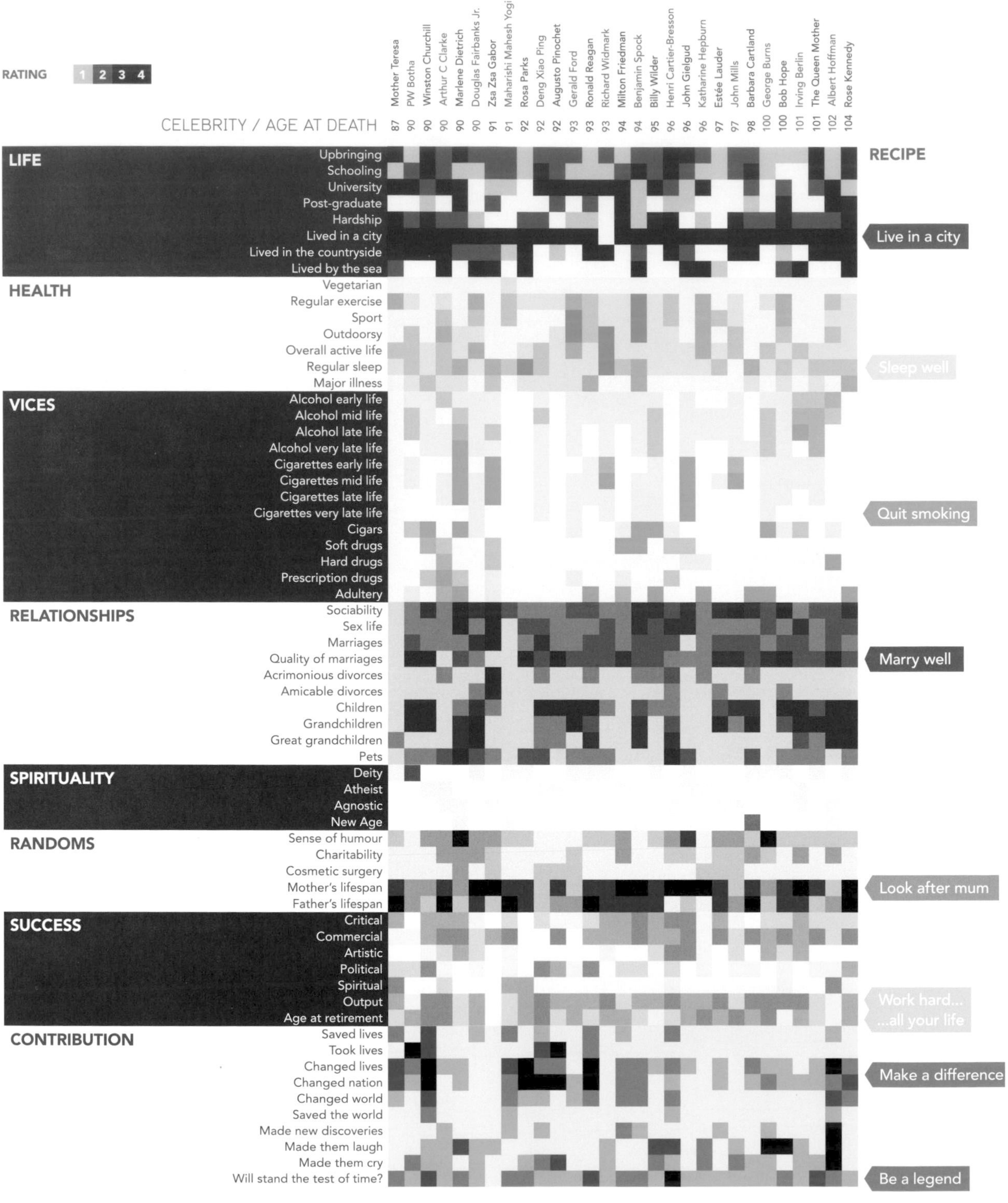

RATING
1 2 3 4
CELEBRITY / AGE AT DEATH
Mother Teresa 87
PW Botha 90
Winston Churchill 90
Arthur C Clarke 90
Marlene Dietrich 90
Douglas Fairbanks Jr. 90
Zsa Zsa Gabor 91
Maharishi Mahesh Yogi 91
Rosa Parks 92
Deng Xiao Ping 92
Augusto Pinochet 92
Gerald Ford 93
Ronald Reagan 93
Richard Widmark 93
Milton Friedman 94
Benjamin Spock 94
Billy Wilder 95
Henri Cartier-Bresson 96
John Gielgud 96
Katharine Hepburn 96
Estée Lauder 97
John Mills 97
Barbara Cartland 98
George Burns 100
Bob Hope 100
Irving Berlin 101
The Queen Mother 101
Albert Hoffman 102
Rose Kennedy 104
LIFE
Upbringing
Schooling
University
Post-graduate
Hardship
Lived in a city
Lived in the countryside
Lived by the sea
HEALTH
Vegetarian
Regular exercise
Sport
Outdoorsy
Overall active life
Regular sleep
Major illness
VICES
Alcohol early life
Alcohol mid life
Alcohol late life
Alcohol very late life
Cigarettes early life
Cigarettes mid life
Cigarettes late life
Cigarettes very late life
Cigars
Soft drugs
Hard drugs
Prescription drugs
Adultery
RELATIONSHIPS
Sociability
Sex life
Marriages
Quality of marriages
Acrimonious divorces
Amicable divorces
Children
Grandchildren
Great grandchildren
Pets
SPIRITUALITY
Deity
Atheist
Agnostic
New Age
RANDOMS
Sense of humour
Charitability
Cosmetic surgery
Mother's lifespan
Father's lifespan
SUCCESS
Critical
Commercial
Artistic
Political
Spiritual
Output
Age at retirement
CONTRIBUTION
Saved lives
Took lives
Changed lives
Changed nation
Changed world
Saved the world
Made new discoveries
Made them laugh
Made them cry
Will stand the test of time?
RECIPE
Live in a city
Sleep well
Quit smoking
Marry well
Look after mum
Work hard...
...all your life
Make a difference
Be a legend

source: Wikipedia

War Chests

Who has the biggest military budget per year?

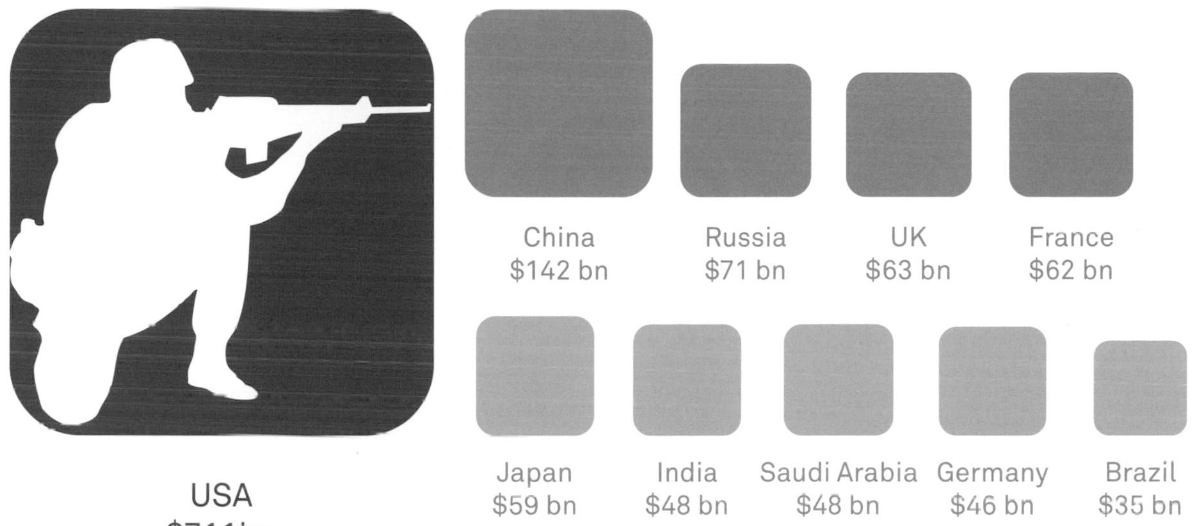
China
$142 bn
Russia
$71 bn
UK
$63 bn
France
$62 bn
Japan
$59 bn
India
$48 bn
Saudi Arabia
$48 bn
Germany
$46 bn
Brazil
$35 bn
USA
$711bn

War Chests II

Who has the biggest military budget as a % of GDP?

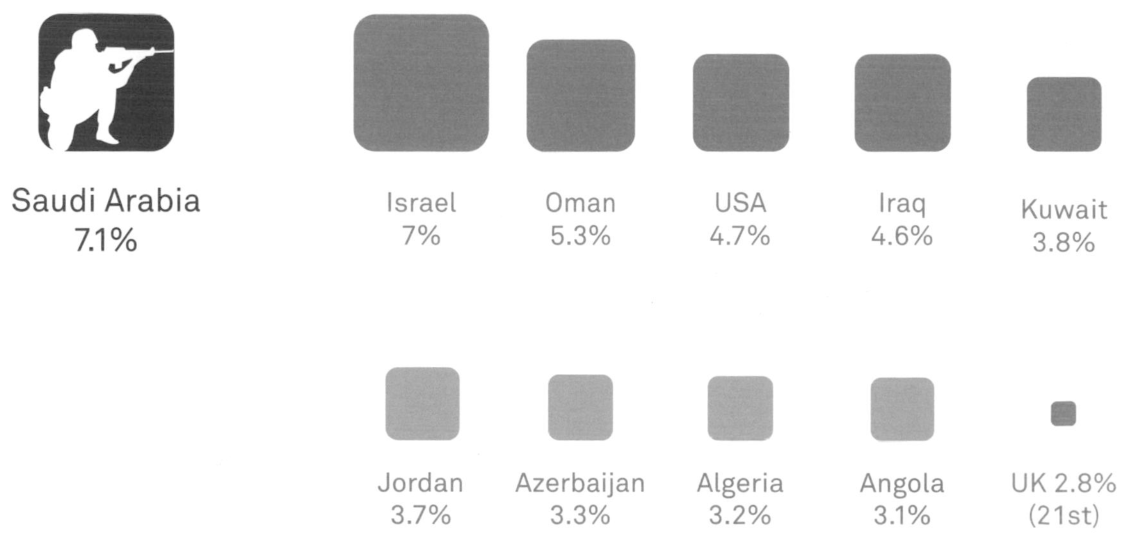
Saudi Arabia
7.1%
Israel
7%
Oman
5.3%
USA
4.7%
Iraq
4.6%
Kuwait
3.8%
Jordan
3.7%
Azerbaijan
3.3%
Algeria
3.2%
Angola
3.1%
UK 2.8%
(21st)

source: Stockholm International Peace Research Institute, sipri.org

2012: The End of the World?

Sceptics vs Believers

2012 BELIEVERS

We believe cataclysmic or transformative events will occur in the year 2012

Mayan archaeological, mythological, and numerological sources all point to December 21st 2012 as a momentous date in the history of humanity.

The planet and its inhabitants may undergo a positive physical or spiritual transformation. Or the date may mark the beginning of an apocalypse...

2012 SCEPTICS

We do not believe anything significant, transformative or apocalyptic will happen in the year 2012

The idea of a global event occurring in 2012 based on any interpretation of the Mayan calendar is rejected as pseudoscience by the scientific community.

It is also considered a misrepresentation of Mayan history by Mayanist scholars.

2012 MAYAN PROPHECY? 2012

BELIEVERS

The ancient Mayans predicted the end of the world in 2012

The Mayan's longest calendar, The Long Count, lasts approximately 5,125 years (13 baktuns) and ends around December 21st 2012.

The end of the calendar signifies the end of a great cycle and the end of the world.

SCEPTICS

The Mayans did not predict the end of the world in 2012

Scholars disagree about the end date. Also different Mayan city states had different Long Counts. Some lasted 7,886 years (20 baktuns).

The end of the calendar did not mean the end of creation. Mayans celebrated the ends of cycles. Predictions were also made for events after the calendar ended.

BELIEVERS

The Mayan's "Hunab Ku" symbol signifies their understanding of cosmic forces on humanity

This Hunab Ku, the name of Mayan diety, is a leading symbol of the 2012 movement. The Hunab Ku bears a resemblance to both a ying-yang symbol and a spiral galaxy. Just an amazing coincidence?

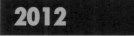

SCEPTICS

This isn't a Mayan symbol. It's Aztec and has no known assocation to "Hunab Ku" or the Mayans

This symbol was originally rectangular and used by the Aztecs, not the Mayans, as a ritual cloak design known as "The Mantle of Lip Plugs". It was turned into a circular symbol and associated with the Milky way by the New Age author Jose Arguelles in 1987.

THE MAYAN LONG COUNT CALENDAR

THE MAYANS COUNTED IN BASE 20 (fingers & toes) ⬭ = 0 • = 1 ▬ = 5

3,200,000's						•••• ▬▬ ▬▬ *
160,000's					•• ▬▬ ▬▬ ▬▬	⬭
8000's				•• ▬▬ ▬▬ ▬▬	⬭	⬭
400's			•• ▬▬ ▬▬ ▬▬	⬭	⬭	⬭
20's		•	⬭	⬭	⬭	⬭
1's	•	⬭	⬭	⬭	⬭	⬭
mayan	kin	winal	tun	katun	baktun	13 x baktuns
solar time	**1** day	**20** days	**360** days	**19.7** years	**394.3** years	**5125.36** years

*N.B. this final Mayan number may be incorrect

START DATE: **AUG 11th or 13th 3113 BCE** END DATE: **DEC 21st or 23rd 2012 AD**

Image: S. Gronemeyer

TORTUGUERO MONUMENT 6

SOME OF THE INSCRIPTION IS ILLEGIBLE

BELIEVERS

Mayan texts are full of references to 2012 (date 13.0.0.0.0 in Mayan).

Present-day Mayan elders believe that 2012 is the year of the transformational "shift".

SCEPTICS

The only reference to 2012 is carved in one single monument found in Tortuguero, Mexico. (And the long count calendar used in Tortuguero was a 7,886 year, 20 baktun, version.)

Very few modern day Mayans use the Long Count calendar. It was only recently discovered by archaeologists. "Apocalypse" is a Western concept that has little to do with Mayan belief.

CELESTIAL SIGNIFICANCE?

2012

PRECESSION OF THE EQUINOXES

A wobble in the Earth's axis slowly traces out a cone over approximately 25,685 years. This means the constellations shift by 1 degree every 72 years. A full rotation is called a Precession.

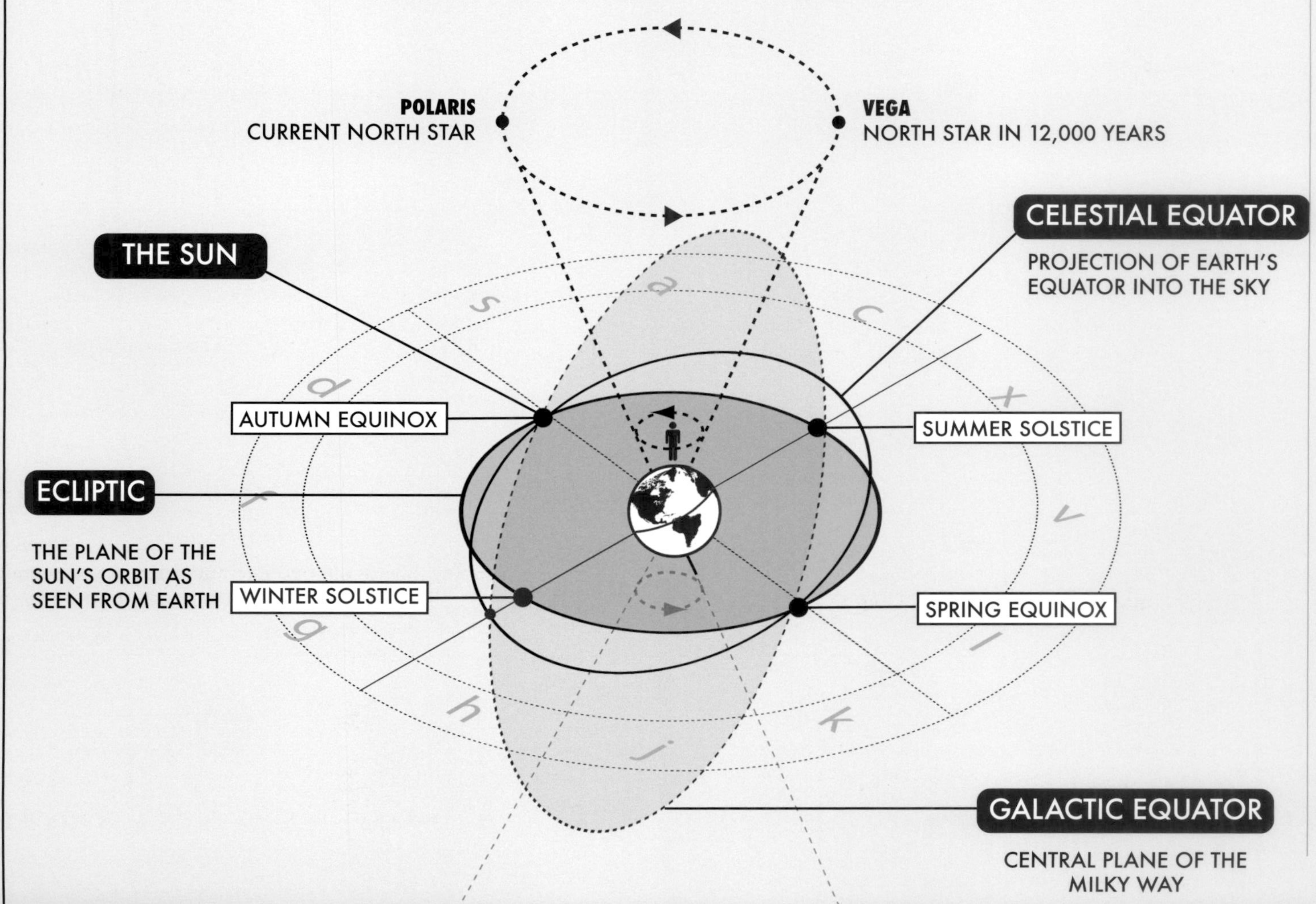
POLARIS
CURRENT NORTH STAR
VEGA
NORTH STAR IN 12,000 YEARS
THE SUN
CELESTIAL EQUATOR
PROJECTION OF EARTH'S EQUATOR INTO THE SKY
AUTUMN EQUINOX
SUMMER SOLSTICE
ECLIPTIC
THE PLANE OF THE SUN'S ORBIT AS SEEN FROM EARTH
WINTER SOLSTICE
SPRING EQUINOX
GALACTIC EQUATOR
CENTRAL PLANE OF THE MILKY WAY

BELIEVERS

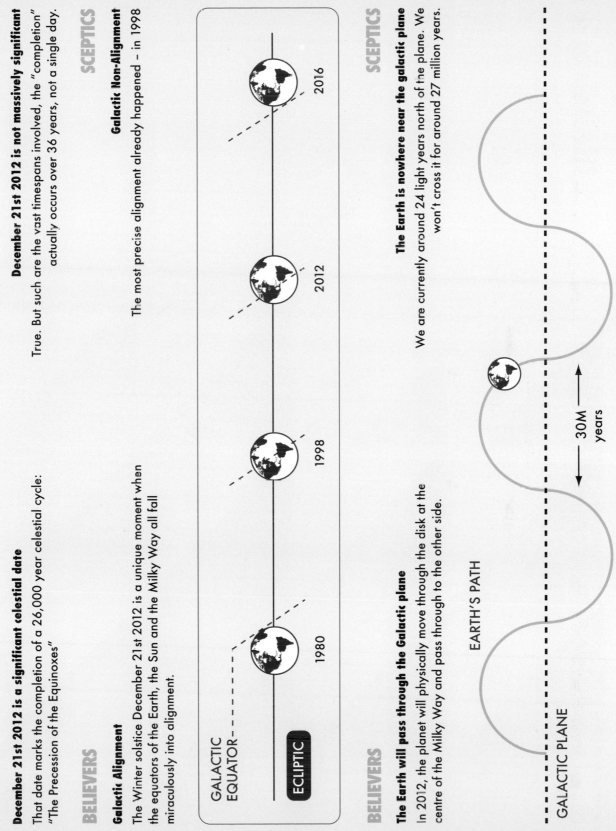

December 21st 2012 is a significant celestial date

That date marks the completion of a 26,000 year celestial cycle: "The Precession of the Equinoxes"

SCEPTICS

December 21st 2012 is not massively significant

True. But such are the vast timespans involved, the "completion" actually occurs over 36 years, not a single day.

BELIEVERS

Galactic Alignment

The Winter solstice December 21st 2012 is a unique moment when the equators of the Earth, the Sun and the Milky Way all fall miraculously into alignment.

SCEPTICS

Galactic Non-Alignment

The most precise alignment already happened – in 1998

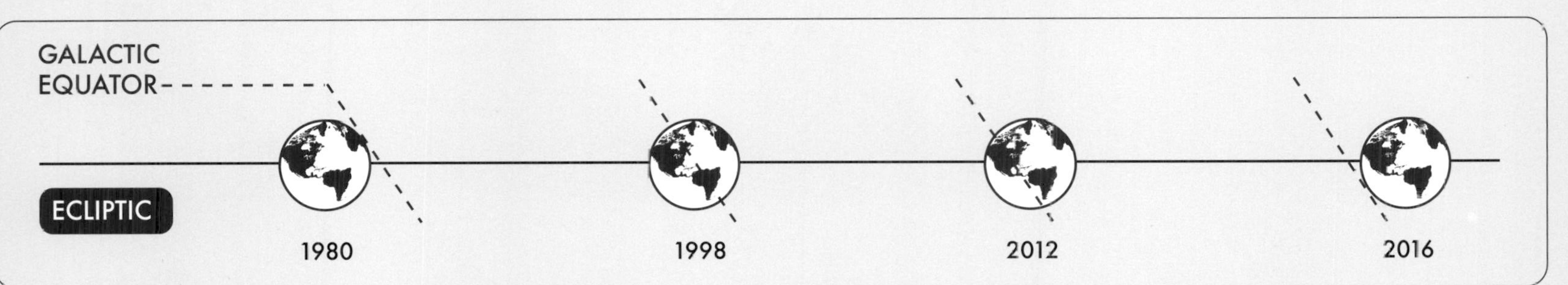
GALACTIC EQUATOR
ECLIPTIC
1980
1998
2012
2016

BELIEVERS

The Earth will pass through the Galactic plane

In 2012, the planet will physically move through the disk at the centre of the Milky Way and pass through to the other side.

SCEPTICS

The Earth is nowhere near the galactic plane

We are currently around 24 light years north of the plane. We won't cross it for around 27 million years.

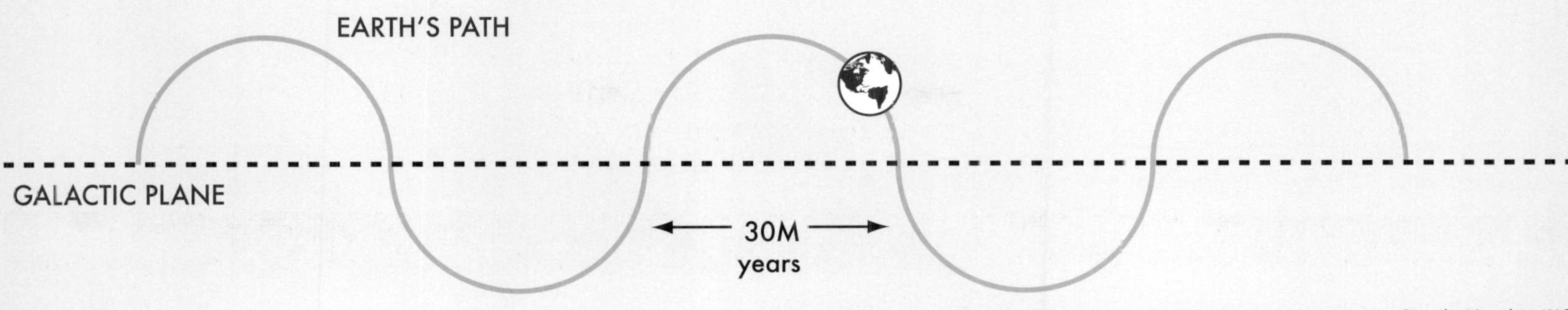
EARTH'S PATH
GALACTIC PLANE
30M years

source: diagnosis2012.co.uk, realitysandwich.com, Associated Press, Astronomy Answers, Skeptical Inquirer, NASA

Red vs Blue

Scientists have discovered that when two evenly matched teams compete, the team wearing red wins most often

American Football
San Francisco 49ers — Denver Broncos

Handball
Norway — France

Rugby Union
Gloucester — Bristol

American Football
Kansas City Chiefs — Tennessee Titans/ Houston Oilers

Baseball
LA Anaheim Angels — Toronto Blue Jays

Ten Pin Bowling
USA — Europe

Football
Arsenal — Chelsea

Ice Hockey
Detroit Red Wings — Columbus Blue Jackets

Politics
Republican — Democrats

Football
Bayern Munich — Schalke

Rugby League
Wigan Warriors — Leeds Rhinos

Politics
Labour — Conservative

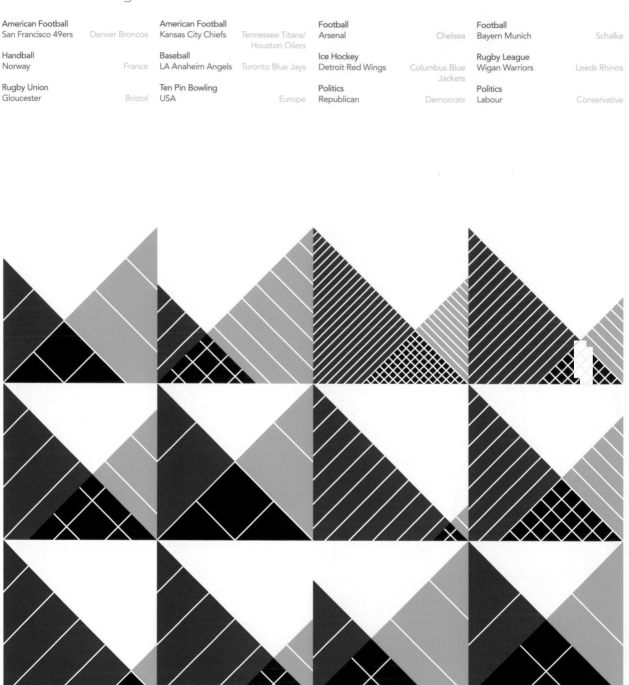

Red win 8

Blue win 2

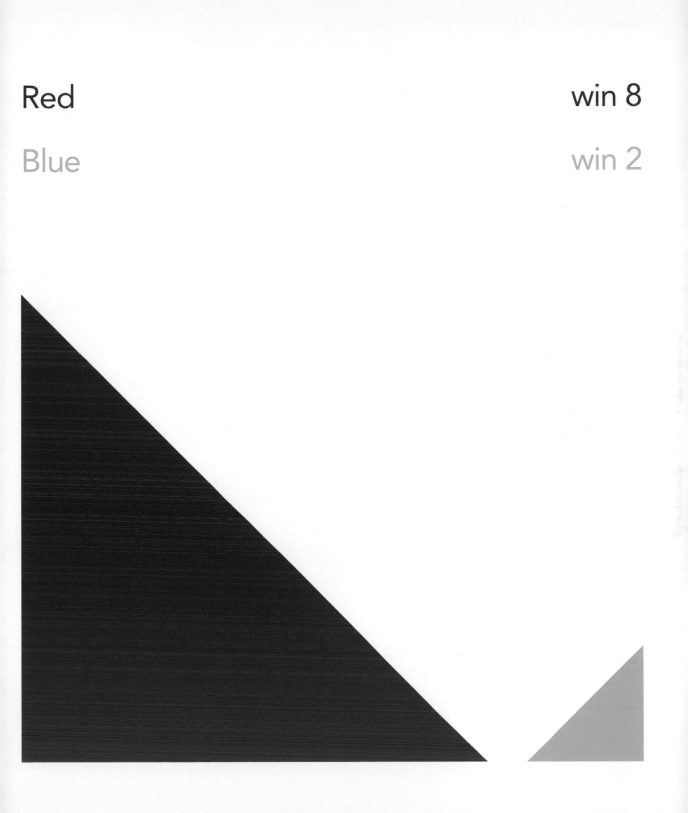

source: Hill & Barton, University of Durham, Journal of Sports Sciences [via Nature], Wikipedia

Man's Humanity to Man

Ah, that's better

Live Aid
$283m

9/11 concert
$35m

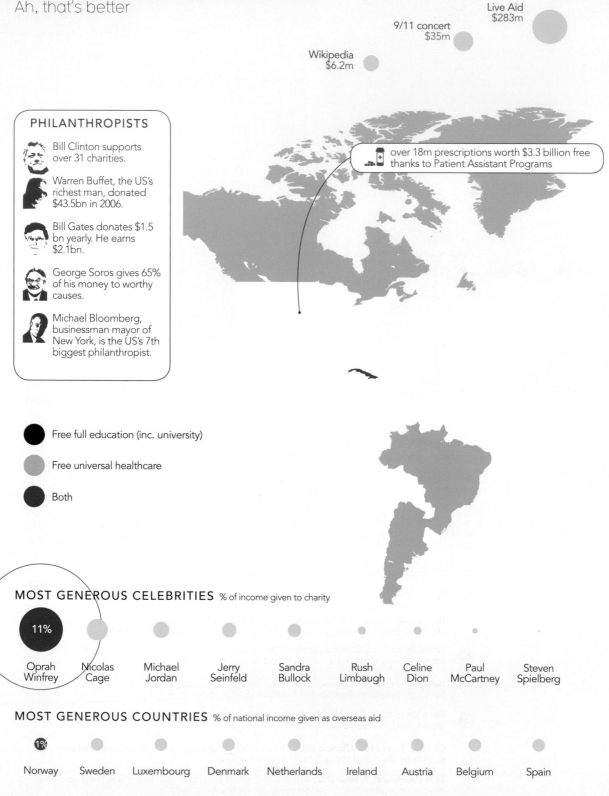

Wikipedia
$6.2m

PHILANTHROPISTS

Bill Clinton supports over 31 charities.

Warren Buffet, the US's richest man, donated $43.5bn in 2006.

Bill Gates donates $1.5 bn yearly. He earns $2.1bn.

George Soros gives 65% of his money to worthy causes.

Michael Bloomberg, businessman mayor of New York, is the US's 7th biggest philanthropist.

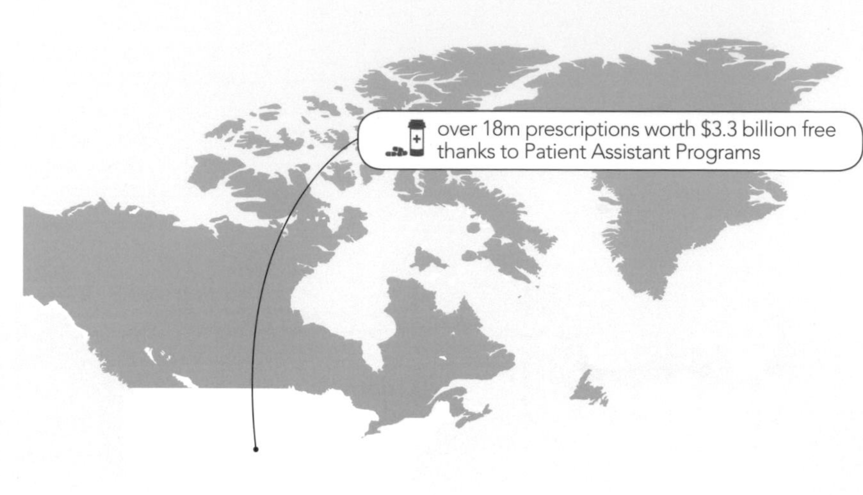
over 18m prescriptions worth $3.3 billion free thanks to Patient Assistant Programs

Free full education (inc. university)

Free universal healthcare

Both

MOST GENEROUS CELEBRITIES % of income given to charity

11%

Oprah Winfrey | Nicolas Cage | Michael Jordan | Jerry Seinfeld | Sandra Bullock | Rush Limbaugh | Celine Dion | Paul McCartney | Steven Spielberg

MOST GENEROUS COUNTRIES % of national income given as overseas aid

1%

Norway | Sweden | Luxembourg | Denmark | Netherlands | Ireland | Austria | Belgium | Spain

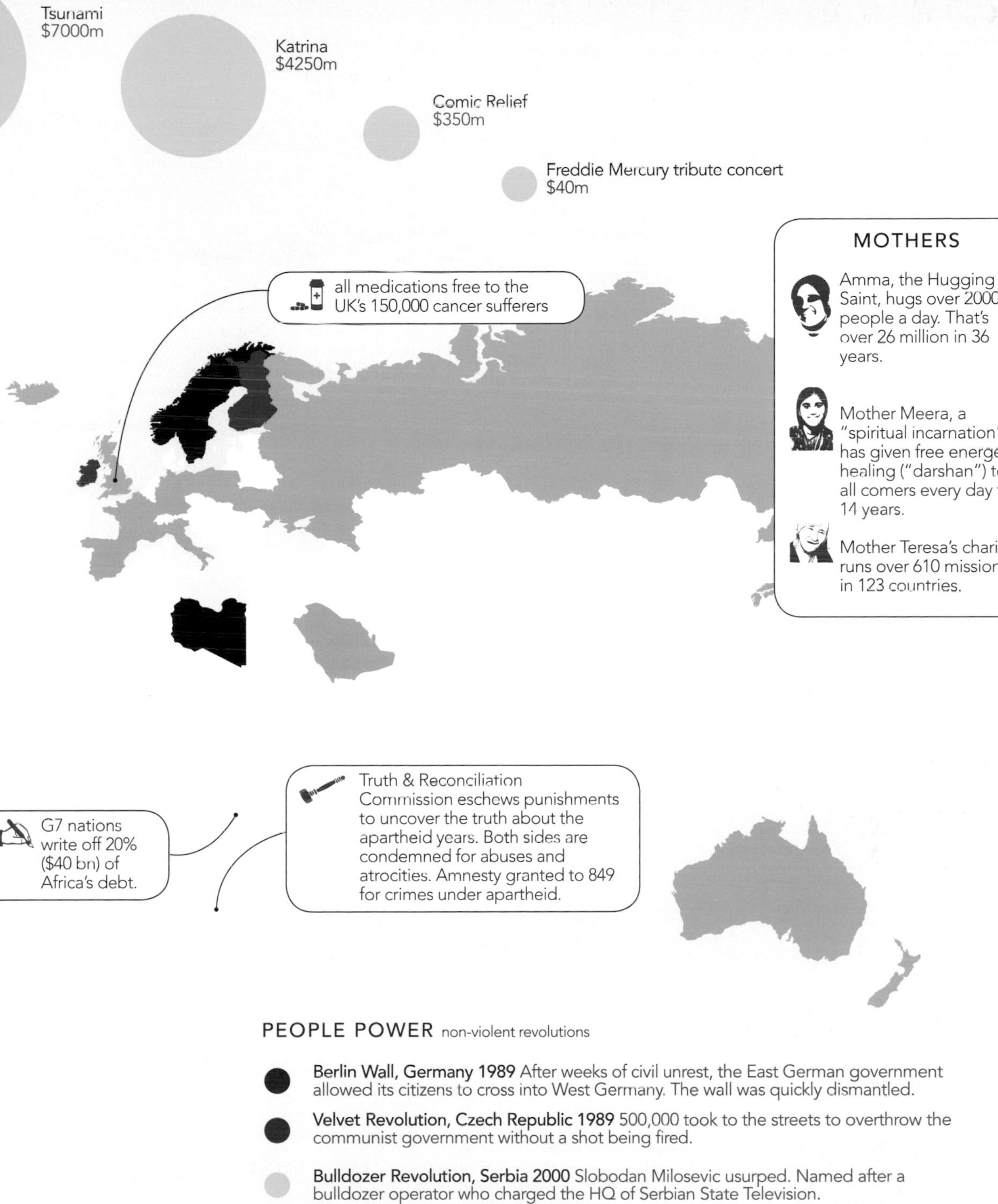

Tsunami
$7000m
Katrina
$4250m
Comic Relief
$350m
Freddie Mercury tribute concert
$40m
all medications free to the UK's 150,000 cancer sufferers
G7 nations write off 20% ($40 bn) of Africa's debt.
Truth & Reconciliation Commission eschews punishments to uncover the truth about the apartheid years. Both sides are condemned for abuses and atrocities. Amnesty granted to 849 for crimes under apartheid.

MOTHERS

Amma, the Hugging Saint, hugs over 2000 people a day. That's over 26 million in 36 years.

Mother Meera, a "spiritual incarnation", has given free energetic healing ("darshan") to all comers every day for 14 years.

Mother Teresa's charity runs over 610 missions in 123 countries.

PEOPLE POWER non-violent revolutions

Berlin Wall, Germany 1989 After weeks of civil unrest, the East German government allowed its citizens to cross into West Germany. The wall was quickly dismantled.

Velvet Revolution, Czech Republic 1989 500,000 took to the streets to overthrow the communist government without a shot being fired.

Bulldozer Revolution, Serbia 2000 Slobodan Milosevic usurped. Named after a bulldozer operator who charged the HQ of Serbian State Television.

Rose Revolution, Georgia 2003 A disputed election led to the peaceful overthrow of president-elect Eduard Shevardnadze.

Orange Revolution, Ukraine 2004 Thousands protested against a presidential election marred by fraud and corruption. Election annulled.

Blue Revolution, Kuwait 2005 Kuwaitis protested in support of giving women the vote. The government gave in and women voted for the first time in 2007.

source: Wikipedia, Unicef.org, Forbes.com, Un.org

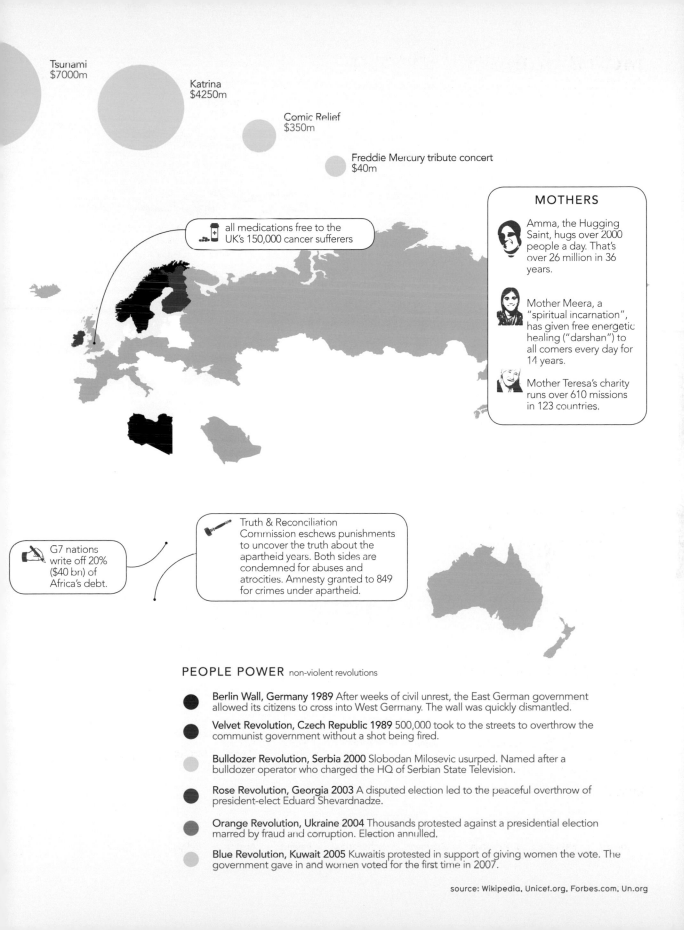

Fast Internet

Most popular search terms 2006

love
world cup 2006
jessica alba
Футбол
в кредит
Päasiäien
Juhannus
царские часы
Lordi
lordi
blocket
eniro
Krak
Ofir
Arto
ebay
argos
big brother
casino
ryanair
hartpatientensichting
routeplanner
wm 2006
marktplaats
wikipedia
wetter
skyblog
pages jaunes
coppa del monda fifa
meteo
juventus
marca
as
rebelde way

Most popular search terms 2008
iphone
wikipedia
iltasanomat
youtube
rovaniemi
tube
borlange
tampere
swedbank
stockholm
aland
trondheim
iltalekti
malmo
kart
spill
lyrics
torrent
video
karte
delfi
one
games
BBC
Bebo
News
Ebay
Facebook
Cardiff
wetter
rapidshare
berlin
you tu
radio
google
schulervz
opole
opisy
o2
mp3
corse
pages jaunes
Yahoo
YouTube
wkw
ebay
bratislava
iwiw
Jeux
Video
Y Tu
tirol
miskolc
terkep
budapest
tv
libero
roma
Bordeux
Correo
Hotmail
hotm
marca
Madrid
Marca
juegos
Hi5
Madeira
Sport
you tu
badoo
tiscali

idea: Christian Lange coccu.de source: Google Zeitgeist.
Years after 2009 not plotted due to dominance of Facebook.

Most popular search terms 2009

rovaniemi
youtube
ostersund
oulu
lyrics
kuopio
trondheim
borlänge
stockholm
ordbok
norge
facebook
iltalehti
eesti
bergen
download
kristiansand
google
in
video
zaidimai
one
viborg
BBC
Bebo
nasza klasa
białystok
wetter
berlin
gry
rzeszów
opole
hyves
erfurt
jena
netlog
wkw
mp3
orange
wer
saarland
seznam
tv
iwiw
letöltés
játékok
wien
miskolc
klagenfurt
terkep
lyon
bern
gmail
bon coin
libero
tuenti
hotmail
bilbao
correo
barcelona
Hi5
girona
jogos
valencia
roma
napoli
palermo
cagliari

Most popular search terms 2006

seattle
MySpace
lyrics
weather
games
youtube
Yahoo
Las Vegas
wyoming
omaha
albuquerque
yahoo
Myspace
my
new orleans
boston
you

Most popular search terms 2008

Most popular search terms 2009

idea: Christian Lange coccu.de source: Google Zeitgeist.
Years after 2009 not plotted due to dominance of Facebook.

Simple Part II

Time to Get Away

Legally required paid annual leave in days per year

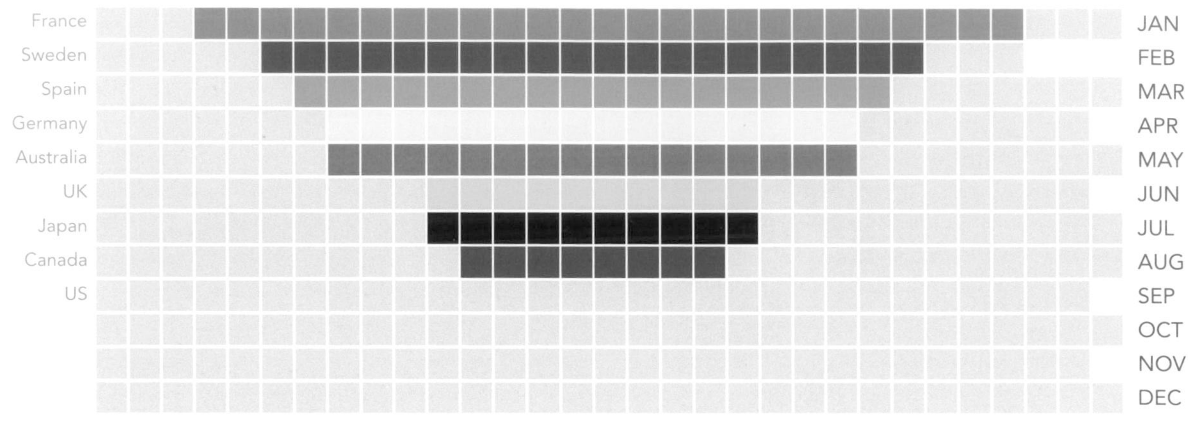
France
Sweden
Spain
Germany
Australia
UK
Japan
Canada
US
JAN
FEB
MAR
APR
MAY
JUN
JUL
AUG
SEP
OCT
NOV
DEC

source: Centre for Economic & Policy Research, 2007

Lack of Conviction

Rape in England and Wales

Reports
Prosecutions
Convictions
2542
690
5.7%

source: UK Home Office

Trafficking

World internet bandwidth usage

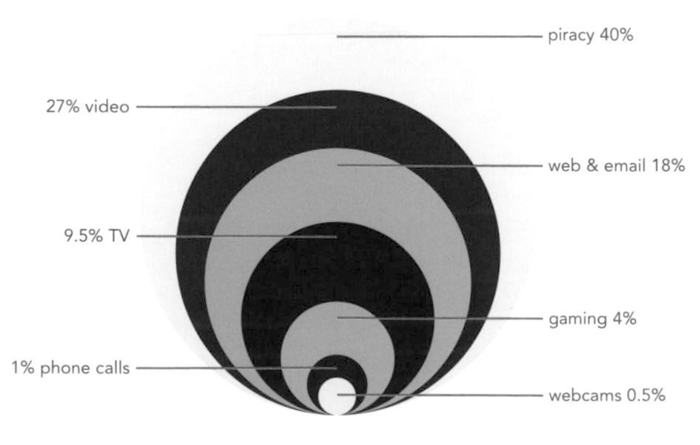
piracy 40%
27% video
web & email 18%
9.5% TV
gaming 4%
1% phone calls
webcams 0.5%

source: Cisco visual networking index

Fat Chance

Who has the most influence on your weight?

Shooting Stars

Worldwide yearly arms sales

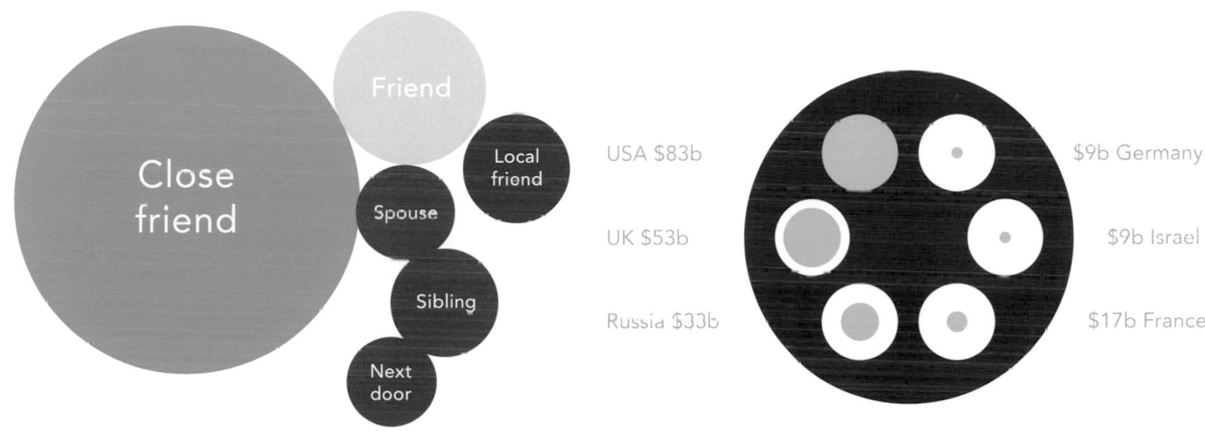

Friend
Close friend
Local friend
Spouse
Sibling
Next door
USA $83b
UK $53b
Russia $33b
$9b Germany
$9b Israel
$17b France

source: N.Fowler, J.Christakis, N. England Journal of Medicine [via New Scientist]

source: Guardian.co.uk

Caused by Global Warming

according to media reports

CLIMATE CHANGE Alaska reshaping, oak deaths, ozone repair slowing, El Niño intensification, Gulf Stream failure, new islands, sinking islands, melting alps, mud slides, volcanic eruptions, subsidence, wildfires, earthquakes, tsunamis RANDOMS witchcraft executions, violin decline, killer cornflakes, tabasco tragedy, truffle shortage, tomato rot, fashion disasters, gingerbread house collapse, mammoth dung melt, UFO sightings, mango harvest failure ANIMALS cannibal polar bears, brain-eating amoebas, aggressive elephants, cougar attacks, stronger salmon, rampant robins, shark attacks, confused birds THE EARTH! light dimming, slowing down, spins faster, wobbling, exploding SOCIAL PROBLEMS floods of migrants, suicides, drop in brothel profits, civil unrest, increased taxes, teenage drinking, early marriages, crumbling roads, deformed railways, traffic jams FOOD soaring prices, sour grapes, shop closures, haggis threat, maple syrup shortage, rice shortage, beer shortage! THE TREES! growth increase, growth decline, more colourful, less colourful HEALTH PROBLEMS dog disease, cholera, bubonic plague, airport malaria, asthma, cataracts, smaller brains, HIV, heart disease, depression LESS moose, geese, ducks, puffins, koalas EVEN LESS krill, fish, glaciers, antarctic ice, ice sheets, avalanches, coral reef MOUNTAINS shrinking, taller, flowering, breaking up INVASIONS cat, crabgrass, wasp, beatle, midge, cockroach, stingrays, walrus, giant pythons, giant oysters, giant squid MORE HEALTH PROBLEMS salmonella, kidney stones, anxiety, childhood insomnia, frostbite, fainting, dermatitis, fever, encephalitis, declining circumcision, diarrhoea, fever, dengue, yellow, west nile, hay DISASTER! boredom, next ice age, cannibalism, societal collapse, release of ancient frozen viruses, rioting and nuclear war, computer models, terrorism, accelerated evolution, conflict with Russia, billions of deaths, the end of the world as we know it

source: UK and US media reports [via numberswatch.co.uk]

Life Times

How will you spend your 77.8 years?

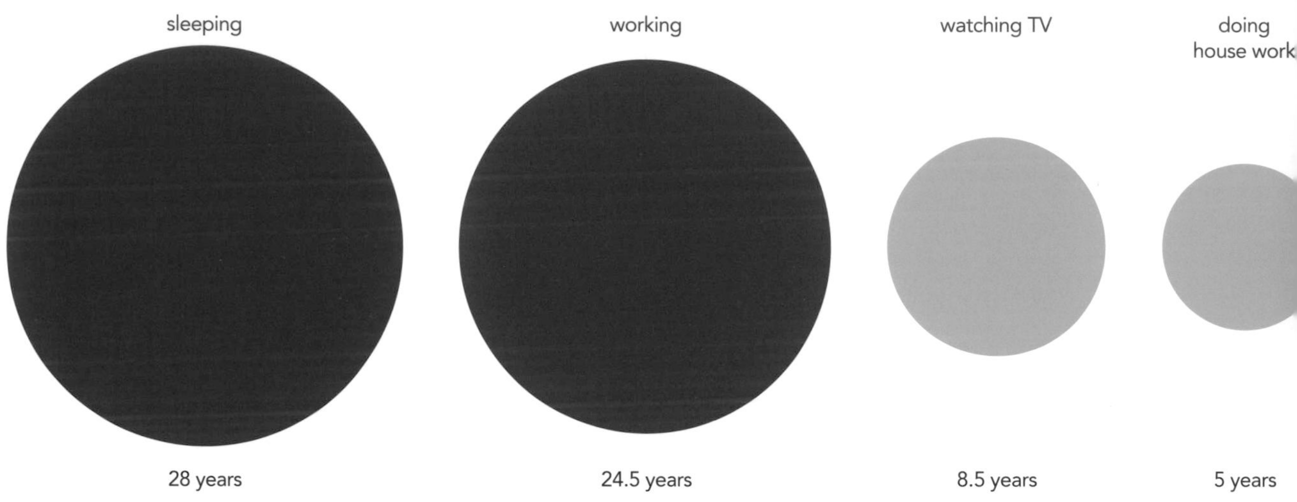

sleeping
working
watching TV
doing
house work
28 years
24.5 years
8.5 years
5 years

Visible Spectrum

Current best guess for the composition of the universe Dark energy // Dark matter // Intergalactic gas // Normal ma

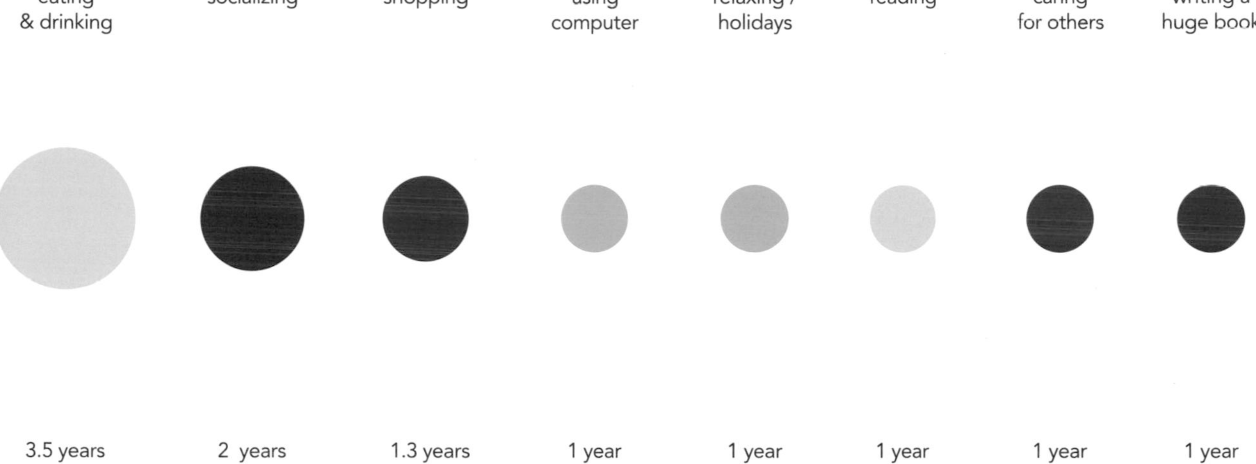
eating & drinking
socializing
shopping
using computer
relaxing / holidays
reading
caring for others
writing a huge book
3.5 years
2 years
1.3 years
1 year
1 year
1 year
1 year
1 year

source: American Bureau of Labor Statistics 2007

s, planets, us etc)
78%
22%
3.6%
0.4%
Visible

source: Wikipedia

Peters Projection

The true size of the continents

The standard "Mercator" world map inflates the size of nations depending on their distance from the equator. This means that many developing countries end up much smaller than they are in reality (i.e. most of Africa). The Peters Projection corrects this.

source: Wikipedia

Alternative Medicine

Scientific evidence for complementary therapies

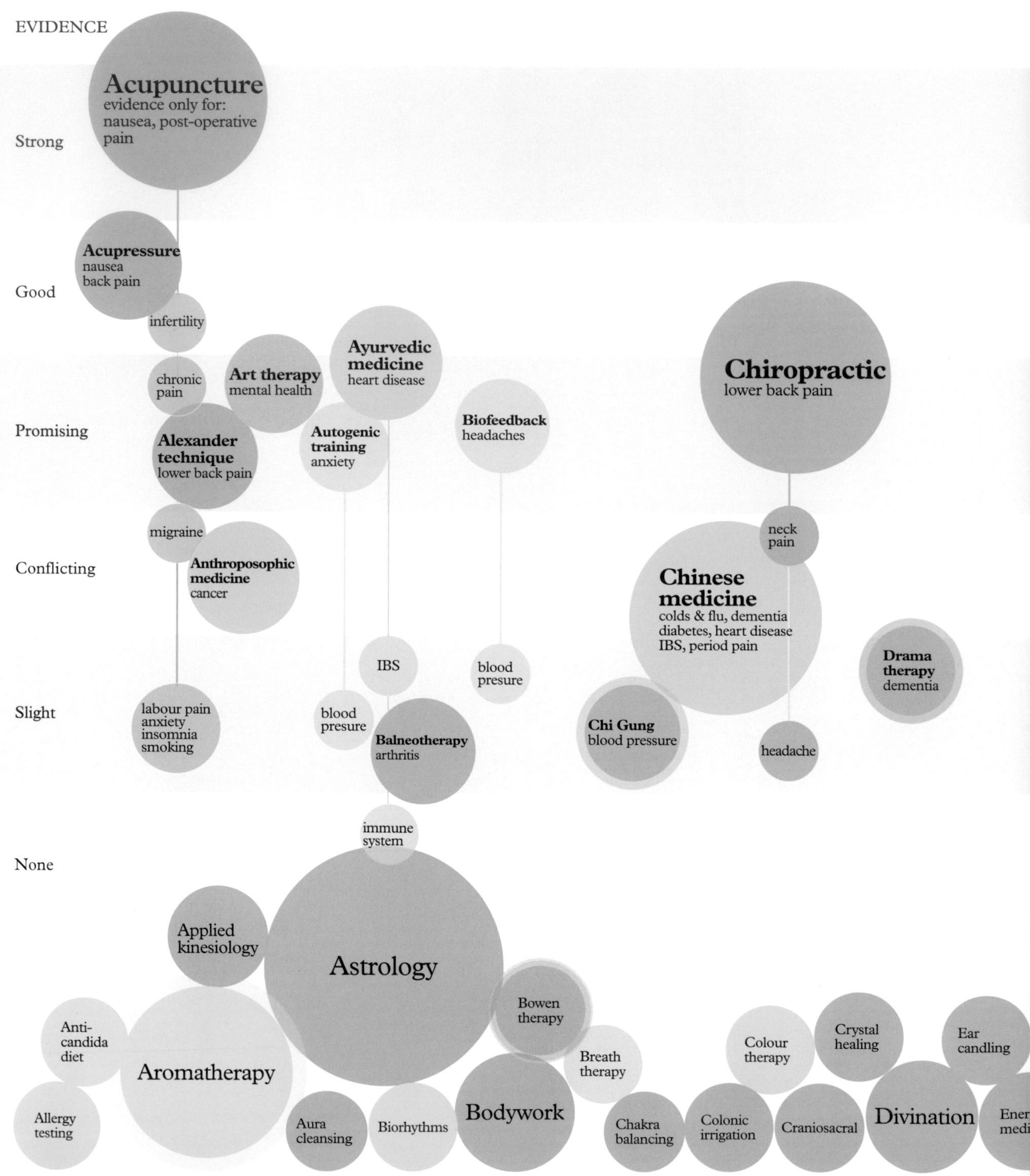

EVIDENCE
Strong
Good
Promising
Conflicting
Slight
None
Acupuncture
evidence only for: nausea, post-operative pain
Acupressure
nausea
back pain
infertility
chronic pain
Art therapy
mental health
Ayurvedic medicine
heart disease
Alexander technique
lower back pain
Autogenic training
anxiety
Biofeedback
headaches
Chiropractic
lower back pain
migraine
Anthroposophic medicine
cancer
neck pain
Chinese medicine
colds & flu, dementia
diabetes, heart disease
IBS, period pain
IBS
blood presure
Drama therapy
dementia
labour pain
anxiety
insomnia
smoking
blood presure
Balneotherapy
arthritis
Chi Gung
blood pressure
headache
immune system
Applied kinesiology
Astrology
Bowen therapy
Anti-candida diet
Aromatherapy
Breath therapy
Colour therapy
Crystal healing
Ear candling
Allergy testing
Aura cleansing
Biorhythms
Bodywork
Chakra balancing
Colonic irrigation
Craniosacral
Divination

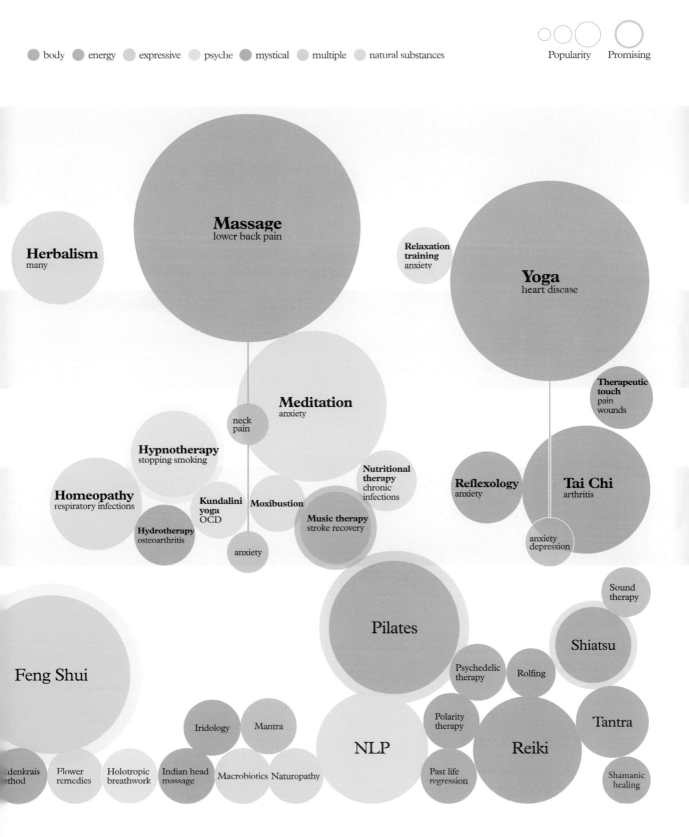

body
energy
expressive
psyche
mystical
multiple
natural substances

Popularity
Promising

Massage
lower back pain

Herbalism
many

Relaxation training
anxiety

Yoga
heart disease

Meditation
anxiety

neck pain

Therapeutic touch
pain
wounds

Hypnotherapy
stopping smoking

Nutritional therapy
chronic infections

Reflexology
anxiety

Tai Chi
arthritis

Homeopathy
respiratory infections

Kundalini yoga
OCD

Moxibustion

Music therapy
stroke recovery

Hydrotherapy
osteoarthritis

anxiety

anxiety
depression

Sound therapy

Pilates

Shiatsu

Feng Shui

Psychedelic therapy

Rolfing

Tantra

Iridology

Mantra

Polarity therapy

NLP

Reiki

denkrais
ethod

Flower remedies

Holotropic breathwork

Indian head massage

Macrobiotics

Naturopathy

Past life regression

Shamanic healing

source: Cochrane.org and other English-language meta-studies (via Pubmed.org)

Radiation Dosage

Risk of harm is dependent on both the **dose** and the **dose rate** (the time the body is exposed to that dose).

So a dose of 1,000 mSv over an hour is considerably more damaging than a dose of 1,000 mSv over a year.

Exposure Time

Instant · **Hours** · **One Day** · **One Year**

microsieverts (μSv)

0.1 μSv

0.1 — Airport security scan (backscatter X-ray)
Eating a banana

0.25 — Airport security scan maximum permitted

1.0 μSv

1.0 — Using a cathode-ray computer monitor for a year

5.0 — Dental X-ray

7.5 — Per day in Tokyo, 250km SW of Fukushima plant (+107 days after the disaster, 28 June 2011)

10 μSv

10 — Background dose received by an average person on an average day (varies wildly)

40 — Flight from New York to LA

70 — Living in a stone, brick or concrete building for a year

80 — Average total dose per person within 10 miles of the Three Mile Island Accident (1979)

100 μSv

100 — Chest X-ray — One hour dose 3km SW of Fukushima plant (+83 days after the disaster, 3 June 2011)

250 — Release limit for a nuclear power plant for a year

400 — Yearly dose per person from food

1000 μSv

1,000 — **US government yearly limit on artificial radiation exposure to a member of the public**

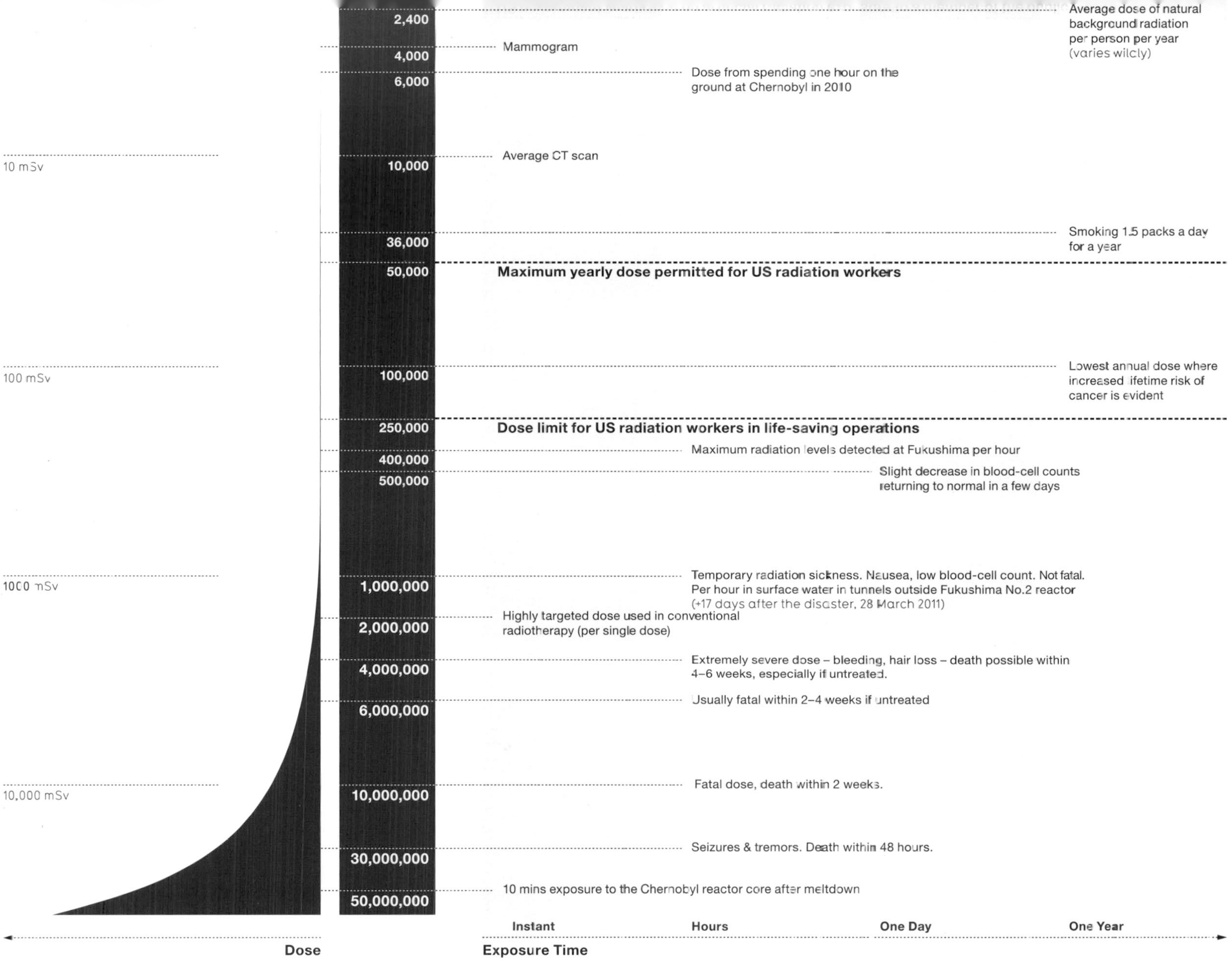

10 mSv

100 mSv

1000 mSv

10,000 mSv

Dose

Dose	
2,400	Average dose of natural background radiation per person per year (varies wildly)
4,000	Mammogram
6,000	Dose from spending one hour on the ground at Chernobyl in 2010
10,000	Average CT scan
36,000	Smoking 1.5 packs a day for a year
50,000	**Maximum yearly dose permitted for US radiation workers**
100,000	Lowest annual dose where increased lifetime risk of cancer is evident
250,000	**Dose limit for US radiation workers in life-saving operations**
400,000	Maximum radiation levels detected at Fukushima per hour
500,000	Slight decrease in blood-cell counts returning to normal in a few days
1,000,000	Temporary radiation sickness. Nausea, low blood-cell count. Not fatal. Per hour in surface water in tunnels outside Fukushima No.2 reactor (+17 days after the disaster, 28 March 2011)
2,000,000	Highly targeted dose used in conventional radiotherapy (per single dose)
4,000,000	Extremely severe dose – bleeding, hair loss – death possible within 4–6 weeks, especially if untreated.
6,000,000	Usually fatal within 2–4 weeks if untreated
10,000,000	Fatal dose, death within 2 weeks.
30,000,000	Seizures & tremors. Death within 48 hours.
50,000,000	10 mins exposure to the Chernobyl reactor core after meltdown

Instant — Hours — One Day — One Year

Exposure Time

source: EPA, BBC, Guardian Datablog

Being Defensive

How psychotherapy sees you

common issues
anger, self-destructive behaviour, addictions, sado-masochism
low self-esteem
feelings of worthlessness
"I don't deserve love."

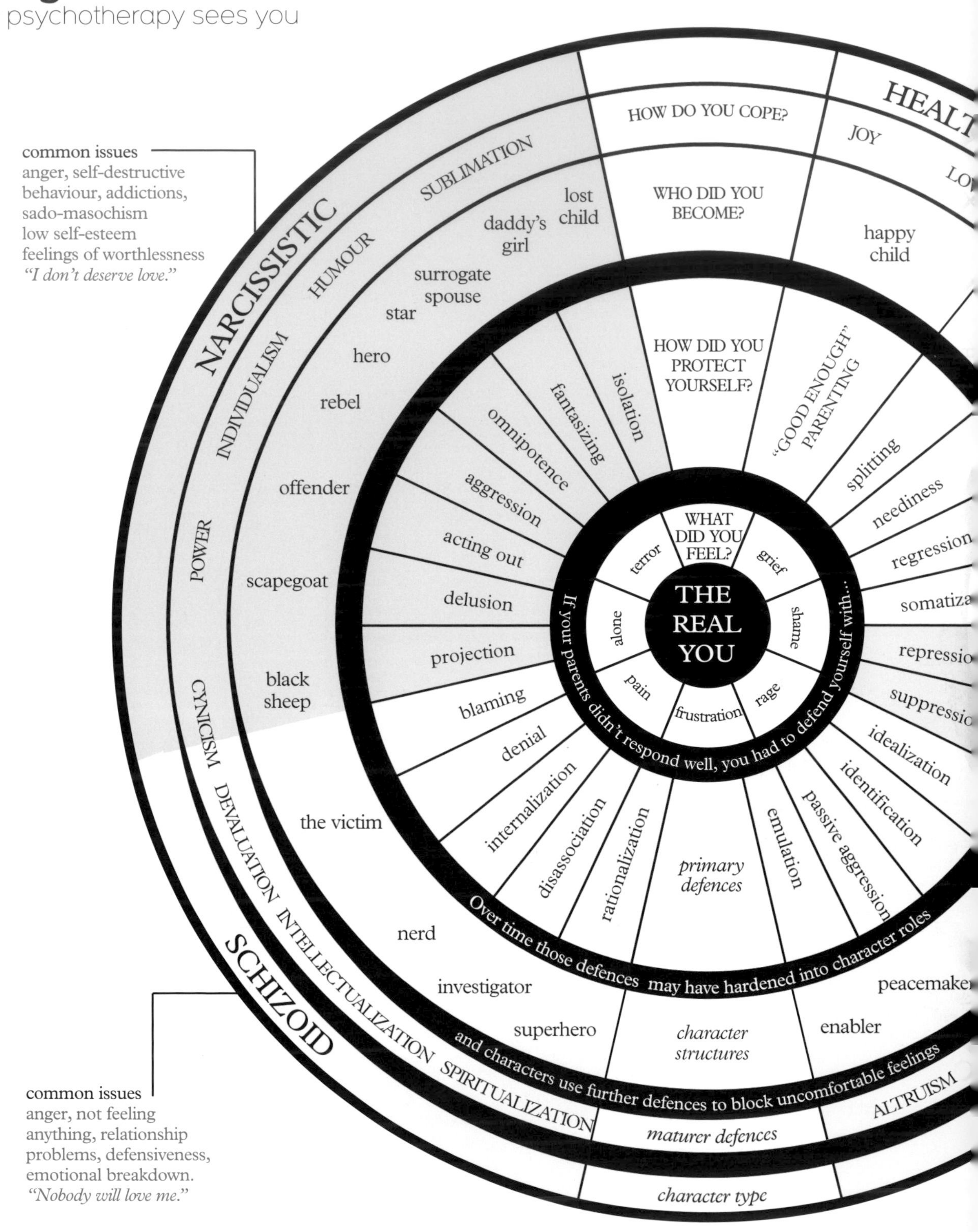

NARCISSISTIC
SCHIZOID
HEALT
HOW DO YOU COPE?
JOY
LO
SUBLIMATION
HUMOUR
INDIVIDUALISM
POWER
CYNICISM
DEVALUATION
INTELLECTUALIZATION
SPIRITUALIZATION
ALTRUISM
WHO DID YOU BECOME?
lost child
daddy's girl
surrogate spouse
star
hero
rebel
offender
scapegoat
black sheep
the victim
nerd
investigator
superhero
happy child
peacemake
enabler
HOW DID YOU PROTECT YOURSELF?
"GOOD ENOUGH" PARENTING
isolation
fantasizing
omnipotence
aggression
acting out
delusion
projection
blaming
denial
internalization
disassociation
rationalization
primary defences
emulation
passive aggression
identification
idealization
suppressio
repressio
somatiza
regression
neediness
splitting
WHAT DID YOU FEEL?
terror
grief
alone
shame
pain
frustration
rage
THE REAL YOU
If your parents didn't respond well, you had to defend yourself with...
Over time those defences may have hardened into character roles
character structures
and characters use further defences to block uncomfortable feelings
maturer defences
character type

common issues
anger, not feeling anything, relationship problems, defensiveness, emotional breakdown.
"Nobody will love me."

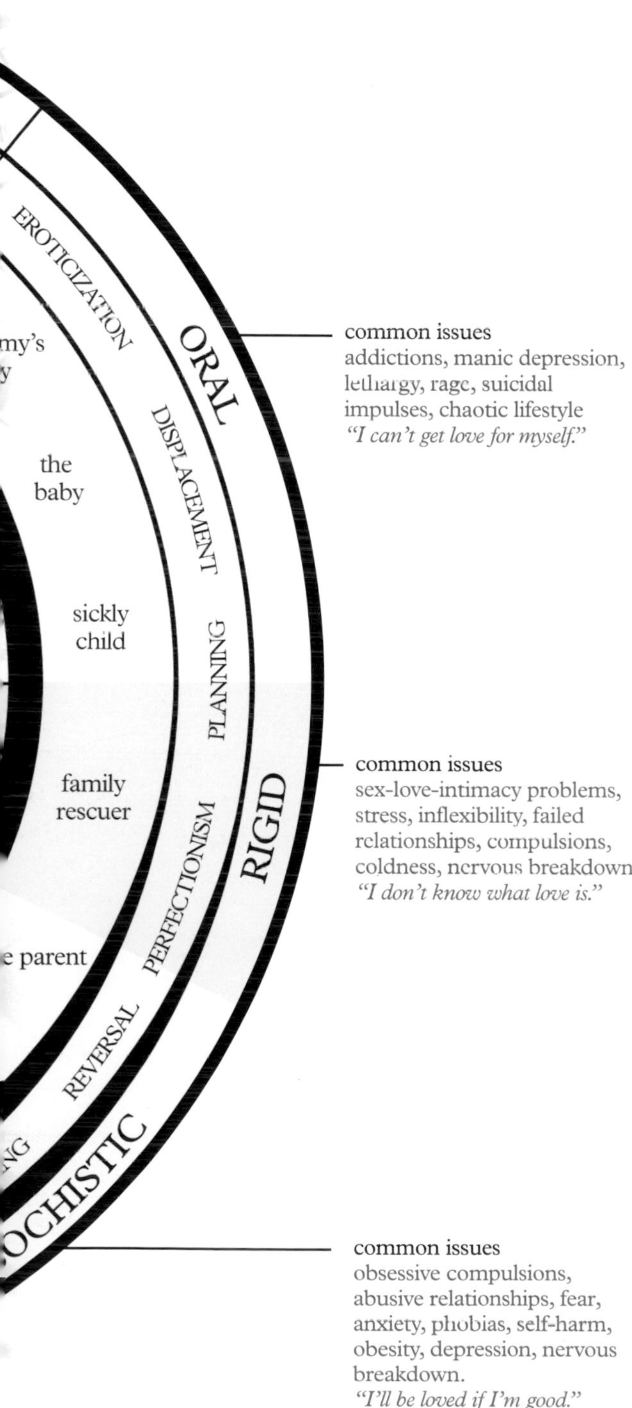

EROTICIZATION
ORAL
DISPLACEMENT
the baby
sickly child
PLANNING
family rescuer
RIGID
PERFECTIONISM
parent
REVERSAL
OCHISTIC

common issues
addictions, manic depression, lethargy, rage, suicidal impulses, chaotic lifestyle
"I can't get love for myself."

common issues
sex-love-intimacy problems, stress, inflexibility, failed relationships, compulsions, coldness, nervous breakdown
"I don't know what love is."

common issues
obsessive compulsions, abusive relationships, fear, anxiety, phobias, self-harm, obesity, depression, nervous breakdown.
"I'll be loved if I'm good."

PRIMARY DEFENCES

acting out
turn it into behaviour

aggression
attacking

blaming
someone else's fault

delusion
lie to yourself & believe it

denial
it's not happening

disassociation
go numb

distortion
changing the story to fit

emulation
copy what you know

fantasizing
go into other worlds

idealization
over-regard for others

identification
forge an alliance

internalization
holding it all in

isolation
separate off feelings

neediness
over-dependence on another

omnipotence
all powerful, no weakness

passive aggression
indirect & concealed attacks

projection
put your feelings on someone

regression
revert back to immaturity

rationalization
a false but plausible excuse

repression
unconsciously burying it

somatization
turn it into a physical illness

splitting
good/bad, love/hatred

suppression
consciously burying it

MATURER DEFENCES

altruism
efface it with good deeds

cynicism
everything is false

devaluation
it doesn't matter

displacement
find a teddy bear

eroticization
safety in sex

humour
deflect with jokes

individualism
celebrate it

intellectualization
turn it into safe concepts

perfectionism
never slip up again

planning
safety in organization

power
control everyone

reversal
do the opposite of how you feel

spiritualization
it's all a divine purpose

sublimation
make art out of it

undoing
constant acts of compensation

source: the work of Freud, Heinz Kohut, John Bradshaw and A.H. Almaas

Being Defensive

How psychotherapy works

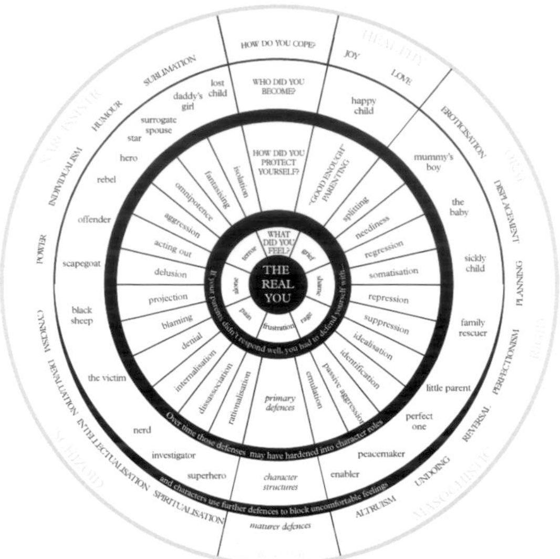

HOW DO YOU COPE?
JOY
LOVE
EROTICISATION
DISPLACEMENT
PLANNING
PERFECTIONISM
REVERSAL
UNDOING
ALTRUISM
maturer defences
SPIRITUALISATION
INTELLECTUALISATION
DEVALUATION
CYNICISM
POWER
INDIVIDUALISM
HUMOUR
SUBLIMATION
WHO DID YOU BECOME?
lost child
daddy's girl
surrogate spouse
star
hero
rebel
offender
scapegoat
black sheep
the victim
nerd
investigator
superhero
character structures
enabler
peacemaker
perfect one
little parent
family rescuer
sickly child
the baby
mummy's boy
happy child
HOW DID YOU PROTECT YOURSELF?
"GOOD ENOUGH" PARENTING
isolation
fantasising
omnipotence
aggression
acting out
delusion
projection
blaming
denial
internalisation
disassociation
rationalisation
primary defences
emulation
passive aggression
identification
idealisation
suppression
repression
somatisation
regression
neediness
splitting
WHAT DID YOU FEEL?
grief
shame
rage
frustration
pain
alone
terror
THE REAL YOU
If your parents didn't respond well, you had to defend yourself with...
Over time those defences may have hardened into character roles
and characters use further defences to block uncomfortable feelings

You slowly build a relationship of trust and intimacy with the therapist. That allows you to investigate, explore and ultimately learn to drop your outer defences without feeling threatened.

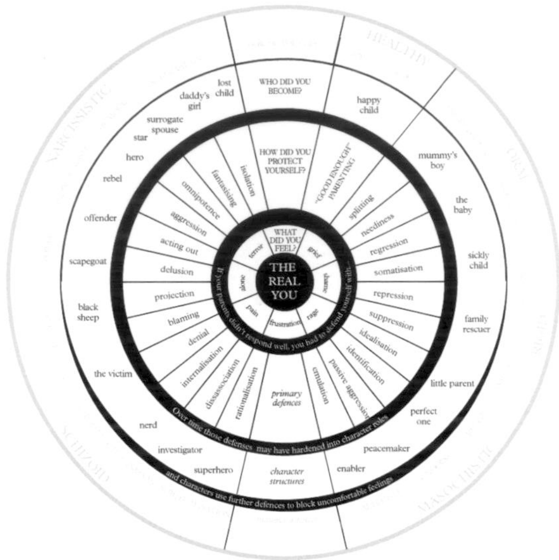

WHO DID YOU BECOME?
lost child
daddy's girl
surrogate spouse
star
hero
rebel
offender
scapegoat
black sheep
the victim
nerd
investigator
superhero
character structures
enabler
peacemaker
perfect one
little parent
family rescuer
sickly child
the baby
mummy's boy
happy child
HOW DID YOU PROTECT YOURSELF?
"GOOD ENOUGH" PARENTING
isolation
fantasising
omnipotence
aggression
acting out
delusion
projection
blaming
denial
internalisation
disassociation
rationalisation
primary defences
emulation
passive aggression
identification
idealisation
suppression
repression
somatisation
regression
neediness
splitting
WHAT DID YOU FEEL?
grief
shame
rage
frustration
pain
alone
terror
THE REAL YOU
If your parents didn't respond well, you had to defend yourself with...
Over time those defences may have hardened into character roles
and characters use further defences to block uncomfortable feelings

Exploring your life history, you re-experience situations and relationships from childhood in slow motion with the therapist. This way you can bring adult awareness and understanding to those experiences.

Some types of therapy and their target areas

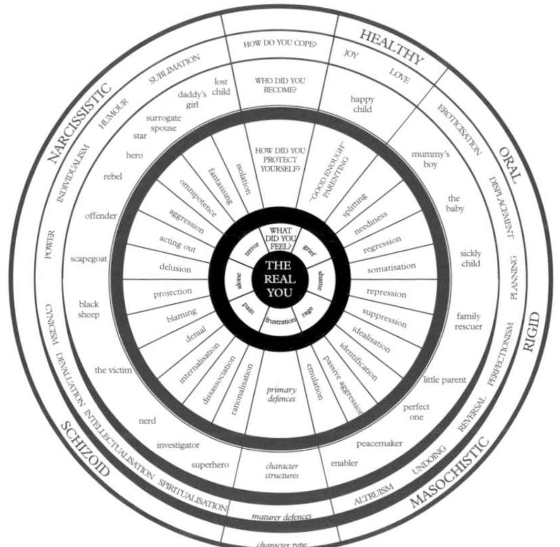

HEALTHY
ORAL
RIGID
MASOCHISTIC
SCHIZOID
NARCISSISTIC
character type
HOW DO YOU COPE?
JOY
LOVE
EROTICISATION
DISPLACEMENT
PLANNING
PERFECTIONISM
REVERSAL
UNDOING
ALTRUISM
maturer defences
SPIRITUALISATION
INTELLECTUALISATION
DEVALUATION
CYNICISM
POWER
INDIVIDUALISM
HUMOUR
SUBLIMATION
WHO DID YOU BECOME?
lost child
daddy's girl
surrogate spouse
star
hero
rebel
offender
scapegoat
black sheep
the victim
nerd
investigator
superhero
character structures
enabler
peacemaker
perfect one
little parent
family rescuer
sickly child
the baby
mummy's boy
happy child
HOW DID YOU PROTECT YOURSELF?
"GOOD ENOUGH" PARENTING
isolation
fantasising
omnipotence
aggression
acting out
delusion
projection
blaming
denial
internalisation
disassociation
rationalisation
primary defences
emulation
passive aggression
identification
idealisation
suppression
repression
somatisation
regression
neediness
splitting
WHAT DID YOU FEEL?
grief
shame
rage
frustration
pain
alone
terror
THE REAL YOU

PSYCHOANALYSIS Explores the connection between (possibly "forgotten") events in early life and current disturbances and stress. Talking freely allows fantasies, feelings, dreams and memories to emerge more easily.

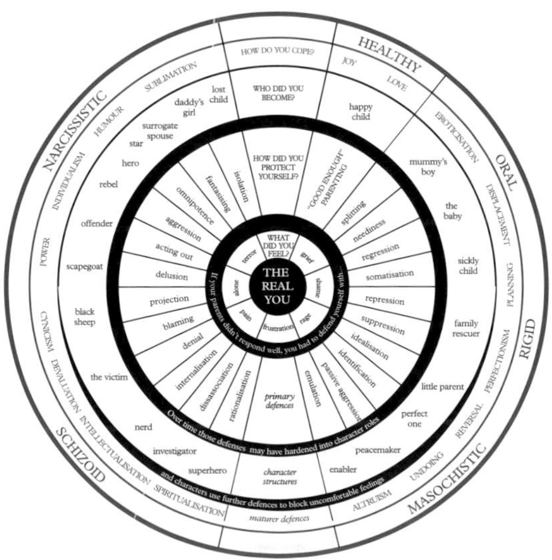

HEALTHY
ORAL
RIGID
MASOCHISTIC
SCHIZOID
NARCISSISTIC
HOW DO YOU COPE?
JOY
LOVE
EROTICISATION
DISPLACEMENT
PLANNING
PERFECTIONISM
REVERSAL
UNDOING
ALTRUISM
maturer defences
SPIRITUALISATION
INTELLECTUALISATION
DEVALUATION
CYNICISM
POWER
INDIVIDUALISM
HUMOUR
SUBLIMATION
WHO DID YOU BECOME?
lost child
daddy's girl
surrogate spouse
star
hero
rebel
offender
scapegoat
black sheep
the victim
nerd
investigator
superhero
character structures
enabler
peacemaker
perfect one
little parent
family rescuer
sickly child
the baby
mummy's boy
happy child
HOW DID YOU PROTECT YOURSELF?
"GOOD ENOUGH" PARENTING
isolation
fantasising
omnipotence
aggression
acting out
delusion
projection
blaming
denial
internalisation
disassociation
rationalisation
primary defences
emulation
passive aggression
identification
idealisation
suppression
repression
somatisation
regression
neediness
splitting
WHAT DID YOU FEEL?
grief
shame
rage
frustration
pain
alone
terror
THE REAL YOU
If your parents didn't respond well, you had to defend yourself with...
Over time those defences may have hardened into character roles
and characters use further defences to block uncomfortable feelings

COGNITIVE-BEHAVIOURAL THERAPY Uncovering and understanding how inaccurate thoughts, beliefs and assumptions can lead to inaccurate interpretations of events and so to negative emotions and behaviours.

WHAT DID YOU FEEL?
terror
grief
alone
shame
pain
rage
frustration
THE REAL YOU

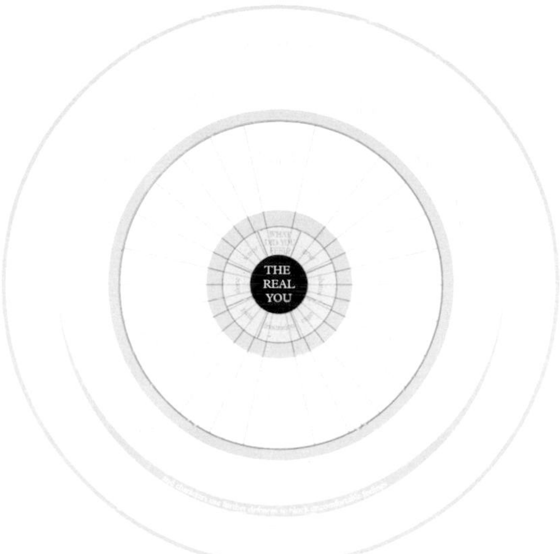
THE REAL YOU

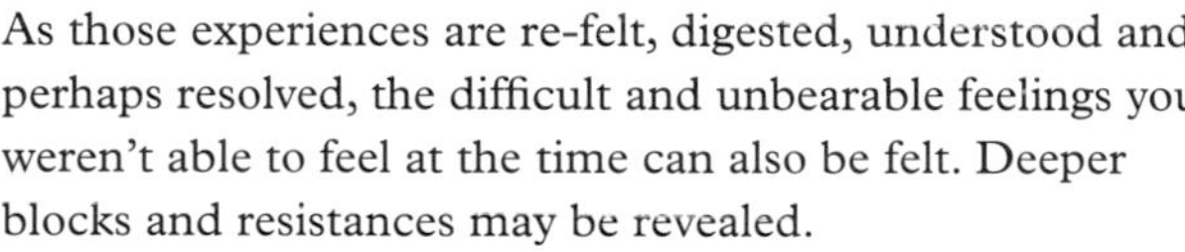

As those experiences are re-felt, digested, understood and perhaps resolved, the difficult and unbearable feelings you weren't able to feel at the time can also be felt. Deeper blocks and resistances may be revealed.

As those feelings are repeatedly felt, you learn to understand, tolerate and deal with them. The "real you", underneath all the defences, can be felt. Nothing really changes. All your defences are still there. You just feel less blocked and become more "transparent".

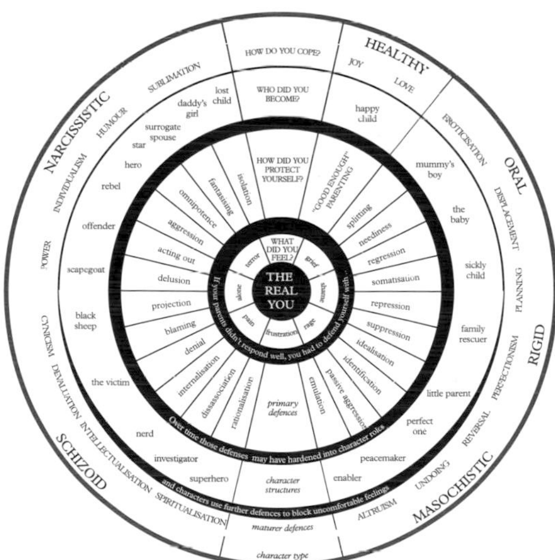
HOW DO YOU COPE?
WHO DID YOU BECOME?
HOW DID YOU PROTECT YOURSELF?
WHAT DID YOU FEEL?
THE REAL YOU
terror
grief
alone
shame
pain
rage
frustration
If your parents didn't respond well, you had to defend yourself with...
Over time those defenses may have hardened into character roles
and characters use further defences to block uncomfortable feelings
HEALTHY
JOY
LOVE
happy child
"GOOD ENOUGH" PARENTING
ORAL
EROTICISATION
mummy's boy
the baby
sickly child
family rescuer
DISPLACEMENT
PLANNING
splitting
neediness
regression
somatisation
repression
suppression
idealisation
identification
passive aggression
emulation
RIGID
PERFECTIONISM
little parent
perfect one
peacemaker
enabler
REVERSAL
UNDOING
ALTRUISM
MASOCHISTIC
primary defences
character structures
maturer defences
character type
SCHIZOID
SPIRITUALISATION
INTELLECTUALISATION
DEVALUATION
CYNICISM
nerd
investigator
superhero
the victim
rationalisation
dissasociation
internalisation
denial
blaming
projection
delusion
acting out
aggression
omnipotence
fantasising
isolation
black sheep
scapegoat
offender
rebel
hero
star
surrogate spouse
daddy's girl
lost child
POWER
INDIVIDUALISM
HUMOUR
SUBLIMATION
NARCISSISTIC

ANTI-DEPRESSANTS Reducing the intensity of symptoms of depression and anxiety and other symptoms of psychological disturbance and distress through regular use of psychiatric medicine.

source: Wikipedia, psychotherapy.org.uk

Most Popular US Girls' Names

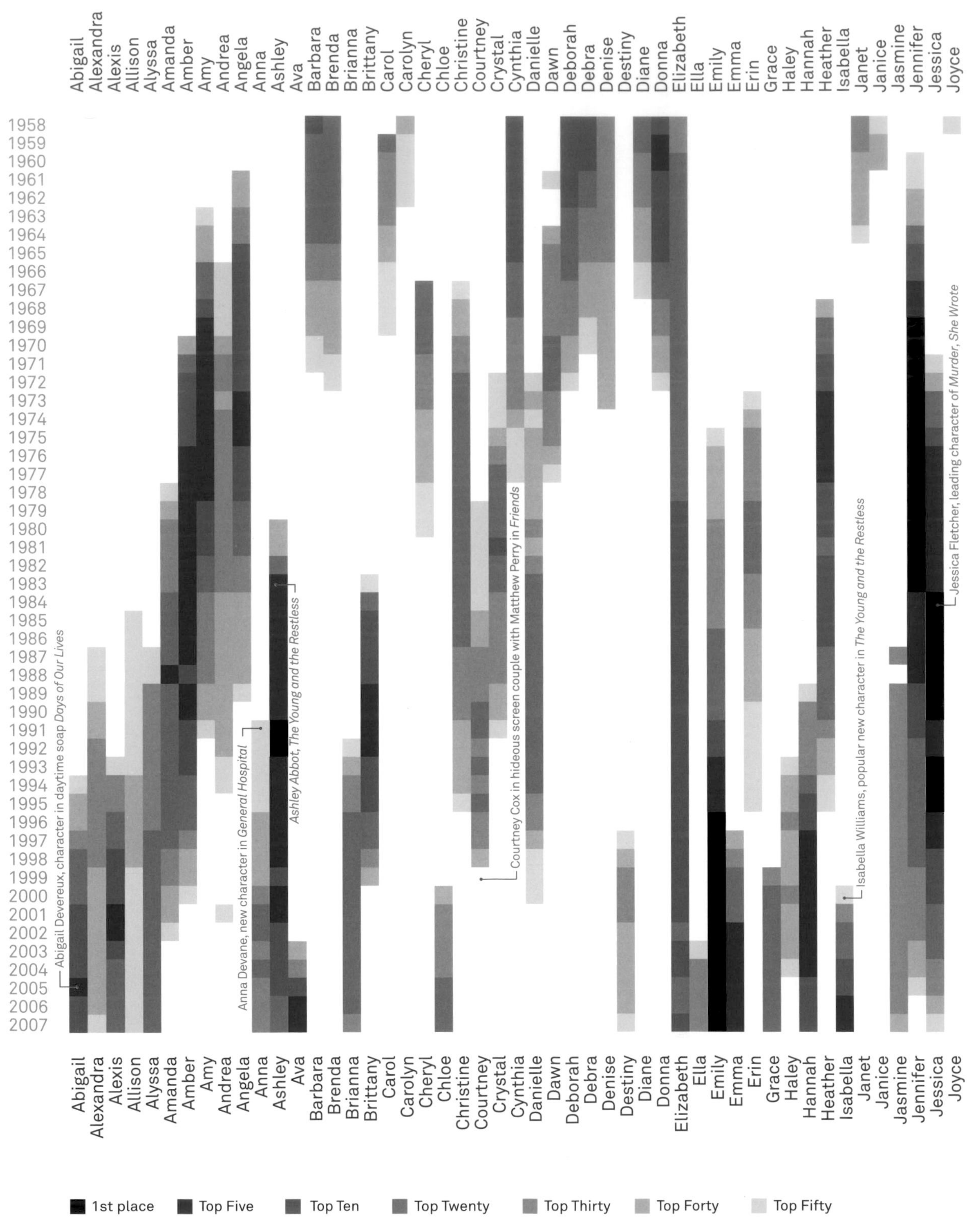

Abigail
Alexandra
Alexis
Allison
Alyssa
Amanda
Amber
Amy
Andrea
Angela
Anna
Ashley
Ava
Barbara
Brenda
Brianna
Brittany
Carol
Carolyn
Cheryl
Chloe
Christine
Courtney
Crystal
Cynthia
Danielle
Dawn
Deborah
Debra
Denise
Destiny
Diane
Donna
Elizabeth
Ella
Emily
Emma
Erin
Grace
Haley
Hannah
Heather
Isabella
Janet
Janice
Jasmine
Jennifer
Jessica
Joyce
1958
1959
1960
1961
1962
1963
1964
1965
1966
1967
1968
1969
1970
1971
1972
1973
1974
1975
1976
1977
1978
1979
1980
1981
1982
1983
1984
1985
1986
1987
1988
1989
1990
1991
1992
1993
1994
1995
1996
1997
1998
1999
2000
2001
2002
2003
2004
2005
2006
2007
Abigail Devereux, character in daytime soap *Days of Our Lives*
Anna Devane, new character in *General Hospital*
Ashley Abbot, *The Young and the Restless*
Courtney Cox in hideous screen couple with Matthew Perry in *Friends*
Isabella Williams, popular new character in *The Young and the Restless*
Jessica Fletcher, leading character of *Murder, She Wrote*
1st place
Top Five
Top Ten
Top Twenty
Top Thirty
Top Forty
Top Fifty

Judy
Julie
Karen
Katherine
Kathleen
Kathy
Kayla
Kelly
Kimberly
Laura
Lauren
Linda
Lise
Lori
Mackenzie
Madison
Margaret
Mary
Megan
Melissa
Mia
Michelle
Morgan
Nancy
Natalie
Nicole
Olivia
Pamela
Patricia
Rachel
Rebecca
Samantha
Sandra
Sara
Sarah
Savannah
Shannon
Sharon
Sophia
Stephanie
Susan
Sydney
Tammy
Taylor
Teresa
Tiffany
Tina
Tracy
Victoria
1958
1959
1960
1961
1962
1963
1964
1965
1966
1967
1968
1969
1970
1971
1972
1973
1974
1975
1976
1977
1978
1979
1980
1981
1982
1983
1984
1985
1986
1987
1988
1989
1990
1991
1992
1993
1994
1995
1996
1997
1998
1999
2000
2001
2002
2003
2004
2005
2006
2007
Kayla Brady, very popular character on *Days of Our Lives*
Lauren Fenimore Williams, *The Young and the Restless*
Olivia Morley from soap *Port Charles*
Taylor Hayes, glamorous psychiatrist, *The Bold & The Beautiful*

source: US Social Security Administration @ ssa.gov

Most Popular US Boys' Names

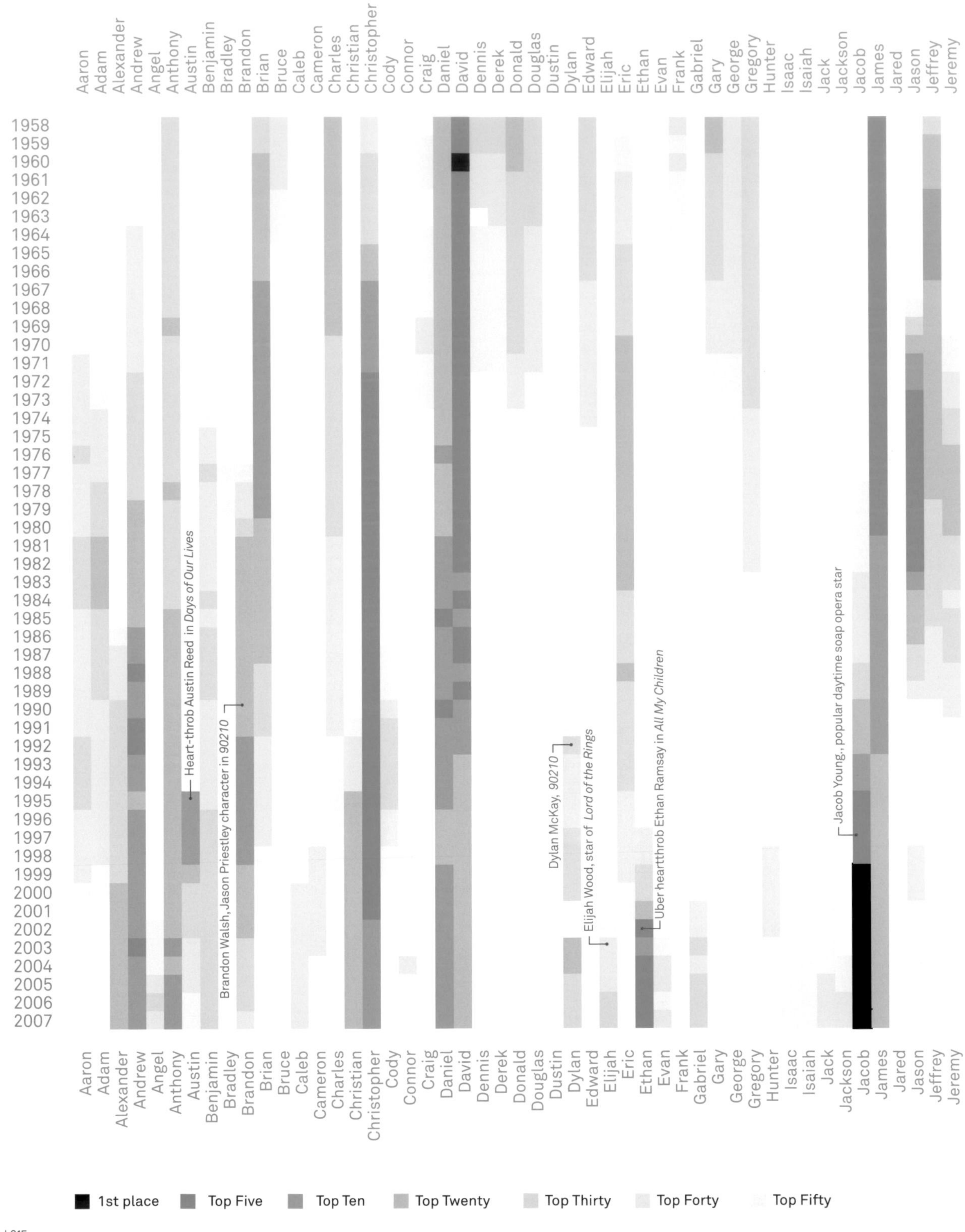

Aaron
Adam
Alexander
Andrew
Angel
Anthony
Austin
Benjamin
Bradley
Brandon
Brian
Bruce
Caleb
Cameron
Charles
Christian
Christopher
Cody
Connor
Craig
Daniel
David
Dennis
Derek
Donald
Douglas
Dustin
Dylan
Edward
Elijah
Eric
Ethan
Evan
Frank
Gabriel
Gary
George
Gregory
Hunter
Isaac
Isaiah
Jack
Jackson
Jacob
James
Jared
Jason
Jeffrey
Jeremy
1958
1959
1960
1961
1962
1963
1964
1965
1966
1967
1968
1969
1970
1971
1972
1973
1974
1975
1976
1977
1978
1979
1980
1981
1982
1983
1984
1985
1986
1987
1988
1989
1990
1991
1992
1993
1994
1995
1996
1997
1998
1999
2000
2001
2002
2003
2004
2005
2006
2007
Heart-throb Austin Reed in *Days of Our Lives*
Brandon Walsh, Jason Priestley character in *90210*
Dylan McKay, *90210*
Elijah Wood, star of *Lord of the Rings*
Uber heartthrob Ethan Ramsay in *All My Children*
Jacob Young, popular daytime soap opera star
1st place
Top Five
Top Ten
Top Twenty
Top Thirty
Top Forty
Top Fifty

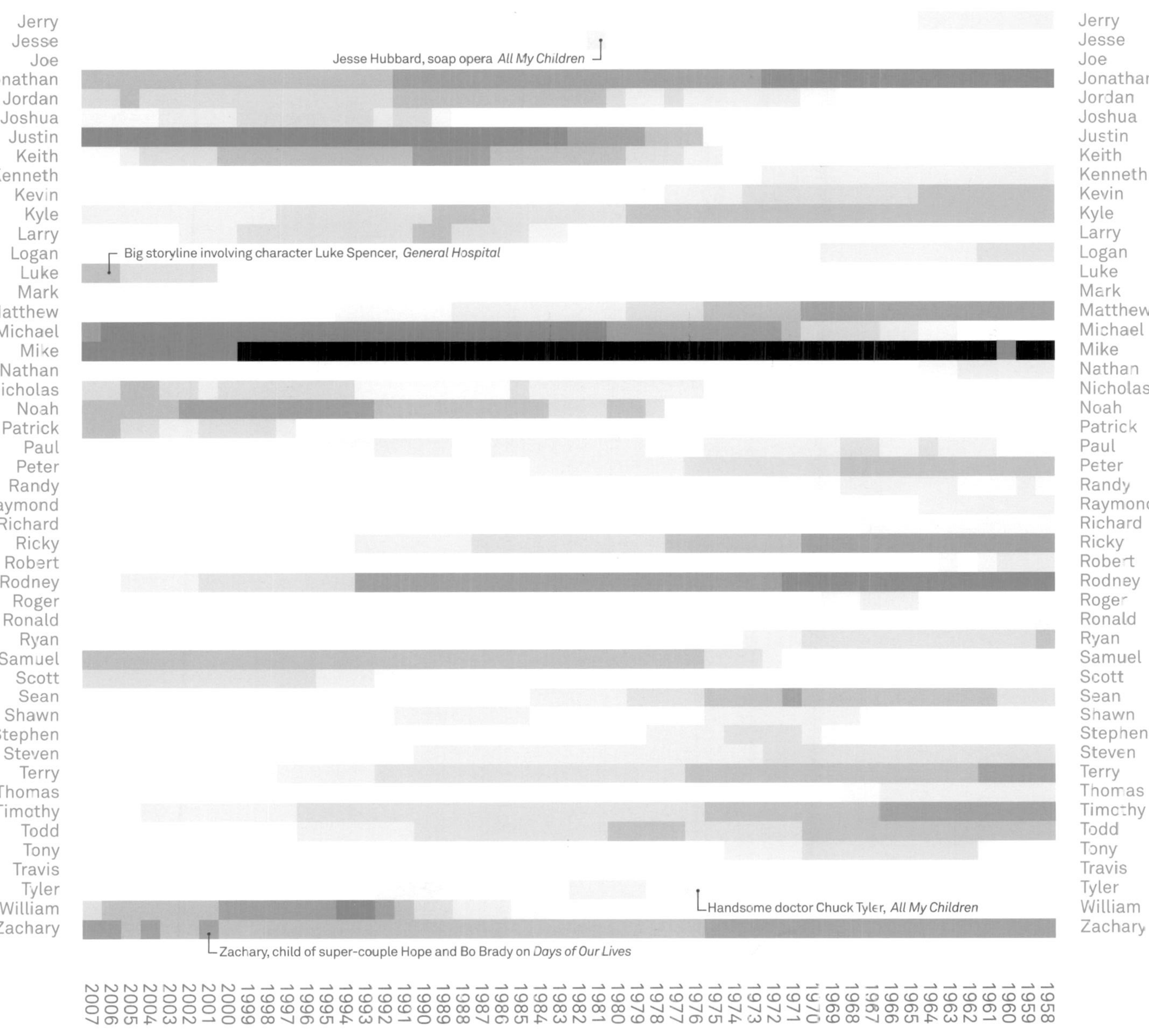
Jerry
Jesse
Joe
Jonathan
Jordan
Joshua
Justin
Keith
Kenneth
Kevin
Kyle
Larry
Logan
Luke
Mark
Matthew
Michael
Mike
Nathan
Nicholas
Noah
Patrick
Paul
Peter
Randy
Raymond
Richard
Ricky
Robert
Rodney
Roger
Ronald
Ryan
Samuel
Scott
Sean
Shawn
Stephen
Steven
Terry
Thomas
Timothy
Todd
Tony
Travis
Tyler
William
Zachary
Jesse Hubbard, soap opera *All My Children*
Big storyline involving character Luke Spencer, *General Hospital*
Handsome doctor Chuck Tyler, *All My Children*
Zachary, child of super-couple Hope and Bo Brady on *Days of Our Lives*
2007
2006
2005
2004
2003
2002
2001
2000
1999
1998
1997
1996
1995
1994
1993
1992
1991
1990
1989
1988
1987
1986
1985
1984
1983
1982
1981
1980
1979
1978
1977
1976
1975
1974
1973
1972
1971
1970
1969
1968
1967
1966
1965
1964
1963
1962
1961
1960
1959
1958

source: US Social Security Administration @ ssa.gov

The Middle East
A relationship map
EU
GERMANY
UK
TURKEY
IRAN
AL-QAEDA
SYRIA
ISLAMIC JIHAD
LEBANON
HEZBOLLAH
IRAQ
GAZA / HAMAS
ISRAEL
JORDAN
WEST BANK
KUWAIT
USA
SAUDI ARABIA
EGYPT
QATAR
UAE
OMAN
YEMEN
relationship
GOOD (trade & mutual interests)
STRONG (allies)
STRAINED
BAD (enemies)

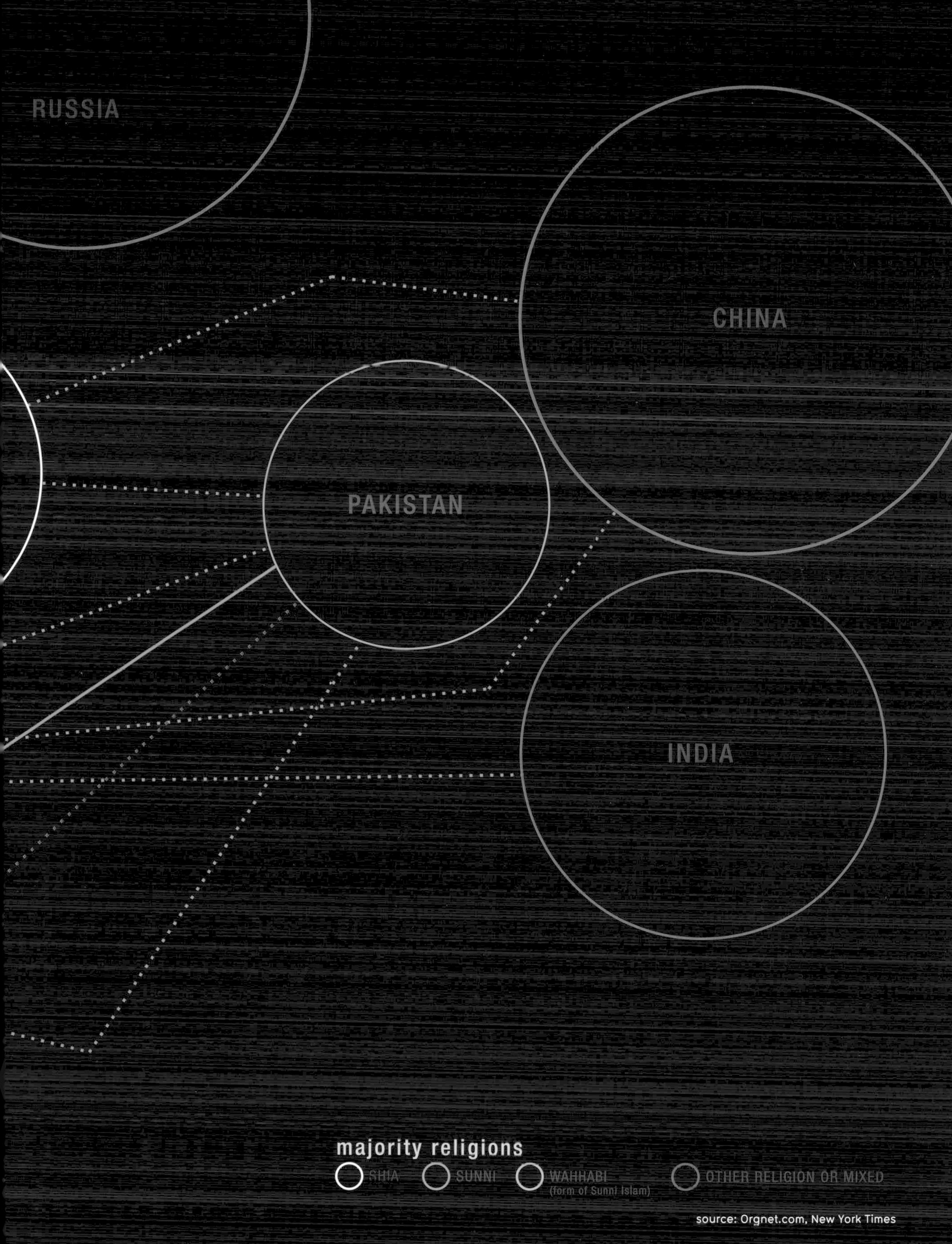
RUSSIA
CHINA
PAKISTAN
INDIA
majority religions
SHIA
SUNNI
WAHHABI
(form of Sunni Islam)
OTHER RELIGION OR MIXED
source: Orgnet.com, New York Times

The Middle East: Some Context
Palestinian territories

1946
1947
1999
2007
MILLION

Oil States
Who has the world's oil?

Oil States
Who'll have the world's oil?

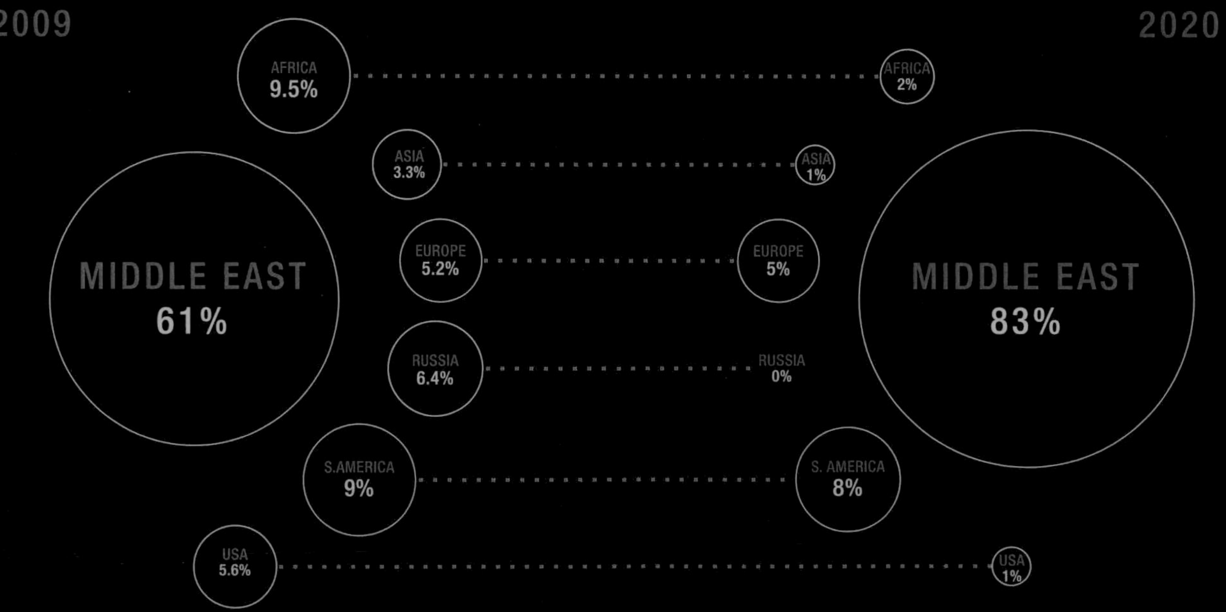
2009
2020
AFRICA 9.5%
AFRICA 2%
ASIA 3.3%
ASIA 1%
MIDDLE EAST 61%
EUROPE 5.2%
EUROPE 5%
MIDDLE EAST 83%
RUSSIA 6.4%
RUSSIA 0%
S.AMERICA 9%
S. AMERICA 8%
USA 5.6%
USA 1%

source: BP Statistical Review of the Year 2008, Wikipedia

The Future of Energy

Place your bets

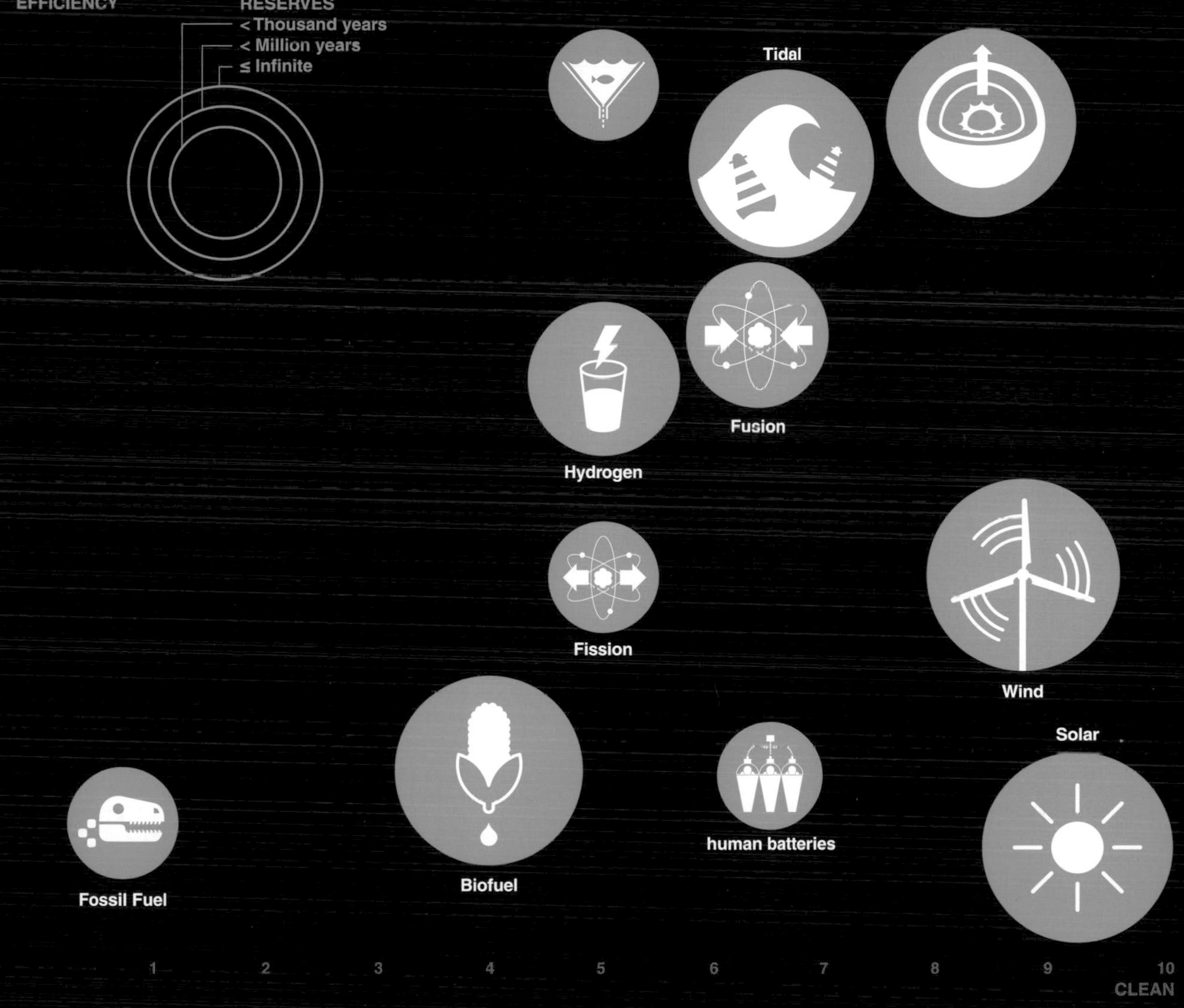

EFFICIENCY
RESERVES
< Thousand years
< Million years
≤ Infinite
Tidal
Hydrogen
Fusion
Fission
Wind
Solar
human batteries
Biofuel
Fossil Fuel
1
2
3
4
5
6
7
8
9
10
CLEAN

Biofuel – To replace all of America's petrol consumption with bio-fuel from plants would take three-quarters of all the cultivated land on the face of the Earth.

Fossil Fuel – By products: sulphur dioxide, carbon monoxide, methane, poisonous metals like lead, uranium and, of course, CO_2.

Geothermal – Drilling for free heat under the earth's surface has lots of advantages and is pollution-free. Iceland gets 20% of its energy this way. But watch out for earthquakes!

Human Batteries – The energy in the food needed to feed human power sources is greater than the energy generated. D'oh!

Hydroelectric – There's an unavoidable built-in limit to dams. There are only so many places you can put them. And space is running out...

Hydrogen – Currently 96% of hydrogen is made using fossil fuels.

Nuclear Fission – To meet the world's electricity needs from nuclear power would require 2230 more nuclear power stations. There are currently 439 in operation. They can take 5–10 years to build.

Nuclear Fusion – Recreates the temperatures at the heart of the sun. Generates much less nuclear waste than fission. But no one can work out how to do it. "At least 50 years away"

Solar – To replace all current electricity production in the US with solar power would take an area of approximately 3500 square miles (3% of Arizona's land area) covered in solar panels. In most areas of the world, solar panels would cover 85% of household water heating needs.

Tidal – Several question marks remain. Mostly related to its impact on environment and biodiversity.

Wind – Turbines covering about 0.5% of all US land would power the entire country. Around 73,000 to 144,000 5-megawatt wind turbines could power electric cars for every single American.

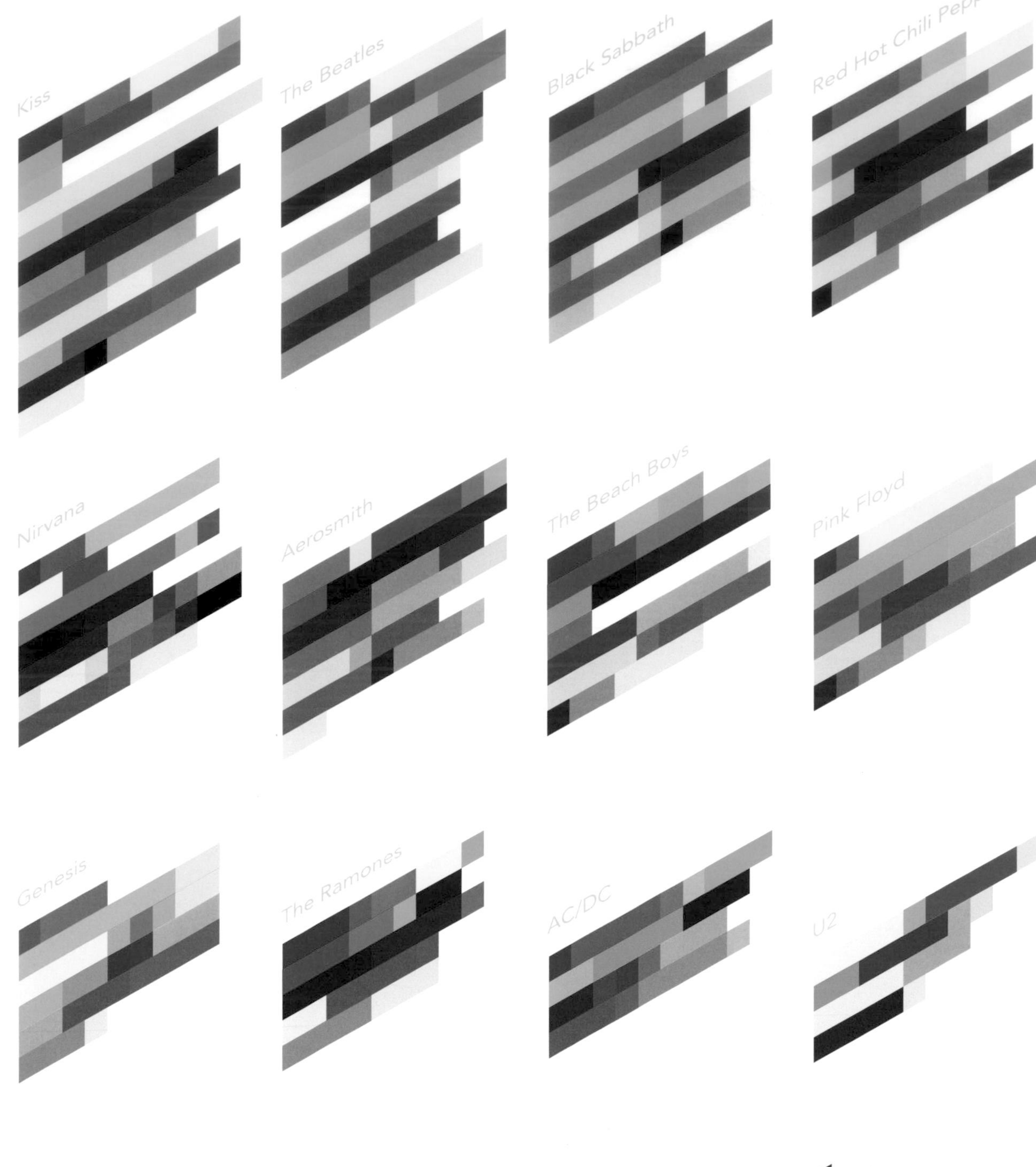

Kiss
The Beatles
Black Sabbath
Red Hot Chili Peppers
Nirvana
Aerosmith
The Beach Boys
Pink Floyd
Genesis
The Ramones
AC/DC
U2

Dead members
Sacked members
Members who just gave up
Replaced drummers
Extra lead guitarists
Changes in musical direction
Classical music pretensions
Albums disowned by band
Number of concept albums

Most Successful Rock Bands

True rock success got nothin' to do with selling records

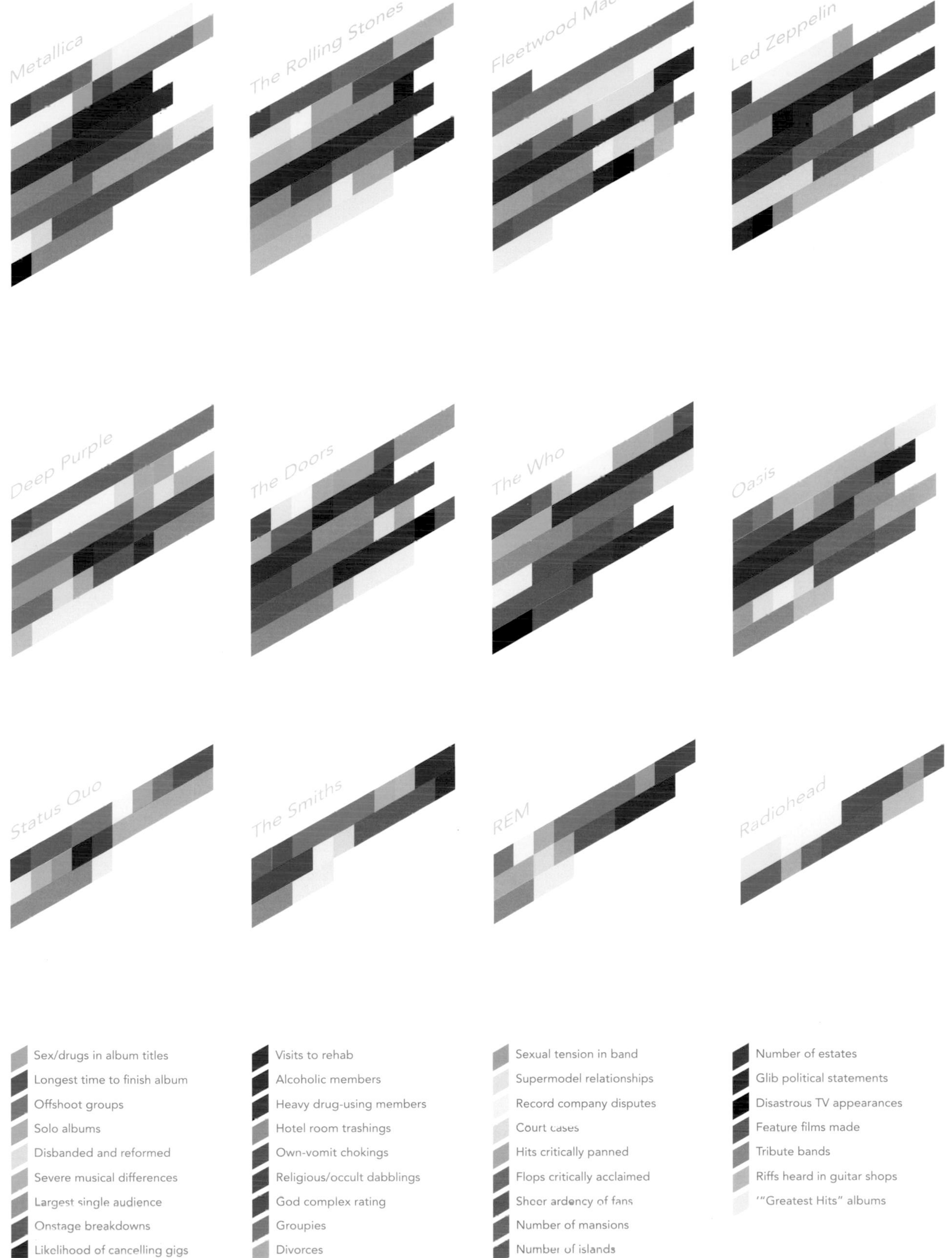

Metallica
The Rolling Stones
Fleetwood Mac
Led Zeppelin
Deep Purple
The Doors
The Who
Oasis
Status Quo
The Smiths
REM
Radiohead
Sex/drugs in album titles
Longest time to finish album
Offshoot groups
Solo albums
Disbanded and reformed
Severe musical differences
Largest single audience
Onstage breakdowns
Likelihood of cancelling gigs
Visits to rehab
Alcoholic members
Heavy drug-using members
Hotel room trashings
Own-vomit chokings
Religious/occult dabblings
God complex rating
Groupies
Divorces
Sexual tension in band
Supermodel relationships
Record company disputes
Court cases
Hits critically panned
Flops critically acclaimed
Sheer ardency of fans
Number of mansions
Number of islands
Number of estates
Glib political statements
Disastrous TV appearances
Feature films made
Tribute bands
Riffs heard in guitar shops
"Greatest Hits" albums

source: Wikipedia

22 Stories

P=The Protagonist

Fish out of Water P tries to cope in a completely different place/ time/world.
Mr Bean, Trading Places

Discovery Through a major upheaval, P discovers a truth about themselves and a better understanding of life.
Close Encounters, Ben-Hur

Escape P trapped by antagonistic forces and must escape. Pronto.
Poseidon Adventure, Saw

Journey & Return P goes on a physical journey and returns changed.
Wizard of Oz, Star Wars

Temptation P has to make a moral choice between right and wrong.
The Godfather, The Sting

Rags to Riches P is poor, then rich.
Trading Places, La Vie en rose

The Riddle P has to solve a puzzle or a crime.
The Da Vinci Code, Chinatown

Metamorphosis P literally changes into something else (i.e. a werewolf, hulk, giant cockroach).
Spiderman, Pinocchio

Rescue P must save someone who is trapped physically or emotionally.
The Golden Compass, Die Hard

Tragedy P is brought down by a fatal flaw in their character or by forces out of their control.
One Flew Over the Cuckoo's Nest, Atonement

Love A couple meet and overcome obstacles to discover true love. Or – tragically – don't.
Titanic, Grease

Monster Force A monster / alien / something scary and supernatural must be fought and overcome.
Jaws, The Exorcist

Revenge P retaliates against another for a real or imagined injury.
Batman, Kill Bill

Transformation P lives through a series of events that change them as a person.
Pretty Woman, Muriel's Wedding

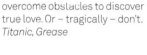

Maturation P has an experience that matures them or starts a new stage of life, often adulthood.
The Graduate, Juno

Pursuit P has to chase somebody or something, usually in a hide-and-seek fashion.
Goldfinger, Bourne Ultimatum

Rivalry P must triumph over an adversary to attain an object or goal.
Rocky, The Outsiders

Underdog Total loser faces overwhelming odds but wins in the end.
Slumdog Millionaire, Forrest Gump

Comedy A series of complications leads P into ridiculous situations.
Ghostbusters, Airplane

Quest P searches for a person, place or thing, overcoming a number of challenges.
Raiders of the Lost Ark, Lord of the Rings

Sacrifice P must make a difficult choice between pleasing themselves or a higher purpose (e.g. love, honour).
300, 3:10 to Yuma

Wretched Excess P pushes the limits of acceptable behaviour, destroying themselves in the process.
There Will Be Blood, Citizen Kane

source: Tennesse Screenwriting Association, Robert McKee's *Story*

Most Profitable Hollywood Stories 2007

Average profitability: 301% Average quality: 51% Most common stories: Love Pursuit

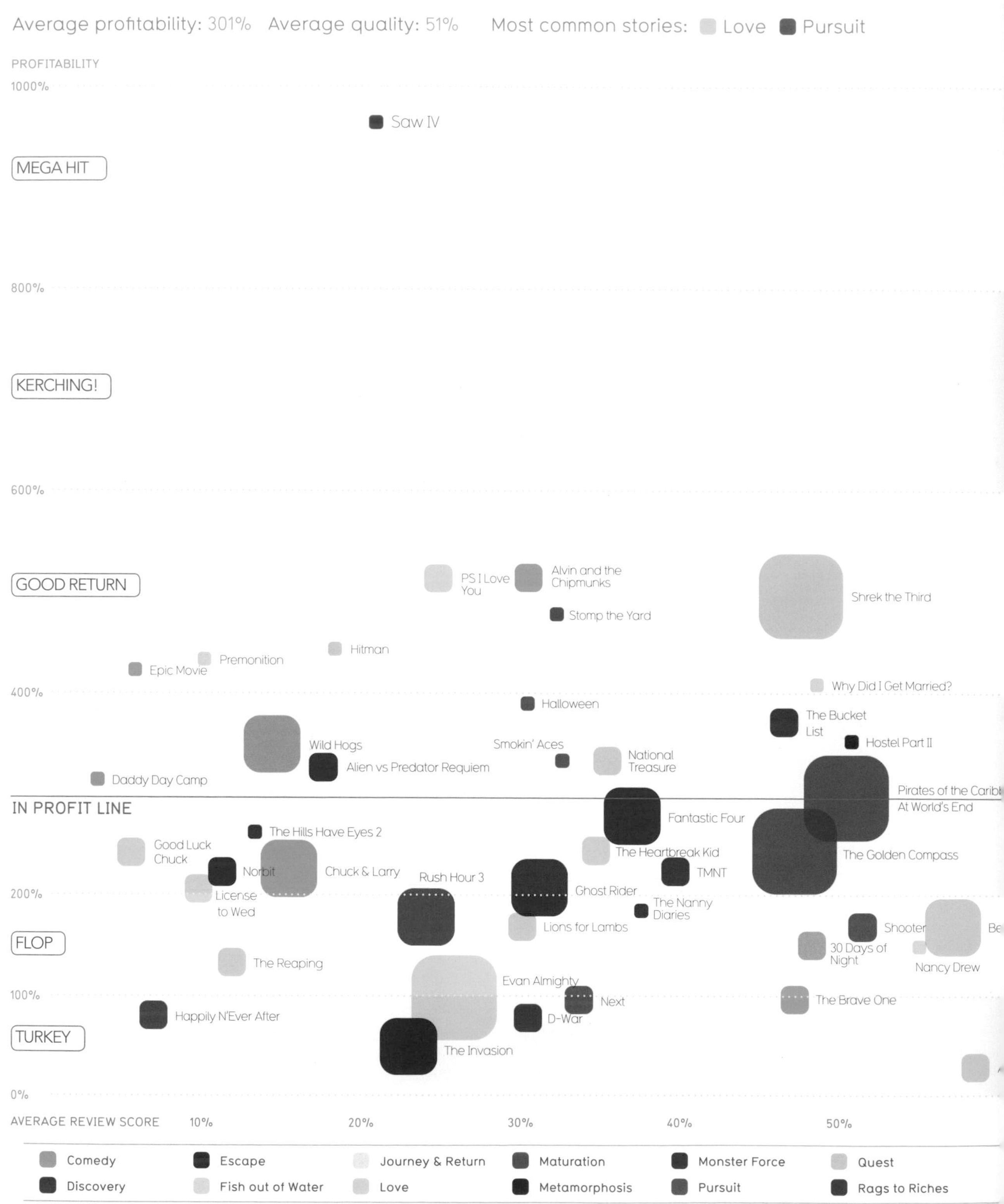

PROFITABILITY
1000%
800%
600%
400%
200%
100%
0%
MEGA HIT
KERCHING!
GOOD RETURN
IN PROFIT LINE
FLOP
TURKEY
Saw IV
PS I Love You
Alvin and the Chipmunks
Stomp the Yard
Shrek the Third
Hitman
Premonition
Epic Movie
Why Did I Get Married?
Halloween
The Bucket List
Hostel Part II
Wild Hogs
Smokin' Aces
National Treasure
Alien vs Predator Requiem
Daddy Day Camp
Pirates of the Caribb
At World's End
Fantastic Four
The Hills Have Eyes 2
Good Luck Chuck
The Heartbreak Kid
The Golden Compass
Norbit
Chuck & Larry
Rush Hour 3
TMNT
Ghost Rider
License to Wed
The Nanny Diaries
Lions for Lambs
Shooter
Be
30 Days of Night
Nancy Drew
The Reaping
Evan Almighty
Next
The Brave One
Happily N'Ever After
D-War
The Invasion
AVERAGE REVIEW SCORE
10%
20%
30%
40%
50%
Comedy
Discovery
Escape
Fish out of Water
Journey & Return
Love
Maturation
Metamorphosis
Monster Force
Pursuit
Quest
Rags to Riches

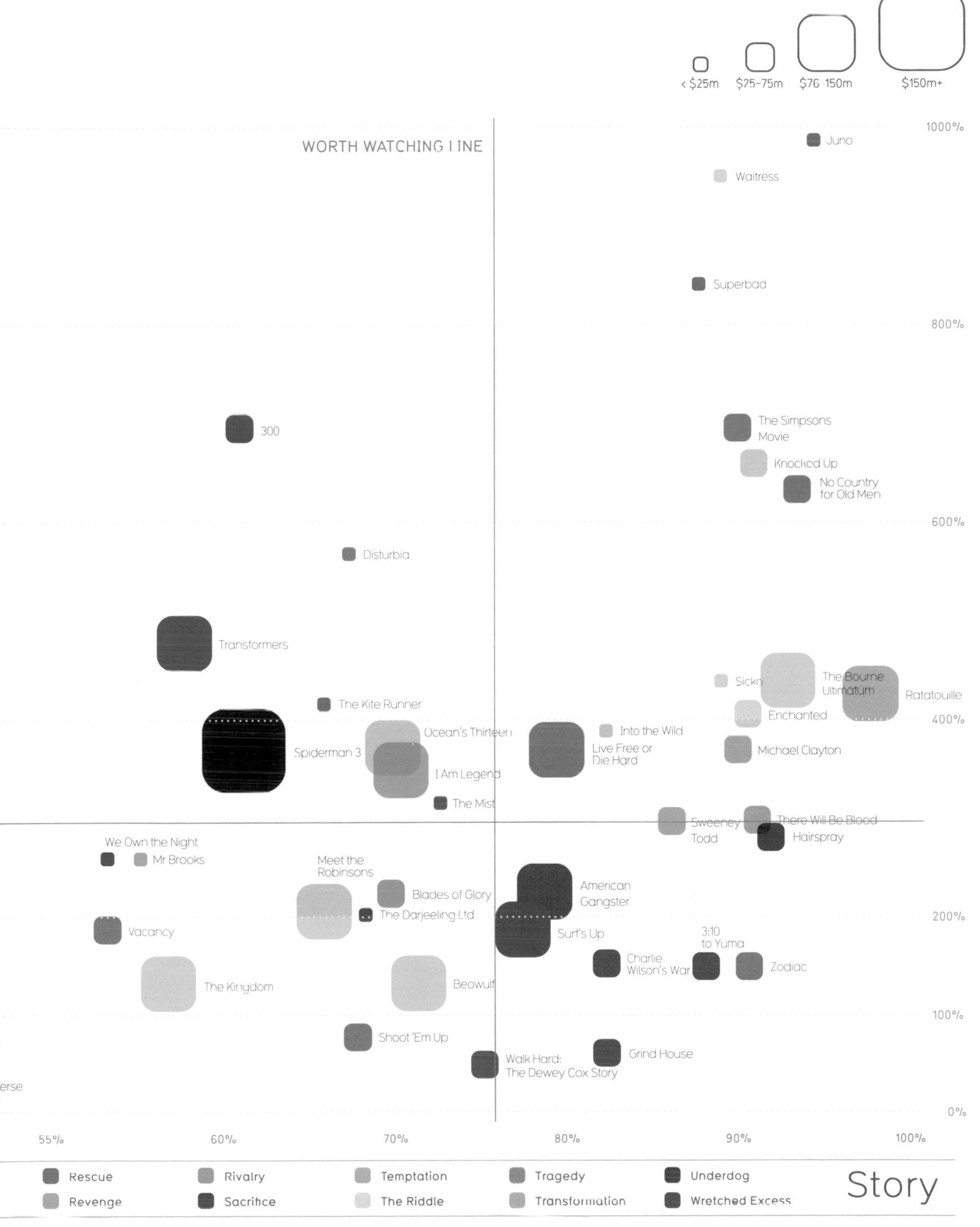
BUDGET
< $25m
$25-75m
$76 150m
$150m+
WORTH WATCHING LINE
1000%
800%
600%
400%
200%
100%
0%
Juno
Waitress
Superbad
300
The Simpsons Movie
Knocked Up
No Country for Old Men
Disturbia
Transformers
Sicko
The Bourne Ultimatum
Ratatouille
Enchanted
The Kite Runner
Spiderman 3
Ocean's Thirteen
I Am Legend
The Mist
Live Free or Die Hard
Into the Wild
Michael Clayton
Sweeney Todd
There Will Be Blood
Hairspray
We Own the Night
Mr Brooks
Meet the Robinsons
Blades of Glory
The Darjeeling Ltd
American Gangster
Surf's Up
Vacancy
3:10 to Yuma
Charlie Wilson's War
Zodiac
The Kingdom
Beowulf
Shoot 'Em Up
Walk Hard: The Dewey Cox Story
Grind House
verse
55%
60%
70%
80%
90%
100%
Rescue
Revenge
Rivalry
Sacrifice
Temptation
The Riddle
Tragedy
Transformation
Underdog
Wretched Excess
Story

source: BoxOfficeMojo.com, The-Numbers.com, Wikipedia, IMDB.com & RottenTomatoes.com. Note: reported film budgets are notoriously unreliable (especially for flops)

Most Profitable Hollywood Stories 2008

Average profitability: 278% Average quality: 46% Most common stories: Love Discovery

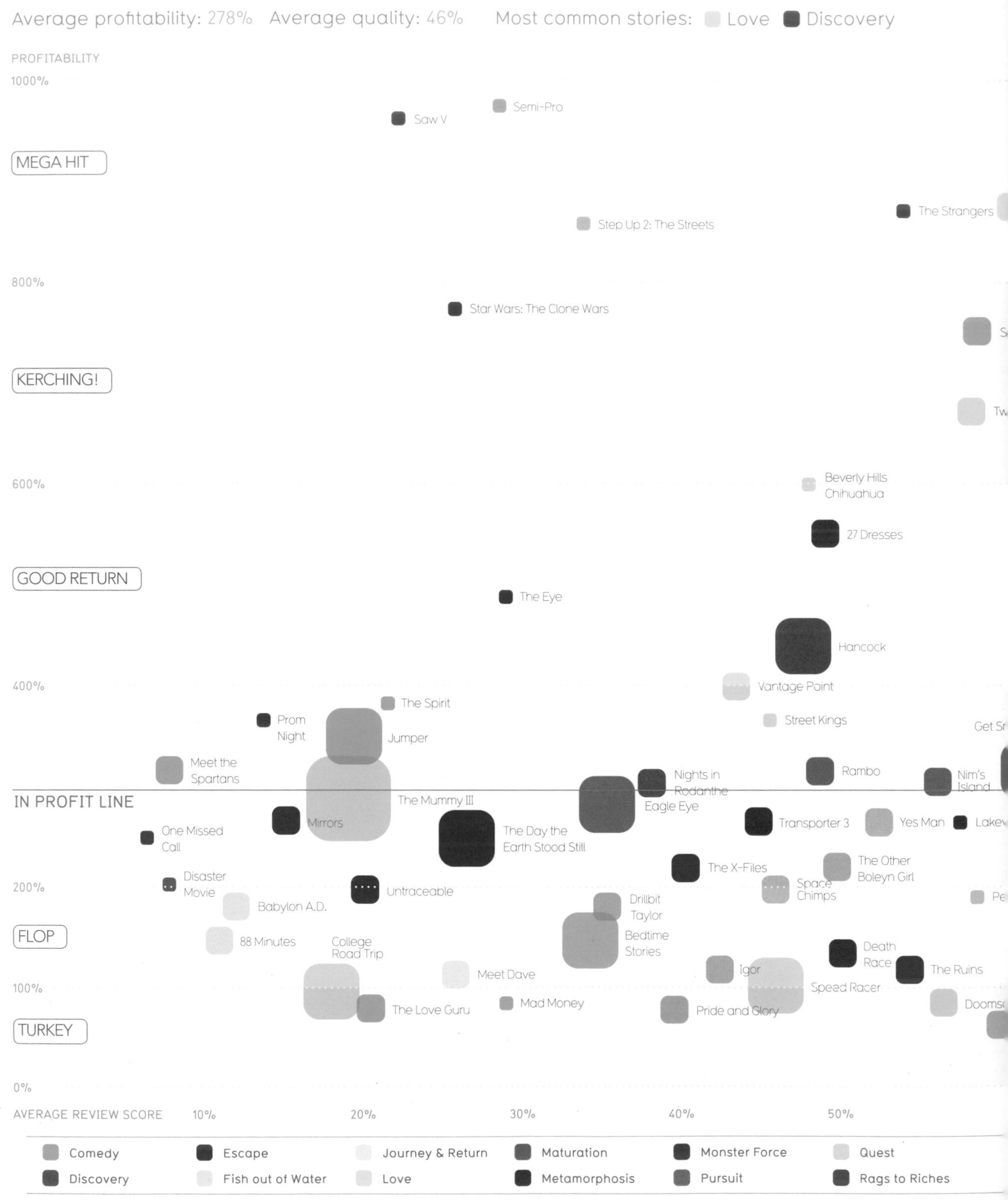

PROFITABILITY
1000%
Saw V
Semi-Pro
MEGA HIT
The Strangers
Step Up 2: The Streets
800%
Star Wars: The Clone Wars
KERCHING!
600%
Beverly Hills Chihuahua
27 Dresses
GOOD RETURN
The Eye
Hancock
400%
Vantage Point
The Spirit
Prom Night
Jumper
Street Kings
Meet the Spartans
Nights in Rodanthe
Rambo
Nim's Island
IN PROFIT LINE
The Mummy III
Eagle Eye
Mirrors
Transporter 3
Yes Man
One Missed Call
The Day the Earth Stood Still
The X-Files
The Other Boleyn Girl
Disaster Movie
Space Chimps
200%
Untraceable
Babylon A.D.
Drillbit Taylor
FLOP
88 Minutes
College Road Trip
Bedtime Stories
Death Race
Meet Dave
Igor
The Ruins
100%
Speed Racer
The Love Guru
Mad Money
Pride and Glory
TURKEY
0%
AVERAGE REVIEW SCORE
10%
20%
30%
40%
50%
Comedy
Escape
Journey & Return
Maturation
Monster Force
Quest
Discovery
Fish out of Water
Love
Metamorphosis
Pursuit
Rags to Riches

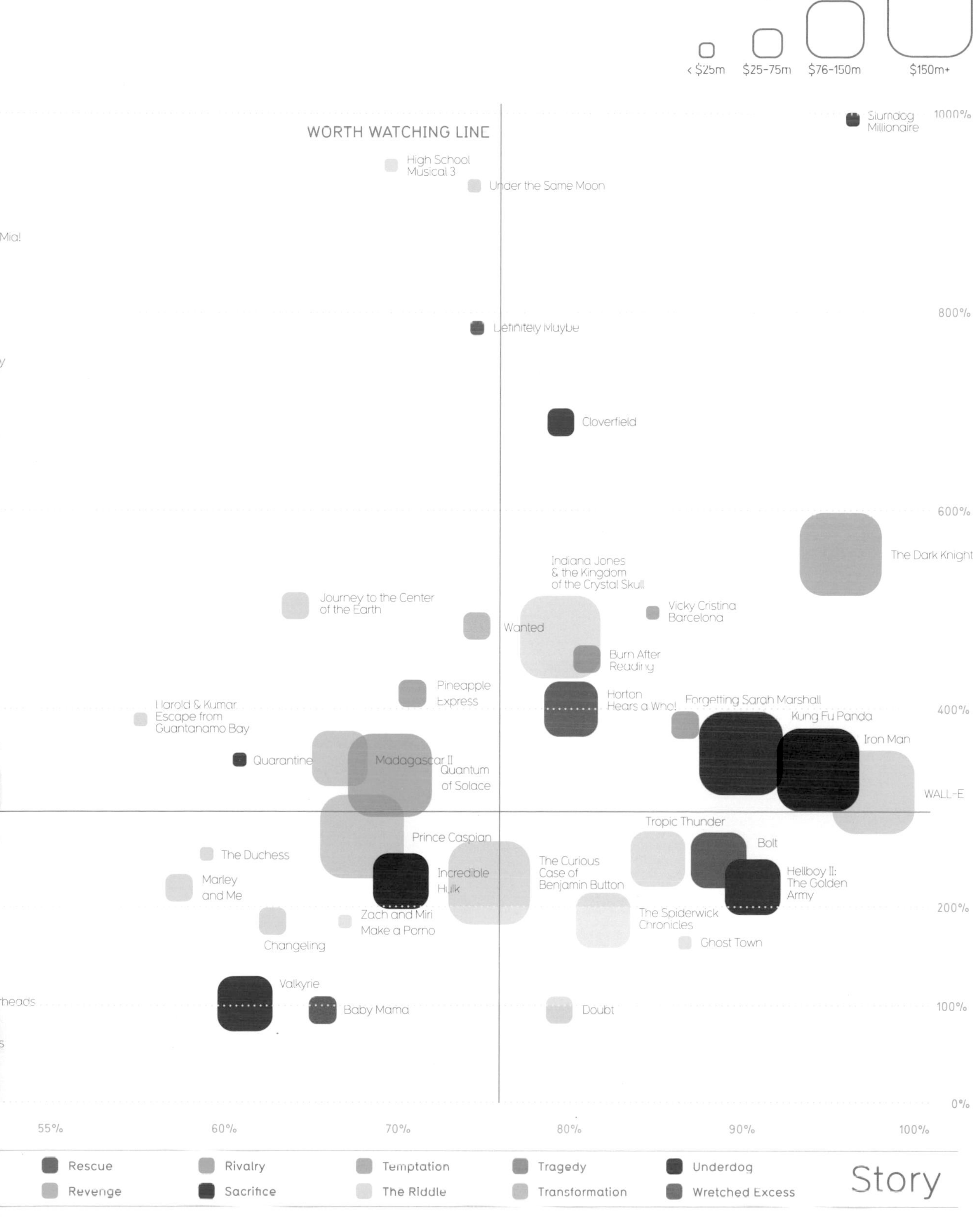

BUDGET
< $25m
$25-75m
$76-150m
$150m+
WORTH WATCHING LINE
Slumdog Millionaire
High School Musical 3
Under the Same Moon
Definitely Maybe
Cloverfield
The Dark Knight
Indiana Jones & the Kingdom of the Crystal Skull
Journey to the Center of the Earth
Vicky Cristina Barcelona
Wanted
Burn After Reading
Pineapple Express
Horton Hears a Who!
Forgetting Sarah Marshall
Harold & Kumar Escape from Guantanamo Bay
Kung Fu Panda
Iron Man
Quarantine
Madagascar II
Quantum of Solace
WALL-E
Tropic Thunder
Prince Caspian
Bolt
The Duchess
The Curious Case of Benjamin Button
Incredible Hulk
Hellboy II: The Golden Army
Marley and Me
Zach and Miri Make a Porno
The Spiderwick Chronicles
Changeling
Ghost Town
Valkyrie
Baby Mama
Doubt
1000%
800%
600%
400%
200%
100%
0%
55%
60%
70%
80%
90%
100%
Rescue
Revenge
Rivalry
Sacrifice
Temptation
The Riddle
Tragedy
Transformation
Underdog
Wretched Excess
Story

source: BoxOfficeMojo.com, The-Numbers.com, Wikipedia, IMDB.com & RottenTomatoes.com. Note: reported film budgets are notoriously unreliable (especially for flops)

Most Profitable Hollywood Stories 2009

Average profitability: 308% Average quality: 47% Most common stories: Quest Comedy

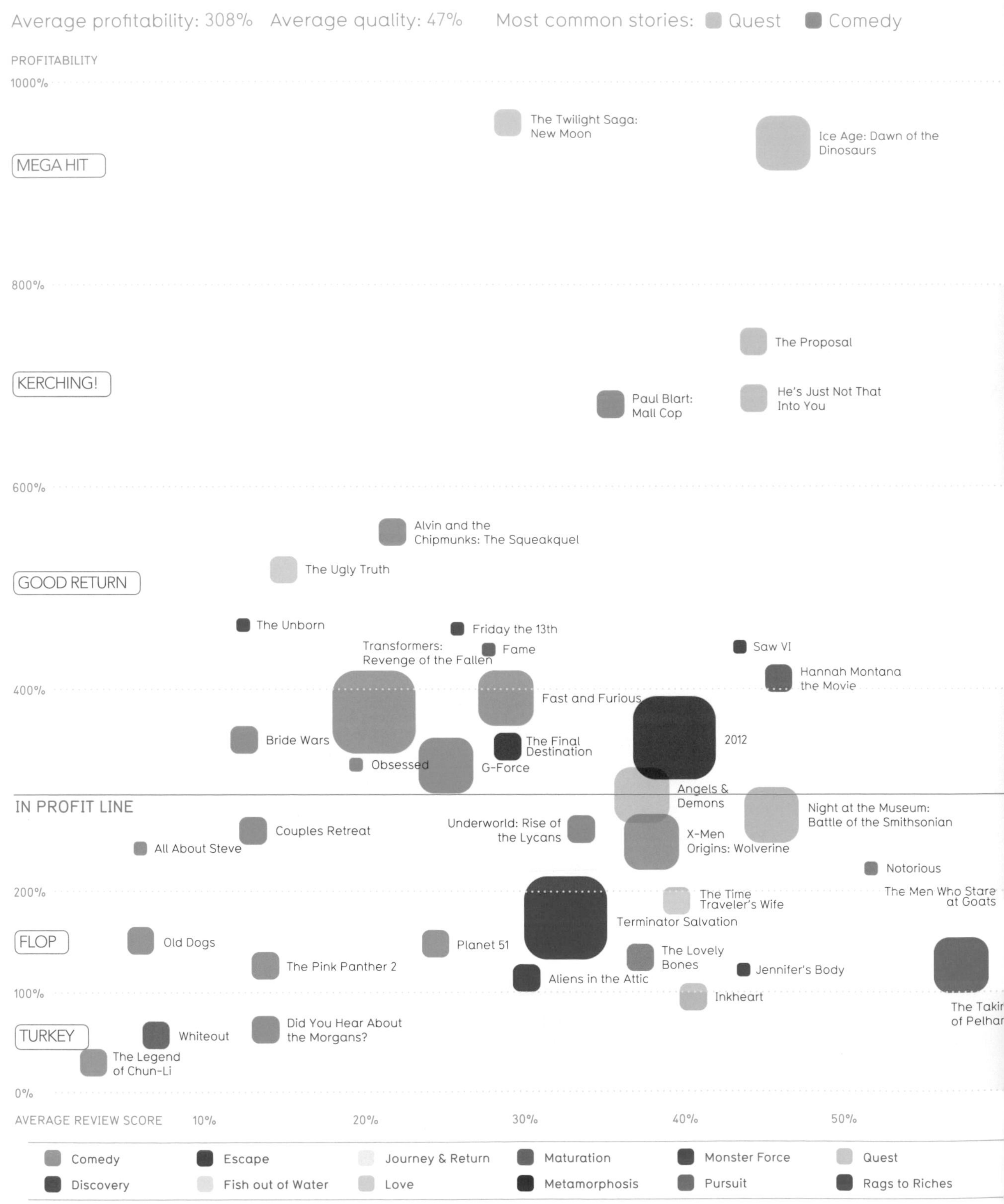

PROFITABILITY
1000%
800%
600%
400%
200%
100%
0%
MEGA HIT
KERCHING!
GOOD RETURN
IN PROFIT LINE
FLOP
TURKEY
The Twilight Saga: New Moon
Ice Age: Dawn of the Dinosaurs
The Proposal
Paul Blart: Mall Cop
He's Just Not That Into You
Alvin and the Chipmunks: The Squeakquel
The Ugly Truth
The Unborn
Friday the 13th
Transformers: Revenge of the Fallen
Fame
Saw VI
Hannah Montana the Movie
Fast and Furious
2012
Bride Wars
The Final Destination
Obsessed
G-Force
Angels & Demons
Night at the Museum: Battle of the Smithsonian
Couples Retreat
Underworld: Rise of the Lycans
X-Men Origins: Wolverine
All About Steve
Notorious
The Men Who Stare at Goats
The Time Traveler's Wife
Terminator Salvation
Old Dogs
Planet 51
The Lovely Bones
The Pink Panther 2
Jennifer's Body
Aliens in the Attic
Inkheart
The Takir of Pelhar
Did You Hear About the Morgans?
Whiteout
The Legend of Chun-Li
AVERAGE REVIEW SCORE
10%
20%
30%
40%
50%
Comedy
Escape
Journey & Return
Maturation
Monster Force
Quest
Discovery
Fish out of Water
Love
Metamorphosis
Pursuit
Rags to Riches

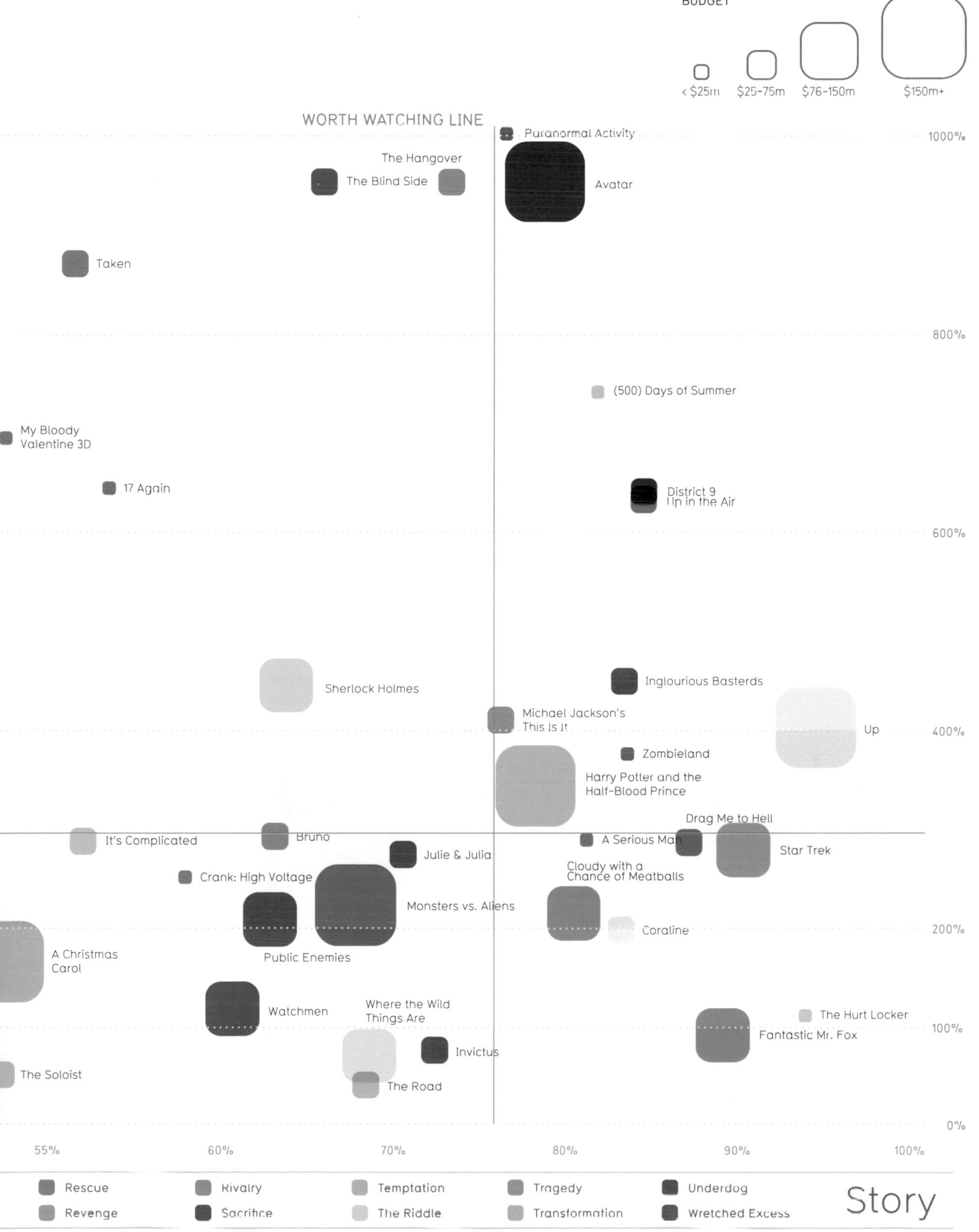

BUDGET
< $25m
$25-75m
$76-150m
$150m+
WORTH WATCHING LINE
Paranormal Activity
The Hangover
The Blind Side
Avatar
Taken
(500) Days of Summer
My Bloody Valentine 3D
17 Again
District 9
Up in the Air
Sherlock Holmes
Inglourious Basterds
Michael Jackson's This Is It
Up
Zombieland
Harry Potter and the Half-Blood Prince
Drag Me to Hell
It's Complicated
Bruno
A Serious Man
Star Trek
Julie & Julia
Cloudy with a Chance of Meatballs
Crank: High Voltage
Monsters vs. Aliens
Coraline
A Christmas Carol
Public Enemies
Watchmen
Where the Wild Things Are
The Hurt Locker
Fantastic Mr. Fox
Invictus
The Soloist
The Road
1000%
800%
600%
400%
200%
100%
0%
55%
60%
70%
80%
90%
100%
Rescue
Revenge
Rivalry
Sacrifice
Temptation
The Riddle
Tragedy
Transformation
Underdog
Wretched Excess
Story

source: BoxOfficeMojo.com, The-Numbers.com, Wikipedia, IMDB.com & RottenTomatoes.com. Note: reported film budgets are notoriously unreliable (especially for flops)

Most Profitable Hollywood Stories 2010

Average profitability: 277% Average quality: 49% Most common stories: Love Comedy

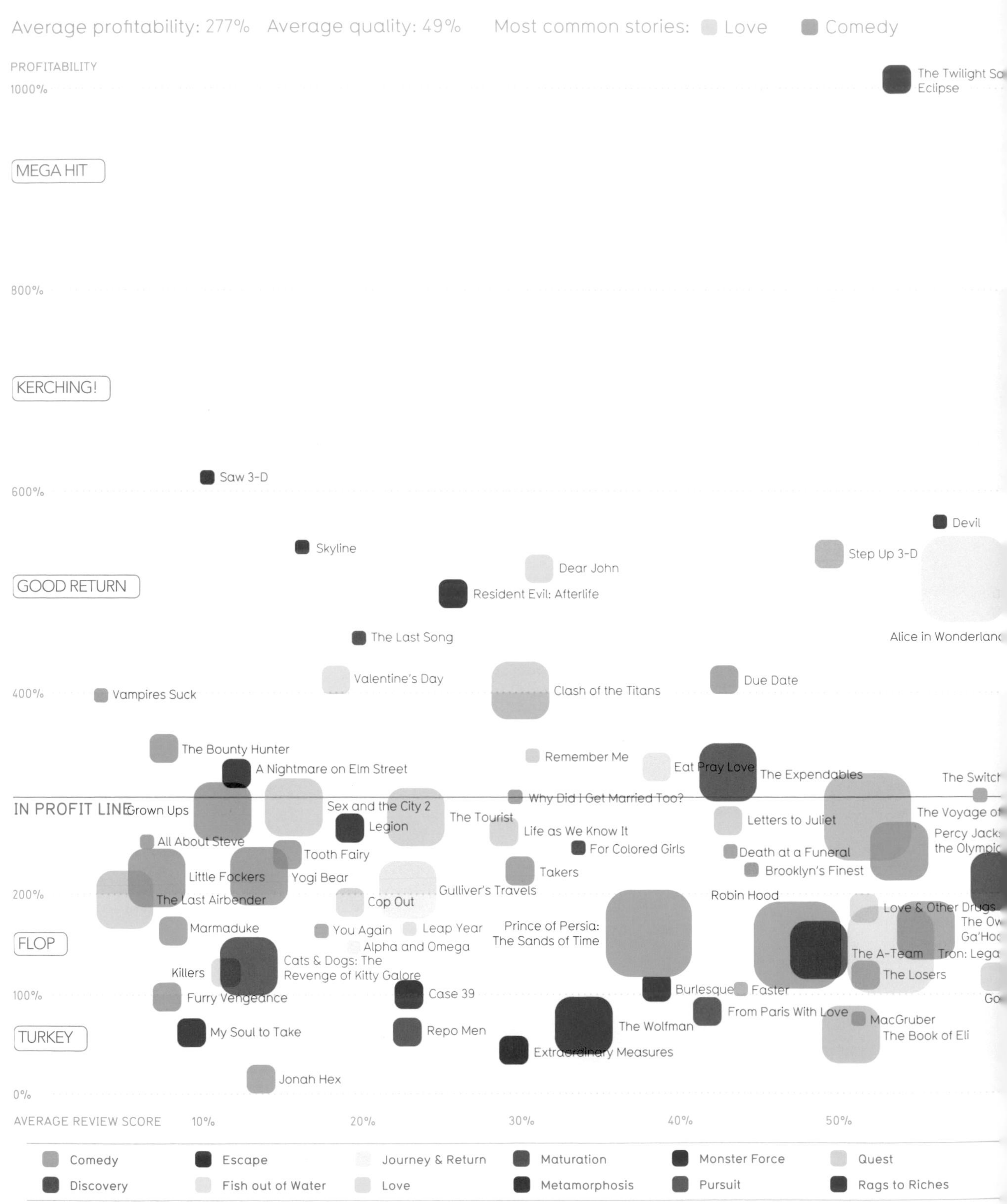
PROFITABILITY
1000%
The Twilight Sa
Eclipse
MEGA HIT
800%
KERCHING!
Saw 3-D
600%
Devil
Skyline
Step Up 3-D
Dear John
GOOD RETURN
Resident Evil: Afterlife
The Last Song
Alice in Wonderlanc
Valentine's Day
Due Date
Clash of the Titans
400%
Vampires Suck
The Bounty Hunter
Remember Me
A Nightmare on Elm Street
Eat Pray Love
The Expendables
The Switch
Why Did I Get Married Too?
IN PROFIT LINE
Grown Ups
Sex and the City 2
The Tourist
Legion
Letters to Juliet
The Voyage of
Life as We Know It
All About Steve
Percy Jack
the Olympic
For Colored Girls
Tooth Fairy
Death at a Funeral
Takers
Little Fockers
Yogi Bear
Brooklyn's Finest
Gulliver's Travels
The Last Airbender
Robin Hood
200%
Cop Out
Love & Other Drugs
Marmaduke
Prince of Persia:
The Sands of Time
The Ow
Ga'Hoo
You Again
Leap Year
FLOP
Alpha and Omega
The A-Team
Tron: Lega
Cats & Dogs: The
Revenge of Kitty Galore
Killers
The Losers
100%
Furry Vengeance
Case 39
Burlesque
Faster
Go
From Paris With Love
MacGruber
The Wolfman
TURKEY
My Soul to Take
Repo Men
The Book of Eli
Extraordinary Measures
Jonah Hex
0%
AVERAGE REVIEW SCORE
10%
20%
30%
40%
50%
Comedy
Escape
Journey & Return
Maturation
Monster Force
Quest
Discovery
Fish out of Water
Love
Metamorphosis
Pursuit
Rags to Riches

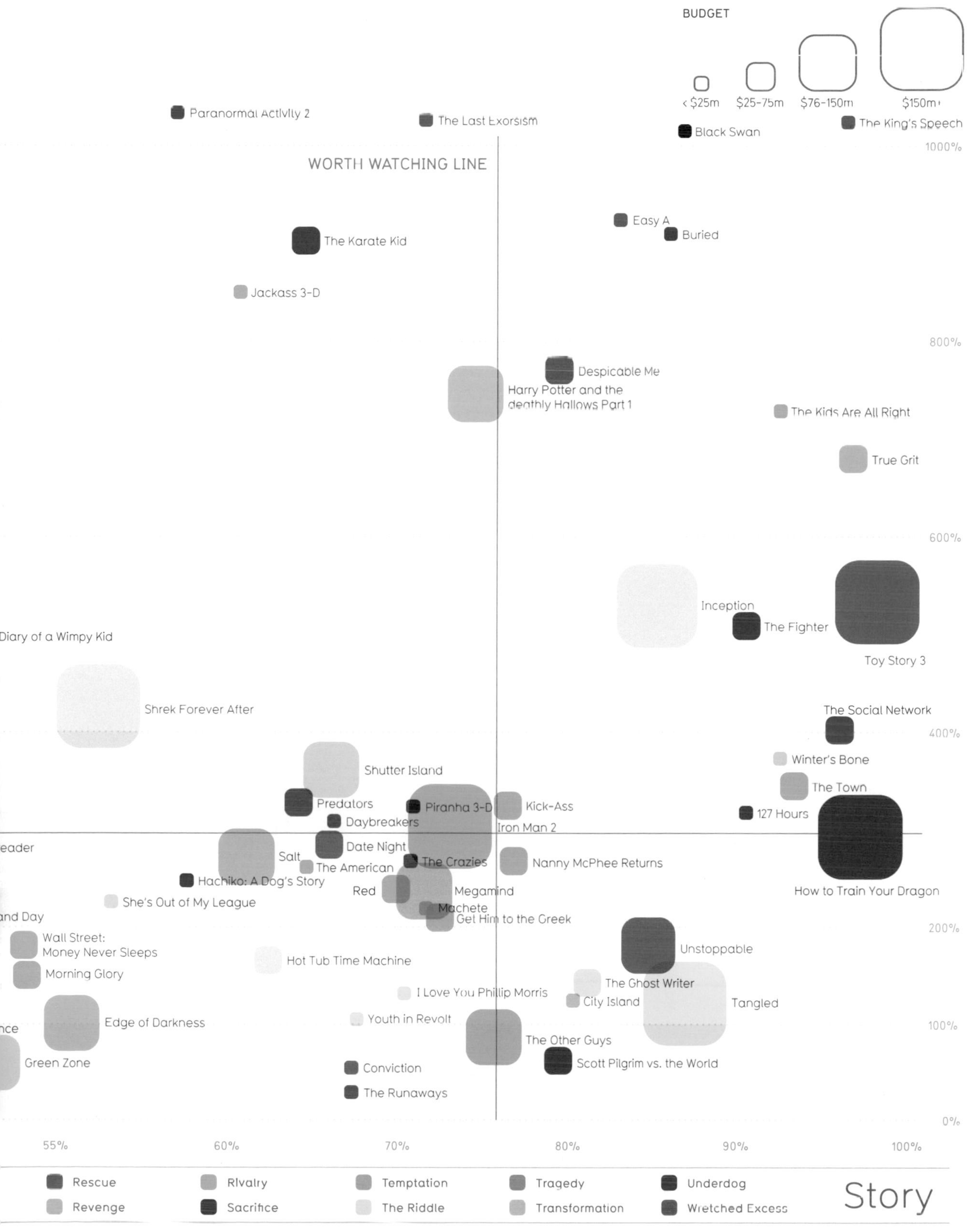
BUDGET
< $25m
$25–75m
$76–150m
$150m+
Paranormal Activity 2
The Last Exorsism
Black Swan
The King's Speech
1000%
WORTH WATCHING LINE
Easy A
Buried
The Karate Kid
Jackass 3-D
800%
Despicable Me
Harry Potter and the deathly Hallows Part 1
The Kids Are All Right
True Grit
600%
Inception
The Fighter
Toy Story 3
Diary of a Wimpy Kid
Shrek Forever After
The Social Network
400%
Winter's Bone
Shutter Island
The Town
Predators
Piranha 3-D
Kick-Ass
127 Hours
Daybreakers
Iron Man 2
Date Night
Salt
The Crazies
Nanny McPhee Returns
The American
Hachiko: A Dog's Story
Red
Megamind
How to Train Your Dragon
She's Out of My League
Machete
Get Him to the Greek
Wall Street: Money Never Sleeps
200%
Unstoppable
Hot Tub Time Machine
Morning Glory
The Ghost Writer
I Love You Phillip Morris
City Island
Tangled
Edge of Darkness
Youth in Revolt
100%
The Other Guys
Green Zone
Conviction
Scott Pilgrim vs. the World
The Runaways
0%
55%
60%
70%
80%
90%
100%
Rescue
Revenge
Rivalry
Sacrifice
Temptation
The Riddle
Tragedy
Transformation
Underdog
Wretched Excess
Story

source: BoxOfficeMojo.com, The-Numbers.com, Wikipedia, IMDB.com & RottenTomatoes.com. Note: reported film budgets are notoriously unreliable (especially for flops)

Most Profitable Hollywood Stories 2011

Average profitability: 289% Average quality: 54% Most common stories: Quest Monster

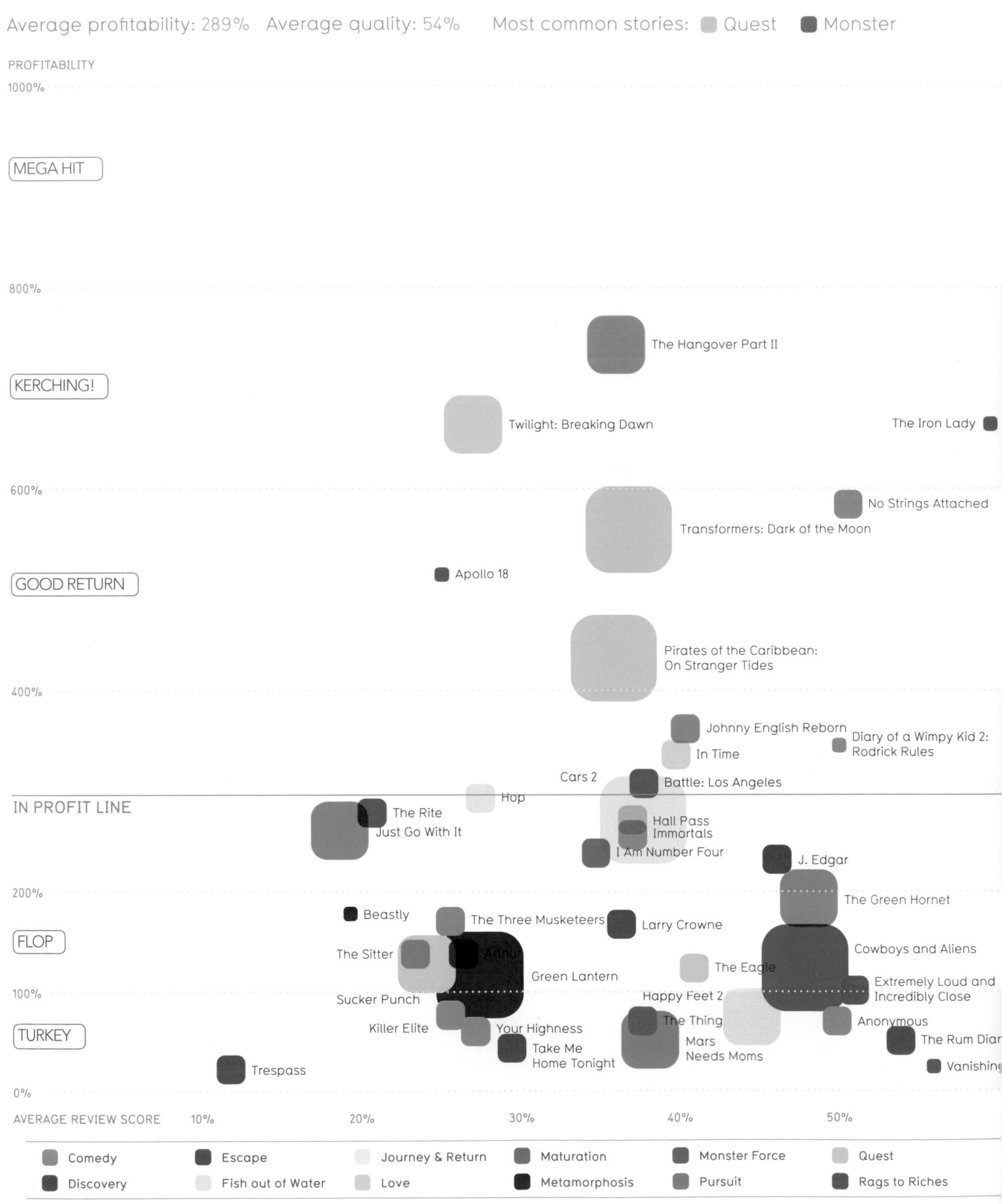

PROFITABILITY
1000%
MEGA HIT
800%
KERCHING!
600%
GOOD RETURN
400%
IN PROFIT LINE
200%
FLOP
100%
TURKEY
0%
AVERAGE REVIEW SCORE
10%
20%
30%
40%
50%
The Hangover Part II
Twilight: Breaking Dawn
The Iron Lady
No Strings Attached
Transformers: Dark of the Moon
Apollo 18
Pirates of the Caribbean: On Stranger Tides
Johnny English Reborn
In Time
Diary of a Wimpy Kid 2: Rodrick Rules
Cars 2
Battle: Los Angeles
Hop
The Rite
Just Go With It
Hall Pass
Immortals
I Am Number Four
J. Edgar
The Green Hornet
Beastly
The Three Musketeers
Larry Crowne
Cowboys and Aliens
The Sitter
Green Lantern
The Eagle
Extremely Loud and Incredibly Close
Sucker Punch
Happy Feet 2
The Thing
Anonymous
Killer Elite
Your Highness
Take Me Home Tonight
Mars Needs Moms
Trespass
Comedy
Discovery
Escape
Fish out of Water
Journey & Return
Love
Maturation
Metamorphosis
Monster Force
Pursuit
Quest
Rags to Riches

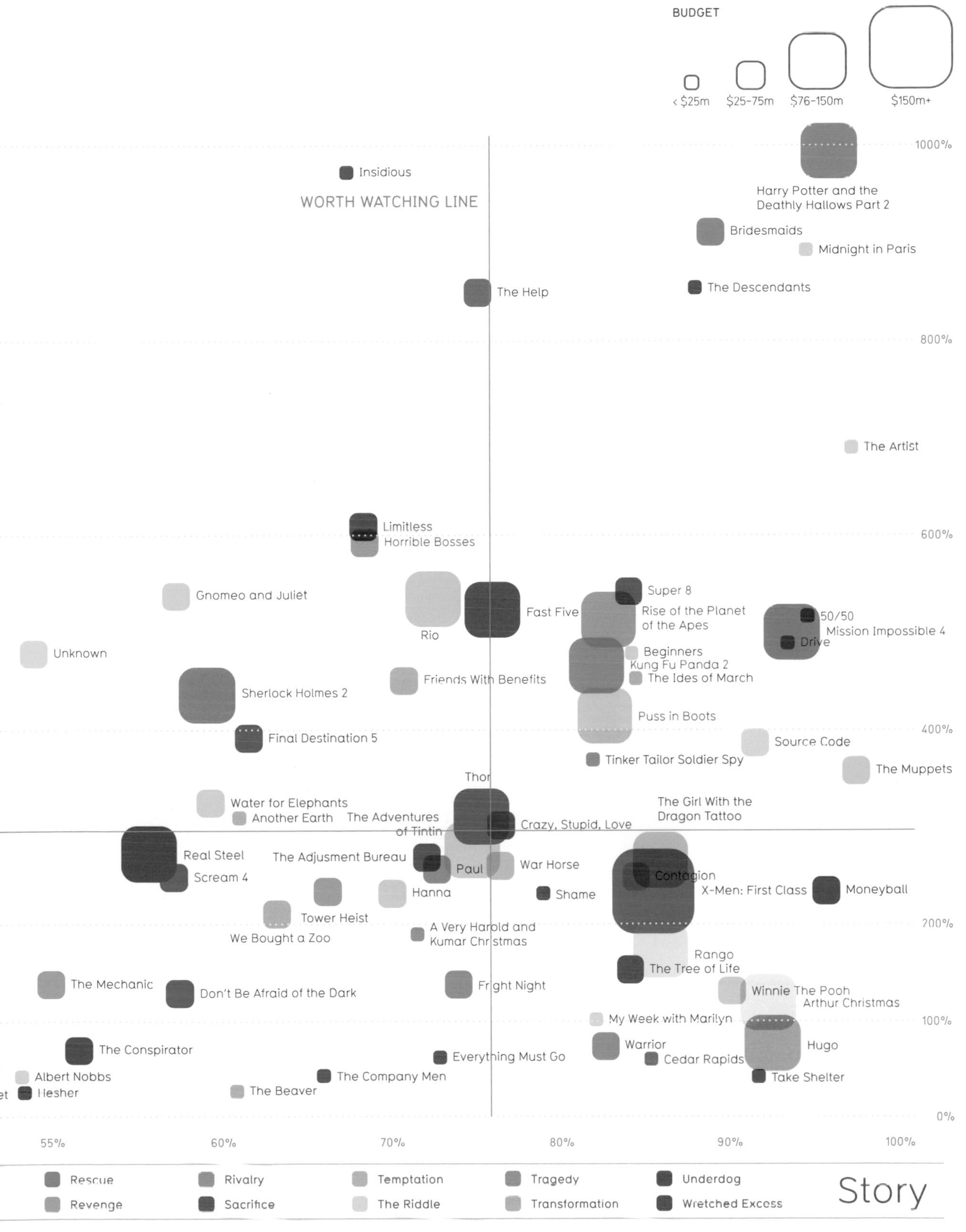

BUDGET
< $25m
$25-75m
$76-150m
$150m+
1000%
800%
600%
400%
200%
100%
0%
WORTH WATCHING LINE
Insidious
Harry Potter and the Deathly Hallows Part 2
Bridesmaids
Midnight in Paris
The Descendants
The Help
The Artist
Limitless
Horrible Bosses
Gnomeo and Juliet
Rio
Fast Five
Super 8
Rise of the Planet of the Apes
50/50
Mission Impossible 4
Drive
Unknown
Beginners
Kung Fu Panda 2
The Ides of March
Friends With Benefits
Sherlock Holmes 2
Puss in Boots
Final Destination 5
Source Code
Tinker Tailor Soldier Spy
The Muppets
Thor
Water for Elephants
Another Earth
The Adventures of Tintin
Crazy, Stupid, Love
The Girl With the Dragon Tattoo
Real Steel
The Adjusment Bureau
Paul
War Horse
Scream 4
Contagion
X-Men: First Class
Moneyball
Hanna
Shame
Tower Heist
We Bought a Zoo
A Very Harold and Kumar Christmas
Rango
The Tree of Life
The Mechanic
Don't Be Afraid of the Dark
Fright Night
Winnie The Pooh
Arthur Christmas
My Week with Marilyn
Hugo
Warrior
Cedar Rapids
The Conspirator
Everything Must Go
Take Shelter
Albert Nobbs
The Company Men
Hesher
The Beaver
55%
60%
70%
80%
90%
100%
Rescue
Revenge
Rivalry
Sacrifice
Temptation
The Riddle
Tragedy
Transformation
Underdog
Wretched Excess
Story

source: BoxOfficeMojo.com, The-Numbers.com, Wikipedia, IMDB.com & RottenTomatoes.com. Note: reported film budgets are notoriously unreliable (especially for flops)

Most Profitable Stories of All Time

Average budget: 43m Average quality: 83% Most common stories: Quest Monster Force

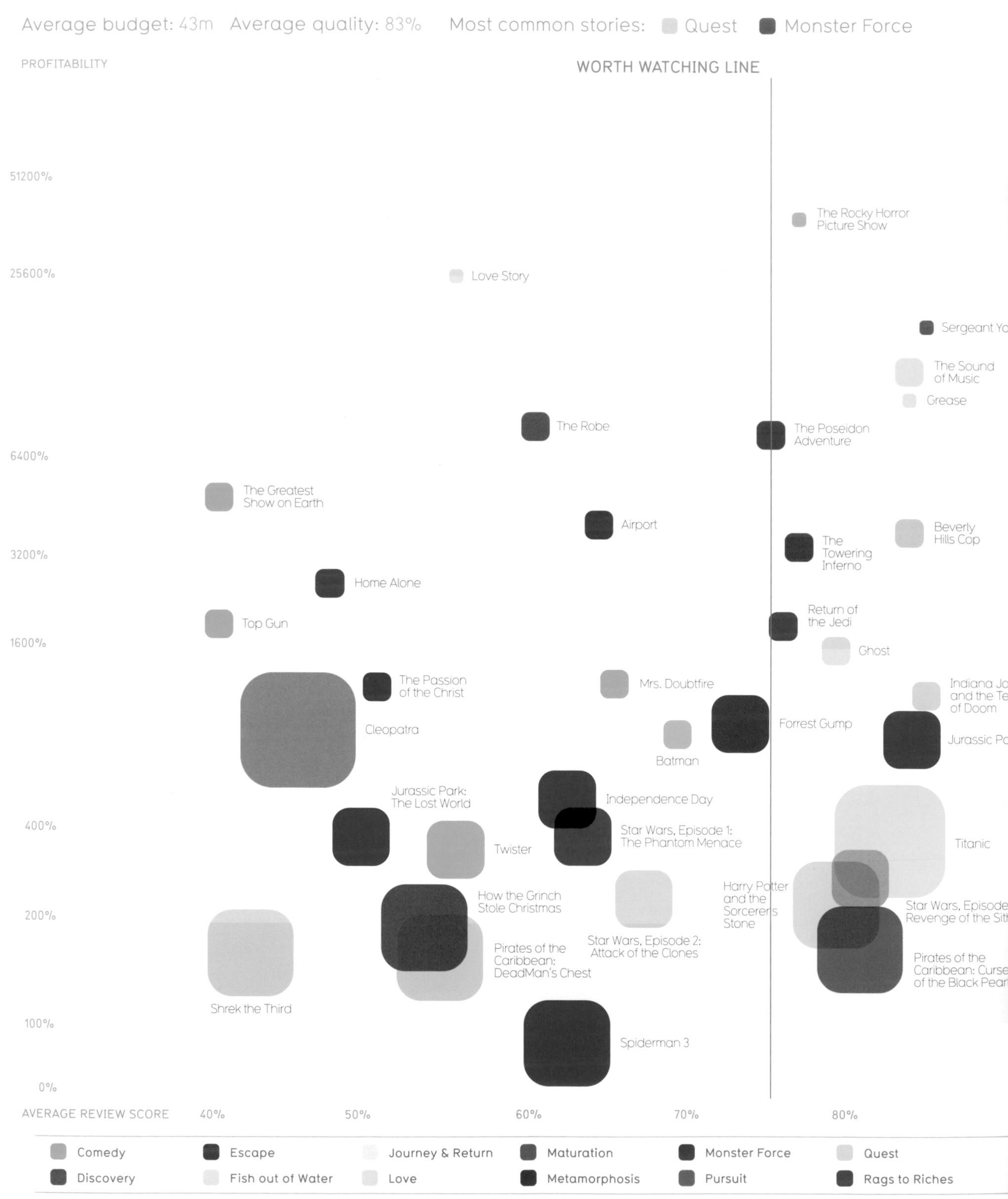

PROFITABILITY
WORTH WATCHING LINE
51200%
25600%
6400%
3200%
1600%
400%
200%
100%
0%
The Rocky Horror Picture Show
Love Story
Sergeant Yor
The Sound of Music
Grease
The Robe
The Poseidon Adventure
The Greatest Show on Earth
Airport
Beverly Hills Cop
The Towering Inferno
Home Alone
Return of the Jedi
Top Gun
Ghost
The Passion of the Christ
Mrs. Doubtfire
Indiana Jo and the Ter of Doom
Cleopatra
Forrest Gump
Batman
Jurassic Pa
Jurassic Park: The Lost World
Independence Day
Star Wars, Episode 1: The Phantom Menace
Titanic
Twister
Harry Potter and the Sorcerer's Stone
How the Grinch Stole Christmas
Star Wars, Episode Revenge of the Sith
Pirates of the Caribbean: DeadMan's Chest
Star Wars, Episode 2: Attack of the Clones
Pirates of the Caribbean: Curse of the Black Pearl
Shrek the Third
Spiderman 3
AVERAGE REVIEW SCORE
40%
50%
60%
70%
80%
Comedy
Escape
Journey & Return
Maturation
Monster Force
Quest
Discovery
Fish out of Water
Love
Metamorphosis
Pursuit
Rags to Riches

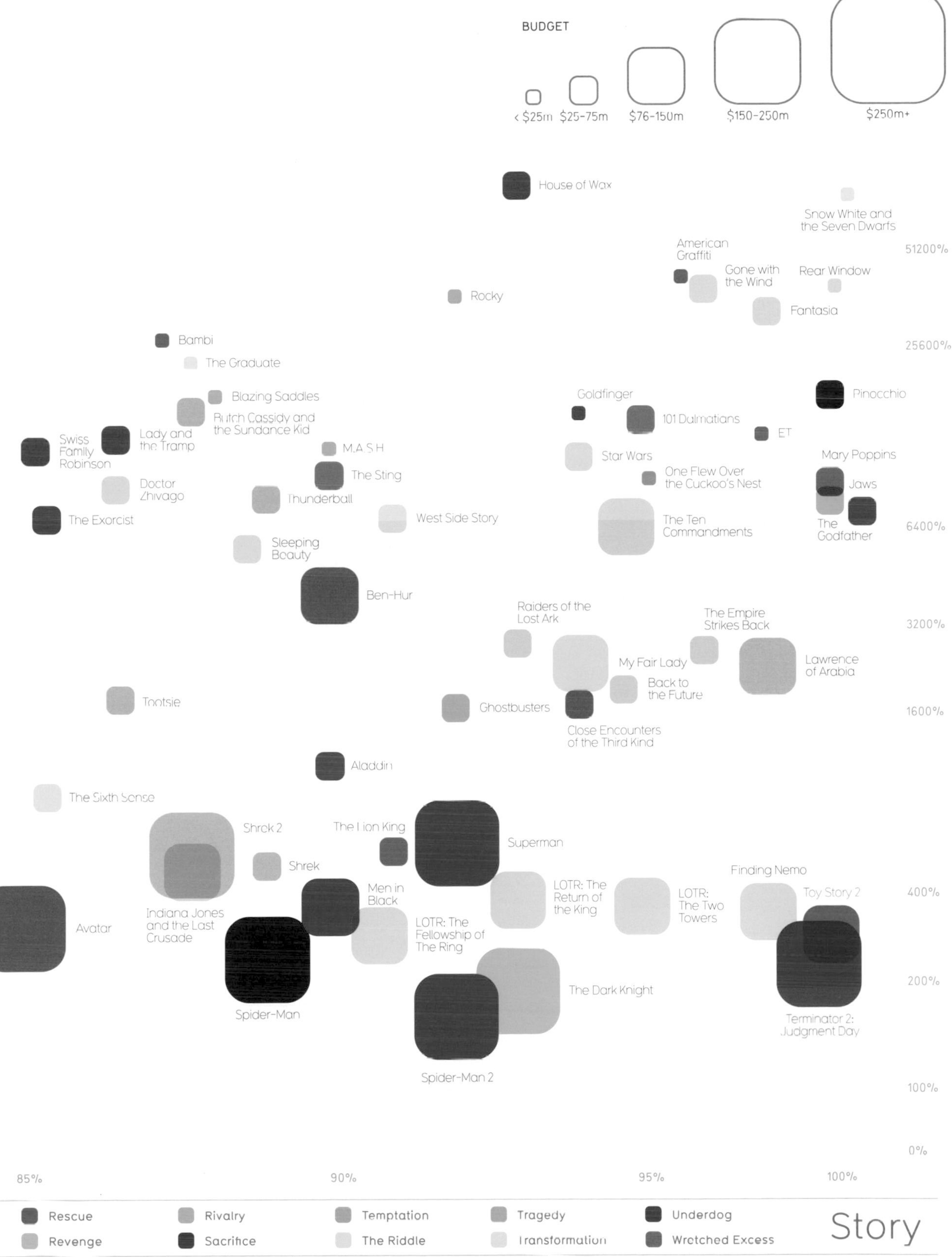
BUDGET
< $25m
$25-75m
$76-150m
$150-250m
$250m+
House of Wax
Snow White and the Seven Dwarfs
American Graffiti
Gone with the Wind
Rear Window
Rocky
Fantasia
Bambi
The Graduate
Blazing Saddles
Butch Cassidy and the Sundance Kid
Goldfinger
Pinocchio
101 Dalmatians
ET
Swiss Family Robinson
Lady and the Tramp
M.A.S.H
Star Wars
Mary Poppins
The Sting
One Flew Over the Cuckoo's Nest
Jaws
Doctor Zhivago
Thunderball
The Exorcist
West Side Story
The Ten Commandments
The Godfather
Sleeping Beauty
Ben-Hur
Raiders of the Lost Ark
The Empire Strikes Back
My Fair Lady
Lawrence of Arabia
Back to the Future
Tootsie
Ghostbusters
Close Encounters of the Third Kind
Aladdin
The Sixth Sense
Shrek 2
The Lion King
Superman
Shrek
Finding Nemo
LOTR: The Return of the King
LOTR: The Two Towers
Toy Story 2
Men in Black
Indiana Jones and the Last Crusade
Avatar
LOTR: The Fellowship of The Ring
The Dark Knight
Spider-Man
Terminator 2: Judgment Day
Spider-Man 2
51200%
25600%
6400%
3200%
1600%
400%
200%
100%
0%
85%
90%
95%
100%
Rescue
Revenge
Rivalry
Sacrifice
Temptation
The Riddle
Tragedy
Transformation
Underdog
Wretched Excess
Story

source: BoxOfficeMojo.com, Wikipedia. Budgets inflation adjusted to 2010 dollars

Enneagram

A personality-type system based around an ancient symbol of perpetual motion. Each type is formed from a key defence against the world. Which one are you?

		I am...	I want to...	Virtue
1	**Reformer**	Reasonable and objective	Be good and have integrity	Serenity
2	**Helper**	Caring and loving	Feel love	Humility
3	**Achiever**	Outstanding and effective	Feel valuable	Honesty
4	**Individualist**	Intuitive and sensitive	Be myself	Balance
5	**Investigator**	Intelligent, perceptive	Be capable and competent	Detachment
6	**Loyalist**	Committed, dependable	Have support and guidance	Courage
7	**Enthusiast**	Reasonable and objective	Be satisfied and content	Sobriety
8	**Challenger**	Strong, assertive	Protect myself	Innocence
9	**Peacemaker**	Peaceful, easygoing	Have peace of mind	Action

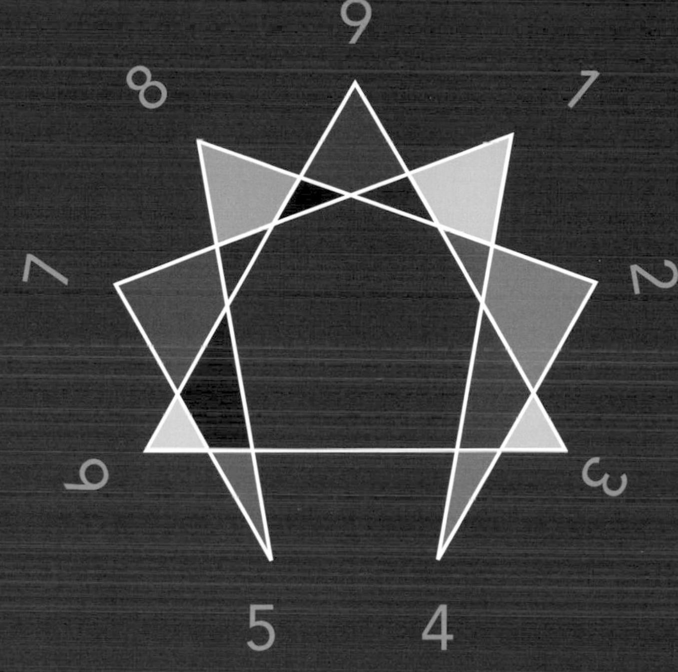
9
8
1
7
2
6
3
5
4

Hidden complaint	I fear being...	Flaw	Saving grace
I am usually right. Others should listen to me.	Bad, wrong	Resentment	Sensible
I'm always loving. Others take me for granted.	Unloved	Flattery	Empathic
I am a superior person. Others are jealous	Worthless	Vanity	Eagerness
I don't really fit in. I am different from others.	Insignificant	Melancholy	Self-aware
I'm so smart. Others can't understand me.	Helpless or incompetent	Stinginess	No bullshit
I do what I'm told . Others don't	Without support	Worrying	Friendly
I'm happy. But others don't give me enough.	In pain	Over-Planning	Enthusiasm
I'm fighting to survive. Others take advantage.	Harmed or controlled	Vengeance	Strength
I am content. Others pressure me to change.	Lost and separated	Laziness	Fluidity

source: Wikipedia, EnneagramInstitute.com

Selling Your Soul

Workers on Amazon.com's Mechanical Turk asked to draw their souls

female

UMASS
13
HAPPY
male

Amazon's Mechanical Turk is a "cloud workforce" of people happy to do microjobs for micropayments ($0.25 and up). 200 people were asked to draw a picture of their soul for the author's ongoing collection. Muhahahahahahahaha...

source: Mturk.com. Thanks to all Turkers who took part!

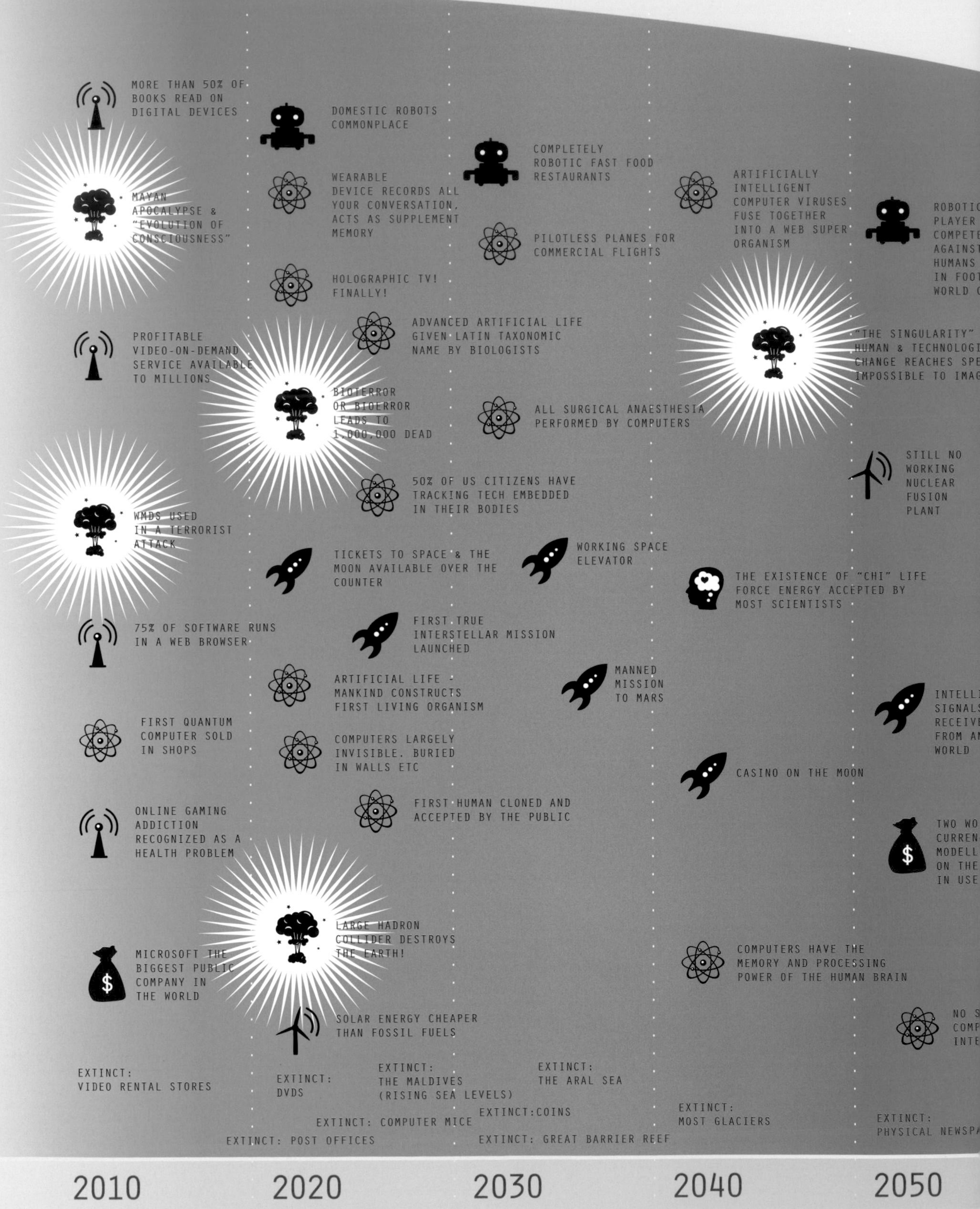
MORE THAN 50% OF BOOKS READ ON DIGITAL DEVICES
MAYAN APOCALYPSE & "EVOLUTION OF CONSCIOUSNESS"
PROFITABLE VIDEO-ON-DEMAND SERVICE AVAILABLE TO MILLIONS
WMDS USED IN A TERRORIST ATTACK
75% OF SOFTWARE RUNS IN A WEB BROWSER
FIRST QUANTUM COMPUTER SOLD IN SHOPS
ONLINE GAMING ADDICTION RECOGNIZED AS A HEALTH PROBLEM
MICROSOFT THE BIGGEST PUBLIC COMPANY IN THE WORLD
EXTINCT: VIDEO RENTAL STORES
DOMESTIC ROBOTS COMMONPLACE
WEARABLE DEVICE RECORDS ALL YOUR CONVERSATION, ACTS AS SUPPLEMENT MEMORY
HOLOGRAPHIC TV! FINALLY!
ADVANCED ARTIFICIAL LIFE GIVEN LATIN TAXONOMIC NAME BY BIOLOGISTS
BIOTERROR OR BIOERROR LEADS TO 1,000,000 DEAD
50% OF US CITIZENS HAVE TRACKING TECH EMBEDDED IN THEIR BODIES
TICKETS TO SPACE & THE MOON AVAILABLE OVER THE COUNTER
FIRST TRUE INTERSTELLAR MISSION LAUNCHED
ARTIFICIAL LIFE - MANKIND CONSTRUCTS FIRST LIVING ORGANISM
COMPUTERS LARGELY INVISIBLE. BURIED IN WALLS ETC
FIRST HUMAN CLONED AND ACCEPTED BY THE PUBLIC
LARGE HADRON COLLIDER DESTROYS THE EARTH!
SOLAR ENERGY CHEAPER THAN FOSSIL FUELS
EXTINCT: DVDS
EXTINCT: THE MALDIVES (RISING SEA LEVELS)
EXTINCT: COMPUTER MICE
EXTINCT: POST OFFICES
COMPLETELY ROBOTIC FAST FOOD RESTAURANTS
PILOTLESS PLANES FOR COMMERCIAL FLIGHTS
ALL SURGICAL ANAESTHESIA PERFORMED BY COMPUTERS
WORKING SPACE ELEVATOR
MANNED MISSION TO MARS
EXTINCT: THE ARAL SEA
EXTINCT:COINS
EXTINCT: GREAT BARRIER REEF
ARTIFICIALLY INTELLIGENT COMPUTER VIRUSES FUSE TOGETHER INTO A WEB SUPER ORGANISM
THE EXISTENCE OF "CHI" LIFE FORCE ENERGY ACCEPTED BY MOST SCIENTISTS
CASINO ON THE MOON
COMPUTERS HAVE THE MEMORY AND PROCESSING POWER OF THE HUMAN BRAIN
EXTINCT: MOST GLACIERS
ROBOTIC
PLAYER
COMPETE
AGAINST
HUMANS
IN FOOT
WORLD C
"THE SINGULARITY"
HUMAN & TECHNOLOGI
CHANGE REACHES SPE
IMPOSSIBLE TO IMAG
STILL NO WORKING NUCLEAR FUSION PLANT
INTELL
SIGNALS
RECEIVE
FROM AN
WORLD
TWO WO
CURREN
MODELL
ON THE
IN USE
NO S
COMP
INTE
EXTINCT:
PHYSICAL NEWSPA
2010
2020
2030
2040
2050

The Future of the Future

At longbets.org leading thinkers gather to place bets on future predictions

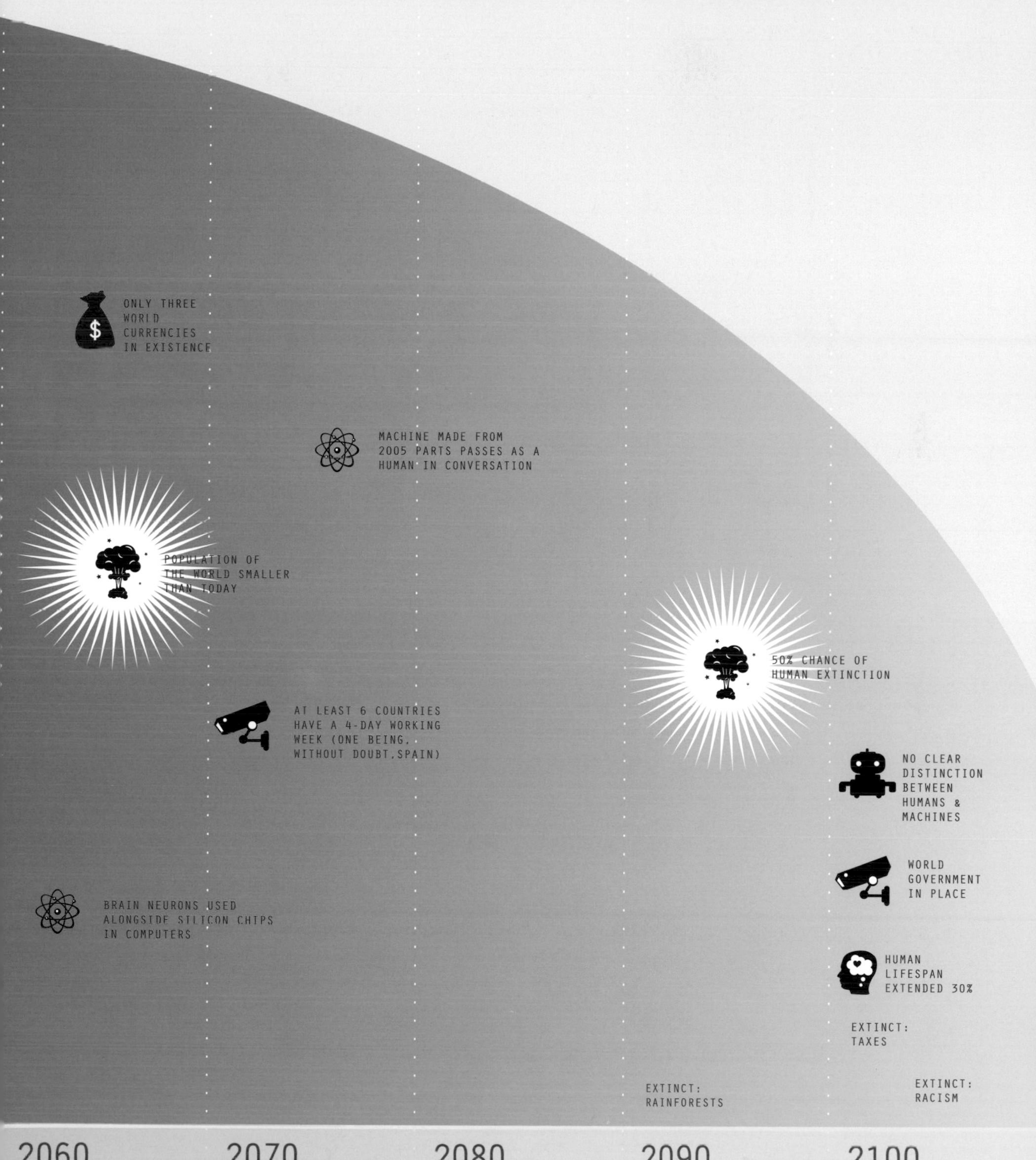

ONLY THREE WORLD CURRENCIES IN EXISTENCE
MACHINE MADE FROM 2005 PARTS PASSES AS A HUMAN IN CONVERSATION
POPULATION OF THE WORLD SMALLER THAN TODAY
50% CHANCE OF HUMAN EXTINCTION
AT LEAST 6 COUNTRIES HAVE A 4-DAY WORKING WEEK (ONE BEING, WITHOUT DOUBT, SPAIN)
NO CLEAR DISTINCTION BETWEEN HUMANS & MACHINES
WORLD GOVERNMENT IN PLACE
BRAIN NEURONS USED ALONGSIDE SILICON CHIPS IN COMPUTERS
HUMAN LIFESPAN EXTENDED 30%
EXTINCT: TAXES
EXTINCT: RAINFORESTS
EXTINCT: RACISM
2060
2070
2080
2090
2100

source: longbets.org

Making the Book

The first six months

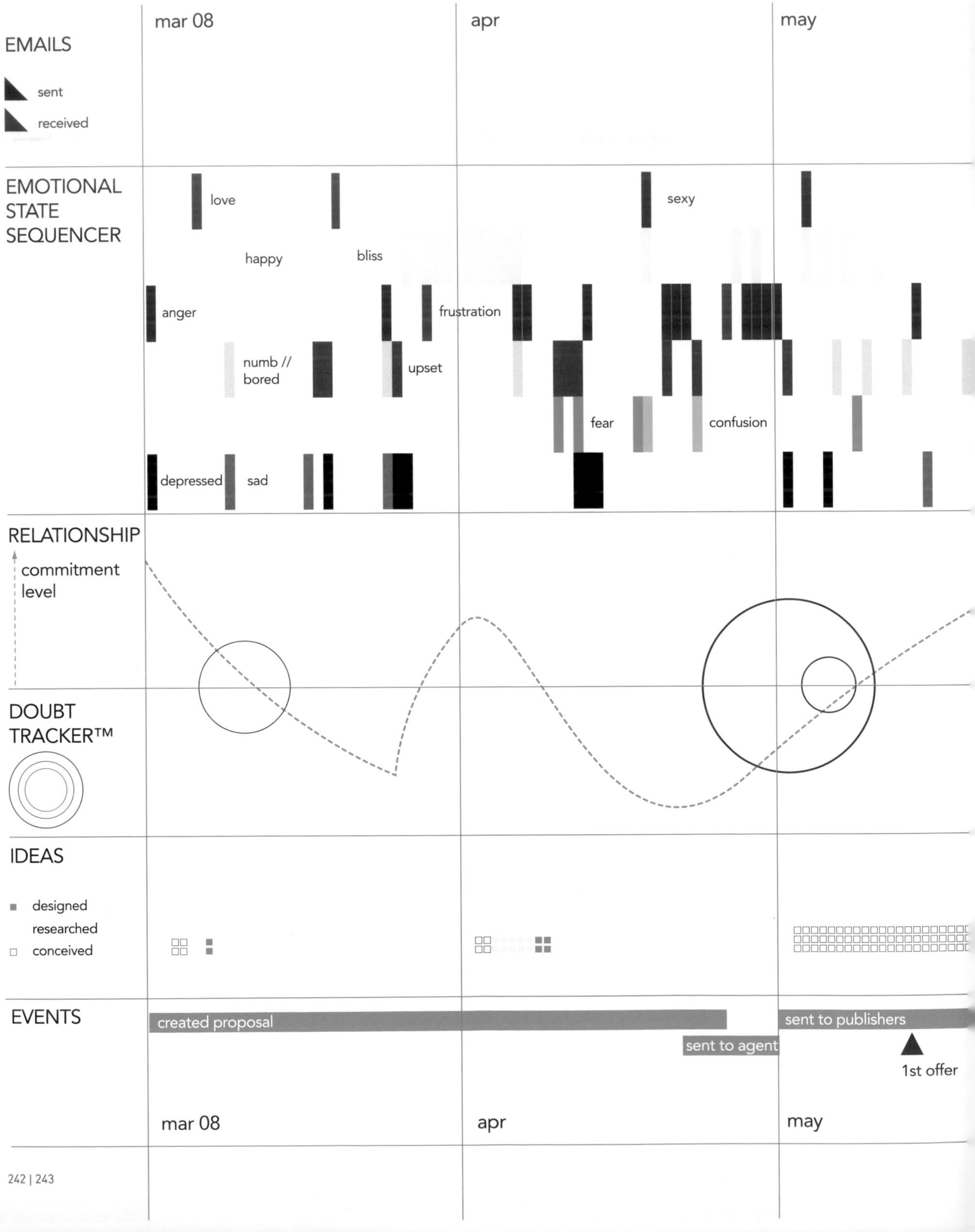

mar 08
apr
may
EMAILS
sent
received
EMOTIONAL STATE SEQUENCER
love
happy
bliss
sexy
anger
frustration
numb // bored
upset
fear
confusion
depressed
sad
RELATIONSHIP
commitment level
DOUBT TRACKER™
IDEAS
designed
researched
conceived
EVENTS
created proposal
sent to agent
sent to publishers
1st offer
mar 08
apr
may

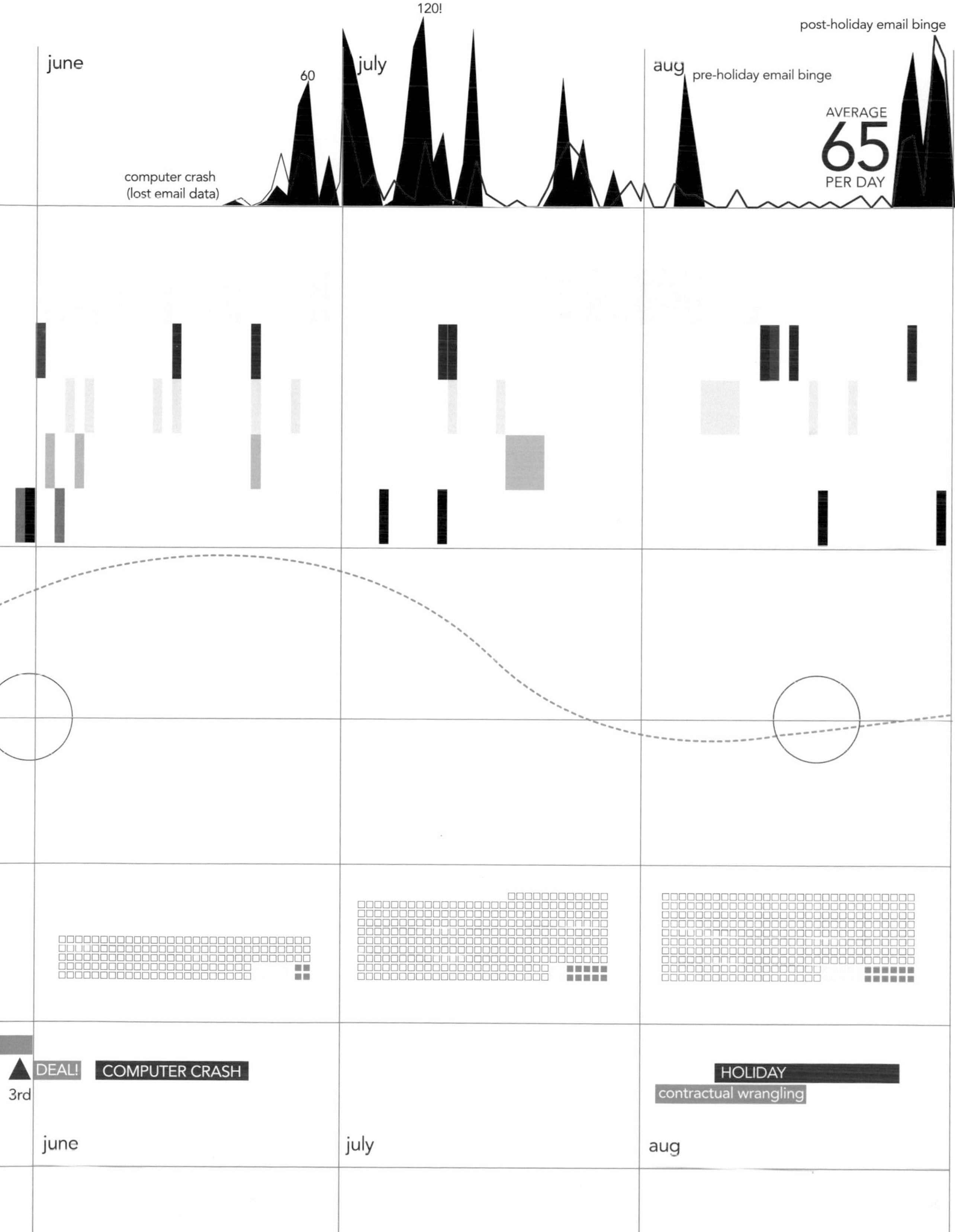

120!
post-holiday email binge
june
60
july
aug
pre-holiday email binge
AVERAGE
65
PER DAY
computer crash
(lost email data)
DEAL!
COMPUTER CRASH
3rd
HOLIDAY
contractual wrangling
june
july
aug

Making the Book

The last six months

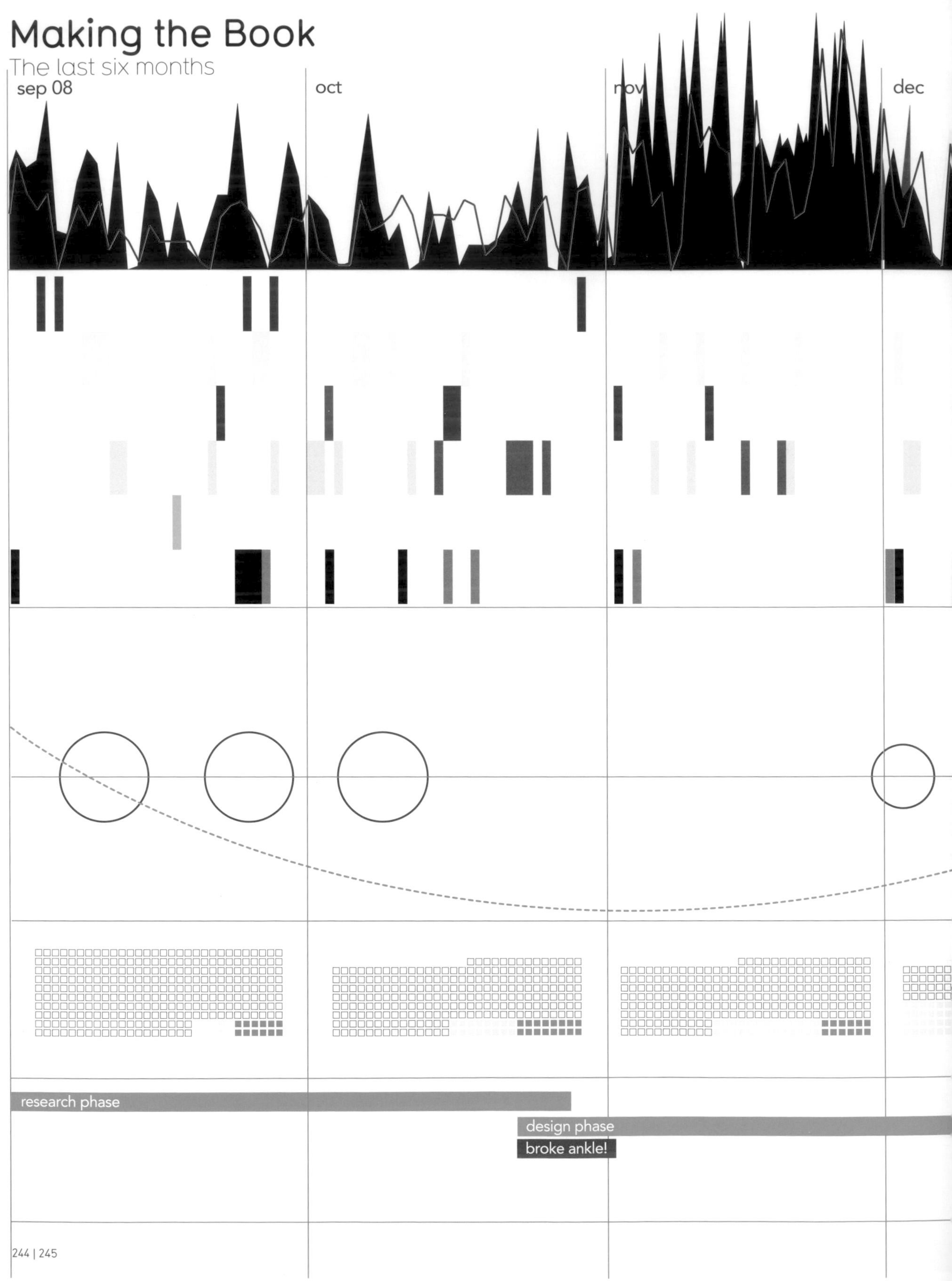

sep 08
oct
nov
dec
research phase
design phase
broke ankle!

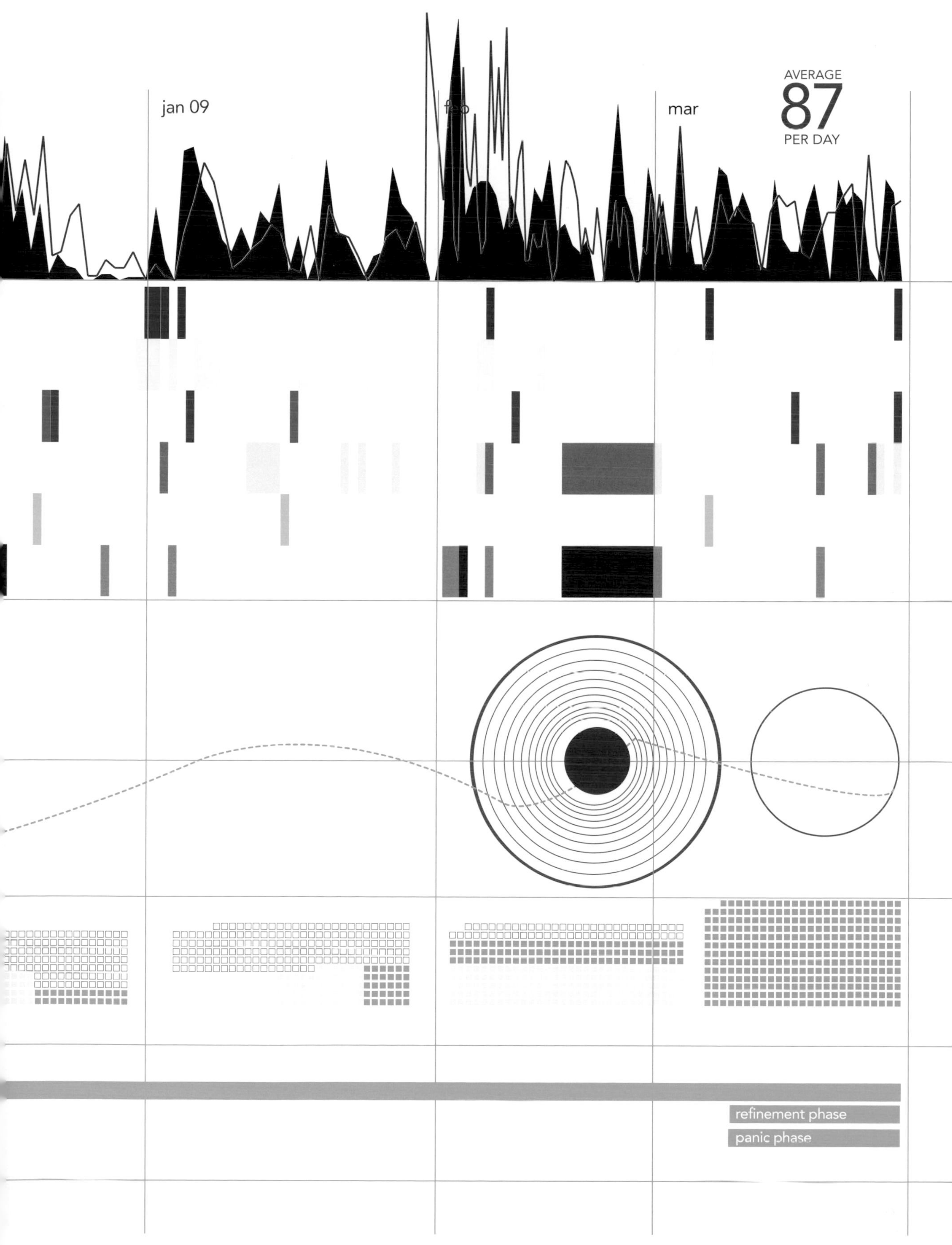

jan 09
feb
mar
AVERAGE
87
PER DAY
refinement phase
panic phase

Acknowledge Map

Thanks to all who helped and supported

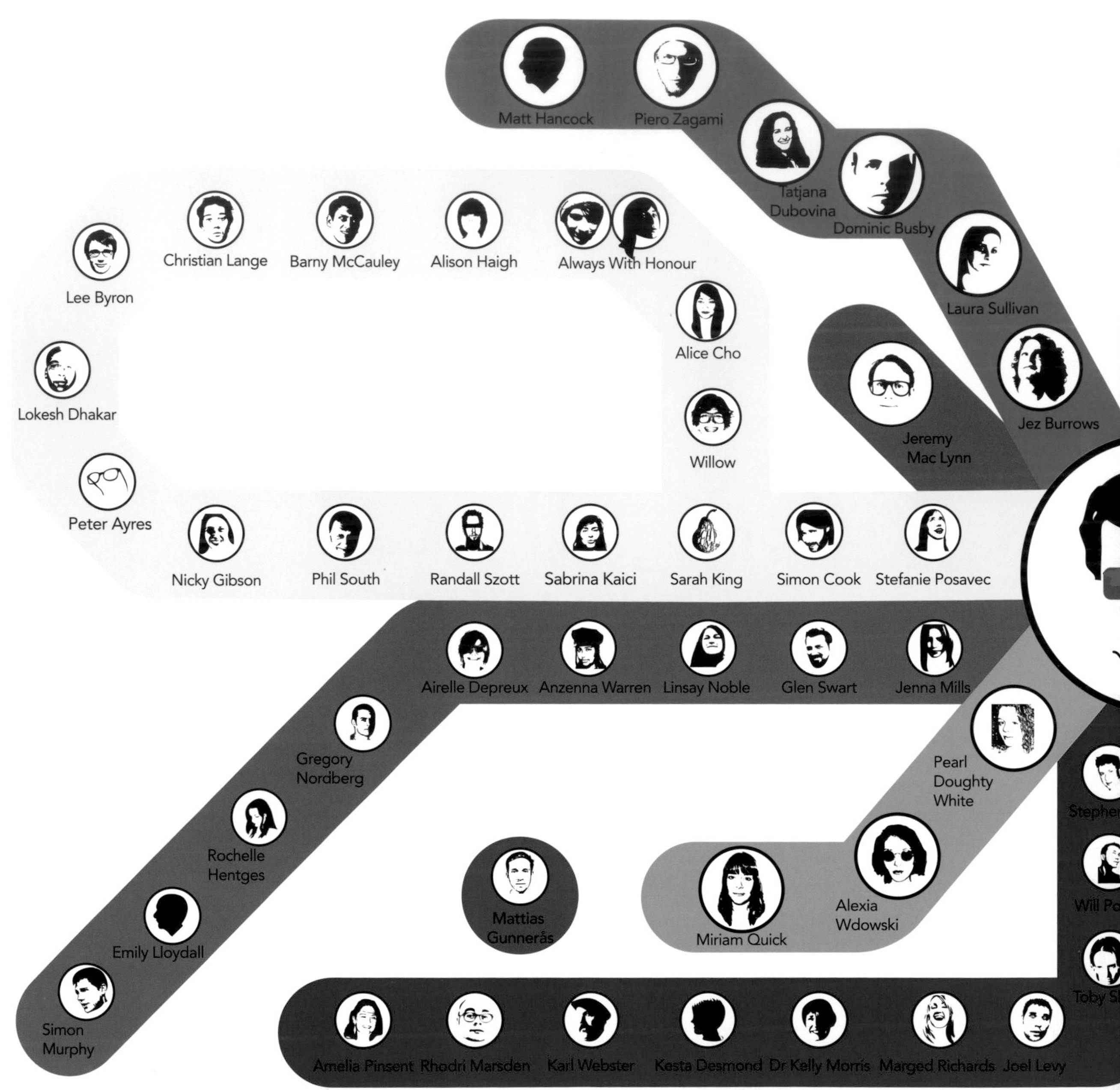

Matt Hancock
Piero Zagami
Tatjana Dubovina
Dominic Busby
Laura Sullivan
Jez Burrows
Jeremy Mac Lynn
Lee Byron
Christian Lange
Barny McCauley
Alison Haigh
Always With Honour
Alice Cho
Willow
Lokesh Dhakar
Peter Ayres
Nicky Gibson
Phil South
Randall Szott
Sabrina Kaici
Sarah King
Simon Cook
Stefanie Posavec
Airelle Depreux
Anzenna Warren
Linsay Noble
Glen Swart
Jenna Mills
Gregory Nordberg
Rochelle Hentges
Emily Lloydall
Simon Murphy
Mattias Gunnerås
Pearl Doughty White
Alexia Wdowski
Miriam Quick
Amelia Pinsent
Rhodri Marsden
Karl Webster
Kesta Desmond
Dr Kelly Morris
Marged Richards
Joel Levy

MANY THANKS TO: Vincent Ahrend, Kathryn Ariel, Dr David Archer, Steve Beckett, Delfina Bottesini, Laura Brudenell, Candy Chang, Susanne Cook Greuter, Dave Cooper, Kesta Desmond, Robert Downes, Danielle Engelman, Edward Farmer, Richard Henry, Dr Phil Howard, Claudia Hofmeister, Aegir Hallmundur, Becky Jones, Dongwoo Kim, Jenny McIvor, Priscila Moura, Mark O'Connor, Kate O'Driscoll, Dr. Lori Plutchik, Laura Price, Richard Rogers, Miriam Quick Twitter Army, Mechanical Turkers.

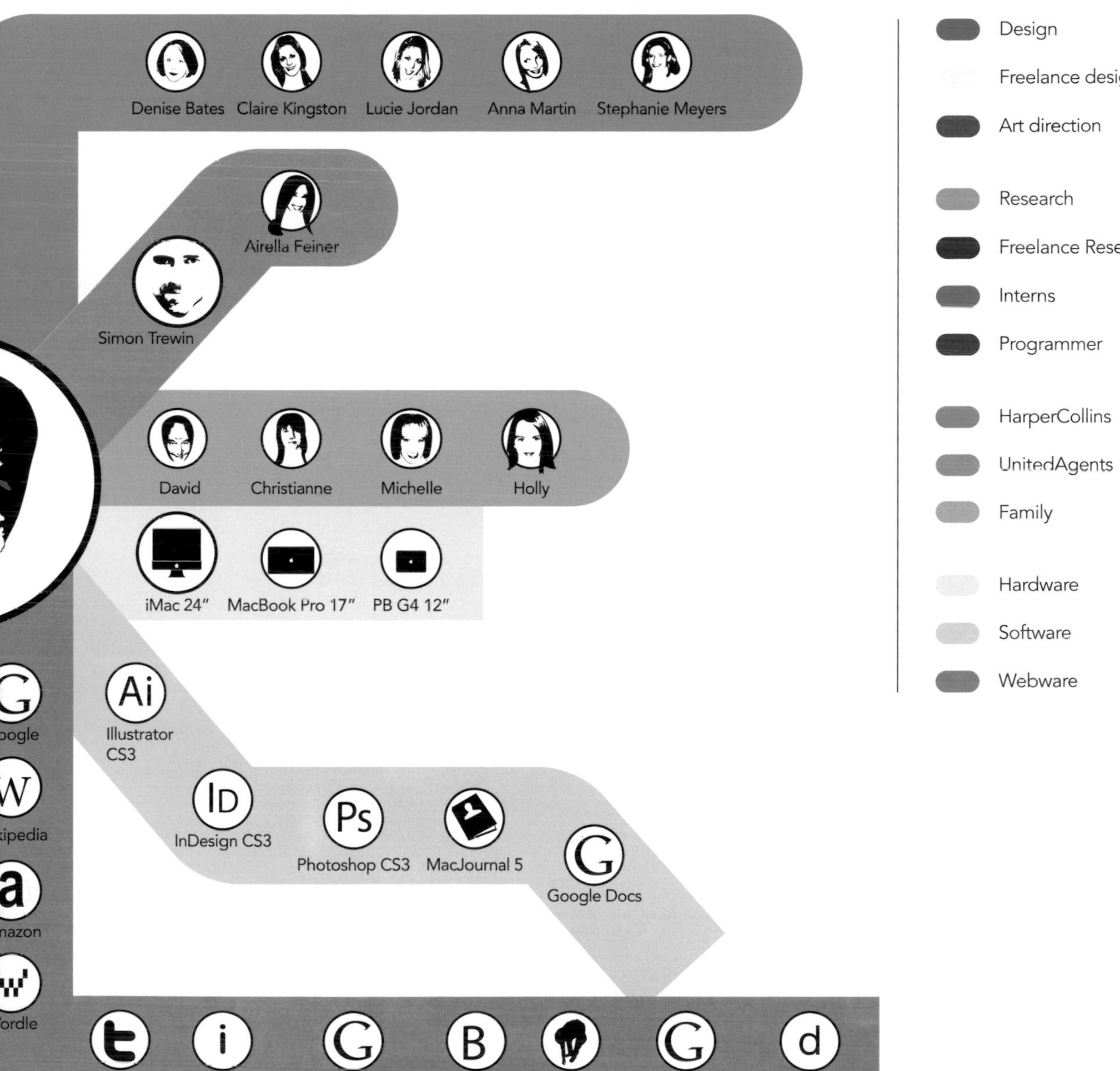

Denise Bates
Claire Kingston
Lucie Jordan
Anna Martin
Stephanie Meyers
Airella Feiner
Simon Trewin
David
Christianne
Michelle
Holly
iMac 24"
MacBook Pro 17"
PB G4 12"
Ai
Illustrator CS3
ID
InDesign CS3
Ps
Photoshop CS3
MacJournal 5
Google Docs
oogle
kipedia
mazon
Vordle
Twitter
iStockPhoto
Google Insights
Britannica
Ffffound
Google Reader
Decodeme
Design
Freelance design
Art direction
Research
Freelance Research
Interns
Programmer
HarperCollins
UnitedAgents
Family
Hardware
Software
Webware

Bibliograph

Inspiration and source material

Tufte, Edward R., *Envisioning Information* (Cheshire, Connecticut: Graphics Press LLC, 2005)

Schott's Almanac
2006
BEN SCHOTT

Schott, Ben, *Schott's Almanac* 2007 (London: Bloomsbury Publishing Plc., 2007)

Visualizing Data
O'REILLY

Fry, Ben, *Visualizing Data* (Sebastopol, CA: O'Reilly Media, Inc., 2008)

Abrams, Janet and Peter Hall, *Else/Where: Mapping* (Minneapolis: University of Minneapolis Design Institute, 2006)

SUFI

Bakhtiar, Laleh, *Sufi* (New York: Thames and Hudson Inc., 2004)

SECOND EDITION
The Visual Display
of Quantitative Information
EDWARD R. TUFTE

Tufte, Edward R., *The Visual Display of Quantitative Information* (Cheshire, Connecticut: Graphics Press LLC, 2006)

FREAKONOMICS
A Rogue Economist Explores the Hidden Side of Everything
STEVEN D. LEVITT &
STEPHEN J. DUBNER

Levitt, Steven D. and Stephen J. Dubner, *Freakonomics* (London: Penguin Books, 2006)

YOU
ARE
HERE
PERSONAL GEOGRAPHIES

Harmon, Katharine, *You Are Here* (New York: Princeton Architectural Press, 2004)

SUPER CRUNCHERS
HOW ANYTHING CAN BE PREDICTED
IAN AYRES

Ayers, Ian, *Super Crunchers* (London: Random House, Inc., 2008)

THE DENIERS
LAWRENCE SOLOMON

Solomon, Lawrence, *The Deniers* (Richard Vigilante Books, 2008)

Image Credits

STOCK IMAGES neubauwelt.com

STOCK IMAGES istockphoto.com

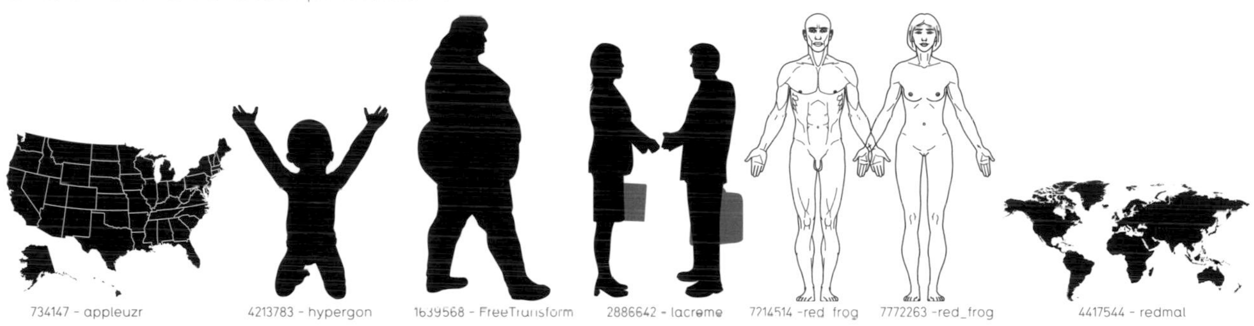

734147 - appleuzr   4213783 - hypergon   1639568 - FreeTransform   2886642 - lacreme   7714514 -red_frog   7772263 -red_frog   4417544 - redmal

DINGS dafont.com

4YeoSport

WC Fonts Sold Out B

WC Fonts Sold Out C

FONTS lineto.com

Type 1451 - ABCDEFGHIJKLMNOPQRSTUVWXYZabcdefghijklmnopqrstuvwxyz1234567890

Akkurat - ABCDEFGHIJKLMNOPQRSTUVWXYZabcdefghijklmnopqrstuvwxyz1234567890

FONTS linotype.com

Avenir - ABCDEFGHIJKLMNOPQRSTUVWXYZabcdefghijklmnopqrstuvwxyz1234567890

InformationIsBeautiful.net

Visit the website for the book

discover more

our blog covers visual journalism, unusual infographics, far-out data visualizations

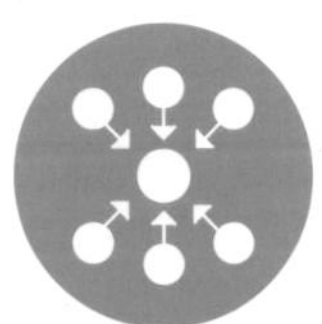

be involved

crowdsource and help us investigate, research and unearth facts and information for new designs

get animated

play with interactive visuals and animations

cc

have a play

access the data and research used in this book and find editable versions of some images

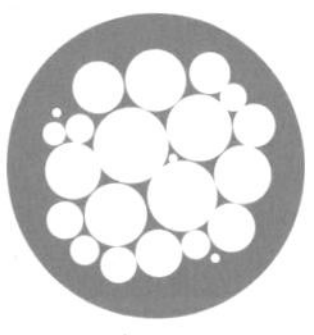

find extra stuff

tons of new diagrams, idea maps, bubble charts, factoramas, knowledgescapes and infomaps...

twitter: @infobeautiful // facebook.com/pages/Information-Is-Beautiful

Can Drugs Make You Happy?

DRUGGIEST Largest % of population using illegal drugs (7% or more)

Argentina, Australia, Belize, Canada, Chile, Czech Rep, Denmark, England & Wales, Estonia, France, Ghana, Ireland, Israel, Italy, Jamaica, Kyrgyzstan, Latvia, Lebanon, Luxembourg, Madagascar, New Zealand, Nigeria, Spain, Switzerland, Uruguay, USA, Venezuela, Zambia, Zimbabwe

source: Guardian Data blog, UN

HAPPIEST by Happiness Index Rating (above 6.8/10)

Argentina, Australia, Austria, Belgium, Belize, Brazil, Canada, Chile, Colombia, Costa Rica, Cyprus, Denmark, El Salvador, England & Wales, Finland, Guatemala, Iceland, Ireland, Italy, Luxembourg, Malta, Mexico, Netherlands, New Zealand, Norway, Saudi Arabia, Singapore, Spain, Sweden, Switzerland, Thailand, Trinidad & Tobago, UAE, USA, Venezuela

source: Erasmus University Rotterdam, Worlddatabaseofhappiness.eur.nl

BLISSED OUT! where happiness strongly correlates with drug use

Argentina, Australia, Belize, Canada, Chile, Denmark, England & Wales, Ireland, Italy, Luxembourg, New Zealand, Spain, Switzerland, USA, Venezuela

42%

just for fun, correlation is not cause

Ain't Nothing Going On But The Rent

money and divorce in a co-dependent relationship?

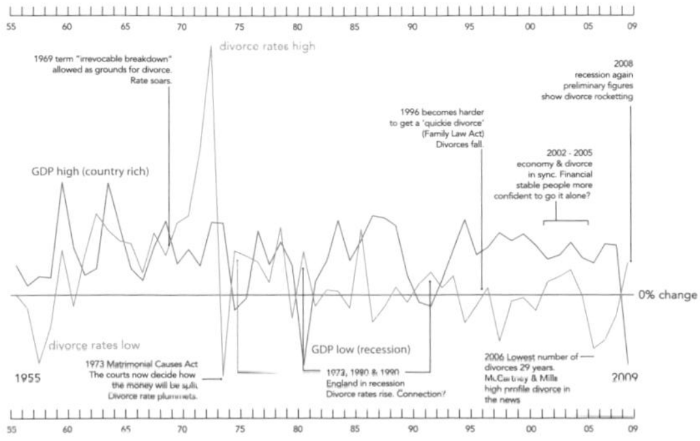
55 60 65 70 75 80 85 90 95 00 05 09
divorce rates high
1969 term "irrevocable breakdown" allowed as grounds for divorce. Rate soars.
2008 recession again preliminary figures show divorce rocketting
1996 becomes harder to get a 'quickie divorce' (Family Law Act) Divorces fall.
2002 - 2005 economy & divorce in sync. Financial stable people more confident to go it alone?
GDP high (country rich)
0% change
divorce rates low
GDP low (recession)
1955
2009
1973 Matrimonial Causes Act The courts now decide how the money will be split. Divorce rate plummets.
1973, 1980 & 1990 England in recession Divorce rates rise. Connection?
2006 Lowest number of divorces 29 years. McCartney & Mills high profile divorce in the news

Selling Out

How much do music artists earn online?

For solo artist to earn US monthly min. wage $1,160

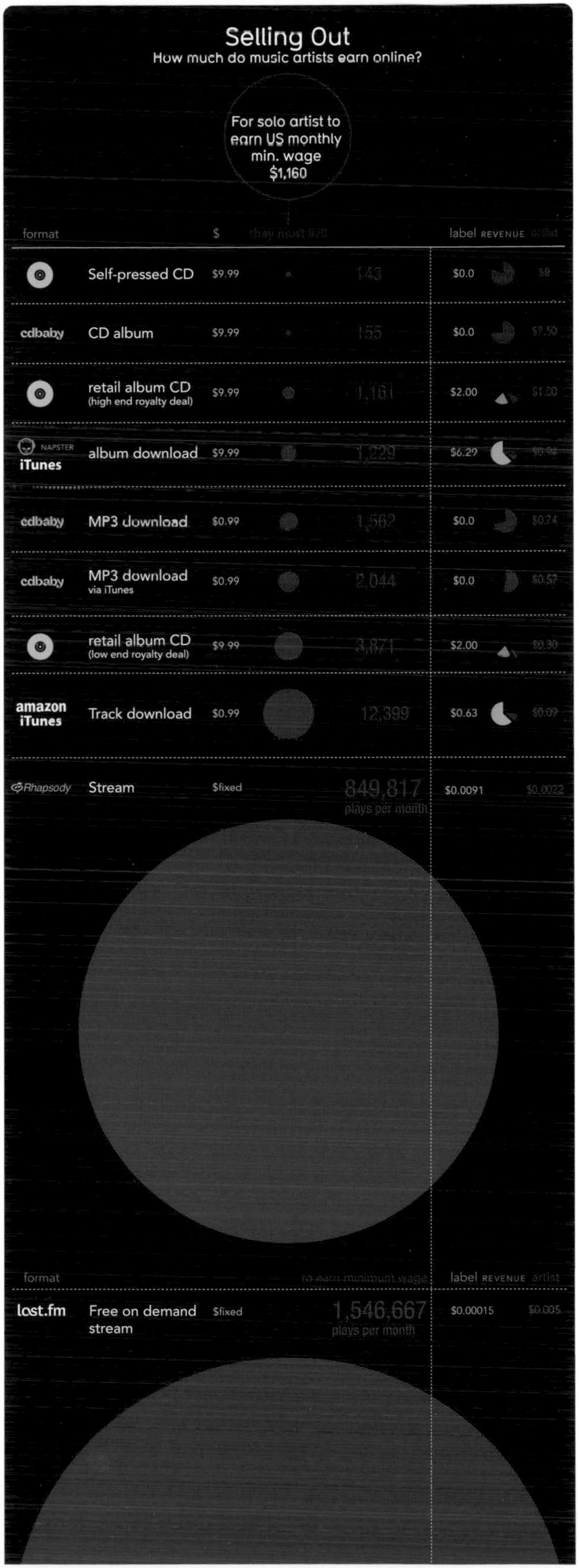

format		$	they must sell	label REVENUE	artist
	Self-pressed CD	$9.99	143	$0.0	$8
cdbaby	CD album	$9.99	155	$0.0	$7.50
	retail album CD (high end royalty deal)	$9.99	1,161	$2.00	$1.00
NAPSTER iTunes	album download	$9.99	1,229	$6.29	$0.94
cdbaby	MP3 download	$0.99	1,562	$0.0	$0.74
cdbaby	MP3 download via iTunes	$0.99	2,044	$0.0	$0.57
	retail album CD (low end royalty deal)	$9.99	3,871	$2.00	$0.30
amazon iTunes	Track download	$0.99	12,399	$0.63	$0.09
Rhapsody	Stream	$fixed	849,817 plays per month	$0.0091	$0.0022

format			to earn minimum wage	label REVENUE	artist
last.fm	Free on demand stream	$fixed	1,546,667 plays per month	$0.00015	$0.005

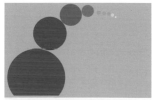